DATE DUE

			PRINTED IN U.S.A.

Children's Literature Review

Guide to Gale Literary Criticism Series

For criticism on	Consult these Gale series
Authors now living or who died after December 31, 1959	*CONTEMPORARY LITERARY CRITICISM (CLC)*
Authors who died between 1900 and 1959	*TWENTIETH-CENTURY LITERARY CRITICISM (TCLC)*
Authors who died between 1800 and 1899	*NINETEENTH-CENTURY LITERATURE CRITICISM (NCLC)*
Authors who died between 1400 and 1799	*LITERATURE CRITICISM FROM 1400 TO 1800 (LC)* *SHAKESPEAREAN CRITICISM (SC)*
Authors who died before 1400	*CLASSICAL AND MEDIEVAL LITERATURE CRITICISM (CMLC)*
Black writers of the past two hundred years	*BLACK LITERATURE CRITICISM (BLC)*
Authors of books for children and young adults	*CHILDREN'S LITERATURE REVIEW (CLR)*
Dramatists	*DRAMA CRITICISM (DC)*
Hispanic writers of the late nineteenth and twentieth centuries	*HISPANIC LITERATURE CRITICISM (HLC)*
Native North American writers and orators of the eighteenth, nineteenth, and twentieth centuries	*NATIVE NORTH AMERICAN LITERATURE (NNAL)*
Poets	*POETRY CRITICISM (PC)*
Short story writers	*SHORT STORY CRITICISM (SSC)*
Major authors from the Renaissance to the present	*WORLD LITERATURE CRITICISM, 1500 TO THE PRESENT (WLC)*

ISSN 0362-4145

R

volume 39

Children's Literature Review

Excerpts from Reviews,
Criticism, and Commentary
on Books for Children
and Young People

Alan Hedblad
Editor

Sharon R. Gunton
Associate Editor

GALE

an International Thomson Publishing company I(T)P®

STAFF

Alan Hedblad, *Editor*

Sharon R. Gunton, *Associate Editor*

Linda R. Andres, Shelly Andrews, Joanna Brod, Elizabeth A. Des Chenes, Motoko Huthwaite, Sean McCready, Thomas F. McMahon, Gerard J. Senick, Diane Telgen, *Contributing Editors*

Marilyn Allen, *Assistant Editor*

Marlene S. Hurst, *Permissions Manager*
Margaret A. Chamberlain, Maria Franklin, *Permissions Specialists*
Michele Lonoconus, Maureen Puhl, Kimberly F. Smilay, *Permissions Associates*
Edna Hedblad, Lori Schoenenberger, *Permissions Assistants*

Victoria B. Cariappa, *Research Manager*
Donna Melnychenko, *Project Coordinator*
Andy Malonis, Gary Oudersluys, *Research Specialists*
Michele Pica, Tracie Richardson, Norma Sawaya, *Research Associates*
Julia Daniel, Michelle Lee, Cheryl L. Warnock, Amy Wieczorek, *Research Assistants*

Mary Beth Trimper, *Production Director*
Deborah Milliken, *Production Assistant*

C. J. Jonik, *Desktop Publisher*
Randy Bassett, *Image Database Supervisor*
Robert Duncan, *Imaging Specialist*
Pamela A. Hayes, *Photography Coordinator*

This book is printed on acid-free paper that meets the minimum requirements of American National Standard for Information Sciences—Permanence Paper for Printed Library Materials, ANSI Z39.48-1984.

Library of Congress Catalog Card Number 76-643301
ISBN 0-8103-9286-0
ISSN 0362-4145
Printed in the United States of America

Gale Research, an International Thomson Publishing Company.
ITP logo is a trademark under license.

I(T)P™

10 9 8 7 6 5 4 3 2 1

Contents

Preface   vii
Acknowledgments   xi

Preface

Literature for children and young adults has evolved into both a respected branch of creative writing and a successful industry. Currently, books for young readers are considered among the most popular segments of publishing. Criticism of juvenile literature is instrumental in recording the literary or artistic development of the creators of children's books as well as the trends and controversies that result from changing values or attitudes about young people and their literature. Designed to provide a permanent, accessible record of this ongoing scholarship, *Children's Literature Review (CLR)* presents parents, teachers, and librarians—those responsible for bringing children and books together—with the opportunity to make informed choices when selecting reading materials for the young. In addition, *CLR* provides researchers of children's literature with easy access to a wide variety of critical information from English-language sources in the field. Users will find balanced overviews of the careers of the authors and illustrators of the books that children and young adults are reading; these entries, which contain excerpts from published criticism in books and periodicals, assist users by sparking ideas for papers and assignments and suggesting supplementary and classroom reading. Ann L. Kalkhoff, president and editor of *Children's Book Review Service Inc.,* writes that "*CLR* has filled a gap in the field of children's books, and it is one series that will never lose its validity or importance."

Scope of the Series

Each volume of *CLR* profiles the careers of a selection of authors and illustrators of books for children and young adults from preschool through high school. Author lists in each volume reflect:

- an international scope.

- representation of authors of all eras.

- the variety of genres covered by children's and/or YA literature: picture books, fiction, nonfiction, poetry, folklore, and drama.

Although the focus of the series is on authors new to *CLR*, entries will be updated as the need arises.

Organization of This Book

An entry consists of the following elements: author heading, author portrait, author introduction, excerpts of criticism (each preceded by a bibliographical citation), and illustrations, when available.

- The **Author Heading** consists of the author's name followed by birth and death dates. The portion of the name outside the parentheses denotes the form under which the author is most frequently published. If the majority of the author's works for children were written under a pseudonym, the pseudonym will be listed in the author heading and the real name given on the first line of the author introduction. Also located at the beginning of the introduction are any other pseudonyms used by the author in writing for children and any name variations, including transliterated forms for authors whose languages use nonroman alphabets. Uncertainty as to a birth or death date is indicated by question marks.

- An **Author Portrait** is included when available.

- The **Author Introduction** contains information designed to introduce an author to *CLR* users by presenting an overview of the author's themes and styles, biographical facts that relate to the author's literary career or critical responses to the author's works, and information about major awards and prizes the author has received. The introduction begins by identifying the nationality of the author and by listing the genres in which s/he has written for children and young adults. Introductions also list a group of representative titles for which the author or illustrator being profiled is best known; this section, which begins with the words "major works include," follows the genre line of the introduction. For seminal figures, a listing of major works about the author follows when appropriate, highlighting important biographies about the author or illustrator that are not excerpted in the entry. The centered heading "Introduction" announces the body of the text.

- **Criticism** is located in three sections: **Author's Commentary** (when available), **General Commentary** (when available), and **Title Commentary** (commentary on specific titles).

  - The **Author's Commentary** presents background material written by the author or by an interviewer. This commentary may cover a specific work or several works. Author's commentary on more than one work appears after the author introduction, while commentary on an individual book follows the title entry heading.

  - The **General Commentary** consists of critical excerpts that consider more than one work by the author or illustrator being profiled. General commentary is preceded by the critic's name in boldface type or, in the case of unsigned criticism, by the title of the journal. *CLR* also features entries that emphasize general criticism on the oeuvre of an author or illustrator. When appropriate, a selection of reviews is included to supplement the general commentary.

  - The **Title Commentary** begins with the title entry headings, which precede the criticism on a title and cite publication information on the work being reviewed. Title headings list the title of the work as it appeared in its first English-language edition. The first English-language publication date of each work (unless otherwise noted) is listed in parentheses following the title. Differing U. S. and British titles follow the publication date within the parentheses. When a work is written by an individual other than the one being profiled, as is the case when illustrators are featured, the parenthetical material following the title cites the author of the work before listing its publication date.

    Entries in each title commentary section consist of critical excerpts on the author's individual works, arranged chronologically by publication date. The entries generally contain two to seven reviews per title, depending on the stature of the book and the amount of criticism it has generated. The editors select titles that reflect the entire scope of the author's literary contribution, covering each genre and subject. An effort is made to reprint criticism that represents the full range of each title's reception, from the year of its initial publication to current assessments. Thus, the reader is provided with a record of the author's critical history. Publication information (such as publisher names and book prices) and parenthetical numerical references (such as footnotes or page and line references to specific editions of works) have been deleted at the discretion of the editors to provide smoother reading of the text.

- Centered headings introduce each section, in which criticism is arranged chronologically; beginning with Volume 35, each excerpt is preceded by a boldface source heading for easier access by readers. Within the text, titles by authors being profiled are also highlighted in boldface type.

- Selected excerpts are preceded by **Explanatory Annotations,** which provide information on the critic or work of criticism to enhance the reader's understanding of the excerpt.

- A complete **Bibliographical Citation** designed to facilitate the location of the original book or article precedes each piece of criticism.

- Numerous **Illustrations** are featured in *CLR*. For entries on illustrators, an effort has been made to include illustrations that reflect the characteristics discussed in the criticism. Entries on authors who do not illustrate their own works may also include photographs and other illustrative material pertinent to their careers.

Special Features: Entries on Illustrators

Entries on authors who are also illustrators will occasionally feature commentary on selected works illustrated but not written by the author being profiled. These works are strongly associated with the illustrator and have received critical acclaim for their art. By including critical comment on works of this type, the editors wish to provide a more complete representation of the author's career. Criticism on these works has been chosen to stress artistic, rather than literary, contributions. Title entry headings for works illustrated by the author being profiled are arranged chronologically within the entry by date of publication and include notes identifying the author of the illustrated work. In order to provide easier access for users, all titles illustrated by the subject of the entry are boldfaced.

CLR also includes entries on prominent illustrators who have contributed to the field of children's literature. These entries are designed to represent the development of the illustrator as an artist rather than as a literary stylist. The illustrator's section is organized like that of an author, with two exceptions: the introduction presents an overview of the illustrator's styles and techniques rather than outlining his or her literary background, and the commentary written by the illustrator on his or her works is called "illustrator's commentary" rather than "author's commentary." All titles of books containing illustrations by the artist being profiled as well as individual illustrations from these books are highlighted in boldface type.

Other Features: Acknowledgments, Indexes

- The **Acknowledgments** section, which immediately follows the preface, lists the sources from which material has been reprinted in the volume. It does not, however, list every book or periodical consulted for the volume.

- The **Cumulative Index to Authors** lists all of the authors who have appeared in *CLR* with cross-references to the biographical, autobiographical, and literary criticism series published by Gale Research. A full listing of the series titles appears before the first page of the indexes of this volume.

- The **Cumulative Index to Nationalities** lists authors alphabetically under their respective nationalities. Author names are followed by the volume number(s) in which they appear.

- The **Cumulative Index to Titles** lists titles covered in *CLR* followed by the volume and page number where criticism begins.

A Note to the Reader

CLR is one of several critical references sources in the Literature Criticism Series published by Gale Research. When writing papers, students who quote directly from any volume in the Literature Criticism Series may use the following general forms to footnote reprinted criticism. The first example pertains to material drawn from periodicals, the second to material reprinted from books.

[1]T. S. Eliot, "John Donne," *The Nation and the Athenaeum,* 33 (9 June 1923), 321-32; excerpted and reprinted in *Literature Criticism from 1400 to 1800,* Vol. 10, ed. James E. Person, Jr. (Detroit: Gale Research, 1989), pp. 28-9.

[1]Henry Brooke, *Leslie Brooke and Johnny Crow* (Frederick Warne, 1982); excerpted and reprinted in *Children's Literature Review,* Vol. 20, ed. Gerard J. Senick (Detroit: Gale Research, 1990), p. 47.

Suggestions Are Welcome

In response to various suggestions, several features have been added to *CLR* since the beginning of the series, including author entries on retellers of traditional literature as well as those who have been the first to record oral tales and other folklore; entries on prominent illustrators featuring commentary on their styles and techniques; entries on authors whose works are considered controversial; occasional entries devoted to criticism on a single work or a series of works; sections in author introductions that list major works by and about the author or illustrator being profiled; explanatory notes that provide information on the critic or work of criticism to enhance the usefulness of the excerpt; more extensive illustrative material, such as holographs of manuscript pages and photographs of people and places pertinent to the careers of the authors and artists; a cumulative nationality index for easy access to authors by nationality; and occasional guest essays written specifically for *CLR* by prominent critics on subjects of their choice.

Readers who wish to suggest authors to appear in future volumes, or who have other suggestions, are cordially invited to write the editor.

Acknowledgments

The editors wish to thank the copyright holders of the excerpted criticism included in this volume and the permissions managers of many book and magazine publishing companies for assisting us in securing reprint rights. We are also grateful to the staffs of the Detroit Public Library, the Library of Congress, the University of Detroit Mercy Library, Wayne State University Purdy/Kresge Library Complex, and the University of Michigan Libraries for making their resources available to us. Following is a list of the copyright holders who have granted us permission to reprint material in this volume of *CLR*. Every effort has been made to trace copyright, but if omissions have been made, please let us know.

COPYRIGHTED EXCERPTS IN *CLR*, VOLUME 39, WERE REPRINTED FROM THE FOLLOWING PERIODICALS:

Appraisal: Children's Science Books, v. 3, 1970; v. 4, Fall, 1971; v. 5, Fall, 1972; v. 6, 1973; v. 9, 1976; v. 12, Winter, 1979; v. 15, Winter, 1982; v. 18, Autumn, 1985; v. 19, Fall, 1986; v. 25, Winter, 1992. Copyright © 1970, 1971, 1972, 1973, 1976, 1979, 1982, 1985, 1986, 1992 by the Children's Science Book Review Committee. All reprinted by permission of the publisher.—*Best Sellers,* v. 37, November, 1977; v. 40, March, 1981; v. 42, January, 1983; v. 44, March, 1985; v. 46, August, 1986. Copyright © 1977, 1981, 1983, 1985, 1986 Helen Dwight Reid Educational Foundation. All reprinted by permission of the publisher.—*The Book Report,* v. 11, January-February, 1993; v. 12, May-June, 1993. © copyright 1993 by Linworth Publishing, Inc., Worthington, Ohio. Both reprinted with permission of the publisher.—*Bookbird,* v. XVII, March 15, 1980. Reprinted by permission of the publisher.—*Booklist,* v. 73, February 1, 1977; v. 74, December 1, 1977; v. 75, July 15, 1979; v. 76, November 1, 1979; v. 77, November 15, 1980; v. 77, June 1, 1981; v. 78, February 1, 1982; v. 78, June, 1, 1982; v. 78, August, 1982; v. 79, October 1, 1982; v. 79, November 1, 1982; v. 79, January 15, 1983; v. 79, April 15, 1983; v. 79, June 15, 1983; v. 80, September 1, 1983; v. 80, September 15, 1983; v. 80, May 1, 1984; v. 81, September 1, 1984; v. 81, January 15, 1985; v. 81, June 1, 1985; v. 81, July, 1985; v. 81, August, 1985; v. 82, November 15, 1985; v. 82, January 15, 1986; v. 82, March 1, 1986; v. 84, October 15, 1987; v. 84, December 1, 1987; v. 84, May 1, 1988; v. 84, June 1, 1988; v. 85, September 1, 1988; v. 85, September 15, 1988; v. 85, December 1, 1988; v. 85, January 1, 1989; v. 85, February 1, 1989; v. 85, June 15, 1989; v. 86, August, 1990; v. 87, December 1, 1990; v. 87, March 15, 1991; v. 88, February 1, 1992; v. 88, February 15, 1992 ; v. 88, June 15, 1992; v. 88, July, 1992; v. 89, October 15, 1992; v. 89, November 1, 1992; v. 89, February 15, 1993; v. 89, April 1, 1993; v. 89, May 15, 1993; v. 90, May 1, 1994. Copyright © 1977, 1979, 1980, 1981,1982, 1983, 1984, 1985, 1986, 1987, 1988, 1989, 1990, 1991, 1992, 1993, 1993, 1994 by the American Library Association. All reprinted by permission of the publisher.—*The Booklist,* v. 66, September 1, 1969; v. 67, September 1, 1970; v. 69, October 1, 1972; v. 71, April 15, 1975; v. 72, April 15, 1976. Copyright © 1969, 1970, 1972, 1975, 1976 by the American Library Association. All reprinted by permission of the publisher.—*Books and Bookmen,* v. 20, May, 1975 for a review of "Karlson on the Roof" by Sally Emerson. © copyright the author 1975. Reprinted by permission of the author.—*Books for Keeps,* n. 58, September, 1989. © School Bookshop Association 1989. Reprinted by permission of the publisher.—*Books for Young People,* v. 1, October, 1987 for "Past and Present Merge in Painful, Haunting Tales" by Peter Carver. All rights reserved. Reprinted by permission of the publisher and the author.—*Books for Your Children,* v. 16, Spring, 1981; v. 21, Summer, 1986; v. 25, Summer, 1990. © Books for Your Children 1981, 1986, 1990. All reprinted by permission of the publisher.—*Books in Canada,* v. 16, December, 1987 for "Ways to Escape" by Mary Ainslie Smith. Reprinted by permission of the author.—*British Book News Children's Books,* September, 1986. © The British Council, 1986. Reprinted by permission of the publisher.—*Bulletin of the Center for Children's Books,* v. 21, April, 1968; v. 23, December, 1969; v. 26, October, 1972; v. 30, April, 1977; v. 31, February, 1978; v. 31, July-August, 1978; v. 32, January, 1979; v. 32, May, 1979; v. 33, December, 1979; v. 33, April, 1980; v. 34, October, 1980; v. 34, April, 1981; v. 35, November, 1981; v. 35, June, 1982; v. 36, December, 1982; v. 37, September, 1983; v. 37, February,

COPYRIGHTED EXCERPTS IN *CLR,* VOLUME 39, WERE REPRINTED FROM THE FOLLOWING BOOKS:

Anderson, Celia Catlett. From "Kipling's Mowgli and Just So Stories: The Vine of Fact and Fantasy," in *Touchstones: Reflections on the Best in Children's Literature,* Vol. 1. Edited by Perry Nodelman. Children's Literature Association, 1985. © 1985 ChLA Publishers. Reprinted by permission of the publisher.—Avery, Gillian. From "The Children's Writer," in *Rudyard Kipling: The Man, His Work, and His World.* Edited by John Gross. Weidenfeld & Nicolson, 1972. Copyright © 1972 by George Weidenfeld and Nicolson Ltd. All rights reserved. Reprinted by permission of the publisher.—Blount, Margaret. From *Animal Land: The Creatures of Children's*

Children's
Literature
Review

Clayton Bess

1944-

(Pseudonym of Robert Locke) American author of fiction.

Major works include *Story for a Black Night* (1982), *The Truth about the Moon* (1983), *Big Man and the Burn-out* (1985), *Tracks* (1986), *The Mayday Rampage* (1993).

INTRODUCTION

Hailed for his ability to create believable characters and compelling stories, Clayton Bess is best known for young adult novels that examine moral issues without lecturing readers. Using realistic dialogue, evocative language, and fast-paced plots, his books dramatize complex subjects such as prejudice, violence, AIDS, and culture clash. While Bess's works raise important questions, critics observe, they also feature gripping narratives that involve readers in the lives of their characters. These characters are often outsiders who struggle for acceptance or knowledge within their communities; by writing about such individuals, the author hopes he can "open up the minds of people, young or old, to accept people's differences, to cherish them."

Biographical Information

Born in California as Robert Locke—his pseudonym is taken from the first names of his parents as a tribute to them—Bess had early ambitions as an actor and earned a degree in theatre from California State University—Chico. He later turned from acting to playwriting, and supported himself as a librarian while he wrote several plays which were produced under his real name. Bess's stint in the Peace Corps from 1968 to 1971 proved instrumental to his career as a writer for children. As a teacher in Liberia, Africa, Bess was introduced to a woman who had been severely scarred by smallpox; the story of how she contracted the disease deeply moved him, and "finally I told myself I'd just have to write it to get it out of my head." The woman's experience was the genesis of *Story for a Black Night,* which the author spent ten years trying to publish before it finally appeared in 1982. Since then Bess has penned several works for children, always striving to tell "a good story, a meaningful story, keeping readers on the edge of their seats, involving them, moving them, making them think." He continues to work as a librarian and playwright in California, and frequently visits schools to read from both published books and works in progress.

Major Works

The Liberian woman who made such an indelible impression on Bess becomes the central focus of a moral dilemma in *Story for a Black Night,* which is narrated as a

recollection by the woman's son Momo. On a stormy evening, Momo's mother allows two women to take shelter with the family, even though her own mother warns against it. When the visitors abandon a sick baby, Momo's mother nurses the infant through smallpox herself, an act that has dire consequences for the entire family. With a writing style that captures the essence of West African storytelling and dialect, Bess creates a powerful confrontation of opposing beliefs and presents a balanced view of each side of the conflict. The author's experiences in Africa also inspired his only picture book, *The Truth about the Moon.* This gently humorous story of a boy searching for facts about the moon highlights the differing roles of legend and knowledge. The author looked closer to home for *Big Man and the Burn-out,* a novel set in contemporary America about Jess, a motherless boy searching for love and friendship. This novel was not as successful as *Story for a Black Night,* as some critics found the plot burdened with too many themes and events; nevertheless, several reviewers hailed the work as ambitious and involving, with memorable characters.

Bess's third novel, *Tracks,* has received widespread acclaim as an exciting picaresque novel that vividly brings the era of the Great Depression to life. As two brothers hop freight trains to travel from Oklahoma to California, they witness racism and brutality and are confronted with various dangers. Because the story is related in flashback by one of the boys, Bess provides his readers with the historical context needed for deeper understanding. *The Mayday Rampage* has a more direct educational purpose: to inform teens about the dangers of AIDS. Structured as a series of tape recordings with true-to-life dialogue, *The Mayday Rampage* shows the efforts of student reporters Molly and Jess (from *Big Man and the Burn-out*) to explore the effects of AIDS in their community. A dramatic and shocking epilogue ironically reinforces the important lessons the two teens have learned about this deadly disease. Because of its creative approach in exploring and answering questions regarding AIDS, Laura Lent called *The Mayday Rampage* a "superior" book "that every teen (possibly everybody) needs to read."

Awards

Story for a Black Night received a special award in 1983 from the Southern California Council on Literature for Children and Young People for making a "contribution of cultural significance."

TITLE COMMENTARY

📖 *STORY FOR A BLACK NIGHT* (1982)

Hazel Rochman

SOURCE: A review of *Story for a Black Night,* in *School Library Journal,* Vol. 28, No. 7, March, 1982, pp. 144-45.

In modern Liberia one night the electricity fails, evil seems all around, and Momo tells a story of his childhood, before modernization, and before vaccination had eradicated smallpox. It is a story of horror and beauty, of selfishness and heroic sacrifice and of complicated moral choice. On a dread dark night in their isolated hut in the bush, Momo's mother gives shelter to two traveling women with a baby. In the morning the strangers have gone, leaving the baby—who is discovered to have smallpox. Momo's grandmother, blinded herself by the dread disease, hysterically begs Momo's mother to abandon the sick baby, but she cannot. She nurses it, and when the nearby town refuses her own children shelter, her whole family becomes infected. Her own baby dies; the child, Momo, recovers; the mother herself endures terrible agony: the beautiful woman Momo remembered standing proud "holding stranger baby to her breast" becomes a disfigured "Monster. All over running sores . . . her nose was hill of pus, her nostrils blocked up with scab. . . ." Told in dialect by Momo to his son, the story unfolds with intense drama,

each section building to its own climax, with new discoveries of betrayal and grace until the very last page. No simple judgments are made: the mother, the grandmother and the townspeople stand by their various points of view to the end. Nor is "progress" the clear answer: smallpox is gone, but what is the meaning of community? The grandmother rejects Christianity; the mother says the "book" (the Bible) teaches her what she must do; the Christian townspeople drive out the infected children. A story for reading together and talking about for a long time.

Kirkus Reviews

SOURCE: A review of *Story for a Black Night,* in *Kirkus Reviews,* Vol. L, No. 9, May 1, 1982, pp. 553-54.

This is set in Africa (Liberia, per the flap) where a man of 40, on a night the electricity goes out, tells of the evil and good that came on a dark night when he was ten, in the same house but with bush all around, "before the town grew to meet it." At ten, then, Momo lives with his baby sister Meatta, his Ma, and his Old Ma, long blind from the pox. Pa has been killed by a two-step snake. When traveling strangers knock in the night, Old Ma would keep them out, but Ma, taking pity, lets them in. The next morning the visiting young woman and old woman are gone, but they have left behind their baby, who is covered with the red sores of smallpox. And so begins the ordeal, with Meatta dying of the pox, Momo sick and recovering, and Ma, worse hit, emerging from the fever half-blind, bald, and covered with scabs and "folded rot." For Ma has insisted on keeping the strangers' baby, though her Ma would give it to the bush or the river. Ma can't say why she must keep the baby, any more than she can understand Old Ma or her own sister Musu—who comes to help when Ma is sick, but confesses then that it was she who sent the strangers to them. "Musu, if I were well I would kill you," says Ma. Then there's the final irony when the minister's wife sees Ma's pox as punishment for "very bad sin" and Musu's immunity as evidence of "a deep and good heart." Given character and poignance by its setting, an African community to which Christianity had come, making converts and confusion, it's an unabashed moral tale and a crowd-holding story, with the moral content central to the story interest.

Zena Sutherland

SOURCE: A review of *Story for a Black Night,* in *Bulletin of the Center for Children's Books,* Vol. 35, No. 10, June, 1982, p. 183.

"Ain't the night is black tonight? You would like to run playing, but the darkness be too great for you. By force of storm, electric current came to fail. . . ." And so a Liberian father tells his children a story of his childhood. Locked into their house, widowed Ma, baby sister Meatta, blind Old Ma, the grandmother, and the narrator, Momo, are startled when two women beg to be let in with their baby. Old Ma is opposed to taking them in, but Ma insists; in the morning, the women are gone and the baby clearly has been abandoned because she has smallpox. That is how tragedy comes to Momo's family, for Ma insists on nursing the waif. Meatta sickens and dies, while the other baby lives, and Ma herself contracts the disease and almost dies. The villagers nearby won't come near the house, but they solicitously bring food and medicine. Momo, too, gets smallpox and recovers. When the baby's grandmother turns up, her daughter dead, to claim the child, Ma refuses to give her up: the baby was abandoned, she saved the child, it is now her baby. The story is taut and tender, deftly structured, vivid in its depiction of the village community as well as of the family, but it is most distinctive in the writing style, which captures the lovely cadence of the language in its dialogue and has the warmth and sonority of the best kind of storytelling in its exposition. A stunning first novel.

Denise M. Wilms

SOURCE: A review of *Story for a Black Night,* in *Booklist,* Vol. 78, No. 19, June 1, 1982, pp. 1308, 1310.

In this present-day Liberian setting, a storm has brought electrical failure to the village; and as darkness settles in, a father sits with a group of children and begins a story that becomes a riveting meditation on the moral choices that must be made in living. He harks back to his boyhood, to the time his mother sheltered two pleading women from the night and so brought smallpox into the household. The story poignantly contrasts generational values and outlooks. Ma's decision to aid the women, and next morning the sick baby they've stealthily left behind, goes against the warnings of her own mother (who herself has been blinded by smallpox) and is not without dire consequences. Ma loses her own baby to the disease, sees her son through a relatively mild case, and then herself develops a severe case that leaves her blind in one eye. Throughout the story, there is tension between old ways and new, religion and tradition, education and ignorance, and most basically, the good and bad ways people behave. The telling, a congenial, lilting patois, doesn't take much getting used to and reinforces the drama of a tragic but peacefully ending episode.

Nancy C. Hammond

SOURCE: A review of *Story for a Black Night,* in *The Horn Book Magazine,* Vol. LVIII, No. 4, August, 1982, p. 398.

On a night darkened by a power failure, Momo, a Liberian father, tells how evil arrived on another black night in his childhood. Kept awake by a presaging leopard "coming to weep at our house," the child Momo hears the knock of a stranger who, with her mother and crying baby, begs for shelter. Convinced "'they trouble,'" Old Ma, blinded and scarred by smallpox, argues against admitting them, but Ma, educated and exposed to Christian-

ity, opens the door. In the morning the women are gone—the baby deserted and ill with smallpox. Old Ma moves to "'kill it before it kill you,'" but Ma intercedes. The smallpox spreads, the family is quarantined but sustained by the neighboring villagers and, although the baby and Momo live, Ma's own baby dies, and Ma herself is grotesquely disfigured and partially blinded. An heroic figure, dignified and tender, she resolutely continues to do what she feels she must, while humbly responding, "'I don't know'" to the questions of the weaker, less resolute Auntie about why she makes the choices she does. Directness, honesty, and tolerance underlie Ma and Old Ma's relationship and the powerful narrative itself, as it vividly dramatizes—without simplification, proselytizing, or judgment—the moral conflicts and confusion of a culture in transition.

Alex Boyd

SOURCE: A review of *Story for a Black Night,* in *Voice of Youth Advocates,* Vol. 5, No. 6, February, 1983, p. 32.

It is not often that a reader, after completing only a page or two of a book, realizes that he or she has come across an authentic and beautiful, yet tragic tale that transcends national, racial and ethnic boundaries. This is a particularly difficult feat to accomplish in a relatively short work, yet such is the case with *Story For A Black Night* by Clayton Bess. The title is fraught with irony as the central theme of the book concerns evil, deception, and, ultimately, death. But it not only connotes the death of a few innocent, superstitious and frightened individuals, it also symbolizes the death of an innocent and beautiful land and its culture.

The story is set in Liberia and revolves around a tale told by an African father to his son about the disaster that follows a night when a baby with smallpox is abandoned in his family's home. Bess imaginatively captures the rhythms and cadence of the people's speech; but, more importantly, he invokes the horror and tragedy that smallpox and Christianity bring to these people. In actuality, both bring a different kind of death: one to specific individuals, the other to a way of life of an entire society. Regardless, both are just as certain. For the young boy Momo, it is a lesson well taught; for the reader, it is a lesson well learned.

THE TRUTH ABOUT THE MOON (1983)

Kirkus Reviews

SOURCE: A review of *The Truth about the Moon,* in *Kirkus Reviews,* Juvenile Issue, Vol. LI, Nos. 13-17, September 1, 1983, p. J-145.

Small African Sumu is puzzled by the moon: "It followed him around like a dog, always just over his shoulder, yet it had the face of a person. Sometimes it was big and round; at other times small and thin; then gone completely . . . And Sumu wanted it!" What Sumu hears about the moon, from one and another person, leaves him always with questions—and uncertain knowledge. Big sister Fatu scoffs at his talk of a baby moon, and a whole moon family: "There is only one moon. This I know, for our pa told me so." Only one moon? "No, Sumu," says Pa. "There are many, many moons." The moon is reborn, to start all over again. "But Pa," says Sumu, "where does the new moon come from?" And, he wonders, where does it go during the day? His Ma, in turn, laughs at word of many, many moons: "There is only one moon. It is like a woman. And you know how sometimes a woman will grow large and larger, more and more round?" The moon's monthly babies, says Ma, are the stars; the babies' father is the sun. "But Ma, the sun is hot. The moon and stars are cold. Why?" The Chief has a long, ancient tale to explain why—but Sumu queries that too. It is time, the Chief decides, for Sumu to go away to school. Still, the book ends with Sumu grabbing for the moon, as he first did, to put it in a bottle. With [Rosekrans] Hoffman's fond, wry, phantasmagoric illustrations: not didactic, but a teasing, fittingly elusive quest for the truth beyond legend.

Denise M. Wilms

SOURCE: A review of *The Truth About the Moon,* in *Booklist,* Vol. 80, No. 2, September 15, 1983, p. 164.

Samu is fascinated by the moon and is full of questions on whether or not there is only one, and why it changes shapes and even disappears. Answers of a sort come from stories his mother and father tell him of the moon's waxing and waning, but Samu's curiosity is still unsatisfied. He decides to visit the village chief, who spins yet another, more thorough tale of explanation. Samu listens and is as intrigued as ever, but Samu's curiosity is still not fully satisfied. And as he questions yet again, the elderly chief decides that Samu should be sent to a school for formal education. The story gently points up the contrast between modern and traditional beliefs, yet allows room for both. It's good to hear the chief tell Samu that he must decide on the truth of the knowledge he will find. "But whatever you decide, I know you will not forget my story, and I hope one day you will tell it to your child." With stylized charcoal drawings accented in brown.

Cheryl Lynn Gage

SOURCE: A review of *The Truth about the Moon,* in *School Library Journal,* Vol. 30, No. 8, April, 1984, p. 98.

Sumu, an African boy with an insatiable curiosity about the moon, is told several stories about it. Pa tells him the moon is like a child who grows into a man, Ma tells him the moon is like a woman who gives birth to a child. The

village chief tells him yet another tale of how the moon and sun were once married, but he soon realizes that the child needs facts and arranges for him to go to school. The soft pencil sketches [by Rosekrans Hoffman] are well executed and subtly incorporate symbols of fertility which the tales suggest. There are elements of folklore here; however, this gently humorous story is based on stories told to the author by his students while teaching in West Africa and no sources are provided.

BIG MAN AND THE BURN-OUT (1985)

Denise M. Wilms

SOURCE: A review of *Big Man and the Burn-out,* in *Booklist,* Vol. 82, No. 6, November 15, 1985, p. 491.

Deserted by his mother when he was a baby, Jess leads a somewhat sheltered, isolated life on his grandparents' farm. He has a tense relationship with his grandmother, a reticent woman who loves him dearly but whose stern attitude and undemonstrative ways are misread by Jess. He clearly prefers—and needs—his step-grandfather's sunny warmth. When Jess discovers a goose egg on the farm it becomes a challenge to him to hatch it. For his science project, he decides to answer the question, can a goose egg hatch in an incubator set with a temperature for chicken and turkey eggs? More to the point, though, is whether Jess can prove his grandmother wrong and make a success of things. Jess' discontent at home is offset some at school as he works at building a friendship. His first try with a boy named Rob simply doesn't work out; they are too different. What does happen is an accidental rapport with a new boy, Meechum, who is the class tough guy. Silent and surly, but, as it turns out, also very bright, Meechum is the last person Jess would pick for a friend, but they have some important things in common. Like Jess, Meechum is motherless; like Jess, he has someone who loves him but with whom he can't quite connect. Meechum (who is black but doesn't look it) has responded by withdrawing, and Jess tries to reinvolve him in school and in just plain living. Supporting Jess and Meechum is a sensitive teacher, Mr. Goodban, who agrees to work with Meechum so that he will graduate in time to attend high school. The novel is a story of coming of age, of friendship, and of nurturing. It also deals peripherally with emerging sexual identities, and simmering below the surface is the issue of homosexuality. The teacher, Mr. Goodban, is gay, and it's refreshing to see that this does not become an issue in the story. The pertinent development is a sensitive scene in which the boys rest naked after a creek swim and realize their pleasure in looking at each other, though neither articulates or acts on his feelings. Jess' grandmother instantly condemns them, but his grandfather rebukes her, and, when everyone's exploding emotions settle down, a measure of calm returns to Jess' family. An ambitious book that sometimes displays one thread too many, this is nevertheless involving and satisfying; Jess and those around him grow almost despite themselves.

Deborah M. Locke

SOURCE: A review of *Big Man and the Burn-out,* in *School Library Journal,* Vol. 32, No. 4, December, 1985, p. 86.

Jess, who was abandoned at a young age by his unwed mother and left in the care of his elderly grandparents, is now in the eighth grade and is struggling with adolescence, boredom, less-than-competent teachers and the difficulties of an uneasy home life. His self-image improves because of a science project, which involves hatching and raising a young gosling, and through his friendship with Lee Meechum, the class burn-out. His greatest antagonist is his grandmother, who loves him but seems to be unable to show Jess anything but her chilly and critical side. Bess introduces so many themes that some important issues are raised but never fully explored, causing the novel to lose its focus. Jess is unbelievably naive for an eighth grader. Meechum, a supportive English teacher and Jess' grandfather are well-drawn, but some of the other characters are so unconvincing in their behavior and dialogue that they become parodies. The subplot about Kathy the goose, told in alternating chapters, reads like a story for small children and is very likely to turn off what seems to be the intended audience. A badly flawed book.

Bulletin of the Center for Children's Books

SOURCE: A review of *Big Man and the Burn-out,* in *Bulletin of the Center for Children's Books,* Vol. 39, No. 6, February, 1986, p. 103.

The end of Jess Judd's last year in junior high finds him still friendless and fighting his rigid grandmother, bored with school, and chafing against one obnoxious teacher in particular, who insists Jess do a science project. It is this very assignment that proves a water-shed when, partly to defy his grandmother, he understakes to hatch a goose egg he's found on their farm and subsequently connects with a failing classmate, who, like himself, is an orphan harboring bitter loneliness. Both the boys have champions in their corners: Jess, a compassionate step-grandfather, and Meechum, an adoring half-brother stricken with sickle-cell anemia. Meechum's step-father and Jess' grandmother, too, are caring but stiff-necked, and it is an intelligent English teacher who is able to change both boys' discontent with school. This teacher's homosexuality is dealt with openly, as is, in one scene, the two boys' sexual tension. There is a lot going on in this book, including the complex racial mix of Meechum's family. There's also some heavy symbolism, as in the grafted fruit tree that becomes Meechum's redeeming science project. But if the story is slightly overloaded, the characters carry the weight easily. They are vivid and interesting, from the complex protagonist to each barnyard fowl. Jess' maturation comes off convincingly paced and deeply hopeful.

Allan Cuseo

SOURCE: A review of *Big Man and the Burn-out,* in *Voice of Youth Advocates,* Vol. 9, No. 1, April, 1986, pp. 27-8.

Jess, eighth grader, must confront his contempt for his grandmother with whom he lives. His relationship with his peers is no better until he meets Meechum, the burn-out who's flunked so many times he's the oldest student in the eighth grade. Life becomes richer for Jess after he finds a newly laid goose egg which he attempts to hatch in an incubator. The egg has been abandoned as has Jess by his mother.

A gem of a book that is incandescent and fragile with its loving, caring people who are unable to express their emotions. The characters are full of pain and so memorable that the novel begs to be read aloud and cherished. There is so much here to savor: the hypocritical church-goers who frown on Jess because of his bastard status, the bullying peers who abuse classmates, the gay teacher who befriends Jess, and the loving grandmother who lost her daughter (Jess's mother ran away) and now may lose Jess and his step-grandfather.

TRACKS (1986)

Hazel Rochman

SOURCE: A review of *Tracks,* in *Booklist,* Vol. 82, No. 13, March 1, 1986, p. 1014.

Though covering the same subject as [Chester Aaron's] *Lackawanna*—young people hopping the freights with the hoboes during the Depression—this is a far richer novel. In 1934 young Blue Roan, unschooled and runty, runs away from his Oklahoma home to follow his beloved older brother Monroe. At first it is a glorious adventure as the boys learn to survive in the speeding trains and the hobo "jungles" along the tracks. After being caught in a huge Panhandle dust storm, the boys find work in south Texas with the beautiful Italian widow/farmer, Mrs. Landover. But Blue loses his innocence when he and Monroe stumble on Klansmen who are mutilating a Mexican boy they have murdered for courting a white girl. In a stark, terrible gesture, one of the men offers the brothers a knife to join the butchery. Instead, they run, and there is a chase and shootout, a secret surgery performed by Mrs. Landover on the kitchen table, and tense days in hiding until they find safety. Blue and Monroe are wonderfully drawn, their relationship close, funny, and caring—Monroe always in love with some girl; Blue, a sharp observer, but sometimes surprised, as when he discovers that the widow's bigoted son is a sensitive pianist. The story is told, in colorful Oklahoma dialect, by an adult-Blue to his grandson; in doing so, he explains some of the history and comments on the atrocity. Bess's plot transitions are sometimes awkward, and the train adventures seem like a separate book from the episodes with the Klan and the somewhat idealized widow. But in general the picaresque form works well, with sharp vignettes of the period glimpsed by the boys as they stop and move on—a grieving farm woman who harshly mothers them; clusters of the dispossessed huddled in a derelict factory; a teenager's homosexual relationship with two hoboes; a racist's monologue about ending the Depression by sending the "Niggroes" back to Africa. Exciting action, strong relationships, and vivid historical detail are shot throughout with cruelty, prejudice, humor, and brotherhood.

Bulletin of the Center for Children's Books

SOURCE: A review of *Tracks,* in *Bulletin of the Center for Children's Books,* Vol. 39, No. 8, April, 1986, p. 143.

Jess' stepgrandfather in **Big Man and the Burnout** recounts his journey into maturity riding the rails with his brother as a hobo during the Depression. From its opening scene, in which Blue almost gets killed hopping a freight, the book is gripping, with characters making brief but well-defined appearances and action mounting through vivid episodes. There is a cumulatively forceful theme of the dynamics of prejudice, evinced at first in offhand remarks and attitudes and climaxing in the brothers' last harrowing escape from some masked Klansmen whose torture of a Mexican they have witnessed. This is a complex book, perceptive of characters such as the Italian woman who harbors the boys, of the hoboes they ride with, and of the brothers themselves. It's also sharply realistic, a rhythmic first-person narrative told in rural dialect and resonant with the experience of hardship.

Kirkus Reviews

SOURCE: A review of *Tracks,* in *Kirkus Reviews,* Vol. LIV, No. 9, May 1, 1986, p. 718.

The powerful, evocative story of an 11-year-old who journeys with his older brother through the Dust Bowl of Texas and Oklahoma during the Depression.

Blue knows that big brother Monroe will set out after the alluring Starr girls, who have moved to California, and when a freight train passes through town, Blue is ready. The two boys head West through harrowing poverty, dust storms, and a blood curdling encounter with the Ku Klux Klan. Depression hardships are a grim background for the journey, but love, loyalty and Blue's unsullied vision transcend the harsh surroundings.

As narrator, Blue's voice is fresh and unsentimental. His subtle humor and sharp observations draw the reader into the story. The colloquial language is natural and unobtrusive, its perfectly chosen words creating a gentle rhythm. Characterization is vivid, structure superb. Will be popular for its action, but it deserves recognition for its excellent craftsmanship and the beauty of its voice.

Publishers Weekly

SOURCE: A review of *Tracks,* in *Publishers Weekly,* Vol. 229, No. 22, May 30, 1986, p. 69.

Robert Locke (Clayton Bess). Photo by Bob Fong.

The acclaimed author's new novel recreates America during the blighted 1930s, different from but as powerful as Aaron's *Lackawanna.* Bess's story starts in Oklahoma, where the narrator grew up. His name is Blue Roan, and he describes events in a colorful and frank argot that frequently leavens the terror he recalls from his boyhood. At 11, Blue hops his first freight, set on following his older brother Monroe who wants to find the girl he loves (she moved with her family to California). Blue and Monroe narrowly escape death on their travels, the most terrible threat at the hands of members of the Texas Klan. The Klansmen lynch a Mexican youth and blame the murder on the brothers, a situation calling on all of Blue's resources. Running from the criminals, the boys hide out but Monroe is shot and Blue must get help before it's too late. The people who risk their lives to save Monroe as well as others—the cruel and the kind—remain indelibly etched on the reader's mind.

Beth E. Andersen

SOURCE: A review of *Tracks,* in *Voice of Youth Advocates,* Vol. 9, No. 2, June, 1986, p. 76.

Blue Roan, 11-years-old in Oklahoma during the Depression, joins his older brother Monroe on a cross-country trek riding the rails. Monroe has the eye for the ladies in general and three sisters (being moved to Los Angeles by their preacher father) in particular. So the chase is on. Blue narrates this moving lyrical tale of tough times and strong boys of honor. Blue and his brother share the comraderie of the hoboes of the railyard jungle, spend time with an unusual courageous Italian-American widow, and stumble upon a vicious group of KKK clansmen murdering a young Mexican boy. The killers turn their murderous ways on the brothers, who attempt to escape a midnight chase with bullets flying.

Bess is a gifted storyteller, grabbing his reader with his opening lines, and not letting go as the story of Blue's evolution from innocent devoted brother to a too sadly, worldly-wise citizen of the road, unfolds. Highly recommended.

Loralee MacPike

SOURCE: A review of *Tracks,* in *Best Sellers,* Vol. 46, No. 5, August, 1986, p. 196.

Clayton Bess's tale of an eleven-year-old boy riding the rails in the American Southwest of the 1930's is at once sweet and gripping, sad and strong. Blue Roan, following his seventeen-year-old brother Monroe, jumps a train West; by the second page, readers are already fear-deep into Blue's precarious hold on the boxcar ladder as he begins to learn the hobo's trade. Hoboes, not bums: a hobo is "a kind of migrant worker" who works and then rides, works and rides. And so Blue and Monroe set off to work their way to Amarillo to find Monroe's girl friends, Rose Jewel and Marguerite Pearl Starr. But Preacher Clyde Starr has already left for Los Angeles, so the boys stop to work for Mrs. Landover, an Italian opera singer who followed her love to America only to have him lynched by the Ku Klux Klan, leaving her with a big farm and two small children. Mary and Ira Landover, who waste their days practicing scales, seem pretty useless to the fast-growing Blue until they perform a concert, and then his world expands to include the wonder of beautiful music. Forced to move on again when the Klan accuses *them* of a murder they watch Klansmen commit, Blue and Monroe are brought to Black Cully, a healer hobo. They survive a dust storm, a gondola car full of rolling pipes, and a vicious bum out to get them. The story ends in California, the land of gold and Disney, where Blue settles down and writes this book, his reminiscences of youth.

Told in the dialect of 30's Oklahoma, the book re-creates a boyhood on the rails. It manages to be evocative while maintaining the realism of the story; its pace is fast and its philosophy rich. Not least, it's a pleasure to find that a book so interesting can also be totally unobjectionable.

Robert Unsworth

SOURCE: A review of *Tracks,* in *School Library Journal,* Vol. 32, No. 10, August, 1986, p. 98.

This is the Depression-era story of Sidney Australia Roan,

as told by his grandson, who passes it along "just the way he told it." Sid, or Blue Roan as he is called, leaves his dismal Oklahoma town to accompany his big brother, Monroe, to Los Angeles, as Monroe follows the love of his life, Rose Jewel. They ride the rails but never do get to L.A., at least in this novel (which hints at a sequel). They encounter dust storms, prejudices and a brutal KKK murderer, a cattle roundup, nice hobos and at least one mean one and a kindly Italian widow with musical prodigies for children. There is also room for reflections on bad government programs for farmers. The writing is splendid, once readers adjust to the colloquial language and grammar, and the story moves along nicely, with misfortunes awaiting Blue and his brother around each corner. *Tracks* is a well-done, if fanciful, evocation of a slice of the 1930s.

📖 *THE MAYDAY RAMPAGE* (1993)

Publishers Weekly

SOURCE: A review of *The Mayday Rampage,* in *Publishers Weekly,* Vol. 240, No. 4, January 25, 1993, p. 87.

In perhaps no other YA novel to date has the topic of AIDS been dealt with as graphically and thoroughly as in this timely book by the author of *Tracks* and *Big Man and the Burnout.* Structured in the vein of Paul Zindel's *The Pigman,* with two teens chronicling events which have led to a major crisis in their lives, the story begins with seniors Molly and Jess telling how they decided to write a series of articles on the HIV virus for their school newspaper. The young journalists set out to research their topic by interviewing several people in their community, including medical professionals, a prostitute and the mother of a five-year-old AIDS victim. The devastating effects of the disease become even more immediate when the pair learns that the housemate of a favorite teacher has contracted the virus. Although the protagonists' mutual attraction borders on over-cuteness, their dialogues for the most part are compelling and true-to-life. Besides dramatizing the impact of the AIDS epidemic on a high school population, Bess provides facts and statistics which may shock uninformed readers. Most hard-hitting of all is his epilogue, which traces the growth of the disease and reveals the sad, ironic fates of the two students.

Jacqueline C. Rose

SOURCE: A review of *The Mayday Rampage,* in *Kliatt Young Adult Paperback Book Guide,* Vol. 27, No. 2, March, 1993, pp. 3-4.

High school juniors Jess and Molly write a series of articles on AIDS for their school paper. Some school authorities object to the articles' explicitness, and Jess and Molly are forced to apologize. With the help of a sympathetic teacher, they print their own newspaper, which results in their being suspended from school. Meanwhile, Jess and Molly have been developing an intimate relationship. In the end, Molly discovers that she's HIV positive, the result of a past encounter with a gay male friend who was trying to deny his sexuality. Because this story is presented as a transcription of recorded tapes that Jess and Molly made, the text is entirely dialogue, making quick and appealing reading for reluctant readers. The protagonists are extremely funny and they are so realistic that readers will almost experience them as live presences. The storyline is riveting from start to finish, with accurate AIDS information appropriately woven in. While the impact of AIDS on the characters' lives is deeply disturbing, the story is an excellent illustration of the realities of this disease. This book could be a most effective tool for AIDS education and prevention. Bess is a master at capturing the way teens talk. Some adults will probably object to the street language and graphic sexual details. However, the book will grab teens and move them profoundly. A definite "must purchase."

Kathy Fritts

SOURCE: A review of *The Mayday Rampage,* in *School Library Journal,* Vol. 39, No. 5, May, 1993, p. 124.

Molly and Jess, crusading reporters from the Broder High School *Rampage,* are determined to inform the student body about AIDS. This book tells about their experiences and is written in the form of their taped reminiscences about the explosive events that follow the publication of their stories. Their language is explicit, and an uproar ensues: forced apologies, suspensions, expulsion for Jess, departure of the principal, and disaster for a gay teacher. Molly has contracted AIDS from a single encounter with a bisexual and is fading fast in the epilogue; Jess marries her so she can have health insurance. Molly and Jess are endearing and true-to-life characters, but the plot is largely a series of events into which clinically detailed and graphic lessons about AIDS have been inserted. Molly herself, in spite of her exact and detailed knowledge, fails to ask Jess to use a condom ("yeah, well . . . that's different."). The book simply doesn't work as a story; rather it's didacticism at its worst.

Ruth Dishnow

SOURCE: A review of *The Mayday Rampage,* in *The Book Report,* Vol. 12, No. 1, May-June, 1993, p. 38.

The back cover of this book states: ". . . if straight talk about sex offends you, then put this book down right now." Using a dialogue format, this novel presents essential information about AIDS from the viewpoint of Jess and Molly, high school juniors who write a series of articles about AIDS for their school newspaper, *The Rampage.* They talk to medical professionals, a prostitute, the mother of a five-year-old AIDS victim, as well as a mother who campaigned to keep the child out of school. Molly discovers she has contracted the virus from a one-time sexual encounter with another student. Bess describes Molly's fight against the illness, addressing issues such as

her difficulty in obtaining insurance coverage. Students in my school who read this book loved it, finding it "openly honest and frank." They immersed themselves in a moving story about censorship, homosexuality and AIDS. This is a superb title to recommend to students who want AIDS information without delving into a scientific nonfiction book.

Laura Lent

SOURCE: A review of *The Mayday Rampage,* in *Voice of Youth Advocates,* Vol. 16, No. 2, June, 1993, p. 86.

Bess uses this book as a means to thoroughly discuss the AIDS issue and all of its ramifications. Because of his creative approach—having two teenagers, Jess and Molly, record their adventures onto cassette tapes—young adults will be interested enough in the story to actually learn some facts about sex and AIDS that might save their lives.

Jess and Molly try to educate their peers on AIDS through a series of articles in their school newspaper, the *Rampage.* Although their articles are factual, the principal, Mr. Hightower, bows to pressure from the community and makes the two apologize for the latest AIDS articles that were published.

Both Jess and Molly are unwilling to be silenced; therefore, they decide to record on cassette their interviews with people affected by AIDS, their own personal thoughts, and candid questions and answers about AIDS. Since they record these things in the privacy of Molly's home, Jess and Molly are able to speak freely about this subject—as two teenagers would. Although some adults may find their discussions and language lewd, this reviewer feels that the language used by Bess will be easily understood by the majority of today's teenagers. Through this style of writing, Bess is able to provide factual answers to serious questions about sexuality and the AIDS virus that teenagers are prone to wonder about.

In addition, Bess personalizes this book by showing what happens to Jess and Molly because of their sexual relationship. Thus, the author dispels the myth that sex between monogamous, heterosexual teens is safe by revealing Jess's and Molly's problems at the end. Bess's message is powerful. No teen can be absolutely sure about his or her partner, and the only safe sex is *none.*

This book will definitely appeal to a wide variety of young adults because the content deals with two taboo subjects—sex and AIDS. Furthermore, teenagers will understand the information that is provided because Jess and Molly speak the same language (lots of slang) that teens speak. Young adults will appreciate the candor with which specific questions are answered. Once the reader figures out the author's approach—teens talking into a cassette recorder—the story flows easily from page-to-page.

Unfortunately, my review does not begin to show the

positive influence this book can have on our teenagers. Because of the subject and how the author handles it, this book is superior and is a book that every teen (possibly everybody) needs to read because it dispenses badly needed factual information to an at-risk group—the nation's teens. Further, Bess may even save a life or two because of his willingness to write about this subject. In my opinion, many parents will appreciate Bess's mature approach to a life-threatening disease and will be relieved that they do not have to discuss it with their children.

Cathi Dunn MacRae

SOURCE: A review of *The Mayday Rampage,* in *Wilson Library Bulletin,* Vol. 68, No. 1, September, 1993, p. 93.

To reach young adults who feel invulnerable to AIDS, Clayton Bess uses fictional audiotapes in *The Mayday Rampage,* on which high school journalists Jess and Molly record their traumatic experience of censorship of their AIDS articles in their school newspaper, *The Rampage.* (Actual tapes are available.) Within this dialogue, Bess flawlessly characterizes the two speakers and everyone they discuss. As their story emerges, Jess and Molly fall in love, giving readers the sensation of eavesdropping on a private encounter.

Meanwhile, Jess and Molly dispense hard-hitting facts about AIDS in teens' own language, answering questions the author collected from students. Their own censored interviews with a child dying of AIDS, a prostitute, and a gay man are "better," says Molly, "than those pamphlets in the library that look just like schoolwork and that no one reads." When Jess learns that Vic—the lover of his favorite teacher, Mr. Goodban—is dying of AIDS, his refusal to name his gay teacher provokes a riot and his expulsion from school. Molly is also not immune to consequences. Readers who have not missed the irony of Molly preaching the use of condoms while refusing to use them herself will still be jarred at the final twist in her story.

Of all AIDS information available, this novel is most likely to be taken to heart by teenagers, through the voices of peers deeply affected by the disease and the political controversy surrounding it. The taped version targets reluctant readers, and the book format could reach a wider audience if dramatized.

A 1992 report shows an AIDS increase of 70 percent among teenagers in the previous two years. Because the wallop-packing *Mayday Rampage* will arrest even the most resistant young adults, libraries need to purchase multiple life-saving copies and then make sure their YA patrons find them.

Additional coverage of Bess's life and career is contained in the following sources published by Gale Research: *Contemporary Authors,* Vol. 129; and *Something about the Author,* Vol. 63.

Margaret Buffie

1945-

Canadian author of fiction.

Major works include *Who Is Frances Rain?* (1987; U.S. edition as *The Haunting of Frances Rain*), *The Guardian Circle* (1989; U.S. edition as *The Warnings*), *My Mother's Ghost* (1992; U.S. edition as *Someone Else's Ghost*).

INTRODUCTION

A popular and widely respected author of fiction for young adults, Buffie has written supernatural fantasies that are uniquely grounded in thought-provoking explorations of modern family relationships and the growing pains common to adolescents. She is credited with a lively style and engaging, credible protagonists, and her stories are commended as fast-paced and inventive. Ghosts and other apparitions play important roles in Buffie's novels, where past and present come together in unusual and mysterious ways. Buffie has stated: "I don't believe great lives die. There is a link between generations—characteristics passed on, stories told—and I explore those links." Critics have praised the author for effectively blending magic with the mundane, humor with horror, and time-travel with frank contemporary realities in her works, which commonly feature young protagonists who learn from the past how better to cope with and begin to resolve present-day problems. An accomplished painter and illustrator, Buffie is also noted for her vivid descriptions of landscape and her meticulous depiction of time and place. The natural beauties of Long Pine Lake in Ontario, where Buffie spent many of her childhood summers, and her hometown of Winnipeg, Manitoba, figure prominently in her works. Commenting on the relation between Buffie's own experiences and observations and those of her characters, Peter Carver has written: "Sifting through layers of memory and feeling, Margaret Buffie is a kind of literary archaeologist exploring the people who occupy her stories. It's a search that's not likely to disappoint her readers."

Biographical Information

Born and raised in Winnipeg, Manitoba, Buffie and her three sisters lost their father to cancer when Buffie was twelve. Their mother subsequently worked two jobs while attending night school in order to keep the family together. Buffie received her Bachelor of Fine Arts degree from the University of Manitoba in 1967 and married James Macfarlane, a high school art teacher, the following year. She worked as a fashion illustrator for the Hudson Bay Company until 1970. After the birth of her daughter, Christine Anne, Buffie worked part-time as a painting instructor for the Winnipeg Art Gallery from 1974–75; she returned to the university to earn a teaching certifi-

cate in 1976. Buffie taught high school art for one year, then decided to stay home to raise her daughter and do freelance illustration and painting. When Christine Anne became a teenager, Buffie developed an interest in young adult fiction. She began writing stories in a journal, an effort which culminated in the publication of her first young adult novel, *Who Is Frances Rain?*, in 1987.

Major Works

The highly successful *Who Is Frances Rain?* comprises elements of a mystery, ghost story, and time-travel fantasy with Buffie's sensitive depiction of a fractured modern family. In the novel, fifteen-year-old Lizzie, anxious to get away from her moody mother, new stepfather, and quarreling siblings, decides to explore the deserted Rain Island, considered by her grandmother to be unsafe and off-limits. There Lizzie discovers a pair of magic glasses through which she peers more than half a century into the past, viewing two female figures who lived on the island in the 1920s. What she learns from them helps her to appreciate her own family history and to work at resolving her personal problems. In *The Guardian Circle,*

Buffie's fifteen-year-old heroine Rachel is deserted by her mother and feels abandoned by her truck-driving father, who leaves her with his Aunt Irene and the eccentric elderly residents of Irene's haunted house. Gradually Rachel earns the trust of the older people and of her great Aunt, who reveals to her the secret behind the strange happenings, and becomes friends with a boy who lives across the street—gaining a confidant with whom she can share her explorations and discoveries. Commentators note that Buffie has blended humor and romance effectively with the supernatural in this work, contributing to a lively read. *My Mother's Ghost* features two stories from two different times: the story of sixteen-year-old Jess and her parents, on a guest ranch in Alberta in the present, trying to cope with the death of Jess's little brother Scotty, and that of a crippled boy, Ian Shaw, who lived on the same ranch nearly a hundred years before. Jess's grief-stricken mother begins to see an apparition and is convinced it is her dead son. Jess, however, discovers Ian's journal and uses it to reveal the real identity of the ghost her mother sees. In a rare moment, past and present overlap, and both spirits are laid to rest in peace. Thus in all three books, Buffie helps young people resolve conflicts in the present with help from the past, transforming harsh reality by transcending the laws of nature.

Awards

Who Is Frances Rain? won the 1988 Canadian Young Adult Book Award, was runner-up for the 1988 Canadian Book of the Year Award, and was shortlisted for the Ruth Schwartz Children's Book Award 1988–89.

GENERAL COMMENTARY

Dave Jenkinson

SOURCE: "Margaret Buffie," in *Emergency Librarian,* Vol. 16, No. 3, January-February, 1989, pp. 58-62.

As a child, Margaret was afraid of [things] from bugs to big trucks and from Joe, the peddler's horse, to Frank, her great-aunt's budgie. But the greatest fear was reserved for bedtime. "It meant being cut away from that warm light downstairs that my parents basked in while I dealt with the dark and the dreadful things that flickered and slid through the blackness of my room at night." For her ninth birthday, Margaret received a gift from her parents which changed her night-time dread. "It was a big, fat book called *Heidi.*" Margaret's mother read to her nightly, but that practice was replaced by Margaret's being allowed to read by herself. What was initially a way to postpone "lights-out" became something much more significant. "For the first time I went into that cave of darkness with other images in my mind than the dim pictures of horrible, rustling night creepers in my closet. I wasn't afraid anymore because I wasn't going to sleep all alone. I had Heidi with me. I *was* Heidi."

Other "friends" and identifications followed, among them the Bobbsey Twins and Nancy Drew. "I read all the time, and when I didn't have a new book to read, I reread the others." And another change took place. "Sometimes when I went to bed at night, I'd sort of rearrange the stories in my mind and make up my own. But the thought that I might write something some day didn't even enter my mind." Margaret's reason for not seeing herself as a future author lay partly in her discovery of another talent. "I'd found out early that I could take some of those thoughts that were in my mind, and I could put them down on paper in a new and exciting way than just writing. I could draw, and I was pretty good at it too. I remember I used to do caricatures of our teachers to entertain my friends."

Born in Winnipeg, Manitoba on March 29, 1945, the third of four girls, Margaret identifies that her life changed drastically when she was twelve. "In six short months, just before I entered junior high school, my father became very ill and died of cancer. My mother was determined to keep the family together, which she did. She went to secretarial school at night and worked two jobs during the day." Though the period was most difficult, Margaret reflects that "it's a time that's full of really rich memories for me that I've used or tried to use in the writing that I do." Many aspects of life changed including the family's lengthy holidays at their log cabin on Long Pine Lake in Ontario, the future setting of *Who is Frances Rain?* "Instead of the two whole months, we managed to squeeze in a few weeks and some weekends."

"All through junior high and high school, I read books for myself, and I drew pictures for other people." Following graduation, Margaret entered the University of Manitoba where she completed a Bachelor of Fine Arts degree in 1967. Though her married name is Macfarlane, Margaret maintains her maiden name for writing purposes as a tribute to her father. Prior to the birth of her daughter, Christine in 1971, Margaret worked as a fashion illustrator for the Hudson's Bay. Teaching painting part-time at the Winnipeg Art Gallery followed, and then Margaret returned to university, obtaining a teaching certificate in 1976. After a single year as a high school art teacher, Margaret decided she wanted to stay home to raise her daughter and fill "spare" hours by painting and doing freelance illustration.

As daughter Chris approached her teen years, Margaret became reflective. "I began to think about myself at 12 and how similar and different my daughter and I were. And I began to think about my father. I talked about him with my mother and my sisters, and I noticed something amazing. When I was growing up, there had really been five different fathers in our household. One father for my mother, whom I didn't know at all, and one for each of my sisters. It was at that point that I began to write a kind of journal of my life at 1241 Dominion Street in Winnipeg. I wrote everything I could about the father I had known and about my life with my sisters and my mother, before and after his death. And I wrote about our cabin on Long Pine Lake, and when I was done, I put it away."

About the same time, Margaret, as is the custom of many mothers, took a "look" at the content of her daughter's free reading materials. "Another new world opened up for me as I started to read a new breed of young adult novels. I became a secret YA reader as I read books by K. M. Peyton, Susan Cooper, Philippa Pearce, Norma Fox Mazer, John Rowe Townsend and others. And I was well and truly hooked. I began to notice how these writers used language, rich descriptive language used sparingly, yet weaving that language into wonderfully compelling stories about growing up."

The reading of Chris's books and the writing of the Dominion Street journal came together one day when Margaret revisited the journal's pages. "It was while I was looking at it that something struck me. I had never been happier than when I was writing. Painting, it seemed, I was always doing for others, but this wad of paper in my hands was something I'd done for myself. I gave it some thought, and I decided to write a book."

As so many new authors have discovered, the decision to write a book and the act of actually producing one can be separated by a very large time gap. "I can't count the first two years except I suppose I could classify them as 'research.' There aren't a lot of places to go to learn about writing children's literature, at least not in Manitoba. I read every book I could lay my hands on about how to write, and so I read such books as *The fiction writer's handbook, The writer's survival manual,* and I even read *How to become a bestselling author.*"

But Margaret did more than just read about writing; she wrote. Having declared herself a "writer", she "demanded" a place to write in the family home and was given the storage room next to the furnace where, equipped with a cheap portable typewriter, a card table, a folding chair and a few empty shelves, she became, in her words, "a closet writer, too embarrassed to tell my friends that I was 'becoming a writer'." Her secret existence was forced into the open by the actions of an employee at the local library where Margaret borrowed her books on writing. Recognizing what appeared to be a pattern to Margaret's reading, the library staffer asked if Margaret were a writer. When Margaret replied that she was trying to become one, the suggestion was proffered that Margaret should become a member of the Canadian Authors' Association and attend their workshops where she could get some feedback on her work. Most hesitant at reading her manuscript "to a bunch of strangers and having them pick it apart", Margaret tried to beg off by saying that she was "not much of a joiner."

Each library visit, however, brought the same suggestion, and faced with joining this group or changing libraries, Margaret capitulated. Having become a member, Margaret entered one of her short stories in a CAA contest and won a runner-up award. In the first flush of her validation by peers, Margaret ran about telling everyone of the recognition, but then the realization that "one short story does not a novel make, and it does not a writer make

either" set in, and "so now I had to sit down and finish this 'stupid' novel."

The novel was an adult mystery and reflected the fact "I'd read many hundred mystery stories when I was a teenager and I just loved them. I wanted to write a mystery story, and I really wanted it to be published." The finished manuscript was packaged up and sent out, and it came back, not once but several times. With each rejection, Margaret became more dejected. "I figured I'm not a writer at all. There's no hope for me." Her feelings softened when she read an article about rejection and discovered that such well known writers as Agatha Christie and John Creasey had also been on the receiving end of numerous rejection slips.

From the same article, Margaret also gleaned some valuable practical advice. The author counselled would-be authors to research publishers to confirm that those receiving their manuscripts were actually interested in publishing the types of books the authors were producing. Margaret realized that "I hadn't done my homework." At that time, her manuscript "was sitting in a slush pile at McClelland and Stewart. I 'knew' they were going to reject it, and so I thought, 'Am I going, to sit here and do nothing, or am I going to settle down and write another book, or am I going to give up writing altogether?'"

Of the three choices, Margaret elected the middle one. Her reading of young adult novels had caused her to be "fed up with the disease-of-the-week and the young-hormones-in-rampage books that flooded the market. I like a book where the kids come into contact with forces greater than that. I like magic and dark forces, books of self-discovery on a deeper, more universal level." Margaret also had what she considered to be a good concept for a YA novel.

"The idea for *Who is Frances Rain?* came from a decaying garbage dump dating from the 1930's and located on an island near our Long Pine Lake cabin. In 1983, I was looking for old bottles with my sister when I discovered a pair of wire-rimmed spectacles inside an old root beer cup that had been lying under a deep layer of damp green moss and red soil. When I titled the cup over, out fell the spectacles, just like in *Frances Rain,* only for me it wasn't as much fun because I cleaned them up, put them to my eyes, and nothing happened. But I thought, 'Gee! Wouldn't it be really neat if, when you put them up to your eyes, you could see into the past?' And that's when the plot for the book was hatched."

"I took a fifteen-year-old girl, her grandmother's cabin in northern Manitoba, a family that's going through some tough changes, the remains of a prospector's cabin, and put them all together into what I wanted—a combination of a ghost story, a mystery, and a comment on contemporary life's problems as well." Barely pausing when her mystery manuscript was returned, liked by McClelland and Stewart but rejected because the house did not publish mysteries, Margaret spent about a year working on *Frances Rain,* and the spring of 1986 saw the third draft's completion. Letting the manuscript "settle" awhile, Margaret reread it a few weeks later. "I was pretty close to what I'd hoped to achieve by that point. Lizzie, the main character, had finally found her own voice, and my characters had gotten off their flat two-dimensional planes and were walking around on their own now."

Though the novel's setting is northern Manitoba, its basis in fact was Long Pine Lake. Writing the backdrop was probably the easiest part of the book for Margaret for "I'd painted that setting in oils and water colors for thirty years. I knew it intimately, the smells, the colors, and the drama of its many moods." Working in the book's real life setting, Margaret did a final summer long revision and then, with great deliberation, set out in search of a publisher. "I took time and learned the children's book market in Canada. I read *Children's book news,* talked to librarians, and haunted book stores." Liking the work of Kids Can Press, Margaret decided they were going to get her unsolicited manuscript "over the transom."

"In less than two weeks I heard from them. I received a phone call from the publisher, Valerie Hussey. They actually wanted to publish my book! She said, 'Would you be willing to make a few changes?' By that time, I would have cut off one of my two typing fingers for her. 'Yes! Of course I'll make changes!'" When a letter detailing the "few changes" arrived, it included a request to shorten the book by 50 pages. "I had been strutting around telling my husband that I was about to start on book number two any minute now." Since there were no obvious large sections which could be amputated, "I was going to have to suck out little sections of the manuscript. This meant that I'd have to carefully rewrite, lifting a paragraph here, a sentence here, a word here, a word there. Needless to say, I came down with a thump!"

In order to be included in the new catalog, all of the work had to be carried out in just two months. Margaret received a contract, a small advance and an editor, Charis Wahl, plus the name of a courier service to shuttle the revisions. Aided by long distance calls, the last revised manuscript page was completed but not before the old typewriter literally dropped its carriage and had to be replaced by a new one.

As the revisions were being done, a new problem arose. The book's working title had been "Rain Island Ghosts", but Kids Can thought it made the book sound too much like a bubblegum book. "The Lost Farewell", "The Shadow Watcher", "The Final Thread" and others were all tried out but discarded. When *Who is Frances Rain?* was put forth, "we all agreed that it gave just the right degree of mystery and people might wonder about it."

And then there was the need for a cover illustration. Since Margaret was an illustrator, would she like to do the cover?, asked Kids Can. Burdened with revisions and lacking experience in the specialized art of fiction covers, Margaret declined. A photocopy of a proposed cover was sent for Margaret's approval before going into the catalog. "Seeing my book written up in the Kids Can catalog

was the first tangible evidence that this mess of manuscript pages was really going to become a reality."

Copy editing followed, and chunks of manuscript roared back and forth between Winnipeg and Toronto as small changes were made. Galley proofs were then checked by Margaret and two proof readers with this stage being done in three days. "When the pages arrived, I went through them as they suggested, using a ruler and concentrating on actually reading the book and not just skimming it over. And when it was done, I sent it back for the last time. I was actually finished."

"It's a strange feeling to write a book and have it published and suddenly have to step back and watch it go out on its own. For many months, this book, its characters and everything about it were mine, and mine alone. Then I had to share it with a reader at a publisher's, and before I knew it, I was sharing it with strangers all across the country. One of my biggest worries was how it was going to be received by these strangers. Would they see Lizzie and her family the way I did? Would they care what happened to Frances Rain the way I did?"

Though most parents naturally worry about their children as they take their first independent steps into the larger world, Margaret did not have to concern herself long about her literary child for the book received excellent reviews and was named a runner-up for the Canadian Book of the Year for Children Award, a finalist for the Ruth Schwartz Award, and the winner of the Young Adult Canadian Book Award. As well, Penguin purchased the British Commonwealth hardcover and paperback rights and Scholastic (U.S.) has picked up the hardcover rights.

For fifteen-year-old Elizabeth, aka Lizzie, July's arrival had always signalled a summer with her older brother Evan and younger sister Erica at their grandmother's cabin on Rain Lake in northern Manitoba. This year, however, brings the addition of an unwanted stepfather, "Toothy" Tim, and a sullen, cantankerous mother, Connie. Some 18 months earlier, Connie's lawyer husband had deserted the family and, just months before, Connie had remarried. The two older siblings, resenting their stay-at-home potter stepfather, attempt to make his life as unpleasant as possible. Seeking a way to get his new wife out of her funk, Toothy Tim had suggested that the family members vacation together, but Connie, also a lawyer, resents spending time away from her office. Though Connie's stated reason for not wanting to holiday masks the real cause of her unhappiness, her negative behaviors still lead to the family's mood being tense and unpleasant. To escape her sullen mother, nosey stepfather and carping brother, Lizzie decides to find a secret place where she can be alone. The site she chooses is Rain Island, some half mile distant from her Gran's cabin and named after a mysterious woman who had once lived there. On her second visit to the island, Lizzie, while sifting through the remains of an old cabin, uncovers a root beer mug containing a pair of wire-rimmed spectacles with round lenses. Placing the glasses on her face, Lizzie finds the season changed and the cabin restored. Further visits introduce Lizzie to the island's "inhabitants", Frances Rain and a teenage girl, both visible only when Lizzie dons the glasses. Learning that the island's namesake had been dead for over 60 years causes Lizzie to seek to answer the compound question, "Who is Frances Rain, and what is her relationship with the young girl?"

A "Prologue" tantalizes readers by suggesting, "If you don't believe in ghosts, and if you doubt that you could ever be convinced that they exist, it might be best to stop reading right about here." While immediately introducing the fantasy element, *Who is Frances Rain?* operates as both a time fantasy and as realistic fiction. Initially, Kids Can objected to the book's dual structure. "When I first sent the manuscript to the publisher, they didn't want both stories in there. They thought that the family conflict was one novel and that Frances Rain's story was another. They said, 'You can't do two story themes like this in a book without botching it up or without confusing the reader.' That was one of the things that went back and forth between us, and I did slightly lower the family conflict. I felt one story fed right into the other."

Tying the two streams together is the romantic relationship between Lizzie and Alex Bird, a young man from the lake area who had previously viewed her simply as a bothersome girl. "The romantic plot was put in because my daughter 'demanded' it. She was 15 at the time, and she said, 'There's no romance in here. Girls and boys like to read about that, Mom.' So I thought about it, and, of course, many of the books that I'd read always had this sort of undercurrent. I didn't want the relationship to detract from the real story in *Frances Rain,* but I wanted it to have some promise. Those are the memories I had of 15, and so you take little bits and pieces of what you grew up with and what you think the reader will enjoy."

With one of the plot lines dealing with family conflict, Margaret found herself having to make some language decisions. The final version contains a dozen or so cuss words, but "there were a few worse words in there that I edited out myself. All the language that was in the manuscript was fine with the editor, but, as I reedited, I thought, 'Nah! That had better come out.' What's left is real language. It's what people really say. It seems to me that if you're going to whitewash it to the point that it's not real language anymore, then your characters aren't real people in the kids' minds. I thought, 'Everybody I know uses these words, and so this family does too because there's lot of conflict and stress.' I knew that the question of language and school audiences would crop up, and I spoke to the publisher and editor about it. Both were totally supportive."

During the writing process, Margaret finds herself almost driven. "When I'm writing something, I think about it all the time. If I think about the right idea, I have to scurry about like an idiot looking for pen and paper to write it down otherwise it just floats away though it may come back to me later. I bought a tape recorder, and I keep it all set to go. If I think of something as I'm working, I can run over and click it on and speak to it. When I was first working on *Frances Rain,* I was obsessed by it, and I didn't think of anything else except that book. As I got into 'The Overlooking Ring,' I was just living in a world all of my own. It just drives my family crazy."

"Some things come to you when you're not expecting it. The really amazing thing is that sometimes when you're writing, a twist in the plot or something like that just appears on the page, and it's perfect for that spot. It's really strange when you reread something you've written. Sometimes it's hard remembering writing it because you've been working on it so intensely. Sometimes I feel that way about my paintings too when I haven't seen a painting for four or five years. It's like somebody else did it. If I pick up *Frances Rain* now, I can actually read it as a reader, not as the author of it."

The manuscript for Margaret's second book for adolescents is presently with her publisher and carries the working title, "The Overlooking Ring." "It's about a young girl who is left at the doorstep of her great-aunt's big house in Winnipeg. When she enters this home thinking that she's going to be with her elderly aunt, she finds that the place is full of these strange old people. As time goes on, she begins to realize that there's something odd about them." Margaret says that finding the correct voice to use has been difficult. "I've gone from first person to third person and back at least three times. I wrote the first 100 pages about five times until I felt like pulling my hair out." Daughter Chris loved the first book, and functioned as the in-house critic for the second. "I was always shoving pages at her saying, 'What do you think of this?' She thinks she likes the second one better, but. . . ."

Margaret's hesitancy about accepting her daughter's positive judgment can be attributed, perhaps, to authors' common dread of the second book. "There's no guarantee that book number two is going to have the same reception. It's possible that no one's going to like it. I've been told by a number of people that second books are reviewed far more critically and are often not as good as the first book. So I'm working really, really hard to keep that from happening, but you never know. If number two's a big flat flop, then where will I be? I figure I'll just be working on number three."

Peter Carver

SOURCE: "Margaret Buffie's Spirit Circle," in *Quill and Quire,* Vol. 55, No. 11, November, 1989, p. 13.

Few young-adult novelists have enjoyed the charmed entry into their careers that Margaret Buffie has. The first publisher to receive her first manuscript was Kids Can Press, which had never published a young-adult novel before. But within two weeks *Who Is Frances Rain?* was accepted, a decision that started Kids Can and Buffie down an adventurous road together. Now Kids Can is publishing Buffie's second novel, *The Guardian Circle,* which again evokes the world of ghosts and spirits that informed *Frances Rain.*

Conversations with Margaret Buffie often end up as discussions about family, especially about "the Buffie girls": Linda the nurse, Judy the mother, Erna the writer, Margaret the painter. Each sister is aware of her place in the family, all have strong personalities, and all are competitive, loving, but tough. "With us, there's always a wariness about what the other is doing. We're all supposed to occupy certain roles; then I hopped out of my little slot and I wasn't just Margaret the painter anymore."

In fact Buffie has painted since age 13. She holds a degree in fine arts from the University of Manitoba, has shown and sold her work in a Winnipeg gallery, has worked as an illustrator, and spent a year teaching high-school art. She started writing about six years ago, and since then has done less painting. "I like writing better," she says. "It's more personal."

The Guardian Circle is dedicated to "the Buffie girls who once lived at 1241." Buffie's father died when Margaret was 12 and all the sisters were either on the brink or in the midst of adolescence. Her mother worked hard at two jobs to keep the family home at 1241 Dominion Street in Winnipeg's west end. "We were afraid of being homeless," Margaret recalls, "and my mother was determined to hold on to the house."

Buffie also talks about Long Pine Lake, near Ingolf in northwestern Ontario, where Grandfather Leach (Margaret's mother's father), a CPR worker, got off the train one day in 1912 and built a summer home for his family. "All the great memories in my life are associated with the lake," Buffie says. "Winnipeg happens to be where I spend the winter, but the lake is home."

Long Pine Lake provided the setting for *Who Is Frances Rain?,* published in 1987. The novel is marked, above all, by its unmistakably Canadian setting, the woods and water so familiar to Canadian kids who go to summer cottages.

The Guardian Circle was the first manuscript Buffie worked on, but "*Frances Rain* took over." The attention Buffie received for that book was overwhelming. "It took my breath away—suddenly I was off and running with my first book and I couldn't quite believe it all. This second book was harder than anything else I've done in my life. I said to myself: '*No one*'s going to like it! I was just lucky the first time.'"

Set in a dark, creaky old Winnipeg house, *The Guardian Circle* is about teenaged Rachel, who is dumped by her distraught father to live with her great-aunt Irene. Aunt Irene, it turns out, shares the house with a weird assortment of ancient characters whose motives and past Rachel finds unfathomable. Rachel is full of anger at being abandoned, first by her artist mother and then by her father, who has abruptly sold off the family farm to take up the life of a long-distance trucker.

The members of Rachel's new "family" are part of a spirit circle involved in a classic struggle between good and evil, a struggle in which Rachel herself becomes the pivotal figure. While the story itself is not autobiographical, woven into the characters of Aunt Irene and her associates are elements of the figures in Buffie's own family—and her own teenage anger.

"I'm not sure what I was angry at when I was growing up. I was afraid of everything—of school, you name it. If the worst can happen, it'll happen to me—that's what I thought. I was always late in high school. The excuse was that I was looking after my little sister—and I was furious when the teacher took me aside and tried to show understanding of my predicament. 'Get *away* from me,' I'd say. I was terrible—but I felt everything that Rachel feels in this book."

Buffie chuckles at the idea that the therapeutic nature of writing can save the writer the cost of psychoanalysis. She credits her growing sense of humour to her husband, Jim Macfarlane (a high-school art teacher), who has, according to Buffie, a knack for telling a funny story and an upbeat view of life that balances her sometimes overly serious mood. (Their 18-year-old daughter, Christine, is working in a library for a year before starting university.)

In addition to her preoccupation with family, Margaret Buffie has a keen sense of the spiritual world—although she herself has never had a psychic experience. "Jim's a very pragmatic person, but he's had a couple of strong psychic experiences," she says. "I don't have a religion, but I feel the human spirit is strong. I also think that supernatural stories allow kids to take problems in real life and abstract them somewhat. They allow a different experience of life."

The ghostly world of Buffie's novels is not necessarily threatening but rather a manifestation of the strong personalities of those who have gone before—hardly surprising in a writer who has such a strong sense of where she comes from.

Buffie's next book will be set in Alberta, where her sister Linda lives. "I have a very strong sense of the place—in fact I get homesick for it. I have a whole wall of my room covered with illustrations and photos of ranch life."

Sifting through layers of memory and feeling, Margaret Buffie is a kind of literary archaeologist exploring the people who occupy her stories. It's a search that's not likely to disappoint her readers.

TITLE COMMENTARY

WHO IS FRANCES RAIN? (1987; U.S. edition as *The Haunting of Frances Rain*)

Children's Book News, **Toronto**

SOURCE: A review of *Who Is Frances Rain?* in *Chil-*

dren's Book News, Toronto, Vol. 10, No. 2, September, 1987, p. 13.

It's summer, and 15-year-old Lizzie, her elder brother and her younger sister are on their way to stay with their grandmother in her cabin on Rain Lake in northern Manitoba. This time, though, there's a difference: their mother is coming too, and with her their new stepfather ("Toothy Tim", Lizzie's dubbed him), and a lot of domestic tension which threatens to disrupt the family holiday and much more.

To get away from the bickering, Lizzie decides to explore Rain Island which her grandmother has declared off-limits because of the dangerous waters nearby. Almost immediately, about the time she puts on a pair of steelrimmed glasses she finds in the island's clearing, she realizes that others have been on this island many years before and that there are still restless spirits abroad who have something to tell her. As she battles the tricky winds and waves of the lake and explores the paths and the clearing on Rain Island, Lizzie begins to understand that her sorting out of the ghostly world might somehow help her deal with the family discord.

Who Is Frances Rain? is a thoroughly absorbing young adult novel filled with characters who are bound to intrigue teenagers. It's full of the resonance of Canadian summer, the mystique of forest and water, and is sure to linger in the reader's mind long after the last page is turned.

Peter Carver

SOURCE: "Past and Present Merge in Painful, Haunting Tales," in *Books for Young People,* Vol. 1, No. 5, October, 1987, p. 10.

Two impressive new novels give fresh evidence that today's Canadian books for the young are getting better. Each book explores the pain and the resilience of children enduring the stresses of contemporary family life. Each is imbued with the awareness that our present is inevitably influenced by where we have come from, collectively and individually. . . .

[The first is Welwyn Wilton Katz's *False Face.*] Equally haunting is Margaret Buffie's first novel, *Who Is Frances Rain?* . . .

Domestic discord is . . . a starting-point here. Lizzie, her elder brother Evan, and her younger sister Erica have usually spent summers alone with their grandmother in her cabin on northern Manitoba's Rain Lake. But the summer Lizzie is 15 years old, the children are joined by their edgy lawyer mother, Connie, and their new stepfather, Tim, whom they've swiftly dismissed as a hopeless wimp. The mood during the car trip from the city is snappy, even vicious, and the family arrives at Gran's primed for a rotten holiday.

To escape the poisoned atmosphere, Lizzie takes on a personal holiday project: a private investigation of Rain Island, which Gran has always declared off limits because of the treacherous waters surrounding it. Once safe on the island (having been driven off by a storm on her first attempt), Lizzie encounters more than she bargained for, including vivid glimpses of other lives—lives which seem to be reaching out for her. Putting on a pair of wire-rimmed spectacles she found in the wreckage of the island's old cabin, the girl becomes an unwitting observer of events and people of 60 years before: the lonely woman, Frances Rain, who lived and died on the island, and the girl Teresa, who spent one long-ago summer as companion to Frances. Lizzie spends the summer veering back and forth from the island to the tortured explosions of her own family, a course which somehow leads her to solve the mystery of Frances. And like Laney McIntyre of *False Face,* Lizzie is eventually able to find her own special place in the world.

Who Is Frances Rain? is as distinctively Canadian as the intoxicating allure of silent woods and wind-whipped lakes. The textures of the narrative and the well-rounded characters are just as haunting as the ghosts Lizzie finds on Rain Island. It's a ghost story with much to reveal to the thoughtful reader about the turbulent emotions at work within families. It's a novel that makes us grateful for a strong new voice in Canadian literature for young people, a voice we'll want to hear again, soon.

Mary Ainslie Smith

SOURCE: "Ways of Escape," in *Books in Canada,* Vol. 16, No. 9, December, 1987, p. 11.

Two books that make use of all the exhausted mechanisms of time travel, but nevertheless manage somehow to keep fresh and entertaining, are *The Doll,* by Cora Taylor, and *Who Is Frances Rain?,* by Margaret Buffie. . . .

Lizzie, the 15-year-old narrator of *Who Is Frances Rain?,* feels that her family is disintegrating around her. Her father, a successful lawyer, has left the family, and with her mother, also a lawyer, working harder and later than before, Lizzie has struggled to keep things going at home, especially for her little sister Erica. When her mother suddenly remarries, many of Lizzie's responsibilities are lifted, but she resents the intrusion of the big, good-natured Tim, and she and her brother Evan conspire to make his life with them as difficult as possible. By the time Tim decides that the whole family should go together for a summer holiday to Lizzie's grandmother's cottage north of Winnipeg—a holiday traditionally taken by the children alone—his new marriage is on the verge of breaking up, and no one in the family can speak a civil sentence to anyone else.

Lizzie, made even more resentful by this disruption of what has always been a special time at the lake with her beloved grandmother, seeks refuge by exploring a nearby deserted island. There, on the ruins of a long-abandoned cabin, she finds a pair of old-fashioned spectacles. When she puts them on, the scene in front of her subtly changes. The cabin becomes entire again, occupied by two mysterious female figures who move ghost-like into Lizzie's view. As soon as the spectacles come off, all is back to normal. Lizzie, determined to learn the identity of her ghosts, soon finds out that the older woman must be Frances Rain, a reclusive prospector who died alone in her island cabin in 1925. But it is harder to learn anything about the younger figure, a girl close to Lizzie's own age—who she was, what her relationship to Frances could have been, and why they were so unhappily separated. . . .

[Lizzie] acquires an understanding from her glimpses of the past that helps her put her current problems into perspective. But although her exploration of the island's mysteries occupies much of the story, it is really of secondary interest to the parallel story about the clashing of the strong wills in Lizzie's own family and their working out of a tentative truce.

As time-travel books, both *The Doll* and **Who is Frances Rain?** do a good job of re-creating the past—both convey the challenge and isolation facing people alone in the wilderness. However, both books have even more value for their sensitive and realistic treatment of the problems and tensions facing modern families.

Sarah Ellis

SOURCE: "News from the North," in *The Horn Book Magazine,* Vol. LXIV, No. 3, May-June, 1988, pp. 390-94.

[**Who Is Frances Rain?** begins in a] conventional young adult mode. Surly fifteen-year-old Elizabeth recounts in whiny tones her dislike of her mother, her new stepfather, her older brother, and life in general. The only person who escapes her scorn is her beloved grandmother, to whose cabin in rural Manitoba the whole family is traveling to spend a summer by the lake.

Elizabeth changes her outlook quite literally when she canoes over to Rain Island and discovers, in an overgrown ruined cabin, a pair of antique spectacles. When she puts on the glasses, she sees the island in the 1920s. Scenes include the strong and reclusive Frances Rain, a young girl, and the ominous toad-faced visitor. Elizabeth gradually realizes that she is observing a drama of love, manipulation, and independence. The time-travel conventions are handled very delicately. Elizabeth's visions of the past are by no means mechanical but dependent on her own psychological state. Sometimes she sees the cabin in the twenties against the landscape of the eighties in a kind of double perspective that parallels her own increased depth of vision. As she finds out more about the past through asking questions in the present, she finds that her visions become clearer; as she becomes more emotionally linked to the characters on the island, she herself becomes visible in that past. Finally when it becomes evident that she has a role to play in the events of the past, the characters come forward to the present to

beg for her help. The time travel occurs in both directions.

From a basic plot point of view this gradual accumulation of information and emotional connectedness creates superb tension, suspense, and mystery. From the point of view of character it is an original device to show how Elizabeth is coping with her own life. From the first-person whining of the opening chapters, her voice changes as her barriers of anger and stubbornness fall. We get to know her as one is rarely able to know young adults in real life, to hear the real voice under the flippancy.

At one point Elizabeth's hand is superimposed on that of Frances Rain, in a moment that is echoed in a later scene where she touches the hand of her ailing grandmother. Elizabeth says of this experience: "Looking closely at the soft, blurry cabin, I suddenly felt a strange ache deep inside. It's hard to explain, but it was as if the cabin was changing me, as if I was growing outside of me—growing into someone else—someone different and lonely and sad." Growing into someone else is precisely what Elizabeth is doing; the universal experience of adolescence is given literal expression. Elizabeth is Frances Rain, her own great-grandmother, as we discover in a delicious plot twist. She is the past as well all are, linked back through family and nature. But she is also the future, as are all the young, making decisions, changing the world.

Jo-Ann Wallace

SOURCE: "The Power of Story," in *Canadian Children's Literature,* No. 53, 1989, pp. 59-60.

These two novels [**Who is Frances Rain** and Richard Thompson's *The Last Story, The First Story*] have more than an exotic Canadian location in common. In each a young girl must learn, through the healing power of story and through an experience with the other-worldly, to accept the loss of a father and to find new strength in herself. In her struggle to come to terms with her own past, each girl also unearths a deeper social or familial history of maternal love, strength and sacrifice.

The heroine of Margaret Buffie's **Who is Frances Rain?** is fifteen-year-old Lizzie, the eldest child of a newly and unhappily reconstituted family. Her father abandoned the family two years before the action of the novel and her mother, a driven and tense lawyer, has remarried—unexpectedly and seemingly inappropriately—a potter with a yen for "baking after-school cookies and tuna casseroles." Toothy Tim (the nickname with which the children skewer their new stepfather) has forced a family vacation at Lizzie's grandmother's cottage at Rain Lake in Northern Manitoba. While there, Lizzie deals with her own unarticulated sense of abandonment by excavating a ruined cabin site on the nearby Rain Island. There she discovers an old pair of wire-rimmed child's spectacles which mysteriously allow her to *see* the past, to witness the terrible loneliness of an eccentric turn-of-the-century female prospector, Frances Rain, and to situate herself within her own family of very different and very strong women. While the story is moving—the lesson that Lizzie must learn about how pain can be passed from one generation to the next is a difficult one—the first-person, "hard-boiled" narration is not always convincing; it is not clear why Lizzie is writing this story or who she is addressing in her "Prologue," and her continued references to *Alice in Wonderland* occasionally seem contrived.

Mike Hayhoe

SOURCE: A review of *Who is Frances Rain?* in *The School Librarian,* Vol. 37, No. 3, August, 1989, p. 112.

Lizzie's family is in trouble. Her mother's recent remarriage has made all three children uneasy and resentful and the marriage itself is not going particularly well. Like many Canadians, they leave the summer city to return to Nature for a while—in this instance to a lake in northern Manitoba. Their annual escape to this rough Arcadia is important to Lizzie, for she loves the lake in its many moods and finds solace in the slower, deeper wisdoms of those who live there all year, especially her beloved and wise Gran. But this year she is sure will be problematic, because of her mother and stepfather, and she is right. Matters are further complicated by her own sexuality as she falls in love for the first time. Into this tale, the author weaves Lizzie's exploration of an island in the lake, where she time-slips into an earlier part of the century and observes a strong-minded, independent woman who copes with great emotional adversity. Through this experience, Lizzie learns much about growing up and gains further knowledge about her family. The exploration of adolescent troubles through a blend of realism and fantasy is not entirely new, but this novel is quite a lively read. I found the device used for the time-slip a bit implausible and the final explanation of the mystery and its links to the family might be too long for less patient readers; but those who enjoy a sparky, touchy, sensitive narrator will certainly like Lizzie and sharing her tale and increasing maturity.

Tatiana Castleton

SOURCE: A review of *The Haunting of Frances Rain,* in *School Library Journal,* Vol. 35, No. 13, September, 1989, p. 272.

The summers in which she and her brother and sister spend with their grandmother in the lake country of central Manitoba have always been special to 15-year-old Lizzie McGill. This year, however, her mother and stepfather have joined them, and the air is heavy with quarrels and misunderstandings. Lonely and left out, Lizzie decides to explore nearby Rain Island. In the remains of a small cabin she finds a pair of eyeglasses and, looking through them, is able to observe, and later to enter, the troubled world of Frances Rain, who lived and died in the cabin in the 1920s, more than 60 years before. In the end Lizzie unravels the mystery surrounding Frances and her

daughter, and in so doing, learns to confront her own family problems and becomes a participant in finding a solution to them. Buffie builds her fantasy carefully, drawing on a strong sense of time and place. She includes a number of real-life subplots without losing control of her main theme or of the ghost/fantasy world which Lizzie approaches so reluctantly. The cast of characters is large, and generally well-drawn. Lizzie, often prickly, is always understandable; her unfailingly disagreeable mother and brother, on the other hand, are one-dimensional. Ghost story fans should enjoy this first novel.

Kirkus Reviews

SOURCE: A review of *The Haunting of Frances Rain,* in *Kirkus Reviews,* Vol. LVII, No. 19, October 1, 1989, p. 1471.

Spending the summer with her incessantly bickering family on Gran's island in the northern Canadian wilderness, Lizzie McGill unravels the mystery of a ghost—one whose tragedy sheds understanding on her own family's unhappiness.

Mother and Dad are both hard-driven lawyers who were never home much, so when Dad left two years ago it didn't make much difference to Lizzie—though her older brother's anger at being abandoned continues to poison his every word. Mother's anger is also unresolved; nevertheless, she has just married nice, easygoing Tim, who is now the target of all three kids' ill-humor. Meanwhile, Lizzie escapes by exploring the ruins of a cabin on Rain Island, where she finds an old pair of spectacles that allows her to see events of 60 years ago: a girl brought to spend the summer with the recluse who Lizzie learns is Frances Rain; the growing love between Frances and the girl; the girl's forcible removal by the stern, ugly man who seems to be her guardian—leaving behind a sketchbook that Lizzie is able to find and share with Frances on her deathbed before returning it to its original owner in its own time.

A good sense of place and atmosphere; a first romance for Lizzie; the all-too-realistic family friction and its heartening, less-than-perfect resolution, as well as the satisfying ghost-cum-mystery tale that leads to present-day characters—all add up to an unusually entertaining first novel, already a Canadian award-winner.

Barbara Carman Garner

SOURCE: "Lost and Found in Time: Canadian Time-slip Fantasies for Children," in *Children's Literature Association Quarterly,* Vol. 15, No. 4, Winter, 1990, pp. 206-11.

Time-travellers are drawn into the "other world" because they are needed, if not to change history, at least to give strength to some person in the past so that he may accomplish his quest or mission. Authors utilize one of three patterns to enable their protagonist to affect the past: She is either 1) a new character who moves in and influences decisions made in the past; 2) the inhabitant of the body of a person in the past; or 3) an observer of past events who can bring lost knowledge back to the present, and/or carry messages to the past. . . .

Margaret Buffie, using the third pattern, addresses [an] unsolved mystery in the past by having Elizabeth in *Who is Frances Rain?* find the magic talisman, in this case a pair of gold-rimmed spectacles which allow her to see what is happening in the "other world," but restrict her ability to intervene directly in that world. When Elizabeth puts on the spectacles, she can see the cabin in which the mystery woman Frances Rain lived. Elizabeth watches part of the action over one summer of Frances Rain's life in the cabin on Rain Island. Like Rose [from Janet Lunn's *The Root Cellar*] and Meg [from Cora Taylor's *The Doll*], Elizabeth is able to go back in time partly because or her desire to get away from her family, from the unpleasant second marriage of her mother, and her fear of getting too involved with her new stepfather in case he too will desert them as her father did two years earlier. The very strong links with her grandmother, Terry, we realize at the end of the book, are partly responsible for this journey back in time. The superstition that Rain Island is haunted is a common one and the fact that her new stepfather, Tim, and young friend Alex Bird both can sense the sadness, and a presence on the island helps calm some of Elizabeth's fears about the experiences she has while on Rain Island. Buffie modifies the convention of making the character in this type of time-slip either invisible to all but the character she identifies with most, or invisible to everyone in that world of the past. Elizabeth never really becomes a part of the world she observes. She cannot hear the conversations of Frances and the young girl whom she watches and sketches. Once, however, Frances appears in Elizabeth's room at her grandmother's cottage and beckons to her. On the last occasion, when Elizabeth, having retrieved the young girl's sketch book, returns to give it to Frances, Frances speaks directly to her.

Elizabeth talks about her experience as a kind of time warp and on one occasion mentions this "strange time curtain." Her experiences with the past help her to cope better with her mother and her dilemma about her second marriage, and the main plot of the novel with its intricate story of family life and new romance develops in the real world while Elizabeth carries on her scientific experiment with the past on Rain Island. The integrating of story lines is well-handled, and I believe *Who is Frances Rain?* will have a special place among Canadian time-slip fantasies. The message the young Elizabeth is able to give Frances Rain and the one she is able to bring back to her grandmother from the past are important for both Terry and Elizabeth to know. That Elizabeth receives her great-grandmother's signet ring seems a fitting reward both for the acquaintance she made with her great-grandmother in the "other world," and for the certainty of the link of love between Frances and her daughter that she was able to verify for both of them. Elizabeth, after viewing the Toad Man who was Frances's cruel father, is better able to appreciate the family she has been given.

Entering the past by putting on the gold-rimmed glasses always causes Elizabeth to experience a dizzying shimmering world: "Before I could stand up, though, everything around me dipped and swayed. For a second I thought I was going to faint." Elizabeth terms what she sees "visions" and talks about the clarity of the figure coming, like "a Polaroid picture developing." "I could see her so clearly, yet see through her at the same time." One other feature of perspective not encountered in any of the other time-slips occurs when Elizabeth wants Frances Rain to hear her and calls out with great intensity. As she looks down at herself, she realizes that she has become invisible:

> I stepped back, looking down to make sure that I didn't trip over anything. It wouldn't have mattered because my feet weren't there. Or my arms—or my legs. I wasn't anywhere to be seen.

> Frantically I searched for myself. I felt around but couldn't see my hands feeling my body, although I felt a faint pricking of pins and needles at each spot I touched. Horrified, I looked up and saw the same amazement in Frances' eyes. I felt for the glasses and in one hard pull they were off. As I lay in a heap, waiting for the roller coaster to grind to a halt, one thing kept pounding in my head. She saw me. Frances Rain saw me.

The impact of returning from the past is not always so traumatic. When the images end of their own accord while she has the glasses on, she does not suffer from the dizziness and headaches. It is interesting that, although the glasses belonged to Elizabeth's grandmother, Terry, Frances Rain's daughter, it is with Frances that they allow Elizabeth to communicate. It is as though Elizabeth is able to see things again through her grandmother's eyes and is able to convey messages which were never transmitted or properly perceived in the past. May, Terry's friend who is of Cree descent, believes "that if a person hasn't finished something important when they die, sometimes the spirit stays close by until they get the job done." The American title of this book, *The Ghost of Frances Rain,* privileges Frances's attempts to communicate with Elizabeth, whereas the question of the original Canadian title, *Who is Frances Rain?,* could have been partially solved by Terry, Elizabeth's grandmother, had she been willing to tell the sad story of her childhood. I prefer the Canadian title, for Elizabeth herself feels that part of the mystery she has been called back to solve is why she is being used as a "projector," and what it is the mother and daughter want her to see. Through her discovery of the sketch book, Elizabeth is able to rewrite part of the past and set at rest the spirit of the mystery woman, Frances Rain. Hampered though this third type of time-traveller is, she too is on a mission of self-discovery, and benefits personally from her experiences in the past.

Janet Collins

SOURCE: "Buffie Reading Cancelled," in *CM: A Review-*

ing Journal of Canadian Materials for Young People, Vol. XIX, No. 1, January, 1991, pp. 63-5.

If any job description required a warning, school and children's librarians would no doubt be high on the list. Few other positions, except perhaps those of public office, are open to such a barrage of public criticism and debate.

Everyone, it seems, has an opinion concerning what is appropriate reading material for children. The trouble is, few agree on what is appropriate for which age group, and this can lead to problems.

Margaret Buffie's novel *Who is Frances Rain?* forms a case in point.

Frances Rain is described by author, publisher and librarians as being suitable for young adult readers. On that much they agree. However, problems arise with regard to the very definition of that age group.

Too old for picture books, yet too young for adult subject material, these children represent the grayest of markets. Even the chronological age of the children concerned is open to debate.

In Toronto, for example, the young adult seems to be more liberally defined (for example, includes younger children) than in more rural areas. What results is a nightmare for those who are charged with selecting books for these children.

This point may best be illustrated by an examination of events surrounding the recent cancellation of a reading by Margaret Buffie.

Canadian Children's Book Week took place Nov. 3 to 10, 1990. As part of the celebrations, the Canadian Children's Book Centre arranged for a series of talks to be given by well-known authors and illustrators who would travel about the country. Buffie was one such author.

All seemed well with her tour until arrangements were being made for her to speak at Queenswood Public School in Orleans, Ontario (just outside Ottawa).

Like most schools, Queenswood Public knows the value of a visiting author. Yet, in this case, they had reservations. It would seem that the problem was not so much with Buffie herself, but rather in regards to the material from which she would read.

School librarian Diana Gauthier was always on the look-out for authors who would be willing to visit her school. Principal Jim Brown spoke on Gauthier's behalf because "it is school policy that staff not speak directly to the press."

Brown went on to say that Gauthier heard of the tours organized by the Canadian Children's Book Centre through an acquaintance at the local public library. Gauthier no-tified the Centre of her interest and learned soon after that Buffie would be the visiting author.

It must be stressed that Queenswood did not, at that time, have any of Buffie's work in its school library collection. Nonetheless, Gauthier was said to be familiar with her work. After all, it was Gauthier who decided that Buffie's book *The Guardian Circle*, was not appropriate for the planned audience of grades 4 to 6. Another book by the author, *Who is Frances Rain?,* was then acquired.

When a grade 6 teacher read part of this book to his class during a "sharing time," however, he discovered words that he felt were not appropriate for children of that grade level. The passages in question contain the words *damn, hell, shit* and *bastard.* There is also reference made to an illegitimate child.

Brown explained that "as a school, we try to make these author visits available to as many children as possible. For that reason, we prefer to have an author who is able to speak to all of the Primary students, for example, or all the Junior students" (Queenswood is a Kindergarten to grade 6 school).

Once the teacher ruled out the possibility of grade 6 students attending the reading, the question then turned to the book's suitability for grades 4 and 5.

"We had to rule it out as being too complex for them."

And with that, the reading was cancelled.

But Brown felt the reading would have been cancelled because of "logistics" problems even if the book's content had been deemed appropriate.

"The tour organizer said the author insisted on limiting the audience size to sixty students. Nobody else who has come to read at our school has made that sort of demand."

He insisted that many teachers believed their students would feel left out and that led to arguments among the staff. Chris Scott, Mark Thurman, Jan Andrews, Deirdre Kessler and Ann Stephenson are a few of the other authors Brown said had come to Queenswood to read. Apparently, they did not limit the size of their audiences.

For her part, tour co-ordinator Jerrolyn Dietrich-Campbell was surprised by the problems at Queenswood.

"No other school expressed a concern with our limiting the numbers of students the author would speak to, let alone voicing a concern about the book's contents."

Indeed, Buffie's reading went ahead, as scheduled, at D. Roy Kennedy school in Ottawa.

Steve Moretti, public relations officer for the Ottawa Board of Education, noted Buffie would be reading to children in grades 7 and 8—an audience considerably older than that planned for Queenswood.

"We booked her long ago," Moretti confirmed, "and we had no intention of cancelling her" even though Queenswood had done so just days earlier.

It is interesting to note that D. Roy Kennedy not only found *Frances Rain* acceptable for their grades 7 and 8 audience, but they too felt that a smaller number of children was preferable for the author's reading.

Teacher/librarian Bonnie Mabee felt that "smaller groups allow for a more intimate experience than a child is able to gain as part of a group which exceeds, say, fifty participants. Actually, I feel thirty-five children is an ideal maximum."

Mabee appeared to have a different perspective on the book's contents as well.

"I do not see any problem with the words in the book. In the context of the story, they are perfectly acceptable and are very much in keeping with the characters."

She added she was very familiar with the book because she had not only read it, but had also reviewed it for the National Library.

However, one must not conclude that Mabee is willing to read any story to any child—far from it.

"You have to know the children the book is intended for," she cautions. "I would not, for example, read this book to my Grade 4 students. They just aren't ready for it. On the other hand, although I feel Kevin Major's books are very good, I do not think they are suitable for reading aloud. In my opinion, the language of his books just doesn't lend itself to being read aloud."

What this appears to illustrate is the degree to which opinions vary, not only in terms of what constitutes suitable reading material for children, and young adults in particular, but also which of those materials are appropriate for oral reading.

Brown insists that, although Buffie's reading was cancelled, *Francis Rain* has never been banned by the school.

"It was never part of our library collection, and the one copy we obtained as preparation for the author's visit is still available through my office, with parental permission."

Ricky Englander, co-owner of Kids Can Press (publisher of *Who is Frances Rain?*) does not agree with Brown's definition of book banning.

"The fact that the author has been asked not to read at the school, even though arrangements had been made for her to do so, is, in my mind, the same as banning her. Since the author has been banned as a result of a judgment made on her book, does that not also constitute a banning of the book?"

Englander went on to say that this is the only situation of its kind (that she knows of) involving Buffie's work.

Indeed, the problems which surrounded the reading appear even more curious when one considers that *Frances Rain* has received a great deal of attention as a result of winning CLA's 1987/88 Young Adult Canadian Book Award, as administered by the Young Adult Services Interest Group.

The book was also runner-up for the 1988 CLA Book of the Year award and is published in England, Denmark and the United States. But awards alone cannot be the criteria for selecting a book for a school or children's library.

It would be easy to agree with Margaret Coleman, public relations officer for the Carleton Board of Education, to which Queenswood belongs.

She insists that if Gauthier had read the book prior to entering into arrangements for the reading, "much of this could have been avoided."

Whether the book was read at that point in time may or may not be the issue.

Rather, the root of the problem appears to lie in the selection process itself. No two school districts, no two libraries, select their books in exactly the same fashion. . . .

Of course, morals of individual communities will also have much to do with the books a given library may finally select.

In order to account for these variations in community standards, the Ontario Ministry of Education will only give advice regarding text books (by way of *Circular 14*).

The decision regarding the acquisition of other reading materials is left to the local school boards, many of which do not appear to have clear guidelines themselves. Thus, it is left to the librarians to make their own selections.

It would be unrealistic to suggest that only books which have been personally read by the librarian can appear in a school or children's library. There are simply too many books. Thus, many resort to relying on reviews as an aid in deciding which titles to purchase. But that too takes time.

Further, limits on time due to other demands put pressure on any system, no matter how thorough. In the case of teacher-librarians, time is often a precious luxury.

The limited supply of authors willing to speak at a school is certainly another factor that bears some examination. The value of such activities is unquestionable. Not only does a reading by an author provide a child with new insights into a given book, but it may also awaken the child's own creativity—the "if he can write a book, why can't I" attitude.

But enthusiasm for securing willing authors can, in itself, lead to problems. After all, if books are purchased sight unseen, why not book readings in the same manner? The fact is, that does happen, as the Queenswood case has illustrated.

Finally, and perhaps most importantly, is the problem in understanding the classification of children's reading materials. Not all publishers work to the same criteria.

This is especially confusing for librarians, who must largely depend on catalogues and reviews for their prepurchase information.

The fact that the audiences at Queenswood and D. Roy Kennedy were so different underscores this problem. Further, as stated above, the libraries themselves do not appear to have a standard selection process.

Unfortunately, none of these issues is likely to be rectified in the near future. In the meantime, librarians will continue to bear the brunt of the failings of a flawed system, and the children will be the big losers.

Margaret Buffie

SOURCE: "Reflections on a Personal Case of Censorship," in *Canadian Children's Literature,* No. 68, 1992, pp. 43-9.

For writers, librarians and educators, the banning or censoring of a recommended book, even *once,* should ring alarm bells. Loud ones. True, the censoring of literature specifically aimed at young readers is most difficult to deal with. For teachers and librarians, the selection of age-appropriate books can be an ordeal. However, in Canada, many people forget that we have a number of highly-regarded committees who carefully choose and recommend books specifically aimed at certain ages, not only for reading levels but, just as importantly, for their literary qualities as well.

The Canadian Library Association has lists of recommended books, as does the Canadian Children's Book Centre (Our Choice Catalogue), the National Library of Canada, and many individual libraries across Canada. There are magazines such as *Canadian children's literature, Canadian materials, Quill and quire's* "Books for Young People," *Emergency librarian,* and many others that offer insightful analyses of books for young readers. Available from the United States are the esteemed American Library Association "Best Books List," The New York Library "Best Books List," and journals such as *School library, Horn book* and others. I have heard from some librarians that it is impossible to read every book one orders for a school or library. Still, they can't complain that there is nothing on which to base their selections.

Teachers, librarians and school principals presumably use these lists as guidelines for the selection of books from all over the world, as well as for choosing the finest exam-

ples of Canadian literature. One bright note: it has been my experience—talking to a great many teachers and librarians—that a large number *do* buy books on these recommended lists and *do* vigorously defend them against challenges by individual parents or groups who may wish to have one removed from their library or classroom shelves. And a surprising number of these teachers and librarians have read the books they order. Hooray for these involved and committed people!

Sadly, however, there are still those who feel compelled—for various reasons—to remove age-appropriate and highly-recommended books for young people from school library shelves.

Despite the unanimous recommendation from all of the above groups, and despite winning a major Canadian award and being shortlisted for two others, one of my novels, *Who is Frances Rain?* was banned from an Ottawa school during my tour to the Montreal and Ottawa areas for Children's Book Week in the fall of 1990.

Ironically, a few months after my experience in Ottawa, just when I thought the nightmare was over, a long article appeared in the journal *Canadian materials* which described the Ottawa incident and talked sympathetically about the dilemma of selecting age-appropriate materials. A number of people were interviewed for this article. The principal of the Ottawa school, Jim Brown, was once again given space to list the "smokescreen" excuses he'd used to justify cancelling my visit. The only person who was *not* interviewed for this article was "the censored one"— the person most affected by the censoring of her novel— me! I had no opportunity at this crucial time to defend my novel, to defend *myself* against the personal slurs, or to respond to the reasons offered for cancelling the visit.

Shortly before I was to fly east for Book Week, I was told that the Principal of Queenswood Public School in Orleans, Ottawa, had cancelled my prearranged and confirmed visit. His librarian and a grade six teacher were concerned about certain words in *Who is Frances Rain?* When Principal Brown saw these words, he immediately cancelled my visit. He then removed the book from the classroom and locked it in his office. He told reporters later that he would allow students to see it only with parental supervision, stating that this should not be viewed as censorship in any way.

I was flabbergasted. Warned that I might be besieged by the press upon my arrival in Montreal, I laughed this off. Surely the media had better stories to write about than one isolated incident of censorship.

However, after my first presentation in Montreal, I was called to the phone—the first of many calls. A reporter from a large Toronto newspaper asked for my reaction to the banning of my book. Then she asked if I was aware that Principal Brown was maintaining that the language in the book was only *one* reason for the cancellation of my visit. The main reason was that I was simply too difficult and demanding to work with.

I babbled something sophisticated and worldly along the lines of, "Get outta here! No way!", but the reporter insisted that she had talked to him personally. Principal Brown's attack on my professional behaviour was bewildering. After all, I had never spoken or written to this man—and still haven't to this day. Preparations for Book Week are always handled through regional co-ordinators.

What on earth, I wondered as I organized my overheads and books for the next presentation, could he mean when he called me difficult and demanding? It took a few months, but I finally found out—in the *Canadian materials* article by Janet Collins. According to Brown, "the author insisted on limiting the audience to sixty students. Nobody else who has come to our school has made that sort of demand."

Let me explain. The Children's Book Centre asks authors what we consider the "ideal" class size, as a flexible guideline for schools. During that particular 1990 Book Week, I talked to groups ranging from 20 to 130 students and teachers. During my various trips across Canada in the past five years, I have given presentations to auditoriums filled with 200 or more students as well as talking to as few as 15 youngsters from a single classroom. Although, like many authors, I prefer smaller groups, I have never turned down students or teachers eager to sit in on a presentation. I would not have dreamed of turning down any student or classroom teacher at Queenswood School. If I had been approached (which I was not) with a request for more than the *preferred* number of 60 students, there would not have been a problem. Principal Brown, however, said in the *CM* article that "many teachers believed their students would be left out and that led to arguments among the staff." Mmm. Doesn't sound as if everyone was in agreement with my being banned, does it? I felt that this "problem" with class size was an excuse used in order to slip-slide around the real issue—the issue of a school principal banning a highly-recommended book and then having to explain his actions.

On hearing this first excuse, I had a sinking feeling that I was in for a pretty bumpy ride. Most censors get away with their behaviour—usually because they practice "silent" censorship, but the media—print, radio and television—wanted to know all the details. Rather than possibly taking an unpopular stand in the public eye, the censor points the finger at the author. It's all her fault!

The *CM* article states, "Once the [Queenswood] teacher ruled out the possibility of grade six students attending the reading, [because of 'inappropriate' language], the question turned to the book's suitability for grades four and five." Principal Brown is quoted as saying, "We had to rule it out as being too complex for them."

I had been told from the beginning that I would be talking to grade six students at Queenswood School. In an interview with *The Globe and mail* on November 7, the Principal stated that certain passages were "not suitable for Grade 6 students." Then he told the Ottawa *Citizen* on the same day that the grade level was four and five. In the local community newspaper, *The star* (Orleans), November 14, he definitely goes with the "too difficult" excuse, citing the grade levels as four and five, with no mention of grade six classes at all. A small enough point but vital: I had been asked to talk to grade six students.

"Logistics" was another "murky" reason offered for my visit cancellation. In the *Globe and mail* article, Brown is quoted as saying, "I cancelled Buffie's appearance at the school, which was scheduled for mid-November, because of logistical reasons. We couldn't fit her into our schedule." Odd, considering that I had been invited to the school and my acceptance had been confirmed. The school librarian had even arranged to take me to an authors' lunch!

In preparing for this article, wading through Principal Brown's excuses, and once again suffering the slings and arrows of outrageous excuses, I perceive that a great deal of this mess in Ottawa came about through Queenswood School's lack of preparation. Not one of these people had read the book in its entirety before responding with knee-jerk reactions to it. If they had read it, they might have decided against censoring it. And if they were enlightened educators the problem of language could have been addressed in class—a point I will discuss in a moment.

When a school librarian, eager for an author visit—*any* author visit—takes on a writer whose work she is unfamiliar with, there is always plenty of time to familiarize herself with the author's work. Most authors automatically assume, quite rightly I think, that the classroom teacher and the students will be acquainted with at least one of their books when they arrive on the scene. Book Week is exhausting, but it is a job we take on with great energy and pleasure. When I arrive at a school or library, *I am prepared.* It is always disappointing when a writer discovers that a school such as Queenswood is unprepared.

Principal Brown admitted to more than one reporter that he had not read the book before banning it. I believe he felt he didn't have to. Certain words—words which were strung together for the media, making it look as if **Who is Frances Rain?** was one long profanity—had been helpfully highlighted for him by his librarian. Why would he need to read the whole book?

If someone hasn't read a book, can he make a thoughtful decision about its appropriateness for a classroom? Is he in any position to discuss it with anyone? Should he be allowed a platform, such as *Canadian materials,* to discuss what he *doesn't know?* Why was he allowed to prattle on about a demanding and difficult author he had never met, logistical problems and grade level problems, without once having to discuss the actual book? Why wasn't he asked why he banned a book that had been so highly recommended for ages ten and up?

And why wasn't I asked to participate in the debate in the *CM* article? It was titled *Buffie reading cancelled.* Where was Buffie's side of the issue? When I asked for an explanation, it was admitted that only *one* phone call had been made to try to locate me. This article came out over two months after the event. Why didn't someone try to call me in Montreal, or after I returned home in November? Is this a fair look at an issue, when the one most damaged by it is left out of the debate? Being offered a chance to respond in a letter to the *CM* editor two months after the article came out was simply not good enough. The damage had been done.

Sadly, we find that there are other principals and educators out there who ban or restrict books without having read them. In March 1991, a Winnipeg principal encouraged the restriction of **Who is Frances Rain?**. A long-awaited visit was discouraged after the librarian read that *Canadian materials* article and took her concerns to the principal. I wonder if she would have been as worried if I'd had a chance to present my views in that article!

Unfortunately, principals such as this Winnipeg educator are so worried about protecting their position that they find it easier to censor, ban, or restrict a book than to face possible political fallout from a few irate parents (often it is only one parent) or nervous school board members. It saddens me when I see how they can give up or put away, often temporarily, their convictions about intellectual freedom to keep their little boats from bouncing around on an unexpected wave or two. I suppose I can see how this happens, but I will not condone it.

It appears to me—and I have heard this from teachers themselves—there are a growing number of principals and teachers who are taking this easy way out—sometimes anticipating a problem *before* it happens, sometimes moving quickly to stop a conflict in their school by banning an author as soon as one parent complains. Those principals and teachers fail the writer and their own students. These are the educators who we assume have handled censorship problems for years and have a sound selection policy. These are the educators who we assume will crack down on unreasonable censorship.

But they don't. It is *those* educators who anger me the most. It is *those* educators who use their authority in an atmosphere fraught—they claim—with political problems, parental pressures, and questioning school boards to remove a highly-recommended book from the shelves; who decide that a book will not be read to the students; who back down to keep peace; who use words such as "sensitivity" in place of censorship. It seems easier to ban a book and to phone an organizer of an event or the author herself and tell her that she is no longer welcome; that her book has been removed from the shelves; that it will not be read aloud to or read by the students before an author visit, as intended. It seems easier to do all of these things than to expend energy and time fighting school boards, trustees, parents and the growing number of organized censor hounds. Do these principals really think that an author will shrug her shoulders and say, "Oh, well. On to the next school"?

I think they do. As in the case of the Winnipeg principal, they speak so reasonably, you see . . . so apologetically about all of the "political" pressures they are under. And

they ask the writer to understand. Then, if the author speaks out, they use other issues to cloud the real one. If a principal clouds the issues with innuendoes and rumours before sliding back into the shadows, then with luck—he hopes—the author will not respond too loudly and peace will once again reign.

Censorship is often based on fear. I think many of those who press for censorship, whether a parent or a principal or a teacher, do so because of fear. These people believe that the very moral fabric of our society is in grave danger.

The world is a worrisome place. There appears to be more and more violence—especially against women and children. There is growing drug and alcohol abuse and an apparent social acceptance of sexual promiscuity, teenage pregnancies and all of those things that frighten educators and parents. Some feel that disrespect for authority is also being encouraged. (The banning of Robert Munsch's *Thomas's snowsuit* is just one example of this particular fear overcoming common sense.) How can adults guide their children when so much is out of their control? As a parent I have felt these pressures. For some people, however, I think the fear grows and grows until they feel compelled to find something, anything that they can blame—but it has to be something that they can control. One of the things that frightened adults feel they can control, or desperately try to control, is literature that is aimed at young people.

Those who censor highly-recommended quality literature see words—books—as something with the potential to endanger, to frighten and to corrupt the young. I am absolutely certain of one thing: censors of this type believe that what they are doing is right. They have a sense of absolute purpose. They think they are protecting their children's future emotional and spiritual well-being.

Writers of children's literature and many educators do not believe that banning books is the way to go about protecting our young. To deny a student access to a recommended book because of so-called profane language—by counting the number of swear words in it and putting a limit on the acceptable number—one, two, six?—puts a severe limitation on that student's right to read a wide variety of literature by some of the finest writers in the field today. As Dr. David Jenkinson once said to me, "These people seem to presume that innocence and ignorance are synonymous terms."

In a healthy educational atmosphere, we should be able to discuss *why* a writer might use such language. Ask the students. I have. They *know* why it is used. It reflects the world they live in. Writing a certain word does not condone the use of that word. Writers *must* use the language that exists in the world they are writing about. To deny access to a book on these grounds presumes that the rest of the book, the other thousands and thousands of words and sentences and images and conversations and thoughts and feelings are worth absolutely nothing. And as a writer, I refuse to accept that.

So where does this leave the writer who has been censored? If censors and book-banners are allowed to remove my books from the schools and libraries, if they are allowed to define what *all* children read—not just their own children—according to their own narrow vision of what is "moral" or "proper" literature, where will this leave me? What happens to a writer, I wonder, who gives in and accepts the fact that she must now be told what she can and cannot write? Surely the freedom of true creativity will be lost—for she will have to debate within herself what she thinks the censors will want rather than spending time on the literary value of her work.

And where does this leave the possibilities of delving into areas that are controversial or unexplored? I cannot write about a family conflict without using the language that is real to that particular family. It is not possible to write a book that is censor-proof. Beatrix Potter's *Peter Rabbit* was banned in the early 1980's. The *Merriam-Webster dictionary* and *My friend Flicka* have both been the victims of censorship attacks in recent years.

It is not easy to sort out the problems of censorship. Fighting censorship calls for courage and commitment. As a writer, I know I would much rather be writing a novel than writing this article. I hate the personal attacks I have had to endure from people I have never met—from people who have not even taken the time to read my books in their entirety.

I see the true educator's job as transmitting knowledge, ideas, the love of reading and writing—not limiting or restricting those things. Many teachers offer their students a wide range of books to read. And they also offer them the opportunity to openly discuss what they have just read. It can't always be easy. But these are the educators who are truly contributing to the development of confident, tolerant, literate, and astute young adults.

I really do believe that this is probably just the beginning of censorship in our schools. The more that educators use trade books in their whole language curriculum, for example, the more flack they are going to face. More people will be demanding that the schools go back to the bloodless and safe educational texts that can be rigorously scanned for controversial material. But rather than all of us running around, screaming the sky is falling, or avoiding books that might be a problem, teachers and librarians—and principals—will have to arm themselves with carefully-prepared selection policies and guidelines for handling challenges which begin with the all-important question: "Have you read the entire book which concerns you?"

Censorship problems won't stop me from writing. I love writing. I love creating another world. I love outlining plots and describing characters, and developing conflict, and choosing the right name for each character. I love watching those characters get up off their two-dimensional planes and move and walk and talk and react with each other. I love my computer. And my pencils and the smell of paper and ink and cardboard boxes filled with each new draft of a manuscript.

For now, I won't throw away my thesaurus, or my dictionaries, or my *Elements of style,* or my *Elements of grammar,* or my *Fundamentals of clear writing.* With all of the support around me, I will continue to write the book that searches me out and demands to be written. And *I* will decide what words to use—and how and when to use them.

THE GUARDIAN CIRCLE (1989; U.S. edition as *The Warnings*)

Adele M. Fasick

SOURCE: A review of *The Guardian Circle,* in *CM: A Reviewing Journal of Canadian Materials for Young People,* Vol. XVIII, No. 2, March, 1990, p. 71.

Teenage Rachel MacCaw, angry over her mother's desertion, feels even more isolated when her father sells their Manitoba farm and deposits Rachel with his Aunt Irene in Winnipeg while he drives a truck to B.C. Rachel has already been troubled by visions warning her of impending events, and in her attic bedroom at Aunt Irene's house she becomes aware of a hovering dark shadow and of an apparently benign ghost.

The most normal contact in Rachel's new life is Will, a boy from her new school, who lives across the street. Together Rachel and Will decide to try to understand the mysterious events in the MacCaw house. Through a ouija board Rachel learns enough to confront her aunt and persuade her to explain what is going on. Eventually her father returns to play his part in what proves to be a legacy from generations past. At last they can unite against the forces of evil and defeat them. In so doing, Rachel finally comes to accept and understand her father and deal with her mother's desertion.

Buffie's second book has kept the lively style of her first, *Who Is Frances Rain?* This fast-paced story with a touch of the occult will appeal to many young teenagers.

Kirkus Reviews

SOURCE: A review of *The Warnings,* in *Kirkus Reviews,* Vol. LIX, No. 2, January 15, 1991, p. 105.

When red-haired Rachel enters the nutty household of her quaint great-aunt Irene, she is little more than another estranged teen-ager whose mother has walked out on her and whose truck-driver father dumped her so that he can go on the road. But Irene's home is full of dotty old people, and even older spirits; Rachel and her father are the link between one particularly ancient malevolent force and the powerful stone possessed by the old folks (collectively known as "The Guardian Circle"). Rachel prevails, but the ending looks ripe for a sequel.

Buffie creates a wonderful tension between her hard-bitten heroine and the eerie scenes she confronts, while John, the attic-inhabiting ghost who gently aids Rachel, is as fully realized a presence as Irene and the other oldsters. An unusually smooth-rolling romance is worked in with ease. Simple, satisfying, and mistily spooky.

Deborah Stevenson

SOURCE: A review of *The Warnings,* in *Bulletin of the Center for Children's Books,* Vol. 44, No. 7, March, 1991, pp. 160-61.

Fifteen-year-old Rachel MacCaw has a lot to be angry about: her mother has left the family, and now her father has parked her in the city with an unknown Aunt Irene, in a creepy old house filled with alarming old people. It's clear that the house's residents, whom Rachel terms the Fossils ("Sometimes joking helps. Sometimes it doesn't"), are hiding something from her: her Warnings, or alarmingly accurate premonitions of danger, are coming strongly, and a ghostly presence appears to her in her isolated attic bedroom. With the help of an enthusiastic neighbor boy and the gradual trust of the house members, Rachel learns that the elders of the house are part of a Guardian Circle who need her help to prevent an evil ancestral spirit from seizing a magical Stone of power. Although the real-life scenes are less convincing than the ethereal, the book's atmosphere generally lives up to the promise of its terrific read-me cover, with some of the most unusual (and viscerally unappetizing) beneficent elders a supernatural mystery ever had. The last part, unfortunately, fails to live up to the rest of the story; the showdown with the malevolent spirit has too much explanation crammed in and not enough chills. The well-crafted ghostliness of most of the book, however, should keep junior spook fans in happy shivers.

Sally Estes

SOURCE: A review of *The Warnings,* in *Booklist,* Vol. 87, No. 14, March 15, 1991, p. 1464.

Rachel MacCaw, almost 16, is disgruntled, to say the least, when her widower father drops her off to live a while with her Aunt Irene and roars off cross-country in his huge truck. She's even more put off when she meets Aunt Irene's housemates—an odd assortment of elderly people that Rachel soon comes to refer to as the Fossils, even while she becomes more and more fond of each and every one of them. To cap it off, the room she's assigned has a resident ghost! Rachel has long lived with what she calls "The Warnings," augurings of future, not usually happy, events, but has never told anyone about them. After an initial run-in with Will Lennox at her new school, the two become good friends (bordering on romance), and Will helps Rachel and the Fossils (who turn out to be a group of people with special powers monitoring the misuse of power) confront a greedy, wicked spirit. Characters are developed with verve—Rachel and Will are believable teenagers; Rachel's anger, first, at her mother's

desertion, and second, at what she perceives as her father's abandonment, rings true; the Fossils are individuals, not caricatures—and the story is an agreeable mix of the occult and the everyday. It's nice to have a horror story leavened by plenty of humor.

Susan L. Rogers

SOURCE: A review of *The Warnings,* in *School Library Journal,* Vol. 37, No. 4, April, 1991, p. 141.

First Rachel McCaw's artist-mother leaves home to find herself. Then her father—former hippie-farmer, now trucker—sells their Manitoba farm and drives off in his 18-wheeler to sort things out, leaving Rachel in the care of the "Fossils"—Aunt Irene and the odd assortment of elderly characters who share her ramshackled house. Rachel has been plagued by a second sight, or what she calls *The Warnings,* that seems to foretell the future. The Fossils seem to understand this about Rachel, and are inordinately interested in all of her thoughts, dreams, and experiences, as if they are waiting for something to happen. Will, a teenaged neighbor and classmate who is becoming more than a friend, is also drawn into the mystery surrounding a ghost who appears in Rachel's room. Like Buffie's *The Haunting of Frances Rain* this is a compelling story, complex in themes but fast-moving and easy to read. It features a likable but very human heroine faced with meaningful, topical family problems; an unexpected first romance; and unusual supernatural intrigue rooted in her ancestry and guaranteed to keep the pages turning. Fans of Buffie's first novel will not be disappointed in this one, with its surprising and satisfying climax and conclusion; a captivating cover and contents will attract new readers as well.

Catherine M. Dwyer

SOURCE: A review of *The Warnings,* in *Voice of Youth Advocates,* Vol. 14, No. 2, June, 1991, p. 93.

When 15-year-old Rachel McCaw arrives at her Aunt Irene's house in Winnipeg she is greeted by Luther, an ancient circus performer who tumbles down the stairs; Gladys, who is burning the dinner; and assorted other elderly people. Rachel promptly dubs the entire group The Fossils. Living with this strange assemblage is difficult for Rachel because she resents being left with her aunt while her father works as a truck driver. Rachel grudgingly settles into her new surroundings, her attic room, and a new school, and makes friends with Will. She even begins to feel affection for The Fossils. But when Rachel gets the flu, she begins to have a series of strange experiences. She sees a ghost that a Ouija board reveals is someone named John. Luther seems to be drugging her and Aunt Irene won't let Rachel talk to her father. The supernatural encounters escalate until one of The Fossils gets hurt trying to drive away a ghostly thief. Aunt Irene tells Rachel and Will that The Fossils are really a Guardian Circle trying to recover The Gregor Stone, which has supernatural powers and is also being sought by Dunstan Gregor, the ghostly thief. Dunstan wants to use the Stone for evil purposes. When Rachel's father arrives, Aunt Irene finishes the story, explaining that Rachel and her father are descendants of the Gregors. The Guardian Circle, Rachel, her father, and Will, all join together to save the Gregor Stone from Dunstan Gregor.

Buffie has written a wonderful supernatural mystery. Rachel is a well defined character, not too perfect, but smart enough to catch on quickly to what is happening. The Fossils add a comic touch and the character of Will adds a love interest. However, Buffie is careful not to let them distract from the main story lines—Rachel's anger at her father for leaving her, and the recovery of the Gregor Stone. The cover art is eye catching and happily, the description of Rachel in the book matches her portrayal on the cover. Highly recommended, especially for libraries where Lois Duncan's books are in demand.

📖 *MY MOTHER'S GHOST* (1992; U.S. edition as *Someone Else's Ghost*)

Anna Santarossa

SOURCE: A review of *My Mother's Ghost,* in *CM: A Reviewing Journal of Canadian Materials for Young People,* Vol. XX, No. 6, November, 1992, p. 311.

Sixteen-year-old Jess and her parents buy and move to a guest ranch in Alberta. Her family is trying to recover from the death of Jess's little brother Scotty. Jess's father is pretending nothing out of the ordinary is happening. Jess is coping by working very hard on the ranch and by trying to make some sense of what is happening around her. Jess's mother is retreating into her own world, where it seems that no one can reach her, no one except the "ghost" of a little boy that she keeps seeing. Jess's mother thinks that boy is Scotty, but Jess thinks otherwise and gathers as much evidence as she can to prove it.

The reader is familiar with the ghost because, as the story of Jess and her family unfolds, so does the story of Ian Shaw and his family. The author simultaneously tells the two stories. We are introduced to Ian through his journal, in which he records his life as a crippled boy living in the early 1900s on the same Alberta ranch. Ian's main problem is not his injured leg, but his strong-willed mother, who keeps him a virtual prisoner is his own room.

The two stories merge when both families face disaster. Jess's mother is about to slip into the oblivion of her own world when Jess decides to tell her the story of Ian Shaw and to show her his journal. Jess's mother is angry at having her own delusion of the ghost being Scotty shattered. But when Jess and her mother confront their true feelings, they become reconciled. They also help Ian and his mother forgive each other when, in a rare instant, past and present coincide. Ian and his mother can now rest in

peace, while Jess and her family can get on with their lives, despite their grief.

The story was riveting from beginning to end. The fact that it was well written and insightful made the characters seem real. I truly enjoyed the interplay between past and present. Both stories are so interesting they could have easily stood alone. Together the stories create suspense and add another dimension to the novel.

This book is a must. Readers will not be able to put it down.

Valerie White

SOURCE: A review of *My Mother's Ghost,* in *Emergency Librarian,* Vol. 20, No. 4, March-April, 1993, p. 61.

In *My mother's ghost,* Margaret Buffie introduces us to 16-year-old Jess and her family, who are coping with their grief over the death of Jess's younger brother. Jess's father has just quit his job and moved the family from Winnipeg to a guest ranch he's purchased in the Alberta foothills. Her father has no experience with this kind of life. In her grief and despair, Jess's mother has drifted into a world of her own, leaving Jess to do all the work. Jess feels like her life is spinning out of control. She resents her father for uprooting them and also for refusing to get medical attention for her mother's depression. She is also frustrated with her mother because of her inability to help herself. When her mother starts seeing ghosts, Jess thinks she's gone over the edge.

Buffie really tells two stories here: one is Jess's story in the present, the other is Ian's story from the past. Ian had lived at the ranch many years before. He was poetic and sickly: adored by his father and dominated by his mother. Told alternately by Jess and Ian, this book has the page-turning qualities of a good mystery. Yet in ghost story tradition, Ian's ghost finds relief from his torment and is able to help Jess and her parents get on with their lives.

In the author's own words, "I don't believe great lives die. There is a link between generations—characteristics passed on, stories told—and I explore those links."

Linda Soutar

SOURCE: "Angels Watchin' Over Me," in *Canadian Children's Literature,* No. 75, 1994, pp. 73-4.

Following the death of her younger brother Scotty, Jessica Locke's family leaves Winnipeg to start anew in Willow Creek, Alberta. Jessica's father, a former RCMP officer, has chosen to re-start their family's life in the horse ranching and recreation business. No one else is feeling his outdoor enthusiasm, least of all Jeanie Locke, Jessica's mother, who has fallen into a deep depression penetrated from time to time by what she thinks are ghostly visions of Scotty—hence the novel's title.

What is unique and refreshing about this particular ghost story is its linking of two generations—both mother and daughter—in their quest for the supernatural, as opposed to the more standardized plot scenario of the isolated protagonist whose ghostly experiences few would believe. In the context of books for young adults, the novel's culminating in such a partnership is significant in that it breaks away from the alienated teen motif and allows for the incorporation of multiple perspectives while still focusing the story on the experiences of its young protagonist. Interestingly, Jeanie Locke's perspective is highlighted by the extension of her professional career as a photographer into the realization of the novel's supernatural sequences, all of which are seen in photo negative—an effect which simultaneously rationalizes, yet dramatizes, the silhouetted figures and glowing white pupils of the otherworldly characters.

Paralleling the structure of Margaret Buffie's first novel for young adults, *Who Is Frances Rain?*, *My Mother's Ghost* also deals with a modern-day family in crisis which learns to cope by developing an understanding of an historical family, from their home's past, which experienced similar domestic difficulties. In this case the link to the past is Ian Shaw, the young, crippled son of a British remittance man and his bitterly disillusioned wife, Augusta. Augusta's bitterness towards the pioneering life of the Canadian west, combined with her overprotectiveness of Ian, lead to his virtual imprisonment in the family house with only a journal as a temporary means of escape.

While the novel's surrealism is delightful, the realism of its plot construction strains credibility. The overloaded plot includes four families—three present and one past—who have experienced a collapse due to the loss of a family member. Not only are these families all connected with the ranch, but all are well on their way to healing at the end of the novel. Nevertheless, the suspenseful development of each of these plots is riveting, and the novel as a whole has much appeal for both male and female young adults.

Sister Mary Veronica

SOURCE: A review of *Someone Else's Ghost,* in *Voice of Youth Advocates,* Vol. 18, No. 1, April, 1995, p. 19.

The Locke family has moved to a ranch in Alberta, Ontario, in search of a new start in life. Glen Locke tries to distract his wife and daughter from their grief over the accidental death of Jessica's brother Scotty. Instead, thirteen-year-old-Jessica and her mother Jeanie find themselves trapped in a nightmare, haunted by ghosts from a long ago tragedy not unlike their own. What starts out as a simple story of a very unhappy teenage girl and her endlessly grieving mother, becomes the opportunity for healing for them and rest for several unexpected ghostly visitors. *Someone Else's Ghost* will be enjoyed by all young teenagers who love a very scary story with a great ending. The book is a real sit-on-the-end-of-your-seat page turner, worthy of reading late at night for an even better chilling effect.

Additional coverage of Buffie's life and career is contained in the following source published by Gale Research: *Something about the Author,* Vol. 71.

James Haskins

1941-

African-American author of nonfiction.

Major works include *James Van DerZee: The Picture-Takin' Man* (1979), *Black Music in America: A History Through Its People* (1987), *Black Dance in America: A History Through Its People* (1990), *Thurgood Marshall: A Life for Justice* (1992), *Get on Board: The Story of the Underground Railroad* (1993), *The March on Washington* (1993).

For commentary on Haskins's career prior to 1977, see *CLR,* Vol. 3.

INTRODUCTION

A prolific author of nonfiction for young people, Haskins is most highly esteemed for his biographies of prominent African Americans, including those of contemporary entertainers, activists, sports figures, and politicians. In addition, he has written studies of a wide range of topics, including history, international politics, the concerns of disabled Americans, and social issues such as alcoholism and drug abuse that are of special importance to young people. Praised for his simple and lucid prose style and his meticulous approach to his subjects, Haskins seeks to provide his readers with easily accessible books that confront the struggles of African-Americans while acknowledging their frequently unheralded contributions to society. At times inspirational and laudatory, his writings often introduce details that offer a unique perspective on the individuals and events studied. Some critics maintain that many of Haskins's books exhibit a characteristically "pedestrian" or "workmanlike" style and, though utilitarian, are marred by a tendency toward distortion caused by oversimplification. Most commentators, however, value Haskins's works as a much-needed source of insight into the experiences of blacks in America.

Biographical Information

Haskins was born in Montgomery, Alabama. Following early schooling in his home state, he attended Georgetown University and later Alabama State University, where he earned bachelor of arts and science degrees in 1960 and 1962 respectively. Haskins received his master of arts degree from the University of New Mexico in 1963 before moving to New York City, where he was employed until 1965 as a stock trader for Smith Barney & Co. He then returned to graduate study at the New School for Social Research and accepted a teaching position in the New York City public school system. His experiences teaching special education at New York's Public School 92 in the late sixties culminated in the publication of his

first book, *Diary of a Harlem Schoolteacher* (1969). This candid work attracted the attention of several major publishing companies, whose representatives approached Haskins about writing books for young people. In 1970, he published his first work for younger audiences, entitled *Resistance: Profiles in Nonviolence.* He has since written scores of books for young adult readers—including several acclaimed biographies of black Americans—while remaining active as an educator, lecturer, and outspoken proponent of civil rights for minorities.

Major Works

Many of Haskins's most popular works are biographies of noteworthy or well-known African Americans. *James Van DerZee: The Picture-Takin' Man* profiles an obscure black photographer whose pictures captured the bustling life of Harlem in the 1920s and 1930s but were not put before the public until collected in a New York Metropolitan Museum of Art display, "Harlem on My Mind," in 1968. Featuring interviews with Van DerZee, his friends and acquaintances, the book reveals a unique perspective on an important part of American social history through the eyes of a humble, largely unknown artist. *Thurgood Marshall: A Life for Justice* surveys the character and career of the first African American to sit on the Supreme Court bench. The work recounts the racial inequities with which Marshall was forced to contend, and details his battles with segregation as a lawyer for the NAACP and his many contributions to the American civil rights movement. As in his other biographies, Haskins attempts to reveal something of the inner person in *Thurgood Marshall*, placing his subject within the contexts of the social and political upheaval that has occurred in America during the twentieth century and describing the ways in which these forces shaped his life. Other individuals covered by Haskins include political leaders such as South Africa's Winnie Mandela and the Philippines' Corazon Aquino, and entertainers and sports stars including Diana Ross, Michael Jackson, Lena Horne, Julius Irving, Earvin "Magic" Johnson, and Pelé.

In addition to his biographies, Haskins has written a number of nonfiction works on the arts, historical matters, and contemporary social issues. His acclaimed *Black Dance in America: A History Through Its People*, the third in a series that also includes volumes on music and theater, documents the enduring influence of African-American dancers from the beginnings of American slavery early in the seventeenth century through Emancipation and to the present. Vignettes of important figures, including Katherine Dunham, Alvin Ailey, and Bill "Bojangles" Robinson occupy much of the book, which underscores the oppressive racism that confronted all of these individuals. *Get on Board: The Story of the Underground Railroad* examines the clandestine organization of abolitionists, activists, and freed slaves who helped conduct fugitive blacks to the North during the era of American slavery. Along with discussions of Frederick Douglass, Harriet Tubman and other celebrated figures, the book gives substantial space to the personal efforts of African Americans who courageously sought their own freedom. *The March on Washington* outlines the internal workings of the famed 1963 civil rights march, in which one quarter of a million people demonstrated nonviolently in favor of racial equality. The book includes transcripts of important speeches made by Martin Luther King, Jr. and other civil rights leaders, and details the many difficulties which had to be surmounted to organize a protest on such an enormous scale.

Awards

Haskins received the Coretta Scott King Award for *The Story of Stevie Wonder* in 1977. His *Black Music in America: A History Through Its People* earned him the Carter G. Woodson Book Award in 1988. *James Van DerZee: The Picture Takin' Man* was named a Woodson Outstanding Merit book in 1980, while *Lena Horne* and *Black Dance in America: A History Through Its People* were shortlisted as Coretta Scott King honor books in 1984 and 1991, respectively.

AUTHOR'S COMMENTARY

Jim Haskins

SOURCE: "Racism and Sexism in Children's Nonfiction," in *Children's Literature: Annual of the Modern Language Association Seminar on Children's Literature and the Children's Literature Association,* Vol. 5, 1976, pp. 141-47.

A lot of time and paper have been devoted to the subjects of racism and sexism. However, in almost every instance, the time and paper have been devoted only to the area of fiction. Dorothy Broderick, in her *Image of the Black in Children's Fiction,* for example, says much that can be applied to nonfiction, but her primary concern is clearly fiction. Most of the articles that deal with sexism in children's literature in Diane Gersoni-stavn's *Sexism and Youth* also focus on fiction. The same can be said of articles devoted to other minorities in America: the primary concern is fiction.

As a writer of nonfiction, with a special interest in biography, I am concerned with the lack of attention given to racism and sexism in nonfiction. It could be argued that things have improved and undoubtedly will continue to improve in coming years; but that is a cop-out. The point is that enough time has passed already for us to expect substantial progress; yet this progress has not occurred. Racist and sexist books are still being published, kept in print, and stocked by libraries and bookstores. No individual or group can be blamed, but changes are not going to happen until someone takes a stand for them and sticks to it. There undoubtedly will be cries of censorship and denial of children's rights when this stand is taken, but we cannot remain forever in this state of limbo.

Perhaps the limited attention being paid to nonfiction grows out of the belief that factual material presents less opportunity for racism and sexism. Yet the biographer or nonfiction writer is not immune from subjective involvement with a subject. I know when I research the life of a subject, I get totally caught up in his or her time period and daily life. As Judith Thompson and Gloria Woodard state in their article "Black Perspective in Books for Children," appearing in *The Black American in Books for Children,* I try to illuminate the black experience through history and biography. My being black has nothing to do with my approach. I am required, as a former slave commented to Julius Lester, to "wear the shoe" of the subject.

Racism and sexism occur in nonfiction through omission rather than commission. There are exceptions, of course—but they are less likely to be accepted by publishers. Margaret O. Hyde's *Your Brain,* published by McGraw Hill in 1964, serves as a good example of this "sin of omission." The brain is a "colorless" subject—Jensen and Shockley notwithstanding—yet only whites appear in the book's illustrations. Another book, concerning a child's first encounter with a hospital, remains admirably non-sexist throughout the text. However, the illustrations depict only female nurses and male doctors.

Publishers continue to turn out books which purport to represent humanity, but which actually deal only with men. A book about prehistoric mankind for instance will confine itself to a discussion of the first men in the world, when it is obvious that women have contributed a great deal to humanity's growth and development. Such books are not overtly racist or sexist. Hyde never says that black people lack brains, and the "great men of the world" books do not state that there are no great women. Simply by omitting references to other races and sexes, however, they imply and foster these attitudes. The next time you examine a nonfiction children's book, check to see if it includes a mixture of races and if the girls are as actively involved as the boys in scientific experiments, arts and crafts, and sports.

Children themselves are becoming more conscious of these omissions and inequities. I heard recently about two third-grade girls who approached a children's librarian because they were furious about a book entitled *Better Football for Boys*. They enjoyed the sport and played it often. The librarian, sharing their opinion, gave them the publisher's address and they immediately wrote a letter of complaint. I don't know whether they ever received a reply. The point is that they felt strongly enough to take action against an author and a publishing house.

Lothrop, Lee and Shepard, the Juvenile Division of William Morrow and Company, filled a great void with their series "What She Can Be," covering such occupations as veterinarian, lawyer, and architect. Too many girls felt that teaching, secretarial work, and motherhood were their only options. It is unfortunate however that the series couldn't have been "What They Can Be" and that a mixture of races doesn't appear in the books.

Research shows that children develop racist and sexist attitudes before they enter kindergarten. Numerous studies document firmly held opinions among preschoolers of what is appropriate for boys and girls. When asked, "Who drives the car?" most children will answer, "Daddy." This holds true even for children who have seen their mothers drive more frequently than their fathers. Since it's been proven fairly conclusively that sexual differentiation doesn't exist at birth, it's true—as the song says—that "you've got to be carefully taught."

The same song begins "you've got to be taught to hate and fear." Research also demonstrates that white children acquire negative attitudes toward black Americans before they enter kindergarten. Mary Ellen Goodman documents the awareness of racial differences in children between the ages of three and five. Trager and Yarrow have found that whites in kindergarten and in first and second grades were antagonistic toward blacks. A look at recent history makes this understandable. Augusta Baker, in her "Guidelines for Black Books: An Open Letter to Juvenile Editors," wrote that when she was working at the Countee Cullen Branch of the New York Public Library in 1937 and 1938, most of the black children using the library were aware only of Frederick Douglass, Booker T. Washington, and George Washington Carver among great black people. They marveled when they were introduced to Phillis Wheatley and Robert Smalls. She states rightly that: "If black children were so ignorant of their heritage and history, then why expect white children to know?"

The same is true of the awareness of women's contributions through history. If little girls know only about Betsy Ross and Madame Curie, how can little boys know of others? In talking with Shirley Chisholm, my biography of whom will soon be published, I learned how important it had been for her to discover Harriet Tubman, Susan B. Anthony, and, later, Mary McLeod Bethune. They provided a basis for her own hopes to be somebody one day. Had she not been an avid reader and library-goer, she might not have discovered these women until long after her concrete attitudes toward herself had been formed.

Fortunately there are a few valuable books available to those who look for them. In 1947 Shirley Graham's *There Was Once a Slave* introduced Frederick Douglass to thousands of Americans for the first time, and won an award for the best book combating intolerance in America. Ms. Graham followed this book with her biographies of Phillis Wheatley, Benjamin Banneker, George Washington Carver, Booker T. Washington, and Jean Baptiste de Sable. With these books one should contrast Elizabeth Yates' 1951 Newbery Award-winning *Amos Fortune, Free Man*. Throughout this book Amos Fortune says, "No, I'm not ready for freedom, don't give it to me yet." With this attitude in mind, I agree with Dorothy Sterling that the book shouldn't appear on the reading lists of ghetto schools.

After the Supreme Court's decision on school integration, publishers jumped on the bandwagon, bringing out such titles as Langston Hughes' *Famous American Negroes*, Gwendolyn Brooks' *Bronzeville Boys and Girls*, and Dorothy Sterling's *Freedom Train: The Story of Harriet Tubman*. They soon realized, however, that the Court's decision had little impact on the field of children's literature, and retreated to their safe little shells. Dorothy Sterling wrote in *Soul of Learning*, excerpted in *The Black American in Books for Children*, about the problems she faced trying to get her *Captain of the Planter* published. The book was a biography of Robert Smalls and told of Negro disenfranchisement and the birth of Jim Crow.

In 1965 Nancy Larrick wrote *The All-White World of Children's Books*, which greatly altered public opinion regarding the scope of racism in children's literature. She opened her article with a question asked by a five-year-old black girl in a New York nursery school as she looked through a picture book: "Why are they always white children?" A good question—particularly when in 1965 black children comprised 65 percent of the schoolchildren in New York City Public Schools, 53 percent in Cleveland, 56 percent in St. Louis, and 70 percent in the District of Columbia. Some 6,340,000 nonwhite students attended class across the country. Ms. Larrick's main concern was for the 39,600,000 white children learning from their books that they were the "kingfish" of the world—when on a world basis they were actually a minority.

As recently as 1967, John Oliver Killens wrote:

> The American Negro remains a cultural non-entity as
> far as books, television, movies and Broadway are
> concerned. It is as if twenty million Americans do not
> exist. A Negro schoolchild can go into school and
> look into his schoolbooks and children's books and
> come home and watch television and go to an
> occasional movie and follow this routine from day to
> day, month to month and year to year and hardly ever
> see a reflection of himself.

In 1968, when the Kerner report pointed out the facts of
racism and prejudice in America, the publishing industry
suddenly regained its interest in mass-producing books
by and about blacks. Ample federal money for schools
and libraries via LSCA funds kept this movement alive
longer than the first. Now that the economic crunch is on,
however, belts have to be tightened and concern for representative books has waned.

Fortunately this movement had a far-reaching impact and
sparked other concerns such as the treatment of Mexican-
Americans, Native Americans, Puerto Ricans, and most
recently Asian-Americans in juvenile literature. There are
a few articles on this subject: Tony DeGerez's "Three
Times Lonely; The Plight of the Mexican Child in the
American Southwest," in *Horn Book* (Feb. 1970); Mary
Gloyne Byler's "The Image of American Indians Projected by Non-Indian Writers" in *SLJ* (Feb. 1974); "Asian
Images—A Message to the Media" in *Bridge Magazine*
(April 1974). These groups, however, have not enjoyed
the same coverage as anti-black, racism, and sexism
groups. Mary Gloyne Byler's article is perhaps the most
pertinent to my topic. She points out that unlike most
minority groups in America, the Indians have been "represented" in thousands of books since frontier days. The
difficulty of separating fact from fiction seems unimportant—as does the fact that these books portray images of
Indians held by non-Indians. Ms. Byler concludes that
there are too many books about American Indians—featuring painted, whooping, befeathered Indians closing in
on peaceful white settlements. Too many books portray
the childlike Indian saved by white benevolence and give
expert advice on what is "best" for the Indian people. In
other words, these books create a fantasy image of the
American Indian which serves only to sustain the belief
that these barbaric people deserved to lose their lands.
What else can be expected when one publishing house
willingly publishes such a book, originally brought out in
Austria, by a German-born author, educated in Munich,
who lives in Bavaria and raises riding ponies!

Ms. Byler feels that only American Indians can tell non-
Indians what it is to be Indian. There is no longer any
need for non-Indians to "interpret" American Indians for
the American public. The same has been said of whites
writing about blacks—even of white critics evaluating the
work of a black author, but I'm not sure I wholly agree.

I do agree that stereotypes of American Indians should be
withdrawn and forgotten. But being Indian does not in

itself guarantee someone greater competence in writing
about Indians than an outstanding black or white writer
who researches the subject thoroughly and writes the total
picture. Byler feels that publishers should seek out Indian
writers. I agree not only that they should seek out writers
for house-engendered projects, but also that they should
be constantly receptive to the books of Indian writers.
Their chief consideration however must remain a well-
written, balanced, and accurate account.

We are now halfway through the 1970s, and still we discuss racism and sexism over and over again. But there is
no real action. Some changes occur in the publishing and
literary worlds, but frequently backsliding wipes out all
positive achievements. Too often we are so pleased that
February is Black History Month that we forget that most
students never read books by and about blacks during the
other eleven months.

In her article "High John Has Risen Again," in *Horn Book*
(April 1975), Virginia Hamilton describes how busy she
is each February. She also discusses her surprise in learning that many of the students with whom she works and
to whom she lectures wouldn't consider reading a black-
oriented book on their own. She protests, as I do, the
location of Black English in black study departments rather
than in English departments. The same problem exists
with history. Go into any library and ask for a book on
black history. The librarian will go automatically to the
326 shelves where these books are classified. Ask for a
book on American history, however, and the librarian will
take you straight to the 970 shelves.

It is a subtle distinction, but one which encourages children, teachers, and other adults to isolate the study of
blacks and other minorities from the mainstream of American history.

Books about blacks in the armed forces, whether in the
Civil War or World Wars I and II, are similarly separated.
How many knew of Crispus Attucks before the advent of
Black History Week? How many teachers and librarians
over twenty-five knew anything about Chief Joseph before Xerox's TV special "I Will Fight No More Forever?"

A librarian friend of mine once shocked her supervisor by
asking who Benjamin Banneker was, after visiting a Bed-
ford-Stuyvesant school of that name in 1968. She wasn't
stupid—she had majored in American history. But in all
her years of schooling she had never encountered any
other famous blacks than George Washington Carver,
Booker T. Washington, and Frederick Douglass.

Fortunately once she discovered this gap in her education, she began to do some independent study in the area.
How many others never see this gap or realize the need
to fill it? Some must be in publishing—whether as writers, editors, illustrators, or proofreaders.

It has only recently been acknowledged that America's
proud melting-pot includes only Europeans. Blacks, Asian-

Americans, Mexican-Americans, Native Americans and Puerto Ricans have known this for years. More Americans now recognize that history books do not give them the whole story. S. Carl Hirsch pointed this out in his book, *The Riddle of Racism,* and frightened many who realized that he wrote for children.

Gradually more books are dealing with this educational void. In his *Album of Reconstruction,* William Katz discusses the myths surrounding the Reconstruction period—myths making heroes of the Ku Klux Klan, exaggerating the failures while forgetting the contributions of the public school system, women's rights, and tax laws. There are now biographies of Fidel Castro and his hatred of America, Mao-Tse-Tung, Malcolm X, Jesse Jackson, Fanny Kemble, Abby Kelley Foster, and Frances Wright. There are also praiseworthy series such as Crowell's "Women of America," "Crowell's Biographies," and Franklin Watts' "Picture Life of ——."

But we are celebrating our two hundredth birthday. Why are we only now introducing our children to the truths of American history? Will these truths grow and root out earlier falsehoods, or will they wither and fall back? Look over the recent titles of various publishers and the reactions of reviewers with special concern for racism and sexism. We have good reason to worry.

Virginia Hamilton states:

> We need good literature for young people that will bring characters and the past and the present to life through uncontrived situations. I don't care whether this is accomplished through so-called street language or an oneirocritic's nightmares.

She also says:

> Our present experience is not one and the same with the oppression of slave time. While we are not wholly free, neither are we totally captured. For never before has black creative intelligence coincided so opportunely with the development of black pride, the advancement of political cultural awareness, independence, and style to affect black art. My assumption . . . is that non-white literature, defined through its diversity, is as American as white.

Her thoughts apply to any American minority—racial or sexual. The same sentiment echoes in Langston Hughes' poetry:

> I, too, sing America, I am the darker brother.
> (America never was America to me.)

Perhaps someday this second line will no longer reflect the feelings of America's many minorities.

TITLE COMMENTARY

📖 *BARBARA JORDAN: SPEAKING OUT* (1977)

Booklist

SOURCE: A review of *Barbara Jordan,* in *Booklist,* Vol. 74, No. 7, December 1, 1977, p. 607.

Relegating personal information and political criticism to the background, Haskins chronicles the career of Texas-born Barbara Jordan, first black woman to represent a southern state in the U.S. House of Representatives. Garnering information from friends and colleagues as well as Jordan's own published comments and speeches (liberally excerpted throughout), Haskins highlights her college and law school years; details her early political involvement and landmark election to the Texas Senate; and follows her to the House of Representatives, describing, among other things, her role as a member of the House Judiciary Committee investigating Richard Nixon. An astigmatic but absorbing profile of a dedicated, outspoken political leader and her stance on contemporary issues.

Kirkus Reviews

SOURCE: A review of *Barbara Jordan,* in *Kirkus Reviews,* Vol. XLV, No. 23, December 1, 1977, p. 1273.

From childhood Barbara Jordan always wanted to be somebody—she rejected a career in pharmacy because "whoever heard of an outstanding pharmacist?"—and she won respect in the Texas State Senate, just as she got through Boston University Law School, by doing more homework than anyone else. Her political career as chronicled here seems composed of more honors and ovations than hard battles—an impression that doesn't counteract the militants' criticism of Jordan as a "sell-out"—but Haskins appends an impressive list of "legislative accomplishments" while at the same time facing up to the controversy surrounding her fight to extend the provisions of the Voting Rights Act and her evasive performance on the Democratic Compliance Review Committee. Though Haskins lacks Jordan's celebrated talent for direct, forceful speech—and seems unaware that the frequent tribute, "she's one of the most intelligent women I've ever met," is as condescending as the Texas judge's calling her "a credit to her race"—he does come through with an honest, balanced portrait of the formidable Representative who works hard, gets things done, makes a policy of compromise, and as a result of the Impeachment hearings, has assuredly become (as the *U.S. News* described her) one of the Democratic Party's "new luminaries."

Zenata W. Pierre

SOURCE: A review of *Barbara Jordan: Speaking Out,* in

School Library Journal, Vol. 24, No. 5, January, 1978, p. 94.

Haskins' biography of Barbara Jordan—the first Black female representative to the U.S. Congress—gets off to a slow start with an overlong account of the Civil Rights Movement and current events of the 1950's. However, once underway, this turns out to be an interesting account of Jordan's life from her childhood to the present. After receiving her law degree from Boston University, Jordan ran twice for the Texas Senate, winning the second time. She earned respect for her intelligence, fairness, and efforts on behalf of poor people during her tenure in the Texas legislature and was able to wage a successful Congressional campaign. Jordan's life-time desire to excel and to break away from traditional women's roles is well portrayed and the Congresswoman's commanding voice does come through.

Zena Sutherland

SOURCE: A review of *Barbara Jordan,* in *Bulletin of the Center for Children's Books,* Vol. 31, No. 6, February, 1978, p. 95.

In describing Barbara Jordan's career, Haskins gives a vivid picture of her vigorous and forceful personality, achieving this not by effusive prose but by letting her words and her accomplishments tell the story. Her record of "firsts" is impressive: the first black woman to become a Texas senator, to sit in the House of Representatives in Washington, to serve during House impeachment proceedings, to give the keynote address at a Democratic National Convention. The writing is balanced, objective, and candid, and it gives fascinating information about political realities, particularly at the state level, as well as about the subject.

THE GREAT AMERICAN CRAZIES (with Kathleen Benson and Ellen Inkelis, 1978)

Henry Zorich

SOURCE: A review of *The Great American Crazies,* in *West Coast Review of Books,* Vol. 4, No. 2, March, 1978, p. 46.

To compile these odd-ball stories is triumph enough, but Haskins has put all of these short tales into categories, each one proving amusing. These are stories about the strange people in our society, the weirdos of history, those highly individualistic individuals who set out to do something unusual and achieve it. For example, Henry Ford was a great collector; when he died, a look at his personal belongings included a test tube labeled (and presumably containing) "Thomas Edison's Last Breath." And there really *was* a Grizzly Adams who loved to live in the hills and mountains, and whose friend was a bear named Ben Franklin, "Gentle Ben," that is. And in 1960, Movie Star Cary Grant admitted that he found the most functional

and comfortable underwear to be ladies' panties! There are also in-depth profiles of strange people like Ida Wood, who grew from rags to riches, but when she died was concerned about one particular $5 bill, and W.C. Fields who didn't trust any one bank and so, under different names, known only to him, deposited his money throughout the nation in various banks; when he died, millions of dollars were unclaimed, perhaps, to this day, awaiting the fictitious person to turn up to claim them. The stories are all presumably true and that's what makes the book a joy.

WHO ARE THE HANDICAPPED? (1978)

Kirkus Reviews

SOURCE: A review of *Who Are the Handicapped?* in *Kirkus Reviews,* Vol. XLVI, No. 14, July 15, 1978, p. 756.

By explaining the causes, consequences, and nature of different kinds of disabilities and making a plea for understanding and acceptance, Haskins hopes to put a dent in the wall of prejudice he sees holding back all those "whose only social offense is a physical or mental difference over which they have no control." Unfortunately, many of his well-intentioned statements—"The person with a serious disability is every bit as good, as beautiful, as human as the normal person"; it is "what he has to give" that is important—are merely pious or poorly thought out; and he declares too casually that we should take time to listen to the deaf, that the blind have "unique talents," or that we must "assimilate them [the disabled in general] into the social mainstream as full participants." Nevertheless, the little information he gives on each disorder might help to correct some misconceptions, and the specific measures he cites, such as the special Olympics, the successful employment of the retarded, and the legal drive for a barrier-free environment, speak for the cause.

Betsy Gimbel

SOURCE: A review of *Who Are the Handicapped?* in *Interracial Books for Children Bulletin,* Vol. 9, No. 8, 1978, p. 17.

Yet another commercial pot-boiler from a pen that churns out a seemingly endless supply of books on "relevant" topics.

Haskins devotes his energies to reiterating Establishment Medicine's versions of causes, therapies, cures and mental problems connected with the major debilitating diseases, birth defects and injuries, not one of which bears repeating. If intended as a textbook for young people, the book's shallow, ignorant tone is guaranteed to stifle anyone's interest in the subject. If intended for general reading, it fails because it is written in dry textbook style, dwelling on the trite and obvious. Enthusiasm for the subject is displaced by a slick-brochure mentality, hardly commendable when trying to reach any age group with this type of information.

Reflecting the insensitivity of the general contents, the 24 photos (of famous people who are disabled and of activities for the disabled) include no women aside from Helen Keller and Kate Adams (archery champion) and almost no girls in the sports activities. There are no photos of Blacks, except for a few boys involved in sports. The picture that wins first prize for insensitivity is captioned "Scouting is for everyone"—while showing a lily-white bunch of little boys, most of whom do not appear to be disabled.

But the lowest blow of all is the subtle way Haskins puts hearing-impaired, paraplegic Governor George Wallace on a pedestal. Although Wallace is well known for his racist and neo-fascist ideas and actions, Haskins gives him both a photograph and mention in the text as an example to the world of what a disabled person can accomplish. One of Wallace's "accomplishments" has been to help keep Alabama one of the most impoverished states in the nation, as well as one of the worst in terms of its treatment of all minorities, including the disabled minority.

The author concludes by asserting that the solution for all the problems faced by disabled people is "understanding the limitation in order to overcome it. . . . " Even a casual look at history reveals that any improvements in the lot of disabled people in the U.S. have really only come about in the aftermath of huge political, social and economic upheavals in society. Haskins likewise promulgates the myth that "the enemy" is the various myths and preconceived notions about "handicaps," which implies that the disabled person's own worst enemy is actually him- or herself.

Furthermore, every fact of life puts the lie to the author's contention that most disabled people in this country can live "normal" lives—when even so-called normal people cannot live normal lives in the face of high unemployment, inflation, racism, sexism and the general deprivation that is the lot of the "normal" majority.

This book may provide some information to the very uninformed, but its philosophy and overall attitude do a disservice to young readers. We can answer the author's "Who are the handicapped?" with our own question: "What handicapist profits from this drivel?"

Philip Starr

SOURCE: A review of *Who Are the Handicapped?* in *Science Books & Films,* Vol. XV, No. 1, May, 1979, p. 11.

Haskins introduces teenagers to some mental and physical disabilities, stressing the importance of attitudes toward the disabled. Through this primer, the author achieves his objective and makes the reader aware of a few of the aspects of being blind, deaf, epileptic, and so forth. He does stress the fact that we are all different and, in some sense, handicapped. The book's weakness lies in the premise that stories about handicapped persons who have become successful will convince the reader to act differently toward handicapped individuals. I believe the research evidence would not support this premise, as the successful handicapped persons would be treated as exceptions to the general rule. Altogether, the book can be of use as an introductory text on a complex subject.

ANDREW YOUNG: MAN WITH A MISSION (1979)

Joyce Milton

SOURCE: A review of *Andrew Young: Man with a Mission,* in *The New York Times Book Review,* September 23, 1979, p. 26.

Children and teen-agers who know Andrew Young only as our outspoken former Ambassador to the United Nations may well find some revelations in this portrait of the boy who imbibed his father's motto, "Don't get mad, get smart," the aide to whom Martin Luther King Jr. invariably turned for the conservative point of view, and the Congressman who was described by one colleague as "a man of sweet reason." James Haskins, whose biographies of notable blacks range from *The Life of Martin Luther King Jr.* to *The Story of Stevie Wonder,* has built a reputation for books that are strong on social history, and this facility is put to good use here in summing up Young's far-ranging career.

Analyzing Young's performance in his latest endeavor is a trickier assignment, made more difficult by the author's reluctance to ascribe overtly political motivations to either Young or President Carter, the other half of the "peculiar alliance" of Georgians. More mature readers will no doubt sense that there's a dimension missing from this profile; nevertheless, Mr. Haskins is to be commended for his measured and fair-minded assessment of the content and context of the controversial ex-Ambassador's headline-making remarks.

Debra L. Maier

SOURCE: A review of *Andrew Young: Man with a Mission,* in *School Library Journal,* Vol. 26, No. 1, September, 1979, p. 158.

An up-to-date but biased biography of Andrew Young, tracing his life from a comfortable childhood in New Orleans to his current position as U.S. Ambassador to the United Nations. Emphasis is placed on Young's roles during the civil rights movement, as a Congressman from Georgia, and as Ambassador. Controversial remarks made by Young are interpreted by the author in a manner that favors his subject. Little insight is offered into the man's personal life, leaving readers missing a dimension, and Haskins is sometimes simplistic in explaining the intricacies of Young's political career as well.

Ann A. Flowers

SOURCE: A review of *Andrew Young: Man with a Mission,* in *The Horn Book Magazine,* Vol. LV, No. 5, October, 1979, p. 550.

Andrew Young was born into a professional, middle-class Black family; in such a milieu the precocious, self-confident child developed the ability to work with all people without feeling the bitterness that sometimes affects the relationships between Blacks and whites. Not until after his graduation from Howard University did he realize that his vocation was the ministry. His attempts to improve the lot of his poor Black congregation convinced him that social change could be brought about only by coordinated political effort. Committed to nonviolence, he lived in danger as an influential figure in the civil rights movement, as a close friend of Martin Luther King, Jr., and as a leader of the Southern Christian Leadership Conference. The first Black congressman in the United States and later American Ambassador to the United Nations, Andrew Young is portrayed as a vigorous, pragmatic man with a special ability to organize people and to use reason and compromise to reach goals. A sympathetic biography of a man of outstanding achievements.

GAMBLING—WHO REALLY WINS? (1979)

Denise M. Wilms

SOURCE: A review of *Gambling—Who Really Wins?* in *Booklist,* Vol. 76, No. 5, November 1, 1979, p. 449.

According to Dr. Robert Custer of the Veterans Administration's mental services division, nearly all compulsive gamblers started their habit between 12 and 14 years of age; that striking piece of information, plus the fact that gambling is a growing enterprise, indicates a need for coverage of the subject. That the sport is old and widespread comes clear in an introductory look that points to gambling through the ages, including U.S. history. Games both legal and illegal come under brief, systematic review in subsequent chapters. Some moral and philosophical considerations are also probed (gambling raises crime rates but can also make money for a state, for example). Haskins' ultimate concern is gambling abuse; he urges potential players to know the odds, keep a healthy perspective, and most important, be able to recognize signs of developing abuse in themselves. This is useful as an overview; it is generally clear and concise, with a straightforward writing style.

Kathleen W. Craver

SOURCE: A review of *Gambling—Who Really Wins?* in

School Library Journal, Vol. 26, No. 7, March, 1980, pp. 140-41.

Given a dearth of titles covering this increasingly important subject, Haskins' book might be a good bet for this age level, particularly since the text indicates that most gamblers become addicted between the ages of 12 to 14. The text defines gambling and some of the more popular forms such as horse racing, blackjack, professional sports, numbers, bingo, and raffles. It also describes those who gamble and provides information on the treatment of compulsive gamblers. Throughout, the author stresses the pitfalls of the percentages and offers several minicase studies of both the lucky and unlucky. The first chapter is devoted to the history of gambling, while the last closes with advice to would-be betters, accompanied by a questionnaire identifying the personality traits of potential compulsive gamblers.

JAMES VAN DERZEE: THE PICTURE-TAKIN' MAN (1979)

Booklist

SOURCE: A review of *James Van DerZee: The Picture-Takin' Man,* in *Booklist,* Vol. 75, No. 22, July 15, 1979, p. 1619.

He was the official photographer for Marcus Garvey; he snapped such black celebrities as Harry Wills and Bill Robinson; and, as a neighborhood photographer, he recorded the everyday life of the self-respecting Harlem of an earlier day. From his customers he earned the appellation "The Picture-Takin' Man," but his photographic contributions to black American history went sadly unrecognized until he was more than 80 years old. Writing with unashamed admiration Haskins portrays black photographer James Van DerZee, drawing heavily on the man's own reminiscences, to reveal a generous, lively, easygoing individual still surprised at his sudden, belated fame. The first portion of Van DerZee's life is covered more fully, but Haskins gives an adequate review of his later life and career, backgrounding it with editorial perspectives on Harlem's growth and evolution. Numerous black-and-white photographs demonstrate Van DerZee's talent, picture the man and his family, and capture a Harlem that no longer exists.

Kirkus Reviews

SOURCE: A review of *James Van DerZee: The Picture-Takin' Man,* in *Kirkus Reviews,* Vol. XLVII, No. 15, August 1, 1979, p. 862.

A direct, respectful, surprisingly readable biography of the obscure Harlem studio-photographer, now in his nineties, who was suddenly projected into prominence by the 1968 "Harlem on My Mind" exhibit at the Metropolitan Museum. Most laudably, Haskins neither idealizes Van

DerZee nor casts him as a black role-model. Rather, he presents him squarely as the product of a secure, supportive, Lenox, Mass., upbringing (not unaware of his place economically or racially) who for years drifted in and out of elevator-operator jobs and such while hoping to catch on as a musician. Though he'd started taking pictures as a boy (with one of the first two cameras in Lenox), it wasn't until 1915, with the encouragement of his second wife, that he made photography a full-time career. Then, during the so-called Harlem Renaissance of 1920-35 (a white-fostered phenomenon, Haskins acidulously observes), he photographed the literary and theatrical limelighters and the flamboyant doings of black-nationalist Marcus Garvey—but without taking any particular stock of any of them: as he put it, "he made his pictures and left." At the same time, he was recording the "other Harlem" of weddings and funerals, barber shops and drug stores—the sedate existence of the middle class. And he was improvising: the self-styled "Artist and Photographer" was more interested, always, in arranging his subjects—and retouching his negatives—than in the actual picture-taking (a bent Haskins places in the context of photographic history). Sometimes, too, he arranged his subjects in little genre groupings (e.g., the fond parents and the piano-playing tots), sometimes he printed multiple images—in the most famous instance, of a young girl hovering over the casket at her funeral. (All, of course, are represented here.) But in time business fell off. On the eve of the landmark exhibit, the Van DerZees lost their home and shop, and the faithful Gaynella suffered a breakdown and died without fully recovering. His acclaim, says Van DerZee, was "too much, too late." But he lives, without bitterness or loss of interest, on his intermittent income and "meals on wheels"—a lesson in gracious longevity that adds still another facet to this staunchly true-to-life book.

Zena Sutherland

SOURCE: A review of *James Van DerZee: The Picture-Takin' Man,* in *Bulletin of the Center for Children's Books,* Vol. 33, No. 4, December, 1979, p. 71.

A Harlem photographer for over half a century, Van DerZee was "discovered" in 1968, when his work was shown at the "Harlem on My Mind" exhibit at the Metropolitan Museum of Art. Born in 1886 in a small Massachusetts town, Van DerZee had received his first camera as a nine-year-old; a premium for selling sachet, it didn't work, and the next camera (which did) was paid for by money saved from part-time work. As a photographer in Harlem, to which Van DerZee came when he was an adolescent, he recorded for posterity the entertainers, the socialites, the politicians, all the affluent and comfortable world that white society didn't know existed. The book is profusely illustrated with examples of Van DerZee's work: portraits, wedding pictures, group scenes, and family pictures. The writing style is smooth, informal, and carefully researched; there are many interviews with the subject, whose memories are as interesting as his comments are colorful, at times profound. "The years teach much that the days don't even know." This is almost as much a history of photography or of Harlem as it is of the "picture-takin' man."

Laura Geringer

SOURCE: A review of *James Van DerZee: The Picture-Takin' Man,* in *School Library Journal,* Vol. 26, No. 6, February, 1980, pp. 66-7.

Born when Grover Cleveland was President and France sent the Statue of Liberty over to be planted in the New York Harbor, photographer James Van DerZee was "discovered" when he was 83 years old. As a Black child in the mostly white community of Lenox, Mass., he lived on top of a maze of mine shafts, helping his sexton father polish church brass, dust woodwork, and dig graves. Later, in New York City, he worked as a waiter and an elevator operator, nursed ambitions of becoming a musician, and studied French but by the age of 20 was ensconced in the constricted role of husband/provider in a railroad flat with two locks and no furniture ("I felt that if I paid the landlord once or twice he oughta lay off me for awhile, but I found that every month he was right there again, wanting money . . . "). The tide turned when he took a job as darkroom man in a department store portrait concession stand, discovered he had more talent than his boss, and opened his own studio with his second wife, the glamorous Gaynella, thus inaugurating a partnership (Bunny and Baby Doll) that lasted 60 years, and commencing a collection of glass and film negatives that numbered about 75,000 when Reginald McGhee found them for the Metropolitan's Museum of Art's "Harlem On My Mind" exhibition in 1968. Neighborhood riots had replaced renaissance by that time, so the octogenarian's studies of ordinary people going to lodge meetings, beauty parlors and teas while Duke Ellington played and Langston Hughes published his poetry was an eye-opener for many and a valuable historical record. Well-reproduced here are selections from that archive—graduations, confirmations, once-a-year family group shots, soldiers going off to war, athletic clubs, fraternities, as well as views of celebrities of the hour: Marcus Garvey, Florence Mills, Joe Louis, Bill "Bojangles" Robinson, etc. A fine contribution to any library's offerings on urban Afro-American life and photography.

📖 **THE QUIET REVOLUTION: THE STRUGGLE FOR THE RIGHTS OF DISABLED AMERICANS (with J. M. Stifle, 1979)**

Kirkus Reviews

SOURCE: A review of *The Quiet Revolution: The Struggle for the Rights of Disabled Americans,* in *Kirkus Reviews,* Vol. XLVII, No. 24, December 15, 1979, p. 1435.

This is the hard-hitting, brass-tacks argument for the disabled that we missed in Haskins' mushy, platitudinous *Who Are the Disabled?* (1978). Here, the chapter titles refer to different "rights" (the right to prevention, to education, to treatment, to employment, to a barrier-free environment); the content cuts through idealistic rhetoric to document actual conditions. The authors cite specific anti-discrimination laws and court cases—*and* note the gap between law and enforcement. They point to medical advances, but point out that the health care that would prevent disability is unavailable to many. They support deinstitutionalizing the handicapped—but recognize that many discharged retarded persons end up worse off than before. Institutions themselves get a hard look: the authors cite Geraldo Rivera's 1972 exposé of the Willowbrook "snakepit" and show with other examples that this was not an isolated case. Apropos of jobs, we learn that two of three handicapped adults never find permanent jobs though survey findings should have disabused employers of prevailing "myths," that the labor of institutionalized patients is exploited under the heading of "therapy," that "in spite of [cited] regulations a great deal of discrimination occurs within the vocational rehabilitation programs themselves," and that the benefit system also discriminates against those who work. Some disabilities themselves are caused by exposure to toxic substances at the workplace. And just getting to and from work can be a struggle for the disabled, but it could be made easier with architectural, transit, and other reforms. The authors also speak out against compulsory sterilization and for mainstreaming in education, always recognizing the difficulties in applying such principles.

Judyth Lessee

SOURCE: A review of *The Quiet Revolution: The Struggle for the Rights of Disabled Americans,* in *School Library Journal,* Vol. 26, No. 5, January, 1980, p. 70.

A history of the disabled movement from the early 50s to the present. Haskins' discussions parallel the United Cerebral Palsy Association's Bill of Rights for the Handicapped which includes right to treatment, education, employment, etc. The text gives a greater understanding of the militant attitudes of some handicapped people and of the apathetic and sometimes hostile attitudes of the non-handicapped society. New terms are explained well and a concise synopsis of the myriad laws affecting the handicapped passed in the last decade is included. A seven-page bibliography and numerous photographs round out an excellent beginning text for this highly current and controversial subject.

Zena Sutherland

SOURCE: A review of *The Quiet Revolution: The Struggle for the Rights of Disabled Americans,* in *Bulletin of the Center for Children's Books,* Vol. 33, No. 8, April, 1980, p. 153.

This may be considered a companion volume to Haskins'

Who Are the Handicapped? Here the emphasis is not on who the handicapped or disabled citizens are but on what is, or can be, done to solve or alleviate their problems in living in a world in which they encounter not only discrimination but also physical barriers that make it difficult—in some cases, impossible—to live normal lives or take advantage of those rights to which they are entitled. The writing is forceful without being melodramatic, strong in pleading for means to give the disabled human and civil rights, the book a weapon in the quiet revolution that is going on today.

Bruce A. Maloof

SOURCE: A review of *The Quiet Revolution: The Struggle for the Rights of Disabled Americans,* in *Science Books & Films,* Vol. 16, No. 1, September/October, 1980, pp. 8-9.

This volume should make provocative reading for high school and undergraduate students who have had no experience with individuals with severe impairments. It will sensitize them to a wide range of civic and moral responsibilities vis-a-vis disabled persons that have been overlooked in the realms of prevention, treatment, education, employment and compensation, environmental accessibility, and freedom of choice. Although the presentation of the issues occasionally resorts to an inflammatory editorial style and an overtaxing of the rules of logical deduction, the authors commit no grievous factual errors (although the developmental history of consumerism among disabled persons is grossly oversimplified). Perhaps one of the greatest services provided by the authors is the frontal assault on many of the myths regarding the needs and abilities of disabled persons. The authors make very effective use of a combination of survey data, anecdotes and vignettes to "make points" on behalf of the potential of disabled persons and for objectives such as deinstitutionalization, normalization and mainstreaming. However, although there is a chapter on architectural barriers, no distinction is made between impairments, functional disabilities and handicaps. Also, no insight is given into the psychological and sociological reasons why disabled persons have been segregated and disenfranchised so systematically. More of the sociopolitical reasons for the slow progress in the enactment and enforcement of legislation to protect the rights of disabled persons and some of the economic and product liability factors that inhibit the manufacturing and distribution of new assistive aids and devices would have been an asset. Also lacking are such straightforward suggestions as being diligent never to occupy or obstruct parking for disabled persons to more missionary occupations such as promoting sensitivity among parents, peers and teachers.

Kipp Watson

SOURCE: A review of *The Quiet Revolution: The Struggle for the Rights of Disabled Americans,* in *Interracial Books for Children Bulletin,* Vol. 13, Nos. 4 & 5, 1982, p. 16.

The Quiet Revolution gives lip service to the struggle for civil and human rights that is being waged by disabled people but fails to present issues from the perspectives of disabled activists. It is indicative of the author's perspective that a bill of rights for the "handicapped" composed by the United Cerebral Palsy Associations (UCPA) provides the structure for the book. Thus issues are defined by a provider agency rather than by any disabled activists. To give just one example of the distortions that result, the first enumerated right in UCPA's bill of rights is the right to the prevention of disability, whereas the right to travel free of handicapping barriers—an issue of greater importance to activists—is buried within an overall right to barrier-free public facilities.

In yet another example of the author's handicapist perspective, he claims that telethons "destigmatize" disabilities and provide a major impetus for the advancement of disability rights. He fails to mention that disabled activists believe that telethons do precisely the opposite. Adding insult to injury, this book refers to children as "crippled" and to people who use wheelchairs as "confined."

The author's failure to consult or even recognize the leadership of the disability rights movement—let alone mention any disability rights organizations—reflects a perspective that renders his book useless—if not damaging.

📖 *I'M GONNA MAKE YOU LOVE ME: THE STORY OF DIANA ROSS* (1980)

Diane Haas

SOURCE: A review of *I'm Gonna Make You Love Me: The Story of Diana Ross,* in *School Library Journal,* Vol. 27, No. 3, November, 1980, p. 86.

It's refreshing to encounter a biography—particularly of a rock star—which is not only well written but also presents a clear view of the subject's background. Haskins creates a vivid picture of Detroit; of the South and the conditions which forced Blacks to migrate northward; of the music business; and of maintaining a career and family. Through it all, the story is skillfully and entertainingly told without undue adulation or disparagement of anyone involved.

Kirkus Reviews

SOURCE: A review of *I'm Gonna Make You Love Me: The Story of Diana Ross,* in *Kirkus Reviews,* Vol. XLIX, No. 3, February 1, 1981, p. 146.

Is Diana Ross all packaging? That's what critics have said of her act, and Haskins' uncritical but not gushy biography may inadvertently confirm the suspicion. With a little time off to return to charm school for further polishing, Ross spent the militant Sixties under Motown's Berry Gordy's total direction, working hard on success as lead Supreme. In the early Seventies she married and had three unplanned children in rapid succession, but finally gave up the marriage and her sporadic attempts to stay home with the kids. She threw a temper tantrum over the tacky clothes she had to wear in *Lady Sings the Blues,* insisted on designing her own for *Mahogany,* which was less favorably received, and had to sit home pregnant through the premiere of *Lady . . . ,* thus missing "the biggest moment of her life." Now in her thirties, Diana Ross is attempting to project a more natural image, but seems largely reduced to looking back with understandable pride on her early and rapid rise from the Detroit projects. That dream of course still lives; and where Diana Ross still embodies it, Haskins' biography will satisfy at a level a few steps up from fan fodder.

Eugenia Schmitz

SOURCE: A review of *I'm Gonna Make You Love Me: The Story of Diana Ross,* in *Best Sellers,* Vol. 40, No. 12, March, 1981, p. 448.

This biography of Diana Ross, star of rock and blues

Haskins as a teenager.

singer of movies and television, tells an American success story. By dint of beauty, talent, and sheer hard work, she rose from the "Black Bottom" Brewster-Douglass Projects of Detroit to Radio City, Hollywood, and No. 1 billing on the record charts. It is the story of "a skinny high school kid" who became a member of the Primettes, a Black girls' quartet which evolved into a trio, the Supremes. Upon graduation from high school in 1962, the girls received a contract from Berry Gordy of Motown Records. Then, there followed bus tours and one-night stands in the South and finally performances in nightclubs like the Copacabana in New York and others in Las Vegas.

In 1970, the Supremes dissolved as a group, and Diana continued on her own in top nightclubs, as the star in the movie "Lady Sings the Blues" (the biography of Billie Holiday), in "Mahogany," and as Dorothy in "The Wiz." Ms. Ross married Robert Silberstein, a white Jew, in January 1971. They became the parents of three daughters: Rhonda, Tracee, and Chudney. After five years of marriage, they mutually agreed that marriage did not allow either of them the freedom to pursue his/her career, and they were divorced in 1977.

Like most juvenile and teenage biography, this book lacks documentation of primary sources. The acknowledgments mention the use of excerpts from periodical articles and a book, and one assumes that there were interviews with the principals. Missing is a psychological analysis of the person, Diana Ross. The narrative abounds in colloquialisms, such as "lots," "a lot," "so," "all that," contractions, and some split infinitives. A discography and photographs are included.

"MAGIC": A BIOGRAPHY OF EARVIN JOHNSON (1982)

Linda W. Callaghan

SOURCE: A review of *'Magic': A Biography of Earvin Johnson,* in *Booklist,* Vol. 78, No. 11, February 1, 1982, pp. 709-10.

In Haskin's reliable hands, Johnson's life from the playgrounds of Lansing, Michigan, to the ball courts of the Los Angeles Lakers comes alive for the older reader. Thoughtful passages that capture feelings, pressures, triumphs, and tragedies blend with exciting play-by-play accounts of Johnson's growth into a pro star. Coaches, teammates, Johnson, and his family are portrayed with warmth and depth, becoming real people, not just personalities, as Haskins goes behind the star to capture the man whose enthusiasm for his work is inspiring and contagious.

Frances Friedman

SOURCE: A review of *'Magic': A Biography of Earvin Johnson,* in *Voice of Youth Advocates,* Vol. 5, No. 3, August, 1982, p. 45.

A formula sports biography about the 24-year-old basketball superstar, who signed a contract with the Los Angeles Lakers in 1981 for one million dollars a year for 25 years! Born to a blue collar family in Chicago's black ghetto, Earvin began playing organized basketball in fifth grade. He attended integrated Everett High School, was an average student, but basketball brought him offers of scholarships from all over. He attended Michigan State on a basketball scholarship for two years before succumbing to pressures to turn pro. From then on fame and fortune. . . .

Much of the narrative is taken up by game descriptions, otherwise the style is straightforward, easy reading, adorned by occasional b/w photos showing this handsome young star with his infectious smile.

THE CHILD ABUSE HELP BOOK (with Pat Connolly, 1982)

Betsy Hearne

SOURCE: A review of *The Child Abuse Help Book,* in *Booklist,* Vol. 78, No. 22, August, 1982, p. 1525.

The clear, cogent style of reporting here is helpful in reviewing a widespread problem, although the selection of information is more accurate in some cases than in others. The presentation of abusive parents' psychological problems and pressures, for example, is perceptive; but the section on abuse in institutions is very haphazard, and the discussion of father-daughter incest gives only the traditional and highly questionable theory that the blame lies with the mother for having "given up her responsibilities as a wife and parent and turned them over to her daughter." Better sections explore the ways that social stress, poverty, and prejudice contribute to child abuse, and 20 pages are given over to directions for help, including agencies, resource centers, and suggestions for personal action.

Gale Eaton

SOURCE: A review of *The Child Abuse Help Book,* in *School Library Journal,* Vol. 29, No. 1, September, 1982, p. 139.

A survey of physical and emotional abuse and neglect of children, both at home and in institutions, . . . *Help Book* conveys a healthy sense of outrage and suggests turning to Parents Anonymous, state child protection agencies, local counseling services and other responsible sources for aid. Haskins is sensitive to socio-economic stresses that may exacerbate family problems for migrant workers, members of the armed services or urban poor and for members of racial and ethnic minorities. He has a tendency, however, to portray women as more responsible than men; his anecdotal examples of neglecting parents are all mothers, and in describing the sexual abuse of daughters by their fathers he says more about the passivity of mothers (95% of whom fail to report abuse, according to one quoted study) than about the characters and responsibilities of abusing fathers; although he suggests extenuating circumstances for the mothers, the emphasis seems misplaced.

Dean W. Harper

SOURCE: A review of *The Child Abuse Help Book,* in *Science Books & Films,* Vol. 18, No. 3, January/February, 1983, p. 124.

This book, which consists of ten chapters and a series of appendices, is organized into four parts. The first part, with three chapters, focuses on the physical assault, sexual abuse, and physical neglect of children. The second part, also with three chapters, deals with a child's emotional neglect and abuse and abuse in schools and various residential treatment facilities. The author also includes "hidden abuses" that include abuses that result from the lack of medical care or poor care, that occur in families of servicemen that result from the tensions of service life, and that occur among migrant farm workers. In these first two parts of the book Haskins intends to provide readers with information about abuses, but the very brevity of his text results inevitably in a superficial discussion that articulates what those who regularly read newspapers and magazines know already. The third part, "Where and How to Find Help," is presumably the core of the book and reflects the author's motive for writing it. The first three chapters of this part tell parents, children, and concerned bystanders what they can do about abuse in their families, abuse to themselves, or abuse when they think they see it in others. In the final chapter, which is five paragraphs long, the author discusses how to stop child abuse. This book, however, would have been better published as a pamphlet rather than as hardcover book. The information about where to seek help will be outdated quickly since each community will have different facilities for providing help and agencies come and go. Clearly there is a need for both information about child abuse and information about where to obtain help, but the problem is still how to get the appropriate information to those who need it. It is not evident that this book will provide much of an answer to that question.

SUGAR RAY LEONARD (1982)

Denise M. Wilms

SOURCE: A review of *Sugar Ray Leonard,* in *Booklist,* Vol. 79, No. 3, October 1, 1982, p. 251.

Sugar Ray Leonard has drawn more public attention to boxing than anyone since Muhammad Ali. Haskins re-

counts how Leonard came to boxing as a shy, reluctant 14-year-old, how he planned to retire to go to college after winning an Olympic gold medal, and how family obligations pushed him into a pro career and superstardom that, thus far, has meant happiness. Haskins' usual workmanlike style prevails, and his subject is sure to be a popular pick on the sports shelf.

Ann Durbin

SOURCE: A review of *Sugar Ray Leonard,* in *Catholic Library World,* Vol. 55, No. 2, September, 1983, p. 87.

One of the better biographies of its type, this title offers more substance and a more adult format than most of the brief sports biographies which have flooded the market. At the same time a student with reasonably good reading skills should be able to handle it. Haskins focuses primarily on the boxing aspects of Leonard's life and on the people who influenced him. Unfortunately the book is appearing just as Leonard has announced his retirement from boxing, in part due to eye surgery.

KATHERINE DUNHAM (1982)

Sally Estes

SOURCE: A review of *Katherine Dunham,* in *Booklist,* Vol. 79, No. 5, November 1, 1982, p. 361.

Dynamic Katherine Dunham—dancer, choreographer, anthropologist—joins the ranks of the many notable black Americans whose lives have been chronicled by Haskins. This is a loving, admiring profile from which Dunham emerges with few flaws, but the drama of her life and the determination and humanitarianism of her character add up to someone worthy of admiration. Haskins charts her course from childhood, treating her family and personal relationships as well as her studies of the cultural traditions of black dance, her impact as a performer and as a choreographer/teacher, her international fame, and her role in establishing the Performing Arts Training Center in depressed, decayed East St. Louis, Illinois.

Zena Sutherland

SOURCE: A review of *Katherine Dunham,* in *Bulletin of the Center for Children's Books,* Vol. 36, No. 4, December, 1982, p. 69.

A vigorous and dedicated pioneer of the dance, Katherine Dunham is world-famous as a performer, teacher, and choreographer. In this well-balanced biography, there is a good mixture of material about her professional experiences, her personal life, her role as a champion of black culture, and her devotion to the Performing Arts Training Center that she established in East St. Louis in the 1960's. The writing style is variable; indeed, there is a marked difference between the earlier part of the book, in which there are grave errors of style and occasionally syntax, and the concluding pages, which have a rather polished narrative flow.

Amy Kellman

SOURCE: A review of *Katherine Dunham,* in *School Library Journal,* Vol. 29, No. 6, February, 1983, pp. 88-9.

If you have little or nothing about Katherine Dunham in your collection, this book is a perfectly serviceable biography. The path of Dunham's career and varied activities is clearly and accurately charted for the reader to follow. Dunham's work in anthropology, the fortunes of her various companies and schools, her choreography in films and Broadway shows are all interwoven chronologically here. What is missing is the human dimension. For instance, when Dunham's company played in Chicago, it was the first opportunity to introduce to her parents her husband, a white man who was a costume and set designer. What happened and how they related to each other the reader will never know because the author quickly moves on to the next event. Dunham was asked to be dance director for *Pins and Needles,* a well-known show about the International Ladies Garment Workers Union. Alas, that bare fact is all the reader learns about her work on that show. What the author has done is draw a picture of a determined, multi-talented woman whose impact on American dance, and the Black community (especially the young people) is considerable.

BLACK THEATER IN AMERICA (1982)

Zena Sutherland

SOURCE: A review of *Black Theater in America,* in *Bulletin of the Center for Children's Books,* Vol. 36, No. 4, December, 1982, p. 69.

Comprehensive and well-organized, this history of black entertainers, comic or serious, is a useful compendium of information, although the occasional errors (a show that opened in 1908 had a star who fell ill "during its run" and "died in 1907") and the occasional imposition of authorial viewpoint or conjecture ("If he were alive today, DuBois would be amazed . . . ") weaken it somewhat. One of the book's stronger points is the consistency with which Haskins makes connections between what was happening in black theatre to what was happening in the changing status of blacks and to the economic influences on theatre in general.

Michael Thomason

SOURCE: A review of *Black Theater in America,* in *Best Sellers,* Vol. 42, No. 10, January, 1983, pp. 405-06.

While there were black operated theaters with black actors here and there in 19th century America, they were few and far between. Black America did not have the money, even by the end of the century, to support such establishments, lacked the sophistication to demand serious theater, and white America simply ignored the need.

The author points out that theaters require playwrights and there were few blacks in the field. Also while white shows often were bankrolled by sympathetic wealthy patrons (angels), no such resource existed for blacks.

Some of the best dramas involving black themes, actors and actresses, have been written by white playwrights. Haskins is quite even handed in his discussion of the role of white writers and actors. He notes that they have often been more open to black advancement and more willing to accept black equality than the society at large. But in theater the name of the game is money, and authentic black themes have rarely been box-office smashes. Even black audiences have preferred musicals to serious treatment of black themes.

It would be pleasant to report that the era of civil rights solved the major problems of black theater, but it has not. Black theater still suffers from problems of inadequate support both financial and otherwise, hostility or indifference from the white community and the tendency of talented blacks to go for the money in mass appeal shows like "The Wiz." Still black theater survives better than Yiddish theater and its history is probably as good an indicator as any of the course of race relations in America since Colonial times.

Mr. Haskins' book is clearly written and should be of interest to senior high school and college age students. It assumes some knowledge of theatrical matters and presents the subject of black theater with the assumption that the reader has a reasonable understanding of American history. These assumptions may not be valid, particularly for black teenagers educated in marginal inner city schools. Finally the book does not offer a very convincing thesis to explain black theater's failure to blossom as Haskins thinks it should. It may be that black theater, like white theater, survives and prospers by giving people what they want, not what they should have.

Tony Manna

SOURCE: A review of *Black Theater in America,* in *Voice of Youth Advocates,* Vol. 5, No. 6, February, 1983, p. 50.

James Haskins' history of American black drama is as much a tribute to a group of artists—actors, writers, producers, and directors—as it is a celebration of the determination and defiance it took to establish a distinct black theater in light of the racism and prejudice which have burdened its precarious development. It is a candid interpretation of the politics of black theater and the social barriers which initially and consistently forced black dramatists into stereotypical roles expressed through stereotypical material. As Haskins points out, it wasn't until the 1960's " . . . that there finally developed a black theater that was not just white theater in black face but a separate, identifiably *black* theater with subject matter and rhythms and rhetoric that were distinctly black."

Having organized his chapters by decade, Haskins moves from a concentration on the social, political, and economic pressures particular to a specific period, to a series of brief biographies of the most prominent and influential black theater artists and brief sketches of the most influential theater companies. He is a keen observer, who by balancing fact and opinion, proves that literature—in this case, theater literature—does in fact reflect the age in which it is written. *Black Theater In America* is an informative, moving, and deeply concerned book.

Ethel R. Twichell

SOURCE: A review of *Black Theater in America,* in *The Horn Book Magazine,* Vol. LIX, No. 1, February, 1983, p. 63.

The strength and beauty of the portraits on the dust jacket set the tone for a thoughtful and candid, if necessarily brief, history of black theater. In a study beginning with pre-Civil War black productions, the author describes the difficulties encountered in attempting to create a theater which is about, by, for, and accessible to other black Americans. The traditional minstrel format with Mr. Tambo, Mr. Bones, and the interlocutor provided early opportunities for black performers. Next came scattered appearances in the vaudeville era, followed by a flowering of both playwriting and acting during the Depression years under the aegis of the Federal Theater Project. Black musicals, some serious and successful off-Broadway shows, and a painful lack of funding marked the sixties and seventies. The familiar names of Langston Hughes and Eubie Blake appear, as do those of Paul Robeson, Ethel Waters, and Richard Wright. But the book is also emphatically about the lesser-known people who blacked their already black faces and sang and danced even as they tried to escape from the stereotypes. The photographs, many dating from early days, lend both authenticity and nostalgia to a fine portrayal of the extraordinary contribution black actors and playwrights have made to the American theater.

THE NEW AMERICANS: CUBAN BOAT PEOPLE (1982)

Denise M. Wilms

SOURCE: A review of *The New Americans: Cuban Boat People,* in *Booklist,* Vol. 79, No. 10, January 15, 1983, pp. 676-77.

This concise summary of recent history will be useful in current-events units. Haskins describes the exodus of Cuban people from their homeland to the U.S. This includes not only the wave of 1980 but the earlier migration that spanned the years from 1965 to 1971. But it is the most recent wave of Cuban immigration that is at the forefront. Haskins describes stringent conditions in Cuba that prompted it; he also calls attention to the strife that resulted when high expectations of life in the U.S. were dashed in the face of a sluggish economy, high unemployment, and native resentment. Too, he cites tensions generated by opposing value systems that set first-generation immigrants who successfully fended for themselves against the lesser-educated but demanding new wave who are used to being cared for by their government without necessarily having to work. Haskins takes no sides except to spotlight several new immigrants who are doing well and to be sympathetic to the pain of cultural displacement through which these new Americans are going; "in time, each will manage to find a place as an American. American laws and the fine ideas that Americans have about themselves will make that possible."

Evelyn Walker

SOURCE: A review of *The New Americans: Cuban Boat People,* in *School Library Journal,* Vol. 29, No. 7, March, 1983, p. 192.

Haskins portrays the inherent dichotomy in accepting thousands of refugees. He points out that America likes to think of itself as a haven for those seeking freedom; yet while sympathy and compassion are commendable, the staggering economic reality of accepting these "tired, poor . . . huddled masses" makes even the best intentions difficult to fulfill. Haskins' book provides a history of Cuba. It deals with the reasons so many want to leave: poverty, rationing, government control, etc., while also telling the other side of the coin—unrealistic expectations of many of the refugees, the strain placed on the already depressed American economy and the resentment of some Americans who felt their own tenacious hold on the economy threatened by this influx of new immigrants. The obvious attempt to be fair to both sides is well taken but does tend to make the text seem rather belabored. A number of vignettes of the boat people are included. Valuable for its objective, nonemotional treatment of a sometimes controversial subject, this book is a bit plodding in style.

DONNA SUMMER: AN UNAUTHORIZED BIOGRAPHY (with J. M. Stifle, 1983)

Stephanie Zvirin

SOURCE: A review of *Donna Summer: An Unauthorized Biography,* in *Booklist,* Vol. 79, No. 20, June 15, 1983, p. 1331.

What begins as a rather lackluster biography of a determined, self-trained singer who longed for a stage musical career picks up momentum as the authors reveal the controversy surrounding Summer's musical success in the U.S. following the release of her modern torch song "Love to Love You, Baby." Background on Summer (born La-Donna Gaines)—childhood, marriage, motherhood, divorce, early career struggles in Europe, her notoriety in the United States, marriage again, her born-again Christian conversion—is buttressed by the artist's own comments, snippets from *Billboard* and *Variety* reviews of her work, and brief authorial perspective. Not an intimate view of the artist, but the authors provide a good sense of some of the major trends in the music business during the years Summer sought to build a name for herself and mold her musical career, and they clearly identify the difficulties she had shedding the "love goddess" image of her first big success so she could accomplish her goals.

Kay Cassell

SOURCE: A review of *Donna Summer: An Unauthorized Biography,* in *Voice of Youth Advocates,* Vol. 6, No. 3, August, 1983, p. 153.

As Donna Summer said it, "The possibility of a black girl from Boston going to Germany and becoming successful in the American pop field is, like a million-to-one shot." Summer's biography details her rise to stardom. After a traditional family life in Boston, she went to New York where she got a chance to be in *Hair's* German company. Summer spent several years in Germany singing and performing as the opportunity arose. She finally came to the attention of the American popular music scene with her German recording of "Love to Love You, Baby." With the success of that recording she returned to the U.S. where she has become one of the most popular singers of the 1980s. "She wants to become what a *Time* magazine writer suggested in 1980 that she could become: the premier rocker of the eighties." I'm sure many teens will want to read about Donna Summer, but I hope a better biography is on the way. This one is written in such dull style that most teens will not finish it. Recommended only if you must have a book on Donna Summer.

Jack Forman

SOURCE: A review of *Donna Summer: An Unauthorized Biography,* in *School Library Journal,* Vol. 30, No. 2, October, 1983, p. 168.

Getting her start in a minor part in a European production of *Hair,* versatile disco and pop music star Donna Summer has reached the top in the musical world. Haskins and Stifle follow her life and career with accuracy and obvious sympathy, resulting in a book which often reads more like an "authorized" biography than an "unauthorized" one. Some of their generalizations on the pop music scene oversimplify, such as their description of '60s music and the beginnings of disco. And some aspects of Summer's personal life get a too brief once-over—such as her present marriage to Bruce Sudano and her born-again beliefs. However, the authors' careful coverage of the

singer's career, especially the reportage of the many problems Summer has encountered in making records and doing concert tours and the special joys of success she has enjoyed after overcoming the problems add zest to and help flesh out this short biography. This book will whet the appetite of young readers, but is far from the last word.

THE GUARDIAN ANGELS (1983)

Sally Estes

SOURCE: A review of *The Guardian Angels,* in *Booklist,* Vol. 79, No. 20, June 15, 1983, p. 1330.

Offering a rather dry, superficial profile of Curtis Sliwa and the Guardian Angels, the group Sliwa founded to prevent crime on New York subways, Haskins sketches in incidents in Sliwa's childhood and youth leading to his organizing the "Magnificent Thirteen," which began patrolling the subways in February 1979, and charts the group's evolvement into the Guardian Angels, with their red berets and white T-shirts. The author covers the spread of the organization, noting that, though it is difficult to prove or disprove such statistics, the Guardian Angels, by early 1983, claimed 3,000 members in 40 cities in the U.S. and Canada. Though Haskins presents the views of detractors as well as supporters of the group, he himself comes across on the side of the Guardian Angels. Not definitive by any means, but will satisfy the curiosity of readers who have heard about the Guardian Angels and want to know a little bit about them—who they are, their purpose, and their accomplishments.

Kirkus Reviews

SOURCE: A review of *The Guardian Angels,* in *Kirkus Reviews,* Vol. LI, No. 12, June 15, 1983, pp. 667-68.

Readers vaguely aware of the urban youth brigade that rides the subways in red berets may be surprised to learn that Curtis Sliwa, the Guardian Angels' founder and absolute leader, was a model student and student-government president at a Jesuit prep school, with scholarship offers from Harvard, Princeton, and Brown. Instead he became assistant manager of a South Bronx McDonald's, organized local high schoolers in a litter cleanup campaign he made sure got lots of publicity, and finally, on February 13, 1979, with more press releases, shaped twelve recruits into an anti-crime patrol he called the Magnificent Thirteen. Renamed, the Guardian Angels now claim 3000 members in 40 cities across the US and Canada; and many police who resisted them at first now acknowledge that their unarmed presence is a crime deterrent. Still, the group is controversial, and Haskins reports incidents of official harassment, arrest, and worse. All straight kids to begin with (those with police records are not admitted), the largely Hispanic and black Angels have been attacked as vigilantes for behavior which, said New York's Governor Mario Cuomo (then lieutenant governor), would have won them medals had they been "the sons and daughters of doctors from Great Neck or Jamaica Estates." Sliwa has twice been kidnapped and beaten by men who claimed to be police (one group showed him police ID), and, as newspaper readers will remember, 27-year-old Angel Frank Melvin was shot and killed by a Newark policeman firing in what Sliwa maintains was "cold blood." Haskins foresees internal problems stemming from Sliwa's tight one-man (now one-couple) control: he and wife Lisa keep such tight rein on the New York Angels that when both were in Washington on a protest all New York City patrols were suspended. Haskins reports on this interesting group in easy-to-read sentences, evincing sympathy for Sliwa's ideals and achievements without imposing any overall judgment.

Zena Sutherland

SOURCE: A review of *The Guardian Angels*, in *Bulletin of the Center for Children's Books*, Vol. 37, No. 1, September, 1983, p. 9.

A description of the organization of young volunteers who are dedicated to preventing crime begins with the founding, in 1979, of the Magnificent Thirteen. Led by Curtis Sliwa, the group grew, became the Guardian Angels, and has been imitated in other cities than New York, where it began. Most of the members are young males, most are black and Hispanic, and the group has stirred considerable controversy, since some critics feel the Guardian Angels are a paramilitary band who have taken into their own hands matters that should be a police prerogative. Others laud the efforts of the group. After frequent instances of conflict between Sliwa's group and the police, The Guardian Angels were issued identity cards (to be worn on patrol) by the New York Police Department. The leader claimed, in 1983, three thousand members, but there are no statistics to validate this. In fact, one of the weaknesses of the book is that, although Haskins is commendably objective in most of his comments about the Guardian Angels, he tends to accept proffered information without checking it; for example, speaking of Sliwa's academic record (from model student to high school dropout) he says of Sliwa "He says he had acceptances and scholarship offers from Brown, Princeton, and Harvard," but apparently has not investigated the statement. Adequately written, occasionally repetitive, certainly of topical interest.

Steve Matthews

SOURCE: A review of *The Guardian Angels*, in *School Library Journal*, Vol. 30, No. 1, September, 1983, p. 134.

The prolific Haskins has chosen Curtis Sliwa and the Guardian Angels for one of his informative narratives. This journalistic account of the rise of Sliwa's Angels is a favorable portrait of Sliwa as an idealistic if egotistical purveyor of American "bootstraps" philosophy. While criticism of the Angels is discussed, Haskins' portrait is unabashedly admiring. Haskins is redundant in the later

chapters where Sliwa's persecution by police and other detractors is revealed; but basically this is a smooth flowing often exciting account of a youth action group, although no age limit on membership is set.

LENA HORNE (1983)

Kirkus Reviews, Juvenile Issue

SOURCE: A review of *Lena Horne*, in *Kirkus Reviews*, Juvenile Issue, Vol. LI, No. 21, November 1, 1983, p. J212.

Prolific non-fiction-producer Haskins puts the emphasis—appropriately, but perhaps a little too narrowly—on racism and politics in this admiring biography of super-singer Lena Horne. From a middle-class, light-complected black family in Brooklyn, Lena didn't benefit much from that relatively privileged background: her parents divorced; she went on the road with her actress-mother; she was abused, physically and psychologically, by a variety of babysitters. And her career, from the beginning, was shadowed by rough conditions, racism, and Lena's own ambivalence about her relationships with blacks and whites. From the Cotton Club chorus line she went on to band-singing, often suffering demeaning discrimination. ("Sitting alone in those restrooms, Lena developed a prejudice against white middle-class women that would last for years afterward.") An early marriage was rocky from the start—and when it broke up, Lena had to abandon her son. After notable appearances at Cafe Society in the very early 1940s, she became more aware of black history and music ("working for Barney Josephson was like going to school"), soon taking off for Hollywood as an NAACP-encouraged "pioneer"; there, however, she was offered only stereotypes and "specialty" appearances—while many fellow black performers "did not applaud her for demanding a certain dignity in her movie roles." Also a source of guilt: her marriage to white musician Lennie Hayton, which they kept secret for three years. ("Having severed her ties with most of her own family by marrying Lennie, she was unwilling to lose the larger, impersonal family of her race.") And, in the mid-1950s, after blacklisting and Broadway success (*Jamaica*), she "realized that for all of her hardships she had been insulated from much of the anguish of day-to-day life for black people in America": more guilt, anger, and then 1960s activism—followed by deep depression in the early 1970s, when her father, son, and husband all died. But eventually her "pain and grief. . . . opened her up," and "she started to see her audiences as people"—leading to her recent one-woman-show triumphs. Haskins scants personal psychology in this interpretation of Horne's ups and downs. More importantly, he scants her music, with virtually no appreciation of the dramatic changes in her style, no evocation of what now makes her an incomparable vocalist. Still: a solid enough assemblage for those interested in the tribulations, rather than the art, of a great black performer.

Zena Sutherland

SOURCE: A review of *Lena Horne*, in *Bulletin of the*

Center for Children's Books, Vol. 37, No. 6, February, 1984, p. 109.

Spectacular as Lena Horne's career has been, it is rivalled in drama by her personal life: torn from her grandparents' home with its stability and culture to traipse about the country with her mother (an unsuccessful actress) and badgered by her Cuban stepfather, she had an unhappy first marriage that ended with her husband keeping one of their two children. Always a political activist, she was on the *Red Channels* list of banned artists; her marriage to a white man (a marriage that was a long and happy one) brought further problems. Horne struggled throughout her career to improve the image of blacks in the roles she played, and her story is one of battles and triumphs. This has a more even quality in the writing style than some of Haskins' recent biographies, and he writes with a candor that is, like his appreciation of the beautiful Lena Horne, controlled.

Virginia B. Moore

SOURCE: A review of *Lena Horne,* in *Voice of Youth Advocates,* Vol. 7, No. 1, April, 1984, pp. 46-7.

A moving story of a beautiful and sensitive dancer, singer, and actress living today and heralded for the longest-running, one woman show on Broadway. In this highly readable biography, Lena Horne's life of difficulties and success is revealed from her birth to a prominent black middle class family in Brooklyn, New York through her final bows at Nederlander Theater on Broadway to start a new life on her 65th birthday in 1982.

This authoritative narrative details childhood travels with her mother who dreamed of conquering the show business world, her debut at 16 in the chorus line of the famous Cotton Club in Harlem where black entertainers like Cab Calloway achieved fame, and her struggles as Negro America's first "symbol of dignity" to combat the prevailing stereotypes that Hollywood conveyed.

There are chapters which read like a *Who's Who* of musicians, movie stars, educators, civil rights leaders, and government officials that have influenced American cultural enlightenment, political strategies, and social conduct for the past two decades. And accounts of racism, interracial marriage, the Civil Rights Movement along with Hollywood life and personalities are skillfully handled without vindictiveness. Excellent features include historical photographs and a six-page index for use with Social Studies classes and Black History research.

📖 *RICHARD PRYOR: A MAN AND HIS MAD-NESS* (1984)

Kirkus Reviews

SOURCE: A review of *Richard Pryor: A Man and His*

Madness, in *Kirkus Reviews,* Vol. LII, No. 8, April 15, 1984, p. 397.

"Rather than simply tilting at windmills, he grabs hold of the whirling vanes and hangs on, while the world holds its breath and wonders if he will fall." That's how veteran Y-A writer Haskins views Richard Pryor in this YA-ish biography: despite occasional references to his "madness," the Pryor here is essentially—and unconvincingly—an idealistic victim/hero. Raised primarily by his brothel-madam grandma in 1940s Peoria, Ill., Richard discovered racism at school—and didn't get strong family reassurance to counter it. So his "way of coming to terms with his world was to be funny." Street-corner clowning led to local talent shows and the "chitlin' circuit"; early-1960s success came through a toned-down act, modeled on Bill Cosby's. ("If Cosby never mentioned that he was black, then Pryor would get up on stage and be Invisible Man.") But "deep down, he felt like a fake"—and "cocaine seemed to be his only friend." Thus, circa 1970, Pryor "freed himself from the constraints of his Mickey Mouse career"—developing a film-acting career while insisting on doing his ethnic/innovative/profane kind of comedy . . . despite opposition from TV executives and other white-establishment types. ("It seemed that everything about that system was conspiring to keep him down.") And by the late 1970s he was a superstar—"He'd said no to being the white folks' pet and come back bigger than ever"—with strong guilt feelings, emanating, however, from his "supersensitive soul": hence, perhaps, that cocaine-related self-immolation—which he has survived and transcended, complete with spiritual rebirth. Haskins' erratic writing is at its lowest level here—a mixture of the slangy, the stuffy, and the terminally clichéd. His research seems inadequate, with far too much reliance on a small, far-from-authoritative selection of interview-ees. And the Pryor portrait is an unpersuasive mishmash—though some readers will welcome the details on filmings, TV-wrangles, backstage sexual activities, marriages, and drugs.

Publishers Weekly

SOURCE: A review of *Richard Pryor: A Man and His Madness,* in *Publishers Weekly,* Vol. 225, No. 18, May 4, 1984, p. 47.

Haskins, biographer of Bricktop and Lena Horne, combines interviews with press extracts about the complex personality and career of America's best-known black comedian. Brought up by his grandmother in whorehouses in Peoria, Ill., expelled from school for punching a teacher, Pryor by 16 had fathered a child and at 17 had started to work on comedy routines. After a hitch in the army, he joined the "chitlin circuit" and worked in clubs across the Midwest and in Canada, but it was not until he appeared on the *Ed Sullivan Show* that he attained national attention. Thereafter, he achieved extraordinary success in films and at personal appearances, acquired and discarded several wives, and fathered more children, but came to feel that the only love he could count on was the impersonal, if gratifying, love from fans. He became ever more notorious and reached the nadir of self-destruction in 1980, when he was nearly fatally burned in a fire. His comeback would gain him even more acclaim. Dealing with the knotty aspects of Pryor's life is difficult, and on the whole Haskins copes well.

Marcia L. Perry

SOURCE: A review of *Richard Pryor: A Man and His Madness,* in *Library Journal,* Vol. 109, No. 11, June 15, 1984, p. 1250.

Haskins, author of several biographies of black entertainers, has written a well-researched portrait of Pryor, whose brilliant comedy career was almost ended by near-fatal burns in 1980. Pryor is shown as a richly talented comic and writer whose need to keep his biting humor honest to the black experience is at odds with mainstream comedy. Haskins, who believes that Pryor is a reborn man since the fire, does not condone or excuse Pryor's erratic self-destructive behavior. He does detail some of the complicated machinations of the studios and the people around Pryor (including women in his life) who have tended to take advantage of him. Haskins quotes liberally from many of Pryor's acquaintances whom he interviewed. An interesting picture of a complex figure.

SPACE CHALLENGER: THE STORY OF GUION BLUFORD (with Kathleen Benson, 1984)

Denise M. Wilms

SOURCE: A review of *Space Challenger: The Story of Guion Bluford,* in *Booklist,* Vol. 81, No. 1, September 1, 1984, p. 65.

Challenger astronaut Guion Bluford is the first black man to have ridden in space. This smoothly written profile describes his Philadelphia childhood, where he grew up in an integrated neighborhood and attended integrated local schools, and his higher education at Pennsylvania State University and the Air Force Institute of Technology. Interest in flight and airplanes came early, and because his parents had "taught him that he was as good as anyone else," he pursued his dream to become an aerospace engineer, even when a high school guidance counselor told him he wasn't college material and tried to push him into a trade school. Photographs, some in color, are frequent, and there's a glossary that explains many shuttle terms. An efficient introduction to a significant role model for any ambitious child.

Jonathan Gradie

SOURCE: A review of *Space Challenger: The Story of Guion Bluford,* in *Science Books & Films,* Vol. 21, No. 1, September/October, 1985, p. 41.

Guion Bluford has gained a place in history as the first American black astronaut, and *Space Challenger* is a short, inspirational book that includes a brief biographical sketch of him as well as accounts of his adventures aboard the space shuttle *Challenger.* (The 21 black-and-white photographs and drawings depict his training and actual flight experiences, and a useful beginners' glossary is included.) Described are the youthful adventures of an astronaut-to-be and some of the problems Bluford encountered as an ambitious black student during the 1950s and 1960s. These problems tend to be muted and glossed over. Nonetheless, this book will spark the imagination of most of its young readers and inspire them, regardless of sex, race, or socioeconomic class, to follow Bluford's lead—to define and work toward a personal goal in their lives and to ignore the unsolicited advice of others to lower one's sights. I'm not sure that Bluford's somewhat middle-class upbringing is relevant to all those who need a worthwhile role model, but to all children, Guion Bluford should be considered a true American hero.

Barbara Scotto

SOURCE: A review of *Space Challenger: The Story of Guion Bluford,* in *Appraisal: Science Books for Young People,* Vol. 18, No. 4, Autumn, 1985, pp. 24-5.

Space Challenger is the authorized biography of Guion Bluford, the first black American in space. Told in a straightforward manner, the text is detailed and interesting. Bluford's frequent reflections on the events of his life enable the reader to get a sense of the person underneath the facts. In particular his feelings about societal and parental expectations are thought-provoking, and a strong message for young people can be read between the lines. Historical events, especially those related to the space program, are interwoven into the story in such a way that the reader is able to understand the person and his achievements within the context of his time.

Appraisal: Science Books for Young People

SOURCE: A review of *Space Challenger: The Story of Guion Bluford,* in *Appraisal: Science Books for Young People,* Vol. 18, No. 4, Autumn, 1985, p. 25.

Space Challenger is a biography of Guion Bluford, the first black American astronaut to travel in space aboard the space shuttle challenger.

All young people interested in space travel might enjoy this book. It is an excellent example of what a determined individual can do when he or she is willing to work hard toward a desired goal. The reader will find the black-and-white and color photographs in the NASA organization most informative, adding dimension to the text.

Since this is a biography, the emphasis here is on Guion Bluford himself, about his great desire and effort, rather than the scientific aspects of his work.

NAT KING COLE (with Kathleen Benson, 1984)

Kirkus Reviews

SOURCE: A review of *Nat King Cole,* in *Kirkus Reviews,* Vol. LII, No. 21, November 1, 1984, p. 1036.

Haskins and Benson begin this short biography portentously: "It is hard to realize that Cole's effortless delivery and words of love masked a profound tension and unhappiness born of frustrations in abundance, over some of which he had control, over many of which he had none." Ultimately, however, their superficial study fails to bring much illumination to Nat "King" Cole's tangle of racial/ creative/personal problems. A minister's son, growing up poor in Chicago circa 1930, Nat went from high-school to jazz piano-playing, under the primary influence of Earl "Fatha" Hines. By 1937 the King Cole Trio was doing well enough on tour, with a few records aimed at jazz-fans and the Negro market. But, more and more, Nat's singing began to overshadow his musicianship—becoming, along with Billy Eckstine, one of the first black ballad-singers to reach a large white audience. And his crossover became complete with the odd hit "Nature Boy." Thereafter, with the urgings of wife #2 Maria (portrayed here largely as a light-skinned, snobbish, greedy climber), dark-skinned Cole concentrated on expanding and retaining his wide audience appeal, minimizing his ambitious jazz-work and the combo's importance. He avoided "controversial causes because they might hamper his career," staying aloof from the civil-rights movement even in the 1960s. (He did, however, buy a home in a posh white L.A. neighborhood, overcoming lawsuits and harassment.) But attempts to enlarge his career proved that "TV and Hollywood were beyond his reach," so he "was forced to remain a pop artist"—partly in order to sustain a lifestyle that apparently included Las Vegas girlfriends. Despite interview-quotes from two of Cole's children and gossipy others: a spotty, unconvincing portrait, weak on musical matters too—but passable as a source of basic biographical data.

Publishers Weekly

SOURCE: A review of *Nat King Cole,* in *Publishers Weekly,* Vol. 226, No. 20, November 16, 1984, p. 56.

Twenty years after his death at 45, the records of Nat "King" Cole keep him alive as a singer of popular songs for millions of people throughout the world. This short book tells his life story simply but effectively. Born in Montgomery, Ala., in 1919, Nathaniel Adams Coles was brought up in Chicago, experienced that city's rich jazz scene, and became a major jazz pianist by his late teens. But his sense of responsibility to his family, as well as his own need for acceptance by a wider audience, caused him to take up a more commercial and anxiety-provoking life as a pop vocalist. Basically apolitical and long regarded as an Uncle Tom, Cole was charged with "kneeling be-

fore the throne of Jim Crow," yet even one of his most militant critics regarded him as "the most unhating person" she had ever known—and Cole's dignity and basic decency come through in this sympathetic biography.

Martin A. Brady

SOURCE: A review of *Nat King Cole,* in *Booklist,* Vol. 81, No. 10, January 15, 1985, pp. 676-77.

Nearly 20 years after his death from lung cancer at 45, Nat King Cole has maintained a loyal following among aficionados of both jazz piano and mellifluous ballad singing. This anecdotal biography follows Cole's career from his rise as the innovative pianist/star of the King Cole Trio to his later successes as velvet-voiced crooner. Haskins and Benson chart Cole's unflagging popularity as a versatile entertainer, his path-breaking stints as black radio and television performer, his personal disappointment as a failed movie actor, his life as husband and father, his tangles with the IRS, and the unfortunate consequences of his being labeled an Uncle Tom by black activists and colleagues. (Revisionist theory on the latter point marks Cole as a show-business pioneer who demonstrated that multiracial audiences can appreciate the talents of a black man.) Strong on incidental detail and an interesting catalog of the times in which Cole lived, this profile does suffer from a dearth of psychological insight into the man himself. Still, it is very enjoyable reading and fills a void in music historiography.

Carmen P. Collier

SOURCE: A review of *Nat King Cole,* in *Best Sellers,* Vol. 44, No. 12, March, 1985, p. 459.

In sympathy and in simple language the professional life of a man whose fame and success evolved from circumstances rather than plan is recorded in detail. Nat King Cole began his career as a jazz pianist, influenced by Earl Hines, but improving the right hand with strong chords and exciting runs. Few people remember or know of his prowess as an instrumentalist in the climate of his era, the early forties. Audiences demanded more singing than piano playing from touring entertainers, so Cole turned to commercialism. With his showmanship and his renditions of popular ballads he was heard and accepted by white audiences. When he died at the age of forty-five, he was famous in the United States and in Europe, remembered principally for his singing. Today, twenty years later, he is associated with songs like "Mona Lisa," "The Christmas Song," "Nature Boy." His records have sold in the millions; nevertheless he has been one of the most influential of jazz instrumentalists.

The book is strong in the account of Cole's professional life but it brings out the man himself in glimpses and impressions only. Nat King Cole was born in Montgomery, Alabama, in 1919 where and when segregation and racism were the cultural pattern. Cole exceeded his wildest expectations of fame and wealth. Could he have retired at the height of success, he might have lived beyond his mid-forties but his commitment to his luxury-bred family and his debts to the IRS kept him on a strenuous touring schedule.

James Haskins with Kathleen Benson has added a timely biography to their combined lengthy list of biographies of black musicians. The information is apparently based on the recollections of friends, available records, and a biography, *Nat King Cole: An Intimate Biography* written by Maria Cole with Louis Robinson.

DIANA ROSS: STAR SUPREME (1985)

Denise M. Wilms

SOURCE: A review of *Diana Ross: Star Supreme,* in *Booklist,* Vol. 81, No. 18, June 1, 1985, p. 1400.

Ross' childhood retort that "I may be down, but I ain't down" sets the theme of determination that runs through this profile of the black performer and her careers as singer, actress, and entertainer. Haskins looks back on her Detroit childhood, citing Ross' belief that her place as a middle child left her with a hunger for attention that fueled a desire to perform. Besides charting Ross' singing career, Haskins looks at her forays into acting and fashion design, and of late, into independent musical and video ventures. While not overtly adulatory, Haskins is admiring and largely uncritical of his subject, and there is little objective analysis of her abilities. Still, what Ross has accomplished is formidable in view of her beginnings, and that alone makes her story worth reading for young people, whether they be black or white.

Ann W. Moore

SOURCE: A review of *Diana Ross: Star Supreme,* in *School Library Journal,* Vol. 31, No. 10, August, 1985, p. 64.

Haskins has condensed much of the information in his biography of Diana Ross for teenagers (*I'm Gonna Make You Love Me* [1980]) into this short book for younger children. While this book is fairly comprehensive and up-to-date, it suffers from a choppy writing style and a slightly moralistic tone (there are endless references to Ross' refusal to give up). . . . Nevertheless, libraries needing additional material on black history or music may want this biography as there is nothing else currently available on Ross for this age group.

LEADERS OF THE MIDDLE EAST (1985)

Stephanie Zvirin

SOURCE: A review of *Leaders of the Middle East,* in *Booklist,* Vol. 81, No. 21, July, 1985, p. 1539.

Although lacking some of the vigor of the author's previous life histories, this is a distinctive collective biography of nine contemporary, highly controversial Middle East political leaders who have shaped and/or continue to influence events in that volatile area and across the world. Haskins skillfully wades through and condenses the extremely complex history and politics associated with each of his subjects, often relying on repetition of specific key incidents (the massacre of Lebanese citizens by Christian militia, etc.) to demonstrate varied perspectives of the rulers he considers. While his focus is more on politics than on background and personality, he still manages to convey a distinct, well-reasoned impression of each man. Palestine's Zia and Libya's Qaddafi are viewed in the harshest light; Begin's militarism is tempered by emphasis on his role in the Camp David accords; Arafat's terrorist activities are balanced by what Haskins perceives as a selfless devotion to the Palestinian cause; Assad comes across as a clever politician, a new force to be reckoned with. The author does an equally effective job of introducing Khomeini, Mubarak, Fahd, and Hussein. A trenchant overview of the turmoil-plagued Middle East sets the stage for the profiles, and Haskins provides a brief but useful list of further readings as follow-up. An excellent jumping-off place for student research.

Symme J. Benoff

SOURCE: A review of *Leaders of the Middle East,* in *School Library Journal,* Vol. 32, No. 1, September, 1985, p. 145.

Haskins describes the rise of Islam, including the Sunni-Shiite schism, Western imperialism and the political intrigue which plagues the area. The personal lives and motivations of Arafat, Assad, Begin, Fahd, Hussein, Khomeini, Mubarak, Qaddafi and Zia are described in separate chapters. Although Haskins' facts are essentially correct, his tone is, at times, anti-Israel (" . . . the Israelis sometimes exhibit a paranoia about their country, a tendency to shoot first and ask questions later"). The map of Israel shows pre-1967 boundaries; a chapter on the chronology of the Middle East starts with Muhammed. One problem with reading the book straight through is the overlapping coverage of events, albeit from the perspective of the leader covered in that particular chapter. Still, a useful tool for students of history, politics and for understanding the news.

Peter Sanderson

SOURCE: A review of *Leaders of the Middle East,* in *The School Librarian,* Vol. 34, No. 3, September, 1986, p. 288.

James Haskins has written fairly interesting potted biographies of some famous and infamous men here, but with no evidence that the author himself has ever been to their countries, learnt their languages, or done any original research. Such coverage of the 'leaders' has already been done in serious newspapers.

Many details amaze one. I have seen Arab children scuffle, and do not believe that Yasir Arafat when young could or 'would stare down his attackers . . . (who) would soon back off'. Without exception? The UN who tried to partition Palestine in 1947 are 'foreign oppressors', though UNO members did conspicuously nothing about their decision, and later oppressors include King Hussein of Jordan who took over the West Bank. Oddly, the Anglo-French part in the 1956 invasion of Egypt is not mentioned. One cannot write an objective historical biography and survey while both adopting fully the viewpoint of the subject person, and omitting important facts. Arafat may have 'dedicated his life to winning back Palestine', but the point is not made (about 1985-86) that he very obviously did nothing constructive, and has been a ghastly and bloody failure.

The other 'biographies' are similar. In Begin's, the author states 'the Haganah wanted to secure a Jewish state by peaceful negotiation', and there is no mention of Haganah's anti-British atrocities, though there is of one against Arabs. And yet another article about the 'Ayatollah', without explaining what this title means. This is a book too elementary to be read by the sophisticated, who alone could put it into perspective, and too misleading to be put into the hands of unsophisticated readers.

ABOUT MICHAEL JACKSON (1985)

Denise M. Wilms

SOURCE: A review of *About Michael Jackson,* in *Booklist,* Vol. 81, No. 22, August, 1985, p. 1664.

Superstar Michael Jackson is a difficult subject for a credible biography because of limited access; journalists, not to mention writers of biography for children, have had trouble breaking through the shield of privacy that studios, agents, and the star himself keep in firm place. With that caveat in mind, one can say that Haskins succeeds in providing the most complete juvenile profile of Michael Jackson yet. It is longer and deeper than others now available and tries to present a little of Jackson's personality. Haskins addresses some of the singer's problems, most notably the tensions simmering within the family and the quiet divorce between his parents. From a literary standpoint, the text suffers from an occasionally patronizing tone and a general lack of grace. However, readers looking for substance will find a good share of it here, and the straightforward reporting won't bore them.

Tom S. Hurlburt

SOURCE: A review of *About Michael Jackson,* in *School Library Journal,* Vol. 32, No. 5, January, 1986, pp. 67-8.

Revealing no new information concerning the young entertainer, Haskins uses material gathered from Jackson's friends and associates and also quotes liberally from jour-

Haskins's college graduation photo.

nalists who have interviewed him. An attempt is made to dismiss innuendos about Jackson's sexual preference, plastic surgery history, family problems, etc., but these controversial topics are only dealt with in passing. Although the book is generally factual, Haskins does make a glaring error by referring to the moon-walk dance step as the worm, something even the most novice of Jackson fans will pick up on. The black-and-white photos are standard shots found in many Jackson biographies, and the sketches, many of which overlay the text, add little and seem somewhat gimmicky. If the demand for new Jackson biographies is there, Haskins' book is straightforward, up-to-date and does surpass the literary standards of the majority of the mass market paperbacks on the market. . . .

Jerry Grim

SOURCE: A review of *About Michael Jackson,* in *Voice of Youth Advocates,* Vol. 8, No. 6, February, 1986, p. 401.

Haskins may be too late with this one, but I doubt it. MJ has been overexposed and has lost ground in the ratings, but it's not the first time, and a man with such humongous talent (and a multi-talented family to boot) will be on top again, and again. Twenty years is already legendary for a rock star.

I've read several more sophisticated and authenticated books on Motown artists that seem to contradict some of the facts here. And the writing gets trite at times (in an effort to appeal to children, I think). But the coverage is broad and interesting, the photos are good quality, the technical stuff is right (even educational at times), and best of all, the artist comes out looking like a human being, and not a two-dimensional poster. And to a lesser extent, so do the rest of the family (even the real hero, Papa Joe), without whom Michael would likely be just Mike.

BREAK DANCING (1985)

Helen E. Williams

SOURCE: A review of *Break Dancing,* in *School Library Journal,* Vol. 32, No. 3, November, 1985, p. 85.

Haskins has produced a highly readable and entertaining perspective on break dancing which includes its history, profiles of some famous performers and descriptions of some break-dance steps. Clear and attractive color and black-and-white photographs are interspersed throughout this brief book whose format is akin to that of hi/lo books. Terry Dunnahoo's *Break Dancing* (1985) provides more specific how-to information and precautions. However, these books supplement rather than compete with each other. A well-organized explanation of a popular subject.

Bulletin of the Center for Children's Books

SOURCE: A review of *Break Dancing,* in *Bulletin of the Center for Children's Books,* Vol. 39, No. 3, November, 1985, p. 47.

Haskins offers some facts and some conjectures about the several African roots of break dancing, and gives a brief history of how, through disc jockeys and films, the new form of dance was popularized and developed. He discusses some of the people who helped make break dancing famous or who gained attention through their performances. The text, which is on the whole adequately written, is marred by a tendency to accord break dancing the status of a distinguished cultural phenomenon; for example, speaking of the ten-year-old who became an international break dance champion, he says, "Back in November . . . Deena . . . was just an ordinary kid." The book ends with descriptions of some steps and warnings about how strenuous break dancing is.

Denise M. Wilms

SOURCE: A review of *Break Dancing,* in *Booklist,* Vol. 82, No. 10, January 15, 1986, p. 756.

Haskins offers an efficient outline of where break danc-

ing came from, who its stars are, and how some of it is done. He explains that modern break dancing developed as an accompaniment to rap music; it became, under the hand of a New Yorker named Afrika Bambaataa, the means for rival street groups to work out their antagonisms. Then came the national publicity as a result of Michael Jackson and the movie *Flashdance.* Three brief profiles of champion break dancers are provided, and several of the art's more spectacular steps are described and pictured in full-color photographs. It's good to see that Haskins closes with a warning: in essence, break dancing may be hazardous to your health. Serious injuries (including broken backs and necks) have occurred; youngsters game to try are urged to go slow and wear proper clothing to protect themselves.

THE STATUE OF LIBERTY: AMERICA'S PROUD LADY (1986)

Barbara Elleman

SOURCE: A review of *The Statue of Liberty: America's Proud Lady,* in *Booklist,* Vol. 82, No. 13, March 1, 1986, p. 1018.

Haskins provides middle graders with easy access through a spare writing style and explicit index for locating material. In addition to the obligatory highlights concerning the Lady's history, construction, and current rejuvenation, the author makes the interesting point that, while black Americans entered the U.S. mostly through southern slave markets rather than Ellis Island, they also look on the Statue as a symbol of liberty. In Haskins' words— "she stands for what *can* be" in America.

Deborah Vose

SOURCE: A review of *The Statue of Liberty: America's Proud Lady,* in *School Library Journal,* Vol. 32, No. 8, April, 1986, p. 72.

A straightforward account of the people and ideas which inspired Bartholdi's arduous battle to make the Statue of Liberty a reality. . . . Included is information about vital statistics and a plan of repairs. The index is thorough and makes this an excellent book for beginning researchers. It is comparable to two other books, both entitled *The Statue of Liberty,* one by William E. Shapiro (1985), the other by Leonard E. Fisher (1985). However, it has the advantage of being shorter and more manageable for younger readers. As is usual with Haskins' efforts, it is well-written and accurate, but it does lack the liveliness of Coerr's *Lady with a Torch* (1986). Huck Scarry's drawings make Mary J. Shapiro's *How They Built the Statue of Liberty* (1985) a more valuable choice, as she includes all the information offered here as well.

Mary Margaret Pitts

SOURCE: A review of *The Statue of Liberty: America's*

Proud Lady, in *Appraisal: Science Books for Young People,* Vol. 19, No. 4, Fall, 1986, pp. 50-1.

There are a number of recent books on the Statue of Liberty anticipating the centennial celebration of the statue.

This one is geared toward younger readers. The text is quite informative featuring large type and short chapters. Black and white historical photographs which appear on nearly every other page help to document the progress of the statue's construction. The chapters provide a chronology of the statue's history including its design, construction and plans for renovation. Simpler than either William Shapiro's *Statue of Liberty* (1985) or Stephen Krensky's *Maiden Voyage: the Story of the Statue of Liberty* (1985). This book will be a useful addition to most school or public libraries serving younger readers.

BLACK MUSIC IN AMERICA: A HISTORY THROUGH ITS PEOPLE (1987)

Betsy Hearne

SOURCE: A review of *Black Music in America: A History Through Its People,* in *Bulletin of the Center for Children's Books,* Vol. 40, No. 7, March, 1987, p. 125.

Beginning with the slaves who brought with them nothing but their chains and their songs, Haskins traces the dual developments of black musicians who performed in white classical styles and black creators of spirituals, ragtime, blues, jazz, gospel, and soul music. The text alternates between passages giving historical perspective and biographical sketches of great musicians, from Elizabeth Taylor Greenfield, a successful operatic soprano in the 1850s, to Wynton Marsalis, a brilliant trumpet soloist in the 1980s jazz scene. Haskins strikes a comfortable balance between general information and specific facts. He give enough flavor of leading personalities and trends to point young readers toward more in-depth sources, or better still, some listening experiences. Unfortunately, a discography is not included, but there's a bibliography organized by books, articles, and archival sources.

Virginia B. Moore

SOURCE: A review of *Black Music in America: A History Through Its People,* in *Voice of Youth Advocates,* Vol. 10, No. 1, April, 1987, p. 45.

It's an easily readable chronology of black music told through the lives of the black Americans who made it. Beginning with the songs in their hearts as the only possession that the African slaves could bring to America and the instruments which they recreated during nearly 250 years of slavery, Haskins tells how these slaves planted the seeds of the first truly American cultural gift to the world—American music. He chronicles the influence of black music on American popular music, known internationally especially in such forms as blues, jazz, and rock

'n' roll and its acclaim as a source of indebtedness by white performers from Benny Goodman to Frank Sinatra to the Beatles, to Boy George to Rod Stewart.

This account focuses on pioneers and innovators, Afro-Americans who showed that they could make white music and therefore blazed a trail for all black performers as well as those who made genuine black music, to reflect both the obstacles overcome along with the emergence of new musical forms through such individuals and groups as: Elizabeth Taylor Greenfield, concert soprano before the Emancipation; the Fisk Jubilee Singers who preserved black spirituals which made the ragtime and blues of Scott Joplin and W.C. Handy more acceptable to whites; James Reese Europe who ushered in jazz for Louis Armstrong, Duke Ellington, and Billie Holiday; Nat "King" Cole and Mahalia Jackson of the 40s; Bo Diddley, Miles Davis, and Leontyne Price of the 50s; James Brown, Motown artists, and Aretha Franklin of the 60s to the new directions of Michael Jackson, Quincy Jones, and Wynton Marsalis of the 70s and 80s. There are historic photographs on the jacket and within the text along with a selected bibliography to make this a source of reference recommended for school and public libraries.

Helen E. Williams

SOURCE: A review of *Black Music in America: A History Through Its People,* in *School Library Journal,* Vol. 33, No. 10, June-July, 1987, p. 106.

This history of black music provides an admirable parade of musicians and related personalities as it unfolds through their life stories. Linkages and relationships are smoothly styled to move readers from unknown historical figures to contemporary, highly visible performers. A critical aspect of this history is the deplorable social atmosphere of racism, sexism, and economic deprivation which characterized the earliest times, and to some extent, contemporary times. Despite the searing psychological stresses that were imposed by some derogatory stage names, infamously low wages, and inadequate, if any, guest accommodations, these artists persisted to create an amazing range of music that includes jazz, bebop, vocal, gospel, classical, operatic, and music videos. Despite his clear writing style, Haskins appears ambivalent regarding the implication of segregation in the music business. "By and large, people involved in the world of music were more interested in music than in skin color" raises questions when compared to later pages which feature statements such as "very segregated," "considerable white resistance," "music business was still highly segregated." He seems to favor male musicians, as exemplified in the very brief attention given to women including Billie Holiday and Marian Anderson. The basis of Haskins' selections is not explained. Nevertheless, this book will enhance music collections for young readers.

Jeffrey Cooper

SOURCE: A review of *Black Music in America: A His-*

tory Through Its People, in *Kliatt Young Adult Paperback Book Guide,* Vol. 27, No. 3, May, 1993, p. 36.

It's difficult to imagine the library that could not find a place on its shelves for this clear and concise history of African-American music. Haskins has written over 80 books for adult and YA audiences. This lively account of America's music from slave songs and spirituals to ragtime and the blues, from Buddy Bolden and Jelly Roll Morton to Michael Jackson and Wynton Marsalis, was voted a NCSS/CBC Notable Children's Trade Book in Social Studies. By placing the major musical figures of black American music in a social and historical context, the author tells as much about the evolution of American culture as he does about the remarkable men and women who shaped America's music. There are no new and startling revelations on these pages; rather, Haskins's accomplishment is to assemble the vast body of facts about black music in America into one seamless and highly readable volume. Presumably, future editions will include a discussion of rap and other musical developments since the book's original publication in 1987.

📖   *COUNT YOUR WAY THROUGH CHINA;*
      COUNT YOUR WAY THROUGH JAPAN;
      COUNT YOUR WAY THROUGH RUSSIA;
      COUNT YOUR WAY THROUGH THE ARAB
      WORLD (1987)

Kathy Piehl

SOURCE: A review of *Count Your Way Through China* and others, in *School Library Journal,* Vol. 34, No. 1, September, 1987, pp. 174-75.

Four books that introduce a foreign country through counting from one to ten. Each double-page spread shows the number, the character or word for it, the pronunciation, and a full-color illustration. There is also a brief paragraph that gives a few facts about various aspects of life in that country. In the China volume, for example, children read about the two pandas donated to the U.S. in 1972, the five-tone scale, and the ten major dynasties. The kinds of topics vary and seem to be determined in part by what facts Haskins found to illustrate each number. Some information fits well into this format: the importance of prayer five times a day for a Muslim, for example. Others are stretched to fit the point and are not very significant, such as "The [Japanese] character for the words 'how many' requires *seven* strokes." Many of the topics will require further explanation. Haskins does little more than list the seven zones of vegetation in China, for example. The books may find a place as introductory material in social studies, but they are limited by the fact that format determined content.

Barbara Elleman

SOURCE: A review of *Count Your Way Through China*

and others, in *Booklist,* Vol. 84, No. 4, October 15, 1987, p. 395.

Using numbers from one to ten as his method of approach, Haskins introduces a variety of concepts about these four areas of the world. In *Arab World,* for example, "tents with two rooms separated by a curtain are home to most Bedouins," "at least five times a day all Muslims must face Mecca and pray," and "in Arabic there are eight ways to say cousin." These statements are briefly expanded on in double-page spreads embellished by drawings as well as a large, boldface numeral and the Arabic symbol and its pronunciation. Each of the books has the same eclectic presentation with varying degrees of interest. *China* includes information on four important animals in legend, seven zones of vegetation, and a festival honoring the Nine Stars of the Plow. *Japan* describes cultural concepts such as two chopsticks, five kinds of No plays, and seven calligraphic writing strokes. The *Russia* volume features snowshoes, church domes, skating medals, and folk dancers. Useful for introducing other cultures, for short classroom reports, or for teaching children to count in another language. Individual books may also serve where new immigrants are joining a community.

📖   *CORAZON AQUINO: LEADER OF THE*
      PHILIPPINES (1988)

Kirkus Reviews

SOURCE: A review of *Corazon Aquino: Leader of the Philippines,* in *Kirkus Reviews,* Vol. LV, No. 24, December 15, 1987, p. 1732.

Despite some hype, this is a solid, thoughtful look at a stellar political career.

"She took power in the midst of a people's revolution that shed flower petals rather than blood." One hundred and fifty-six people were killed on election day, but let us not quibble: the Philippines is a violent place, as Haskins shows, and Aquino has tried with some success to substitute negotiation for armed confrontation. Benigno Aquino is presented as a brilliant but sometimes opportunistic statesman (not unlike Marcos) who deliberately kept Corazon in his shadow. When she was propelled into the public eye after his assassination, she proved to be a capable politician, as the author's clear, well-organized description of her campaign, the major issues, and her actions in office reveals.

Shirley Wilton

SOURCE: A review of *Corazon Aquino: Leader of the Philippines,* in *School Library Journal,* Vol. 34, No. 7, March, 1988, p. 220.

A clearly written and intelligent political biography of the first woman president of the Philippines. It is Corazon

Aquino's public role which concerns Haskins, and which he describes so well. Mrs. Aquino's family, youth, and private life are treated only briefly. But from the time of her husband's imprisonment in 1972, when she began her arduous campaign to find him and to prevail upon the authorities to release him, Corazon Aquino's education in public affairs becomes the focus of the biography. Haskins deftly describes the various pressure groups and competing individuals who even today make Aquino's control of Philippine events somewhat problematic. Haskins has avoided the twin pitfalls of writing a "woman's story" about the Philippine leader and of focussing on her husband's political career. He has treated Corazon Aquino with the objectivity and political focus that should be granted any public figure, male or female.

Zena Sutherland

SOURCE: A review of *Corazon Aquino: Leader of the Philippines,* in *Bulletin of the Center for Children's Books,* Vol. 41, No. 11, July-August, 1988, pp. 229-30.

In a prefatory note, the author cites sources used in the writing of a biography that is as much up to date as a book can be by the time it is printed, and that gives a sympathetic, if occasionally adulatory, picture of Aquino's early life and her political career. Haskins furnishes adequate background information about the history of the Philippines and the years of the Marcos regime that led to the power struggle, the murder of Benigno Aquino, and the entry of his wife into the tense political arena. The book is, unfortunately, weakened by lapses in writing style that are unlike Haskins at his best; in the same paragraph, for example, are "He did not know if his wife and children were themselves in a prison camp," and "Maybe there was more to life than what he had believed."

MR. BOJANGLES: THE BIOGRAPHY OF BILL ROBINSON (with N. R. Mitgang, 1988)

Publishers Weekly

SOURCE: A review of *Mr. Bojangles: The Biography of Bill Robinson,* in *Publishers Weekly,* Vol. 233, No. 12, March 25, 1988, pp. 57-8.

An elegantly dressed man who could neither read nor write until he was in his 40s, honorary mayor of Harlem and one of the best-known black entertainers of his time, Bill Robinson (1878-1949) grew up an orphan in Richmond, Va., where he earned a living by shining shoes and shelling peas. Based on Robinson's papers and on interviews with his wives and friends, this dutiful biography tries to explain the character and personality of the popular but enigmatic tap dancer but is more successful at chronicling his career. Here are glimpses of his struggles to overcome the color barrier on his way to stardom in white vaudeville, musicals (especially *The Hot Mikado*), films and radio, his addiction to gambling and compulsive need to live on borrowed money, his generosity (he

performed at more than 3000 benefits) and his love for his native city.

Kirkus Reviews

SOURCE: A review of *Mr. Bojangles: The Biography of Bill Robinson,* in *Kirkus Reviews,* Vol. LVI, No. 7, April 1, 1988, p. 515.

Bill "Bojangles" Robinson, who died nearly 40 years ago, was often called the world's greatest tap dancer. His fading image has recently been revived in the video release of his best-known films, those made with seven-year-old dancing partner Shirley Temple: *The Little Colonel, The Littlest Rebel,* and *Rebecca of Sunnybrook Farm.* (His other outings, in *Stormy Weather* and *In Old Kentucky,* are lesser films.)

As a young orphan, Robinson began dancing on Southern street corners and in front of theaters, becoming a compulsive gambler early on. He spent several decades in vaudeville, and was the first black solo act allowed on stage. In later years, he helped black entertainers form a union, was always generous with his time and money, danced for servicemen in WW II, and was named unofficial "Mayor of Harlem" during the rule of Fiorello LaGuardia. Meanwhile, Bojangles (the Bob Dylan song is not about Robinson) was not just dapper, he was fanatical about his clothes, clean dressing rooms, and even tried to patent his famed step dance. Beloved figure though he was, he had flaws that went hand in glove with gambling (but did not drink or smoke), was forever borrowing (sometimes failing to pay back), had a sharp temper, and was a martinet with fellow workers. He did not marry until into his 40s, and at 62 was divorced by his wife for his infatuation with a very young dancer, whom he then married. Robinson's dressing rooms and home always displayed many photos of Shirley Temple (though Haskins and Mitgang are disappointingly scanty about his work with Shirley). His death, at age 72, was followed by the greatest funeral ever held in Harlem.

Haskins, who has limned many black entertainers' lives, and Mitgang see Robinson plain and make clear his sparkle, but—perhaps necessarily—lard their book with large chunks of vaudeville and black theater history.

Peter L. Robinson

SOURCE: A review of *Mr. Bojangles: The Biography of Bill Robinson,* in *Booklist,* Vol. 84, No. 17, May 1, 1988, p. 1469.

For 40 years Bill Robinson reigned as the world's most famous tap dancer. His lighter-than-air descent down a staircase became virtually a trademark (he was denied the patent for it); his fame was immortalized in a song and in a *Vanity Fair* photomontage; and Fred Astaire paid homage in his "Bojangles of Harlem" dance sequence. Amazingly, this is the first biography of Robinson, who suffered several heart attacks prior to death in 1949. His life story, as recounted by Haskins and Mitgang with complete cooperation from the dancer's family and friends, stands as a moving study in bravery and a melancholy portrait of thwarted possibilities. Robinson, who fought determinedly against the color barrier throughout his career, was a longtime gambler and died with an estate valued at only $25,000.

Joseph Boskin

SOURCE: A review of *Mr. Bojangles: The Biography of Bill Robinson,* in *The Journal of Southern History,* Vol. LVI, No. 1, February, 1990, pp. 146-47.

The name has become an artifact in American culture: "Bojangles" symbolizes the artistic movement of tap, an original Afro-American dance, and Bill Robinson was its premier representative. Robinson's nickname developed out of a street joke that involved a tall beaver hat; the title of the popular song actually derives from the southern term meaning mischief maker. From the 1920s through the 1940s, at the height of his popularity, Robinson was one of the most powerful and highly paid black performers. And, it might be said, one of the most criticized for his seemingly Uncle Tom roles, the most cited being the cheerful house butler in those endless roseate antebellum plantation films where he staircase-danced with child star Shirley Temple. In reality, the prevailing Sambo stereotype often locked him in; the stair dance, his own innovation, was his quest for freedom of movement.

In this spritely and informative biography, the authors grapple with the many contradictions in Robinson's life. He was an angry man with a gnawing sense of deprivation, a gambler who packed and openly flashed a revolver; yet he was extremely generous, always optimistic, and exceedingly charming. He was able to cut a path through both white and black worlds. In an intriguing aside, the authors note that in Washington, D. C., the young Robinson had a street partnership with Al Jolson, who sang to Robinson's dances. Behind Robinson's engaging smile, however, was a private fury that drove him to push for actors' rights and against racist practices. Onstage he publicly defied prejudice by "quipping that he was 'having the best time I've had since I was colored.'" In many quiet ways he fought against institutional boundaries and, more often than not, directly confronted racial insults. The overall portrait is of a black man who overcame his harsh beginnings with a determination fueled by rancor, a physical grace that hid various demons, a supreme entertainer caught between separate cultures, and a creative energy that elevated him.

As admirable as the attempt is, this work is too often marred by writing that borders on the melodramatic. The result is a biography that can be categorized as hagiography. It is exasperating to read such sentences as "Sometimes, Bo had to forge his own revolution toward social justice" or "The one thing money could not buy for Bill Robinson was protection from the indignities of racism."

In their zeal to accord him the place he deserves in the history of American entertainment, the authors have not only rationalized Robinson's behavior but also oversimplified the times in which he performed. Robinson's life, in sum, looms larger than this portrayal.

WINNIE MANDELA: LIFE OF STRUGGLE (1988)

Kirkus Reviews

SOURCE: A review of *Winnie Mandela: Life of Struggle,* in *Kirkus Reviews,* Vol. LVI, No. 8, April 15, 1988, p. 618.

The author of vivid, well-written biographies of Lena Horne and Katherine Dunham tells the story of the wife of a long-imprisoned anti-apartheid activist, herself a leader in black Africa's struggle for freedom.

After an opening scene in which Mandela speaks movingly to people massed for a funeral, Haskins flashes back to narrate her earlier life, skillfully interwoven with background information on South African history. Raised in the rural Transkei region, Mandela moved to Johannesburg and became the first black medical social-worker in South Africa. Brought up to be a loyal and dutiful daughter, she matured to become a leader's wife whose first loyalty is to the needs of her people—needs demonstrated in Haskins' description of the barriers erected by the Afrikaners' government. As her father says, she has married not only Nelson Mandela but the struggle. Final chapters deal with her own imprisonments and the harassment that now continues into the next generation.

A painful picture of black South Africa's plight, with more useful historical information than has been included in other biographies of Winnie Mandela. Current through 1985; a story readers won't forget.

Zena Sutherland

SOURCE: A review of *Winnie Mandela: Life of Struggle,* in *Bulletin of the Center for Children's Books,* Vol. 41, No. 10, June, 1988, p. 205.

For a slightly older audience than Meltzer's biography although there is an overlap, this is one of Haskins's best. It is forthright but calm in tone, admiring rather than adulatory, and smoothly written. It gives excellent background (despite one misuse of the derogatory term "kafir") about South African history and politics without overbalancing the text to the detriment of Winnie Mandela's life story. Haskins wisely has let her character and her achievements speak effectively for themselves.

Nancy J. Schmidt

SOURCE: A review of *Winnie Mandela: Life of Struggle,*

in *School Library Journal,* Vol. 35, No. 9, June-July, 1988, p. 123.

This biography, like Milton Meltzer's for younger children (1986), is based primarily on Winnie Mandela's autobiography, *Part of My Soul Went With Him* (1985), and includes background material about the anti-apartheid struggle in South Africa. Its greater length and direction to an older audience permit the inclusion of more details from South African political history that provide the context in which Winnie Mandela has become a national leader and international symbol of the struggle against racial oppression. Haskins skillfully interweaves Winnie Mandela's personal story with that of milestones in the black South African struggle for political freedom and human dignity to create a moving portrait of Mandela as an individual and the "mother" of the nation. Yet he is not overly idealistic and acknowledges that she is unlikely to live to see the struggle in which she has been engaged won. A section of a dozen black-and-white photographs depict members of the Mandela family in events described in the biography, and a one-page bibliography provides reliable sources for learning more about Winnie Mandela and South African political history. The map does not include all of the places mentioned in the text, and there is no glossary to identify important persons, political groups, laws, and institutions mentioned in the text.

Virginia B. Moore

SOURCE: A review of *Winnie Mandela: Life of Struggle,* in *Voice of Youth Advocates,* Vol. 11, No. 3, August, 1988, p. 146.

It's an easy-to-read, fast-paced, and gripping profile of a remarkable Black woman who is the wife of the famous antiapartheid leader, Nelson Mandela, and whose personal life-long endeavor for basic human dignity for herself, her family, and her people in South Africa has won worldwide respect and admiration.

Haskins, noted for his biographies of Katherine Dunham and Lena Horne, relates events from early childhood village life in the remote Transkei through adjustment to city life in Johannesburg, years of hard study to obtain the best education while at the same time learning new ideas about South Africa and Black South African nationalism along with the discovery that all white people were not the enemies described in stories told in the home village to Winnie's becoming the first Black medical social worker in South Africa's history. However, such hardships and achievements could not prepare her for the persistent persecution and difficulties that resulted from her marriage to Nelson Mandela whose leadership role in the outlawed African National Congress caused his arrest soon after their marriage that was followed by a lengthy trial and his imprisonment since 1964 while Winnie was left with two small daughters.

Nevertheless, with a commitment to her husband's ideas and her own desire to help her people fight against apart-

heid, the rigid system of separation of the races with economic and political discrimination that is most severe for Blacks in South Africa, Winnie has endured police harassment, numerous arrests, physical mistreatment, solitary confinement, and banishment to a remote community with a different language from her own. Haskins traces the struggle which both Nelson and Winnie Mandela have shared with their daughters as changes take place in South Africa because of Winnie's courageous effort to overcome the forces posed by family, society, and a brutally strong-willed government in order to make her own choices and to inspire thousands of South Africans who desire to choose their own destiny.

Features such as the attractive photograph on the jacket, thin size, well-researched biographical and historical events which reveal the changing attitudes and practices regarding apartheid along with a bibliography containing books and periodicals combine to make this volume highly recommended for collections on South Africa and women in school and public libraries.

Margaret A. Bush

SOURCE: A review of *Winnie Mandela: Life of Struggle,* in *The Horn Book Magazine,* Vol. LXIV, No. 5, September-October, 1988, p. 645.

"Both Nelson and Winnie Mandela are heroes of a kind rarely seen in human history." Haskins's account, aptly titled as a chronicle of human endurance, does not actually dwell on the heroism of the Mandelas. Rather, his thought-provoking narrative of the events in Winnie Mandela's life becomes a powerful demonstration of the evils of political oppression. The book begins with a rally in late 1985; the story then moves back to her childhood and the historical context into which she was born and continues forward to the present. Although the Mandelas have had limited opportunities for speaking, writing, or interviews, their long years of public life, trials, and imprisonment since the early 1960s have been documented by the international press, and many books have been written about them and the apartheid struggle in South Africa. Winnie Mandela's commitment and survival in the face of unending harassment, surveillance, imprisonment without actual charges, banishment, and separation from family seem nothing short of miraculous. Constructed with skill and restraint, the biography is both sobering and inspiring. It is an unfinished story, and Haskins does not conclude on an optimistic note, though he suggests that the renewed vigor of young black South Africans and the slow surge of international pressure may yet bear fruit. The account will leave the reader informed, troubled, and wanting to know more.

BILL COSBY: AMERICA'S MOST FAMOUS FATHER (1988)

Denise M. Wilms

SOURCE: A review of *Bill Cosby: America's Most Fa-*

mous Father, in *Booklist,* Vol. 84, No. 19, June 1, 1988, p. 1675.

This most famous father and highest paid entertainer in 1987 is diligently profiled by Haskins, who obligingly comments on the social contexts operating as Cosby aspired to show-business success. Haskins describes the entertainer's impoverished upbringing, his lackluster academic record—Cosby was a dropout—and his turnabout in the navy when he realized that education was a necessity. Still, a college degree ultimately took a backseat to comedy, and Cosby's talents have taken him far—far enough to finally complete his education and receive a Ph.D., even as he carried on his comedic endeavors. Haskins acknowledges the criticisms that have been made of Cosby and generally defends him against those who feel his success has been gained by association with whites. Haskins' prose is sometimes lackluster, and a few of his explanations seem patronizing (why, for example, whites were uncomfortable with blacks in the 1960s). Overall, however, this account offers informative coverage that will suit browsers and those looking for biographies to fulfill assignments.

Kirkus Reviews

SOURCE: A review of *Bill Cosby: America's Most Famous Father,* in *Kirkus Reviews,* Vol. LVI, No. 11, June 1, 1988, pp. 827-28.

An unconventional biography of a multifaceted performer: rather than dwelling on Cosby's success, Haskins analyzes his failures and achievements as a black entertainer.

This Algeresque story has been well told several times at this reading level, but Haskins takes a different tack by emphasizing the obstacles and outright barriers Cosby encountered as a black. Of course, Cosby didn't struggle long; his immediate and continuing success is here attributed to talent, hard work, and nonracial material that keeps his white audience from feeling threatened. Haskins describes Cosby's anger at the prejudice he found in the entertainment industry, and the lengths to which he has gone to keep his film and TV shows free of stereotypes; and readers are not allowed to forget Cosby's wealth. Considering the subject, this is remarkably humorless; a few lines from routines are quoted and then explained (rather stolidly). Most of the photos are publicity shots, rather than ones showing Cosby in performance. Cosby's educational concerns and authorship are mentioned, but with little detail. There's a behind-the-scenes look at the production of the *Bill Cosby Show* and a three-page bibliography.

Todd Morning

SOURCE: A review of *Bill Cosby: America's Most Famous Father,* in *School Library Journal,* Vol. 35, No. 9, June-July, 1988, p. 111.

A good overview of the life of the popular comedian, actor, author, and educator. The book, organized chronologically, begins with several chapters on Cosby's childhood that focus on those who proved to be early influences. The development of Cosby's career is covered in detail, but because of Cosby's determination to keep matters relating to his family private, there are far fewer details about this aspect of his life. Haskins does not hide the claims of some people that there is a certain amount of anger and arrogance beneath the affable surface. The writing style is clear and straightforward. This is a more in-depth and complete portrait for an older audience than other recently published biographies. . . .

THE 60s READER (with Kathleen Benson, 1988)

Mary Mueller

SOURCE: A review of *The 60s Reader,* in *School Library Journal,* Vol. 34, No. 11, August, 1988, p. 108.

This outstanding look at the '60s uses readings from original sources to explain and document the various events of the decade. However, it is more than just a book of readings. Haskins and Benson divide the book into large topics and provide background for each, giving readers a good historical grounding. The readings themselves give readers a sense of the passions of the era. They cover the whole spectrum of the '60s, from the SDS Port Huron Statement to Dr. Martin Luther King, Jr.'s eloquent plea for equality written from a Birmingham, Alabama jail, to Dr. Timothy Leary's "turn on, tune in, and drop out" drug message. The authors also bring each reading into perspective by explaining its impact and telling readers what happened to each person after the '60s. There is little bias, with the authors explaining how events affected all types of people. Their style is clear and easy to understand, allowing readers to examine the era while still making the book enjoyable to read. . . . This book is an excellent look at the '60s and provides readers with a feeling of having been there. It deserves a place in any library serving intermediate readers. . . .

Hazel Rochman

SOURCE: A review of *The 60s Reader,* in *Booklist,* Vol. 85, No. 1, September 1, 1988, p. 62.

One of the best of the recent flood of books on the 1960s . . . this smoothly integrates history and analysis with brief biographies of leading figures of the time and excerpts from crucial speeches, articles, documents, and songs. Showing how the direct action civil rights movement set the pattern for much political protest of the decade, the authors devote a chapter to each of the main movements, from student activism to peace and new religion. There are also separate chapters on the music and the drug culture. In each case the authors show both the roots in the past (especially the reaction to the prosperous, comfortable 1950s) and the enduring legacy, positive and negative—for example, the way the drug culture led into the "Me decade" of the 1970s. They also discuss changes within the decade, from civil rights to the black power movement and from polite teach-ins about the war in Vietnam to radical protest. The well-chosen excerpts add vitality and depth, including famous pieces such as King's "Letter from Birmingham Jail" and the song "Little Boxes," as well as a dialogue on transcendental meditation and an underground article on drugs by Timothy Leary. Although the authors talk about polarization, the conservatives get scant attention, nor is there much about science. The focus is on the deep political and social changes. There's a selected bibliography, but though the major excerpts are attributed, the documentation of the main text is thin, making it difficult for readers to follow up particular references. Still, this evokes a crucial decade with immediacy and insight, and it is highly recommended for personal reading and for classes in recent history.

Betsy Hearne

SOURCE: A review of *The 60s Reader,* in *Bulletin of the Center for Children's Books,* Vol. 42, No. 2, October, 1988, p. 38.

With a survey approach and simple prose, the authors report on the political, cultural, and religious movements of the decade that made "it possible for people to ask questions—about their lives, their values, their society—and to challenge the things they did not like." The technique of synthesizing background information as a context for primary materials has been capably handled, with the result that young readers will have easy access to letters, song lyrics, and speech and article excerpts by leaders from Ron Karenga to the Berrigans. The selections are well balanced in scope, if primarily sympathetic to the liberal cause. The Scalapino-Morgenthau National Teach-In debate gives both sides of the Vietnam controversy, and there's a consistent effort at objective summary ("Depending on one's point of view, the bloody confrontations that took place on the streets of Chicago during the 1968 Democratic convention were either a 'police riot' or a 'radicals riot.'"). There are a few quotes that don't seem specifically documented—an interview with Joan Baez, for instance, doesn't appear in the bibliography. However, for junior high and high school students researching the subject, this provides an overview that can lead to more complex analyses in adult literature.

Patrick Jones

SOURCE: A review of *The 60s Reader,* in *Voice of Youth Advocates,* Vol. 12, No. 1, April, 1989, p. 58.

Just look at the tie-dyed t-shirts, the Grateful Dead patches, and the peace-sign earrings to know "something's happening" between 1980s' teens and 1960s' culture.

Haskins and Benson provide a useful volume in the growing literature on the decade which is different from others in many important aspects. First, as a reader it reproduces important documents (Port Huron Statement, lyrics to "Times They Are A Changin'") with a minimum of commentary. Second, it is a nonfiction book which relies on facts and analysis rather than anecdotes or personal narratives. Third, the focus of the book is information as there are few pictures other than often-seen black and white stills. Finally, as a reader, it hits the high points concentrating on certain movements (civil rights, peace) while leaving out others such as the space program, the Great Society, and underground press.

The book is a starting point. Each of the chapters focuses on a movement, then important documents, statements, lyrics, or interviews are presented. There is a bibliography at the end of the book, although a better idea would have been short bibs at the end of each chapter. The book ends with a "legacy" chapter which should have been much longer. Even though the book has these failings, it is still an important work about a subject of great interest to teenagers. Haskins and Benson not only present "what" was said, but also "how."

SHIRLEY TEMPLE BLACK: ACTRESS TO AMBASSADOR (1988)

Ilene Cooper

SOURCE: A review of *Shirley Temple Black: Actress to Ambassador,* in *Booklist,* Vol. 85, No. 2, September 15, 1988, p. 160.

Children who have seen the young Shirley on television or have heard fleeting references to her name should find this well-conceived entry in the Women of Our Times series of interest. Haskins traces Black's life from early days in the movies, as America's Sweetheart, through her phenomenal stardom and describes her transition from actress, to housewife, and later to diplomat. While Haskins has not had the advantage of using recent adult biographies, including Black's own book *Child Star* (out this fall), as source material, his research is very good. He introduces such important issues as the treatment of blacks in the movies and describes how, in Palm Springs, Bill Robinson, little Shirley's co-star in several films, had to live with his chauffeur in servant's quarters while they rehearsed.

Roger Sutton

SOURCE: A review of *Shirley Temple Black: Actress to Ambassador,* in *Bulletin of the Center for Children's Books,* Vol. 42, No. 3, November, 1988, pp. 74-5.

It is unlikely that even the most sophisticated young heart can be hardened against Temple's films of *Heidi* and *A*

Little Princess; this biography shows the sometimes painful real story behind the dimpled melodrama. Temple began her film career in the sleazy "Baby Burlesks" (the kind of films, as Haskins points out, that the grown-up Shirley Temple would crusade against as exploitative) but her star took off after *Stand Up and Cheer,* and she had a phenomenal, though relatively brief, reign as "America's Sweetheart" until 1940. "As a teenager, Shirley didn't have much luck getting more roles. She was not pretty enough to attract movie audiences." Haskins is no sobsister, and his account is candid in discussing the actress' trials and triumphs. He does a good job of placing Temple within historical context—through her relationship with black actor Bill "Bojangles" Robinson, her status as a symbol of better times for Depression audiences, and, more recently, in her role as savvy politician and ambassador. An effective counter to fan magazine hype and an illuminating portrait of young Hollywood.

INDIA UNDER INDIRA AND RAJIV GANDHI (1989)

Kirkus Reviews

SOURCE: A review of *India Under Indira and Rajiv Gandhi,* in *Kirkus Reviews,* Vol. LVII, No. 9, May 1, 1989, p. 692.

A telling look at the contrasting political styles of these two members of India's first family, and at major events during their tenures as Prime Minister.

Indira Gandhi wrote, "[Rajiv's birth] was one of the most joyful moments in my life, although I must say at the time he seemed quite ugly." Throughout this tale of modern India's political and religious turmoil, Haskins never lets readers lose sight of the human dimension, the private lives (or lack thereof) of Indira and her two sons—Rajiv and the ill-fated Sanjay—as they virtually backed into public eminence in the wake of Nehru's death. Indira is the more shadowy figure here, a ruthless matriarch whose loyalties seemed equally split between her country and her children—the "Nation's Grandchildren," as they came to be known. After her assassination in 1984, Rajiv's willingness to hear opposition leaders and to compromise with them came as welcome relief, though—as the author shows—India's racial and religious tensions were only temporarily eased and the era of massive police actions not yet over. Readers may wish for more support for the claim that the British are to blame for India's Hindu/Moslem hostilities, and may wonder why Haskins places such emphasis on the idea that Rajiv is the first of "midnight's children" (a phrase borrowed, with attribution, from Salman Rushdie)—i.e., the post-Empire generation—to rule the country; but the political analysis is clear and incisive here, and the Gandhis emerge as individuals. This excellent supplement to wider-ranging books, such as Traub's *India: The Challenge of Change,* carries the story through 1987.

Zena Sutherland

SOURCE: A review of *India Under Indira and Rajiv Gandhi,* in *Bulletin of the Center for Children's Books,* Vol. 42, No. 11, July-August, 1989, p. 276.

This is Haskins at his best: a thoughtful, moderate tone, a good balance of personal and political material, and enough background to make the chronological narrative more meaningful. The roles of Mohandas Gandhi and, even more, of Jawaharlal Nehru are described in enough detail to make it clear why Nehru's daughter Indira became Prime Minister. Haskins is particularly candid about the careers and philosophies of Rajiv and his brother Sanjay, and the text, which concludes with political events of 1987, reserves judgment about Rajiv's success as Prime Minister.

Ellen D. Warwick

SOURCE: A review of *India Under Indira and Rajiv Gandhi,* in *School Library Journal,* Vol. 35, No. 12, August, 1989, p. 146.

True to its title, this book focuses on the political side of the Gandhi family, with Rajiv emerging as the star and mother Indira and brother Sanjay playing supporting roles. Haskins opens with a brief account of Rajiv's inauguration as prime minister in 1984; subsequent chapters describe his birth, privileged childhood as one of the "nation's grandchildren," and education in India and Great Britain. Frequently, Haskins contrasts Rajiv's modest, unassuming ways with the more flamboyant style of the designated heir apparent, Sanjay. The book includes controversial aspects of the Gandhi reign: Indira's authoritarianism, her coercive sterilization program, and Sanjay's misuse of government funds. Haskins traces Rajiv's transformation from reluctant politician to a respected leader in his own right. The account ends in mid-1987, with the signing of a peace agreement between India and Sri Lanka. Though the author's sympathy is always apparent, he wisely concludes that it's too early to tell how history will judge Rajiv Gandhi. Haskins writes in a clear, pared-down prose; large print adds to the book's readability.

Lola H. Teubert

SOURCE: A review of *India Under Indira and Rajiv Gandhi,* in *Voice of Youth Advocates,* Vol. 12, No. 4, October, 1989, p. 234.

On December 31, 1984, Rajiv Gandhi was inaugurated as Prime Minister of India. After taking office, his first duty was to preside at the funeral service of Indira Gandhi, his mother and former Prime Minister of India.

The generation of Indians born around August 15, 1947, the date of India's Independence, was designated as "Midnight's Children" by author Salman Rushdie in his book by the same title. Rajiv, a Hindu, the more privileged class, was of that generation. The Hindus wanted an independent state in which they held power. The Moslems wanted their own state and the Sikhs felt they should receive the same. According to the author, as a child Rajiv knew nothing of the poverty that existed in his country. He and his younger brother, Sanjay, lived charmed lives. He spent his youth desiring to be a pilot for India Air and showed no interest in politics until the deaths of his father in 1960, and his grandfather, Jawaharlal Nehru, in 1964 (India's first Prime Minister).

After the death of her father, Mrs. Gandhi began commuting between Luchnow, their home, and New Delhi, resorting to nannies for the boys, even though she preferred being a full-time mother. After his matriculation at Doon's School and Trinity College, Cambridge, Rajiv became a commercial pilot in 1972. While Rajiv enjoyed his career, his lovely Italian-born wife, their children, and his social life, Sanjay, who was more ambitious, chose a wife who was a Sikh and pursued his interest in the construction of an automobile plant.

At the same time their mother was desperately trying to consolidate political factions. Even though Mrs. Gandhi favored a democratic government, she signed a peace treaty with Russia, forming a friendship with a non-democratic faction. The author relates that her answer to criticism of her rule was to become more autocratic.

According to Haskins, Sanjay was his mother's favorite and destined to be her successor, but his untimely death in a plane crash left a reluctant Rajiv next in line. Whatever judgment history makes of Rajiv's accomplishments in office, he did become involved in politics when the need arose.

This well-written book, with its very detailed index, pertinent black and white photographs, and inviting print and subject matter will make it a first choice for class papers and India culture enthusiasts.

SPORTS GREAT MAGIC JOHNSON (1989; revised edition, 1992)

Betsy Hearne

SOURCE: A review of *Sports Great Magic Johnson,* in *Bulletin of the Center for Children's Books,* Vol. 42, No. 10, June, 1989, p. 251.

Haskins is almost as practiced a hand at biography as Earvin Johnson is at basketball, so Magic's amiable personality and enviable skills get a smooth introduction. The first half of the book is the most interesting, since it covers the major portion of Johnson's development. Gameplay comprises most of the second half, with an emphasis on Johnson's value as a guard in the rivalry between the Lakers and the Celtics. Black-and-white action photos spice up the coverage, which reveals some of Johnson's hard times as well as highlighting his success. No surpris-

es here, but fans will appreciate the easy-to-read information, enjoy the book's season recaps, and, like Magic, pass it to their buddies.

Phillis Wilson

SOURCE: A review of *Sports Great Magic Johnson,* in *Booklist,* Vol. 85, No. 20, June 15, 1989, p. 1822.

Haskins offers fans a lively, well-balanced profile of the Los Angeles Lakers superstar guard, who won the NBA's Most Valuable Player award in 1987. In tracing Johnson's career, Haskins explores the man's early years on high school and college courts as well as his time with the Lakers. Along with play-by-play excitement, Haskins shares insights on Johnson, characterizing him as a superb ball handler and a staunchly unselfish team player with remarkable "court sense." Johnson's gradual maturing and the buoyant enthusiasm that helped him over the rough spots are revealed through discussion of the pressures of the game, the multi-million-dollar contracts, and the star's ways of dealing with mistakes in crucial moments.

Tom S. Hurlburt

SOURCE: A review of *Sports Great Magic Johnson,* in *School Library Journal,* Vol. 35, No. 11, July, 1989, pp. 85-6.

The life of a black athlete many believe to be the finest basketball player of his era. "Magic" seems an appropriate nickname for Johnson, as every team he's played on, from high school to the pros, has been amazingly successful. Couple his teams' successes with Johnson's quick and engaging smile and a fairly controversy-free off-court life, and you have a modern-day "superstar." The book provides a fairly straightforward account of Johnson's life. Black-and-white photographs, garnered mainly from the wire services, are interspersed throughout the book. There are no appendixes of Johnson's statistics and teams' records. Mention of Johnson's personal and family life is made, keeping the biography focused on the person rather than just the athlete. This book updates Rich Levin's *Magic Johnson: Court Magician* (1981).

Sally Estes

SOURCE: A review of *Sports Great Magic Johnson,* in *Booklist,* Vol. 89, No. 4, October 15, 1992, p. 413.

The revised edition of *Sports Great Magic Johnson* has been updated and expanded by the inclusion of a seventh chapter that discusses Johnson's HIV status, his November 1991 retirement from the Lakers, and his role in the fight against AIDS; there is no coverage of Johnson's playing on the Olympic "Dream Team" in Barcelona, something that occurred after the update went to press. Also added to the new edition is a page of career statistics. Whether replacement of the first edition is necessary is debatable; Johnson's life and career remain in flux, and there will be a need for further updating in the not-too-distant future. However, this remains a brisk account that evokes a sense of the man, and it also, along with the other volumes in the Sports Great series, will attract older reluctant readers.

📖 *BLACK DANCE IN AMERICA: A HISTORY THROUGH ITS PEOPLE* (1990)

Publishers Weekly

SOURCE: A review of *Black Dance in America: A History Through Its People,* in *Publishers Weekly,* Vol. 237, No. 13, March 30, 1990, p. 65.

Despite the enduring influence of black dance on American culture, few writers have documented it. Haskins (*Mr. Bojangles: The Biography of Bill Robinson*) fills this curious void admirably. Without assuming a previous knowledge of dance, he begins at the beginning—the compulsory dancing African slaves were forced to do on board ships bound for the New World in the 17th and 18th centuries—and follows the story almost to the present day, discussing the very different achievements of Katherine Dunham, Pearl Primus, Arthur Mitchell, Chubby Checker, Gregory Hines and many others. The author considers the persistent racism faced by black American dancers in pursuing their careers (even today, few are members of major ballet companies, for example), but his account is utterly free of cant, presenting a clear picture of trials endured and triumphs met. The history is inclusive and up-to-date, save for very recent events (the death of Alvin Ailey, Judith Jamison's appointment to head his company, and the current financial woes of the Dance Theater of Harlem). The book should be of interest to young readers and adults alike.

Jeanette Lambert

SOURCE: A review of *Black Dance in America: A History Through Its People,* in *School Library Journal,* Vol. 36, No. 6, June, 1990, p. 141.

Once again Haskins scores with an incisive look at the participation (and exclusion) of blacks in various dance forms in America. Beginning with a description of how slaves were forced to dance aboard slave ships, he describes the roles that dance played in Africa and how it had to be compromised in the New World. Haskins also relates the impact and contributions of historic dance forms and of individual black dancers upon American culture. The book is evenly divided between biographies and historical accounts. Information is provided on famous black dancers such as Katherine Dunham, Alvin Ailey, and Bill "Bojangles" Robinson, as well as lesser-known figures. Haskins shows how the indomitable spirit of these danc-

ers was severely tested by racism and the exploitation of their work by white performers. Tap dancing, modern dance, and jazz dancing receive coverage in depth, while break dancing and popular dancing are given cursory treatment. This examination of the world of dance shows how success in this area often depended on more than just raw talent. The struggles for acceptance and personal tolls are relayed, but are not sensationalized.

Penny Blubaugh

SOURCE: A review of *Black Dance in America,* in *Voice of Youth Advocates,* Vol. 13, No. 2, June, 1990, p. 125.

Spanning the history of black dance in the United States from the slaves to the present, this interesting study intermingles biographies with pieces of more conventional history. Haskins begins with the practice of "dancing the slaves" on the ships coming from Africa; traces the origins of popular dances like the cakewalk, Charleston, tap, and modern dance; and introduces the reader to a host of interesting black dancers who fought through the multiple layers of prejudice in this country to pursue their dreams.

The biographies are not long, but have enough information to give a feel for the different people. They range from Bill "Bojangles" Robinson and the Nicholas Brothers to Charles "Honi" Coles, Alvin Ailey, Debbie Allen, Judith Jamison, and Geoffrey Holder. The emergence of all black ballet and modern dance troupes and dance festivals is also covered.

Haskins' writing is pleasant and will be easily absorbed by a wide-ranging audience. This is an interesting, informal, though somewhat sketchy, history of black dance that should appeal to anyone concerned with any area of dance—black or white.

Stephanie Zvirin

SOURCE: A review of *Black Dance in America: A History Through Its People,* in *Booklist,* Vol. 86, No. 22, August, 1990, p. 2163.

Using the same kind of approach he employed in previous books on black theater and music, Haskins offers a historical survey of black dance, focusing in particular on its influence on American dance as a whole—tap to twist, ballet to break dance. Organized largely in a chronological manner, with an introductory chapter discussing the dances slaves brought with them to the New World, the text follows the art form from minstrel show to modern dance, profiling, along the way, individuals (Pearl Primus, Alvin Ailey, Judith Jamison, Gregory Hines, etc.) who have left their mark as dancers and/or choreographers over the years. Haskins makes an obvious and effective effort to pinpoint past racism and decries the fact that minorities are still poorly represented in some areas of the medium. The result is a substantial, lively history that will interest students of black history as well as dance.

Haskins with author Harry Crews, 1977.

Black-and-white photographs are scattered throughout, and a bibliography, a videography, and an index are appended.

Ruth R. Woodman

SOURCE: A review of *Black Dance in America: A History Through Its People,* in *Kliatt Young Adult Paperback Book Guide,* Vol. 26, No. 3, April, 1992, p. 44.

This fascinating history traces the development of black dance from slave days to the current sophisticated blending of jazz with modern and classic ballet. The first chapter "Dancing the Slaves" describes the cruelty of slave traders forcing slaves to dance on the decks of slave ships because the captains thought exercise would make their captives look healthy and bring a higher price in the market.

Dance was basic to the African way of life, and slaves continued to celebrate their births, deaths, and weddings by dancing. After Emancipation, African-Americans became popular as entertainers in minstrel shows and jazz and tap-dancing productions. Prejudice, however, kept these superbly talented artists from becoming producers and many of them moved to Europe. However, the talent of Katherine Dunham, Pearl Primus, and Alvin Ailey propelled black dance companies into acceptance and acclaim, and the influence of such established white artists as Martha Graham, Ted Shawn, Ruth St. Denis and Agnes DeMille encouraged acknowledgement. The black dance groups have been real innovators in dance, and their sources were the rhythms of Africa. This history is entertaining and informative and valuable as a reference for dance students and students of anthropology.

📖   *COUNT YOUR WAY THROUGH GERMANY;*
        COUNT YOUR WAY THROUGH ITALY
        (1990)

Mary Lou Budd

SOURCE: A review of *Count Your Way Through Germany* and *Count Your Way Through Italy,* in *School Library Journal,* Vol. 36, No. 8, August, 1990, p. 143.

Clever use of the numbers one through ten treats readers to a brief introduction to the culture, geography, and language of each country. The subject matter is integrated smoothly and subtly as each number is presented sequentially in double-page spreads. One page contains succinct, informative text that is complemented on its facing page with an amplifying illustration. Arabic numerals act as chapter headings and each is accompanied with the written number word (and phonetic pronunciation) appropriate to that country. The text is economical and manageable for the older range of readers; younger children will need help with some of the vocabulary. Even so, their interest will be piqued by the expressiveness of the illustrations. [Helen] Byers uses a pastel palette to evoke an "Old World" feeling in . . . *Germany,* while [Beth] Wright's bold colors and designs in modern graphic art explode from the pages of . . . *Italy.* Both are sure to attract attention. Any foreign words used in the texts are followed by their phonetic pronunciations, easing comprehension. There is no in-depth treatment, but these books will surely whet appetites for further investigations.

Lee Galda and Linda DeGroff

SOURCE: A review of *Count Your Way Through Germany* and *Count Your Way Through Italy,* in *The Reading Teacher,* Vol. 44, No. 3, No. 3, November, 1990, p. 243.

Children of the world are alike in many ways, but also different. One of the most obvious differences is language, a topic of special appeal to young children, our most gifted language learners. Each book in the Count Your Way series introduces primary-grade children to an individual nation through that country's language for counting from 1 to 10. For example, in *Count Your Way Through Italy* by Jim Haskins and illustrated by Beth Wright, children learn that there is *uno* Mount Etna, the largest volcano in Europe; that *duo* brothers, Romulus and Remus, are characters in Roman mythology; and finally that *dieci* horses are chosen for special races held twice a year in Siena.

📖 OUTWARD DREAMS: BLACK INVENTORS AND THEIR INVENTIONS (1991)

Kirkus Reviews

SOURCE: A review of *Outward Dreams: Black Inventors and Their Inventions,* in *Kirkus Reviews,* Vol. LXIX, No. 1, January 1, 1991, p. 107.

A prolific author of nonfiction for young people surveys the role of African-American inventors. Bracketed between an opening chapter discussing the early history of patents, as well as the question of issuing them to slaves, and a concluding discussion of the place of the late 20th-century inventor is a chronological roundup of the more prominent figures, including Banneker, James Forten, Elijah McCoy, Madam C. J. Walker, and Carver. Each is presented in historical context, and Haskins carefully notes the significance of their achievements. He concludes with a useful list of inventors and inventions taken from the 1983 *Negro Almanac.*

The style here is pedestrian, but the content is useful and inspiring enough to overcome the workmanlike tone.

Bob Clark

SOURCE: A review of *Outward Dreams: Black Inventors and Their Inventions,* in *Science Books & Films,* Vol. 27, No. 5, June/July, 1991, p. 138.

Outward Dreams: Black Inventors and Their Inventions is a slim, yet solid volume which sketches the lives of several African American inventors and discusses their creations. The writer's fluid, compact style packs a lot of information in a short space. Not only does he discuss black inventors and their inventions, but he also provides background information on the patent office and fills in pertinent details of African American history, such as the fact that for many years slaves could not secure patents since they were not considered citizens. In addition, an appendix lists patents credited to black inventors from 1834 to 1987. Unfortunately, a typo in the appendix's title says that the listing only covers the years 1834 to 1900. Besides this minor, but annoying error, my only other complaint is that I wish his section on black scientists and inventors working today were longer. These contemporary figures seem to get shortchanged. Still, Haskins covers a lot of ground in fewer then 100 pages, and he should be commended for his effort. The real shame is that so much of the information delivered will be new to so many readers. Hopefully, with this book and others, the idea of black inventors and scientists will seem less exotic and more familiar in the days to come.

Kellie Flynn

SOURCE: A review of *Outward Dreams: Black Inventors*

and Their Inventions, in *Voice of Youth Advocates,* Vol. 14, No. 4, October, 1991, p. 260.

The accomplishments of black inventors are presented here within the clear context of general African-American history. After a cogent explanation of patents and patent law and why many blacks were denied patents, Haskins presents short chapters devoted to a single individual or two (Benjamin Banneker, Jan Matzeliger and Elijah McCoy, Lewis Latimer and Granville T. Woods, George Washington Carver, Percy Julian and Garrett Morgan) alternating with chapters containing references to a number of people ("Ingenuity and Conflict," "Ladies of Invention," "Modern Wizards"). These latter chapters not only present biographical information but also concentrate on providing historical context, thus bringing blacks' contributions to American industry and intellect into focus.

This book's success lies in the information it presents—including illustrations and photos of inventors and an appendix listing patents issued to blacks. It promises to be another much needed middle-grade report source, and can be used in tandem with Altman's *Extraordinary Black Americans.*

Melvin S. Kaufman

SOURCE: A review of *Outward Dreams: Black Inventors and Their Inventions,* in *Appraisal: Science Books for Young People,* Vol. 25, No. 1, Winter, 1992, p. 30.

Here is an extremely well-written, fact-filled book, which is nicely presented. Although one may argue about the inclusion of some of the people in this book about inventions, the majority of them are discussed in moderate detail. The pairing of some contemporary personalities provides the reader with additional food for thought.

On the negative side, technical terms and processes are not always clearly explained, and unattributed quotations occasionally appear. The interesting and useful appendix is marred by an incomplete inclusion of some of the post-1900 inventors discussed in the text.

But the vocabulary used and the concepts presented are generally good, the index is accurate, and a reasonable bibliography is included. On balance, then, the quality of the writing far outweighs the minor failings mentioned.

Candace V. Conklin

SOURCE: A review of *Outward Dreams: Black Inventors and Their Inventions,* in *Kliatt Young Adult Paperback Book Guide,* Vol. 26, Nos. 7-8, November, 1992, p. 28.

By 1913, between 800 and 1200 patents were granted to blacks, but very few of these inventors received proper credit for their achievements. The names of many black inventors have been lost, but many are belatedly being remembered. Haskins, author of the Count Your Way series and other books for children and adults, has collected the stories of more than a dozen black inventors. He chronicles not only their extraordinary successes but also the struggles they had to overcome to gain patents and recognition. He includes unknowns like Benjamin Walsh, who built the first clock made in the U.S., and Jan Matzeliger, whose plans for an automatic shoe-lacing machine were too complex for patent officials to understand, as well as the more famous, such as cosmetics manufacturer Madame C. J. Walker and George Washington Carver. Also included are a bibliography, a list of black inventors and their inventions, and many full-page photographs.

ONE MORE RIVER TO CROSS: THE STORIES OF TWELVE BLACK AMERICANS (1992)

Kirkus Reviews

SOURCE: A review of *One More River to Cross: The Stories of Twelve Black Americans,* in *Kirkus Reviews,* Vol. LIX, No. 24, December 15, 1991, p. 1591.

Biographies of eight men and four women who struggled against racial prejudice and other obstacles to distinguish themselves. The line-up includes Crispus Attucks, escaped slave and "the first American to die in the cause of American Revolution," who "had already declared his own independence"; Madam C. J. Walker, the first female self-made millionaire in this country; Ronald McNair, an astronaut who died aboard the *Challenger;* and Eddie Robinson of Grambling State University, the winningest football coach, pro or collegiate, in history. As usual, Haskins writes in a clear, deliberate way, smoothly integrating biographical facts, lessons received from parents and grandparents, and the significance of his subjects' achievements. He doesn't gloss over their imperfections—Malcolm X's criminal record, Matthew Henson's Eskimo offspring—but does present these men and women as models of courage and dignity. Some (Ralph Bunche, Charles Drew, Marian Anderson, Fannie Lou Hamer, Shirley Chisholm) should already be well represented in most biography collections, but Romare Bearden or Eddie Robinson may be less familiar. Haskins draws his information from printed sources and has appended a good, if largely adult-level, bibliography.

Publishers Weekly

SOURCE: A review of *One More River to Cross: The Stories of Twelve Black Americans,* in *Publishers Weekly,* Vol. 239, No. 2, January 6, 1992, p. 66.

In some ways, these dozen notables couldn't represent more diverse lives and more varied times, yet most of the figures have several commonalities: overcoming poverty and discrimination, avid self-education, drive to find a special niche. Haskins's subjects include Revolutionary patriot Crispus Attucks, co-discoverer of the North Pole Matthew Henson and Madam C. J. Walker, whose black hair preparations made her "the first American woman to earn a million dollars." Also profiled are scientists Charles Drew (the isolator of blood plasma) and Ron McNair (an astronaut who perished in the *Challenger* disaster); social and political activists Ralph Bunche, Fannie Lou Hamer, Shirley Chisholm and Malcolm X; and arts figures Romare Bearden and Marian Anderson. Each vignette manages to capture the individual's unique characteristics, particularly regarding his or her uphill battle: e.g., how Henson reacted to the disappointment of being left out of the glory, why Malcolm's adopted last name was X. Spiritedly informative.

Betsy Hearne

SOURCE: A review of *One More River to Cross: The Stories of Twelve Black Americans,* in *Bulletin of the Center for Children's Books,* Vol. 45, No. 8, April, 1992, p. 208.

This collective biography of a dozen African-American heroes is by turn genuinely lively and minimally efficient. The author exhibits enthusiastic detail for millionaire Madam C. J. Walker and explorer Matthew Henson, but slows down to generic descriptions of Charles Drew's scientific and Ralph Bunche's political contributions. The other subjects—Crispus Attucks, Marian Anderson, Romare Bearden, Fannie Lou Hamer, Eddie Robinson, Shirley Chisholm, Malcolm X, and Ronald McNair—fall somewhere in between, with a balance of readable, generalized portraits in the nature of a survey that may lead students to discover an interest and pursue it further (a bibliography of books and articles is appended). One example of Haskins' teasers is a reference to McNair's two-year doctoral study of Lasers. "Then a flood destroyed all his notes. But he spent only a short time worrying about the loss." What flood? How? When? Where? Equally puzzling is a reference to the death of Bunche's mother. On one page, she "felt much better in the new climate" On the next, "In spite of the healthier climate, Olive Bunche's health was getting worse." The problem here is not so much misinformation as a compression of facts that leads to oversimplification. At the same time, there are memorable lines that will startle black and white readers alike into realizing just how many African American "firsts" have been buried outside the memorial pages of official U.S. history books.

Helen E. Williams

SOURCE: A review of *One More River to Cross: The Stories of Twelve Black Americans,* in *School Library Journal,* Vol. 38, No. 4, April, 1992, p. 133.

One would hardly expect that retold, familiar, and abbreviated biographies could be captivating, but this book is hard to put down. Through clear and dramatic writing,

Haskins helps readers to understand the impact of institutional racism on the lives of 12 African-Americans. Included are Crispus Attucks, Madam C. J. Walker, Matthew Henson, Marian Anderson, Ralph Bunche, and Fannie Lou Hamer, all of whom made outstanding achievements in spite of tremendous prejudice. Each biographical segment is about 16 pages long and includes a full-page black-and-white photograph or reproduction. A valuable compilation for reading aloud, for independent recreational reading, and for reports.

Christine Prevetti

SOURCE: A review of *One More River to Cross: The Stories of Twelve Black Americans,* in *Voice of Youth Advocates,* Vol. 15, No. 1, April, 1992, pp. 56-7.

One More River to Cross is a very worthwhile, readable introduction to the lives of 12 African-American women and men of achievement. The deftly drawn profiles range from the Revolutionary War (Crispus Attucks) to the Challenger disaster (Ronald McNair). Included are Madam C. J. Walker, businesswoman; Matthew Henson, explorer; Marian Anderson, opera singer; Ralph Bunche, diplomat; Charles Drew, scientist; Romare Beardon, artist; Fannie Lou Hamer, civil rights leader; Eddie Robinson, football coach; Shirley Chisholm, Congresswoman; and Malcolm X, Black Muslim leader.

While individual biographies (several cited in the helpful bibliography) exist for several of the people, information is harder to find on others, outside of periodicals. Haskins melds the standard biographical data so coveted by students doing reports with well selected anecdotes, quotations, and personal details against a clearly presented historical and political backdrop. Although the backgrounds and fields of activity of his subjects bring home the diversity of the African-American experience, the sad constant is the way in which racism and discrimination inevitably transformed the lives of these men and women of color. Haskins objectively incorporates these individual struggles to provide some involving reading—inspirational but not cloying.

📖 *AGAINST ALL OPPOSITION: BLACK EXPLORERS IN AMERICA* (1992)

Kirkus Reviews

SOURCE: A review of *Against All Opposition: Black Explorers in America,* in *Kirkus Reviews,* Vol. LX, No. 1, January 1, 1992, pp. 52-3.

Enlightening if vaguely documented accounts of black explorers of the American continent, the North Pole, and space, emphasizing the barriers of race that they overcame.

After quoting early Arab documents to show that the emperor of ancient Mali (an accomplished African civili-zation) sent a large fleet across the Atlantic in the 13th century, Haskins speculates that this led to "negroid" features in some Mayan sculptures, similarities between African and American languages, and rumors that helped to inspire Columbus. "It is likely that Columbus had with him either black seamen or black slaves who had knowledge of the ocean and the lands beyond it." Other better-known explorers included here are Estevanico (explorer of New Mexico), Jean Point du Sable (founder of Chicago), York (a member of the Lewis and Clark expedition), James Beckwourth (a half-black mountain man), George Bush (the first American settler in Washington territory), Matthew Henson, and Guion Bluford (the first black astronaut). Most entries are exciting accounts with substantial quotations from early journals, but their power is somewhat diminished by the many extraneous details, while astronaut Ronald McNair's story seems tacked on as an afterthought. Still, the inspirational value balances any stylistic shortcomings.

Randy Meyer

SOURCE: A review of *Against All Opposition: Black Explorers in America,* in *Booklist,* Vol. 88, No. 12, February 15, 1992, p. 1097.

Haskins looks at a group of neglected contributors to history, courageous Africans and African Americans who stretched the physical and sometimes the sociological boundaries of their own worlds to create new ones. From the Maliens (perhaps two centuries before Columbus) to NASA's Ronald McNair, this collective biography covers a handful of explorers and describes the obstacles that stood in the way of their expeditions. Worthwhile though the subject may be, the book's scholarship is thin, and the text is poorly written. What's more, the absence of footnotes makes chapters on the earliest explorers seem padded with conjecture. Resources in this area may be limited, but Haskins makes little attempt to distinguish between fact and speculation. Still, with a dearth of material on black explorers, the short, accessibly written biographies may be useful in schools, particularly the profiles of the more recent explorers.

David A. Lindsey

SOURCE: A review of *Against All Opposition: Black Explorers in America,* in *School Library Journal,* Vol. 38, No. 6, June, 1992, p. 146.

Haskins hits the bullseye again, producing a readable, informative collective biography of black explorers and adventures. Students familiar with his previous work will note once more the crisp, flowing prose that incorporates telling details and cogent quotations, bringing his subjects to life and giving their toils meaning and relevance. In a non-didactic manner, he uses these people's lives to demonstrate that goals, ideals, and hard work can contribute to the expanding of the frontiers of all types of knowledge, regardless of race, gender, or nationality. Included are Estevanico, who searched for Cibola with Cabeza de Vaca; Jean Baptiste Point de Sable, founder of Chicago; York, who accompanied Lewis and Clark; mountain man James P. Beckwourth; Matthew Henson, co-discoverer of the North Pole; and astronauts Guion Stewart Bluford, Jr. and Ronald McNair. These explorers, as well as those of the present and future, says Haskins, " . . . go forth not for glory; rather, they have a vision of the world, a vision of discovery."

Diane Yankelevitz

SOURCE: A review of *Against All Opposition: Black Explorers in America,* in *Voice of Youth Advocates,* Vol. 15, No. 2, June, 1992, p. 125.

Black explorers faced not only the rigors of their environment but also the problems of prejudice, both during their lives and afterwards. Most were denied recognition for their achievements until recent times.

Explorers from the prosperous African country of Mali sailed in search of land beyond the ocean in the 1300s. Black men accompanied English, Spanish, and French explorers to the New World. Estevanico joined a 600-man expedition to the New World in the 1520s as a servant and later explored New Mexico and Arizona.

Many black men moved to the western territories, lived with the Indians, and became trappers and traders. A Haitian, Jean Point du Sable (1750-1818) founded Chicago. York, a slave of William Clark, accompanied his master on the Lewis and Clark Expedition in 1805-6. James P. Beckwourth (1798-1867) discovered a pass through the Sierra Nevada mountains—Beckwourth Pass northwest of Reno, Nevada. George W. Bush went west to Oregon in 1844 from Missouri. Many went to Florida, lived with the Seminole Indians, and were later forced to resettle in Oklahoma.

Also included are Matthew Henson (1866-1955), a co-discoverer of the North Pole in 1909, and astronauts Ronald McNair (1950-1986) and Guion Stewart Bluford, Jr. (1942-). Bluford earned a PhD in aerospace engineering in spite of being told by his high school counselors that he wasn't college material.

The writing style is encyclopedic, but not difficult. The material presented is covered in detail; however, relatively few lives are scrutinized. While the book will be helpful for reports, it's not very interesting general reading. It does give an overview of the diversity of exploration by black men.

AMAZING GRACE: THE STORY BEHIND THE SONG (1992)

Kirkus Reviews

SOURCE: A review of *Amazing Grace: The Story Behind the Song,* in *Kirkus Reviews,* Vol. LX, No. 2, January 15, 1992, p. 115.

The popular hymn whose origins are recounted here is *not* a folk song, but was written by an English minister who distilled his own grim experiences to pen these compellingly consoling verses. Son of a sea captain whose icy discipline made him a rebel with cause, John Newton (1725-1807) tried, unsuccessfully at first, to hold onto the religion instilled by his dead mother. He became a slave trader and, in part because an early employer had treated Newton himself like a slave, was an unusually compassionate member of what was then an acceptable calling. His faith restored after a miraculous response to prayers in a violent storm, Newton still continued as a slaver for years before taking a customs post and then eventually becoming a minister. Still later, he and the poet William Cowper wrote the *Olney Hymns,* including "Amazing Grace."

Haskins's narrative is so simply written that it's almost abrupt, but it's fascinating not only as an outline of an extraordinary spiritual journey but as a glimpse of the period. He includes a simple arrangement for the melody and cleverly uses the verses to introduce chapters, concluding with some recently added lines and mention of the song's popularity in black churches since the 1800's and in contemporary concerts. Fine for its intended level, a book that leaves the reader wanting to know more about this unique man.

Marilyn Long Graham

SOURCE: A review of *Amazing Grace: The Story Behind the Song,* in *School Library Journal,* Vol. 38, No. 4, April, 1992, p. 133.

A different verse of this famous hymn begins each chapter as Haskins skillfully reveals its origins. In the process, readers learn about the life of the composer, John Newton, who was once a slave trader. A small slice of history unfolds, along with the profound changes that made Newton finally speak out against slavery and moved him to share, in song, his faith in God. The writing is fluid and interesting; the archival photographs and full-color reproductions are clear and relevant. A unique and uplifting story.

Ilene Cooper

SOURCE: A review of *Amazing Grace: The Story Behind the Song,* in *Booklist,* Vol. 89, No. 5, November 1, 1992, pp. 506, 508.

"Amazing Grace" is a song familiar to many young people, either through their church or simply through popular recordings. Here, Haskins profiles the man behind the song, John Newton, a British slave trader turned minister who became an ardent abolitionist. The author makes

Newton's story compelling, especially his realization of the injustice of slavery. . . .

The subject may be slightly esoteric, but history and music classes should find uses for Haskins' account. Though each chapter begins with four lines of the song, nowhere in the book are the complete lyrics given together—amazing.

THE DAY MARTIN LUTHER KING, JR., WAS SHOT: A PHOTO HISTORY OF THE CIVIL RIGHTS MOVEMENT (1992)

Hazel Rochman

SOURCE: A review of *The Day Martin Luther King, Jr., Was Shot: A Photo History of the Civil Rights Movement,* in *Booklist,* Vol. 88, No. 11, February 1, 1992, p. 1024.

The title is only meant to grab attention: this is a photo history of the African American struggle from the time of slavery through today. Attractively designed on good paper with large clear print and several stirring pictures on every page, this inexpensive, oversize, well-bound paperback is an exceptionally good buy for libraries. The style is clear and direct, and the history is organized into two- to four-page chapters, beginning with the slaveship revolts and going on with the abolitionist movement, the Underground Railroad, Jim Crow, and the freedom marches, up to current problems and gains. The format encourages browsing, with photos and thumbnail biographies of the important leaders from Sojourner Truth and W. E. B. Du Bois to King and Malcolm X. There are no notes, and the bibliography includes some slight material and doesn't include any adult references, not even photo essays like this one. There's a long detailed chronology and an index for quick reference.

Eunice Weech

SOURCE: A review of *The Day Martin Luther King, Jr., Was Shot: A Photo History of the Civil Rights Movement,* in *School Library Journal,* Vol. 38, No. 5, May, 1992, p. 122.

A readable and attractive photo essay recounting the struggle for civil rights in the U.S. Haskins's clearly written text and archival black-and-white photographs trace the long, hard road to equal rights for African-Americans from the earliest days of the slave trade; through the desegregation battles; to *The Day Martin Luther King, Jr., Was Shot,* which Haskins cites as the "end of the civil rights era." Brief accounts of brave individuals, both black and white, are included: abolitionists; students who integrated Central High School in Little Rock in 1957; demonstrators who sat-in at a lunch counter in Greensboro in 1960; civil right workers who were murdered in Mississippi in 1964; and many, many more. This excellent overview can be read from cover to cover and may lead readers to more detailed texts such as Altman's *Extraordinary Black Americans from Colonial to Contemporary Times* (1989) and Hornsby's *Chronology of African American History* (1991).

Frances Bradburn

SOURCE: A review of *The Day Martin Luther King, Jr., Was Shot: A Photo History of the Civil Rights Movement,* in *Wilson Library Bulletin,* Vol. 67, No. 2, October, 1992, p. 85.

The Day Martin Luther King, Jr., Was Shot: A Photo History of the Civil Rights Movement by Jim Haskins is [a] book that has the potential to trigger middle readers to conduct further research into this period of American history. While the main title may mislead young readers, the subtitle is accurate; the photographs and illustrations are the book's strength. An easy-to-read text amplifies inserts of newspapers' front pages; old black-and-white illustrations; and original photographs of the history of African-Americans, from their arrival in this country as slaves, through the Civil War and Reconstruction, during the struggles of the 1950s and 1960s and King's subsequent death, to the present day. While the text is limited, it fairly adequately places the illustrations and photographs in perspective on a level and in a format that will appeal to middle readers. And it does move young people toward an understanding of where we have been as a nation in this struggle for equal right. . . . [This] work stresses the heroes of the movement, their courage, vision, and example of hope, perseverance, and determination.

I AM SOMEBODY! A BIOGRAPHY OF JESSE JACKSON (1992)

Kirkus Reviews

SOURCE: A review of *I Am Somebody! A Biography of Jesse Jackson,* in *Kirkus Reviews,* Vol. LX, No. 4, February 15, 1992, p. 255.

In a complete but plodding account of his life in politics, a well-known African-American author explains Jackson's decision not to run for President in 1992. While less colorfully written and less detailed than Jakoubek's *Jesse Jackson* (1991), Haskins's book does give more historical background and a better sense of overall trends. Both strongly emphasize the early support of Jackson's family and demonstrate his strength in overcoming many race-based adversities. Neither hesitates to report controversy, particularly concerning Jackson's actions at the time of Martin Luther King's assassination. Both are authoritative and mildly sympathetic. On balance, Jakoubek's gripping use of language will more effectively involve general readers; Haskins just doesn't convey Jackson's "heart" appeal as well.

Sheilamae O'Hara

SOURCE: A review of *I Am Somebody! A Biography of Jesse Jackson,* in *Booklist,* Vol. 88, No. 21, July, 1992, p. 1930.

Haskins makes no attempt to be an objective biographer of Jesse Jackson. He speaks of the late Mayor Daley's "cronies" and "machine" while mentioning Jackson's "followers" and his work with "the ordinary people—the voters." Nonetheless, Haskins does not let his bias blind him to his subject's faults. The author presents a man of intelligence, drive, compassion, and considerable oratorical skill who seeks the limelight, fails to inform colleagues of his plans, and then is hurt by their lack of enthusiasm and is not above bending the truth, as he did in the aftermath of the assassination of Dr. Martin Luther King, Jr. Haskins presents both the public and private Jackson as a man with flaws but a dynamic and charismatic leader in spite of them.

Jeanette Lambert

SOURCE: A review of *I Am Somebody! A Biography of Jesse Jackson,* in *School Library Journal,* Vol. 38, No. 8, August, 1992, pp. 181-82.

An incisive biography that relates its subject's strengths and flaws in a balanced manner. Haskins's title is taken from one of Jackson's speeches in which he emphasized the importance of self-worth despite one's social or economic circumstances. The author uses this concept to describe Jackson's underprivileged childhood and adolescence, and illustrates how, through hard work and determination, he was able to excel in sports and academics and to win a college scholarship. Haskins objectively examines Jackson's rise to international prominence and his impact as a civil rights spokesperson, politician, humanitarian, and social crusader.

This title fulfills the need for current and unbiased information about Jackson.

Alice M. Johns

SOURCE: A review of *I Am Somebody! A Biography of Jesse Jackson,* in *Voice of Youth Advocates,* Vol. 15, No. 3, August, 1992, p. 188.

Jesse Jackson was born October 8, 1941; son of Helen Burns—18 years old and still in high school—and her neighbor Noah Robinson—a cotton grader, a deacon in the Springfield Baptist Church of Greenville, S.C., and a married man. The child was acknowledged and provided for by his father. He acquired the father who helped raise him and adopted him at age 16 when his mother married Charles Henry Jackson in 1943. Helen and Charles nurtured the energetic, inquisitive child. Their involvement in the Longbranch Baptist Church helped give religion an important focus to Jesse's life.

Haskins' biography begins with a brief history of the Civil Rights Movement in the United States from the end of the Civil War to the 1940s, and a more detailed chronology after Jesse Jackson became involved in the 1960s. The reader is led through the struggles of the 1960s with the big gains for black Americans often followed by a return to the conditions thought to be changed. Struggle, hard work, encouragement to his people seemed to place Jesse Jackson where things were happening that would make a difference.

The Rev. Jesse Jackson completed college at Greenville Agricultural and Technical College and enrolled in Chicago Theological Seminary in 1967. He dropped out in the spring of 1968, and was ordained a minister by Rev. C. L. Franklin and Rev. Clay Evans in June, 1968.

This book presents many facts about Jackson and his family. It details the political progress that propelled him to more power in the process because he helped people to participate in full citizenship. Jesse Jackson believes each person is "somebody"; believing helped him find victory in the process, even though his goals and dreams have not always been reached.

THURGOOD MARSHALL: A LIFE FOR JUSTICE (1992)

Karen Hutt

SOURCE: A review of *Thurgood Marshall: A Life for Justice,* in *Booklist,* Vol. 88, No. 21, July, 1992, p. 1939.

Thurgood Marshall, the first African American Supreme Court justice, devoted his life to fighting racism and segregation through the U.S. legal system. Haskins' portrait shows a man unwavering in his commitment to effect change, so devoted to his work that he often collapsed from exhaustion. The account also conveys the risks that were ever-present for the justice, the precautions taken to ensure his personal safety, and the sacrifices Marshall continually made. Young readers will find the account both readable and inspiring and appreciate the explanations of unfamiliar terms and concepts. The historical, social, and political perspective Haskins incorporates makes the work an illuminating, in-depth portrait of a courageous leader as well as an excellent resource for study of the civil rights movement. Though the lack of documentation will frustrate researchers, an extensive bibliography is appended.

Kirkus Reviews

SOURCE: A review of *Thurgood Marshall: A Life for Justice,* in *Kirkus Reviews,* Vol. LX, No. 13, July 1, 1992, p. 848.

Unlike Martin Luther King, Jr. and others, Marshall devotedly pursued civil rights for African Americans through legal channels. Though the style of this sympathetic account is undistinguished, Haskins successfully establishes the social context of Marshall's career, presenting a full outline of major influences and political developments that affected him, as well as details of his personal life. Most enlightening are chapters explaining the strong effect that Marshall's family and the schools he attended had on his attitudes; one doesn't usually think of an eventual Supreme Court justice as a youthful "cut-up." Occasionally, Haskins describes Marshall's thoughts and feelings without clear attribution ("He wondered why there were so many amendments to the Constitution about equal rights when he knew very well that black people did not enjoy equal rights in America"), but he does give credit for direct quotes. Coverage continues through Marshall's retirement, though it doesn't include his pungent comments on his successor.

Publishers Weekly

SOURCE: A review of *Thurgood Marshall: A Life for Justice,* in *Publishers Weekly,* Vol. 239, Nos. 32-33, July 20, 1992, p. 252.

This energetic portrait of the venerable jurist is also an overview of civil rights advances since 1908, the year of Thurgood Marshall's birth. With an eye for telling detail, Haskins describes Marshall's Harlem childhood (signs posted in the neighborhood read, "This part of 135th Street guaranteed against Negro invasions"), education and illustrious career, from serving as chief counsel for the NAACP to becoming the first black justice on the Supreme Court in 1967. Haskins identifies Marshall's involvement with landmark cases like *Brown v. The Board of Education,* also explaining the significance of the cases themselves and the workings of the legal system. At the same time that he injects a sense of Marshall's no-nonsense, down-to-earth character and well-known wit ("Isn't it nice that nobody cares which twenty-three hours of the day I work?"), he also kindles readers' wrath at racial inequality and fosters a genuine appreciation of Marshall's achievements. By the end of this dextrous biography, readers will share Haskins's obvious sadness at Marshall's 1991 retirement from the bench.

Zena Sutherland

SOURCE: A review of *Thurgood Marshall: A Life for Justice,* in *Bulletin of the Center for Children's Books,* Vol. 45, No. 11, July-August, 1992, p. 296.

Although many pages seem heavily filled with almost-solid paragraphs of print, the vitality and ebullience of the subject and the drama of his career make this an exciting story of one man's dedication and of the civil rights struggle in which he played so large a part. Thurgood Marshall may be remembered in the future as a brilliant figure in the landmark *Brown vs. Board of Education of Topeka* and as the first black man to be appointed to the Supreme Court, but the details of his education

and his legal career are also impressive, and Haskins (despite an occasional stylistic lapse) has made a substantial contribution in compiling this informative biography.

Mary Mueller

SOURCE: A review of *Thurgood Marshall: A Life for Justice,* in *School Library Journal,* Vol. 38, No. 8, August, 1992, p. 182.

Haskins emphasizes Marshall's enormous contributions to the civil rights movement and his unending commitment to the achievement of racial and social justice. He shows how his subject developed a deep faith in the constitution and the law and how he learned to use both of them to make lasting changes. He covers the many cases Marshall argued and won and the dangers he faced as he acted as point man for the NAACP as it challenged and eventually dismantled the legal underpinnings of segregation. One real strength is the discussion of the difference between Marshall's constitutional tactics and those used by the Direct Actions Civil Rights Movement, led by Martin Luther King, Jr. The author includes information about Marshall the person, and uses plenty of quotes and anecdotes to bring him to life. This is similar to Aldred's *Thurgood Marshall* (1990), which has almost exactly the same information, interpretations, and conclusions. Thus, libraries that already have it (and the very good video that accompanies it) might not need this one. Haskins's book, however, is slightly easier to read and understand, making it a good choice for libraries that serve younger readers.

Alice Evans Handy

SOURCE: A review of *Thurgood Marshall,* in *The Book Report,* Vol. 11, No. 4, January-February, 1993, p. 52.

This biography portrays the courage and influence of Thurgood Marshall, who in 1991 retired as the first African-American Justice of the Supreme Court. Not only is Haskins an accomplished biographer whose admiration for Marshall lends enthusiasm to the book, he also shows an ability to summarize history in understandable capsules. The reader learns of Marshall's childhood in Baltimore and New York (where he was forced to memorize the Constitution as a school punishment), his education at Lincoln University and law school at Howard University, his exciting days as a civil rights lawyer for the NAACP (culminating in *Brown v. the Board of Education,* which prohibited [segregation in schools]), his service as an appeals court judge and Solicitor General, and finally his distinguished career on the Supreme Court. Marshall is portrayed as a down-to-earth person—likeable, patient, hard-working and fun-loving. Marshall has said he will not write his autobiography, which makes this title especially valuable. The book is moderately difficult because of the complexity of the issues, but the author does not assume the reader has a background in American constitutional or political history. His explanation of events and historical figures is fairly objective, and, while he relates many amusing anecdotes, he also includes the complex and controversial details of Marshall's career. Do what you have to do to lead students and teachers to this excellent biography.

Marian Rafal

SOURCE: A review of *Thurgood Marshall: A Life for Justice,* in *Voice of Youth Advocates,* Vol. 16, No. 2, June, 1993, pp. 112-13.

Thurgood Marshall was born in an America of lynchings, Jim Crow, segregation and discrimination. He was born into a family which encouraged him to push for what was right. In this pushing, Thurgood Marshall changed our country. Believing that "the keys to equality for black people were present in the Constitution" Marshall worked tirelessly to challenge both custom and law. Haskins presents a vivid account of Marshall's life, first as Howard University law student, later as an NAACP attorney, solicitor general of the United States, and finally as the first African American justice of the Supreme Court. Many of Marshall's pivotal civil rights cases are described here. *Morgan v. Virginia* determined that interstate buses could not be segregated. The 1954 landmark *Brown v. Board of Education* decision determined that separate is not equal.

Discussed too are the differences within the civil rights movement itself. Marshall believed that change should come through constitutional means and not necessarily by the use of nonviolent protest favored by Martin Luther King, Jr. This is an accessible, well-written biography of one of the most important figures of the twentieth century. This has less of a textbook quality than Aldred's *Thurgood Marshall* in the *Black Americans of Achievement* series although the lack of photographs may turn off some of the younger readers.

Ann Wagner Ratliff

SOURCE: A review of *Thurgood Marshall: A Life for Justice,* in *Social Education,* Vol. 58, No. 5, September, 1994, pp. 318-19.

Haskin's biography, ***Thurgood Marshall: A Life for Justice*** is a portrait of the life and times of one of America's most outstanding and courageous civil rights leaders. In a highly readable style, Haskins has weaved a complex tapestry of one man's life, hopes, frustrations, and pain, by describing the complicated struggle that compelled Marshall to champion the rights of African Americans.

Marshall, who was born in 1908, was impacted by the racism, segregation, lynching, and injustices of the turbulent era of the 40s, 50s, and 60s. As a backdrop, it was this setting that provided Marshall with the obsessive desire to challenge the "separate but equal" status of America.

From his early years as a young lawyer, Marshall was

committed to righting the wrongs of a racist society that sought to disenfranchise African Americans. As a visionary, he challenged the inequalities of the legal system, which perpetuated second-class citizenship in America's educational systems, public accommodations and other aspects of American society. This compelling story keeps the reader engaged in case after case, following Marshall's victories in numerous civil rights battles and his destruction of barriers that segregated African Americans and denied them equality. Climaxing in the *Brown v Board of Education* decision, Marshall influenced much of today's civil rights legislation. From assuming the office of Solicitor General to becoming the first African American Supreme Court justice, Marshall's uncompromising valor and devotion to equal justice was revolutionary for America.

This book is certainly a worthy contribution to African American and American history. If the students who read this book have only a meager knowledge of its subject and times, they will learn a great deal more from it than is perhaps expected. Students who are more familiar with African American history will appreciate the work for its in-depth portraiture of Thurgood Marshall.

GET ON BOARD: THE STORY OF THE UNDERGROUND RAILROAD (1993)

Publishers Weekly

SOURCE: A review of *Get on Board: The Story of the Underground Railroad,* in *Publishers Weekly,* Vol. 239, No. 52, November 30, 1992, p. 57.

Weaving together poignant personal stories and carefully researched historical data, Haskins has produced a stirring account of the founding and the workings of the Underground Railroad. Excerpts from the journals and letters of "conductors" and "stationmasters" who helped countless slaves escape to freedom bring authenticity and immediacy to this saga. Focusing on the historically understated contributions of African Americans, Haskins tells of the many unsung heroes who ignored legislation and risked an incalculable amount to provide food, shelter and money to fugitives whom they were not likely to see ever again. Also documented is the arduous work of such celebrated figures as former slaves Frederick Douglass and Harriet Tubman. Haskins provides many intriguing details about the operation of the Underground Railroad, noting how the "passengers" used the North Star to navigate their way; describing the beacons and passwords that were used to identify stations; and recounting the inventive ways in which runaway slaves were hidden or disguised on their journey North. The result is a dramatic, heart-rending chronicle that underscores both the horrors of slavery and the enormous courage of many individuals.

Kirkus Reviews

SOURCE: A review of *Get on Board: The Story of the*

Underground Railroad, in *Kirkus Reviews,* Vol. LXI, No. 1, January 1, 1993, pp. 60-1.

The frequently told story of the Underground Railroad has, claims Haskins, all too often "played up the extent of its organization and the efforts of whites, especially Quakers, and played down the less organized efforts of slaves, free blacks and other whites." Here, he focuses more on people than process in his account of the antislavery movement, the increasingly harsh measures against fugitives in the 19th century, and the courageous work of several stationmasters and conductors dedicated to helping escapees; coded songs and other subterfuges designed to spread the word are also discussed. Haskins devotes a chapter to Harriet Tubman, one to John Brown (author of an important fugitive slave narrative), and another to some "passengers" who succeeded in escaping largely on their own, and concludes with the 13th Amendment and the Railroad's transmutation to legendary status. Though this brief account helps set the record straight, its dry, didactic prose limits appeal, especially for collections that already own Shaaron Cosner's *Underground Railroad* (1991).

Hazel Rochman

SOURCE: A review of *Get on Board: The Story of the Underground Railroad,* in *Booklist,* Vol. 89, No. 12, February 15, 1993, p. 1046.

The tracks and stations, conductors and stationmasters, signs and signals, and, above all, the passengers on the Underground Railroad make up Haskins' subject. He points out that because the slave escape network had to be so secret, and because so few written records were kept, most names have been lost and the role of blacks—both those who escaped and those who helped others—has been understated. But hundreds of their stories have survived, and as in Hamilton's *Many Thousand Gone,* the best parts of this book draw on actual slave narratives as well as on general history. Haskins describes the brutal conditions slaves escaped from, even while he focuses on their courage. There's the letter from fugitive slave Jarmain Wesley Loguen to his ex-owner who'd said she'd raised him like her own child: "Woman did you raise your own children for the market? Did you raise them for the whipping post?" The general discussion is sometimes pedestrian, and there's some repetition, as though all the chapters are not quite co-ordinated; but this is dramatic material both for curricular use and for personal reading. The fascinating (but too brief) chapter on the sorrow songs will set kids searching for more. There are no source notes, but Haskins includes a useful time line and an excellent bibliography.

Betsy Hearne

SOURCE: A review of *Get on Board: The Story of the Underground Railroad,* in *Bulletin of the Center for Children's Books,* Vol. 46, No. 7, March, 1993, p. 213.

Like Virginia Hamilton's more general history of slavery

. . . [*Many Thousand Gone*] Haskins' book on the Underground Railroad will hold readers' attention by the sheer drama of the subject, which Haskins has organized and presented with a fine balance between background information and human interest detail. Although there is some factual overlap in the two titles, Haskins' book is geared toward older readers and generally includes more extensive information within his more selective scope. Both sources, for instance, tell the story of Eliza, the slave who escaped across ice floes in the Ohio River, but from Haskins we also learn that she settled happily in Canada with her daughter and was visited by the Quaker couple who helped them through Indiana. In fact, Hamilton's and Haskins' books complement each other: Hamilton tells us that the carpenter who helped Henry Brown mail himself to freedom tried the same trick unsuccessfully with two more slaves and was imprisoned; Haskins tell us that he was a white man, which adds another dimension to the situation. Even more important is the way the two books reinforce each other: Hamilton's story about Jackson, the Alabama slave who disguises himself as his light-skinned wife's maid, finds a rich counterpart in Haskins' story of Ellen Craft, a lightskinned Georgia slave who poses as a planter traveling by steamer with her "slave"—in truth, her husband. Haskins has synthesized a massive amount of information here and has argued forcefully for the often downplayed role that African-Americans played in their own escape networks.

 *I HAVE A DREAM: THE LIFE AND WORDS OF MARTIN LUTHER KING, JR.* (1993)

Janice Del Negro

SOURCE: A review of *I Have a Dream: The Life and Words of Martin Luther King, Jr.,* in *Booklist,* Vol. 89, No. 12, February 15, 1993, p. 1057.

This well-researched biography of Dr. Martin Luther King, Jr., is reinforced and supported by extensive excerpts from his writings and speeches. A straightforward and perceptive text presents people and incidents that shaped the direction of King's life: his parents, his upbringing, and his encounters with the racism he fought until his death. The nicely bound, oversize book boasts an attractive, approachable layout. The excerpts from letters, sermons, speeches, and writings are boxed with gray backgrounds, and several of the many black-and-white photographs are captioned with quotes from King. All quotations are sourced, and Haskins includes a time line of important events in King's life as well as suggestions for further reading.

Jeanette Lambert

SOURCE: A review of *I Have a Dream: The Life and Words of Martin Luther King, Jr.,* in *School Library Journal,* Vol. 39, No. 6, June, 1993, p. 138.

An outstanding book that examines King's life and

achievements. Haskins focuses on the impact of the civil rights movement and the beliefs that King so eloquently espoused. Information about his family, schooling, and civil-rights activities are conveyed in a lively and engaging manner. Inserted at various points throughout the text are excerpts from speeches, letters, or commentaries. They are positioned in gray boxes, and enable readers to see King's perspective on a particular course of action. The many black-and-white photographs are attractively arranged and often compelling. In addition to photographs directly related to King, there are others that convey the mood of the country struggling to come to terms with the yoke of segregation. A touching introduction by Rosa Parks and concluding source notes supplement the book. All in all, this biography provides a balanced portrait of Dr. King, and it clearly portrays his impact on history.

Bette D. Ammon

SOURCE: A review of *I Have a Dream: The Life and Words of Martin Luther King, Jr.,* in *Voice of Youth Advocates,* Vol. 16, No. 2, June, 1993, p. 112.

This photobiography (with an introduction by Rosa Parks) briefly outlines Martin Luther King Jr.'s childhood and upbringing in middle class Atlanta. Without going into too much detail, Haskins describes King's superlative education which began early on—compliments of his educated parents and their extensive home library. Segregation and racism were facts of life from the beginning for King and he grew up as the civil rights movement in the South became more and more intense. While in theology school, King became convinced that following the Mahatma Gandhi's example of nonviolent persistence and resistance was the best way to effect change. King was committed to promoting racial justice and fighting oppression through nonviolence. As he became more involved in the civil rights movement and his own ministry, King discovered his great power as an orator and writer.

King's own words carry much of this history which includes extensive excerpts from King's sermons and speeches. The large format is enhanced by the prolific use of high quality black-and-white photographs, a significant improvement over past juvenile biographies of King primarily illustrated by drawings. Prolific writer Haskins has long been a major contributor of African American literature for children and young adults. This is a good beginning for a *non-critical* study of King and his life since Haskins avoids mentioning any controversy surrounding King. However, the succinct writing, interesting photographs, and fine layout and design guarantee an audience and make this an important purchase for all collections.

📖 *THE MARCH ON WASHINGTON* (1993)

Sheilamae O'Hara

SOURCE: A review of *The March on Washington,* in *Booklist,* Vol. 89, No. 18, May 15, 1993, p. 1691.

In 1963, 250,000 people marched from the Washington Monument to the Lincoln Memorial in Washington, D.C., in support of racial equality and job opportunity. This book tells the story of all that went into organizing that incredible gathering, from the suggestion first proposed in 1941 by A. Philip Randolph, through the uneasy coalition that was formed from disparate civil rights groups, through the jockeying for position and power, the fundraising, the consciousness-raising, the complex logistical problems, the wonder of the day itself with its "I have a dream" speech, to the cleaning up of the litter and the dismantling of the sound equipment. Haskins deals not only with the event, but also with the men (no women were in power positions) who organized it and the politicians who reacted to it. Whitney Young, Bayard Rustin, Martin Luther King, Jr., and Ray Wilkins are among the black leaders who are profiled. The final chapter, which quotes some of the press stories describing the orderliness, dignity, and friendliness of the crowd on that day, also mentions the assassinations of John and Robert Kennedy, Martin Luther King, Jr., and Malcolm X within the next five years. Clear black-and-white photographs are plentiful and well placed. A bibliography and chronology add to the book's reference value, but the narrative is eminently readable as a story of what may be regarded as one of the great days in American history.

Ellen Fader

SOURCE: A review of *The March on Washington,* in *The Horn Book Magazine,* Vol. LXIX, No. 4, July-August, 1993, pp. 477-78.

Haskins provides a lucid, in-depth, and moving study of the 1963 March on Washington for jobs and freedom. He begins with a detailed recounting of the historical contributions of A. Philip Randolph, the organizer of the Brotherhood of Sleeping Car Porters, and goes on to explore the contributions of the major civil-rights leaders and organizations of the 1950s and 1960s. Intriguing details about the actual logistics of organizing the march—such as transportation, food, and sanitary facilities for the more than 250,000 protesters—are provided. Excerpts from some of the most moving and well-received speeches—such as those by Martin Luther King, Jr., and John Lewis, the national chairman of the Student Nonviolent Coordinating Committee—give readers a glimpse into the emotional power of the organizers. The book has an open and attractive appearance, enhanced by a smattering of well-chosen photographs that help put faces to the many personalities involved. A list of "Important Dates," from 1909 to 1990, gives order to the text, which at times unfortunately departs from its chronological arrangement. There is also a minor discrepancy in dates concerning the bombing of the Sixteenth Street Baptist Church in Birmingham in which four teenage girls were killed. These minor faults do not detract from the overall quality of this excellent survey, which gives background and information not easily found in other books for young readers. . . .

Judy Silverman

SOURCE: A review of *The March on Washington*, in *Voice of Youth Advocates,* Vol. 16, No. 3, August, 1993, p. 177.

This book is a fantastic look at a time that is too often dismissed as "ancient history" by today's young people. Beginning with the introduction by James Farmer, the reader is pulled into a story that still hasn't ended. History was made on August 23, 1963, when 250,000 people marched on Washington to demand the change in racial policies, both official and non-official, that had been promised for over twenty years. Black and white Americans descended on the capital in the largest demonstration for human rights in U.S. history.

Demonstrations have become so common now that we forget how incredible it seemed then. Leaders of the civil rights community from all sides of the political spectrum presented a united front in dealing with this idea of equality. The demonstration was totally non-violent (only three arrests made), and the aim of the march, to "get Americans to do more than 'tut-tut' on the plight of Little Rock (Arkansas) school children" made a major impact on the entire country. The march on Washington marked the end of the nonviolent movement, when the new, young leaders of the civil rights movement felt the time had come for a new way of dealing with the same old problems. James Haskins manages to make this history come very much alive.

📖 *BLACK EAGLES: AFRICAN AMERICANS IN AVIATION* (1995)

Colleen Macklin

SOURCE: A review of *Black Eagles: African Americans in Aviation*, in *Voice of Youth Advocates,* Vol. 18, No. 3, August, 1995, p. 182.

Haskins continues to educate and enlighten young adults with his latest collection of profiles of African Americans in aviation. This collection of historical sketches begins with the earliest attempts to fly. Eugene Bullard was an African American who was a pioneer in his attempts to use flight as an effective military strategy. Unfortunately, he had to travel and live in France in order for his ideas to be used by military leaders. When he returned to America, the only job that he was able to get was elevator operator! Over and over again, Haskins not only provides young readers with compelling portraits of courageous men and women, but reminds these same readers of the racial obstacles and road blocks that often stopped these aviators from reaching their full potential. Benjamin O. Davis became the first African American to graduate from West Point in the twentieth century. Unfortunately, he spent that four years of his life hearing statements such as, "it was not 'logical' for a Black officer to command White troops." All of these aviators had one thing in common: they were not going to give up their dreams and aspirations because of racial bias. These are not so much stories of aviators as they are stories of perseverance and courage. Haskins's book includes numerous photos and the cover design is appealing, six attractive photos of the aviators that are included in the book. This is a well designed and well written book.

Additional coverage of Haskins's life and career is contained in the following sources published by Gale Research: *Authors and Artists for Young Adults,* Vol. 14, *Contemporary Authors New Revision Series,* Vol. 25; *Major Authors and Illustrators for Children and Young Adults*; *Something about the Author,* Vols. 9, 69; and *Something about the Author Autobiography Series,* Vol. 4.

Rudyard Kipling

1865-1936

(Full name Joseph Rudyard Kipling) English author of fiction and poetry.

Major works include *The Jungle Book* (1894), *The Second Jungle Book* (1895), *"Captains Courageous": A Story of the Grand Banks* (1897), *Stalky and Co.* (1899), *Kim* (1901), *Just So Stories for Little Children* (1902).

Major works about the author include *Something of Myself for My Friends Known and Unknown* (by Kipling, 1937), *The Life of Rudyard Kipling* (by Charles E. Carrington, 1956), *Rudyard Kipling* (by Frederick Birkenhead, 1978).

The following entry presents criticism on *The Jungle Book* and *The Second Jungle Book.*

INTRODUCTION

Regarded among the finest short story writers in world literature, Kipling is praised as a brilliant literary stylist whose rich, rhythmic prose and creative use of language have delighted generations of readers around the globe. He is best known to modern audiences for his masterful, widely read stories for children, many of which are collected in the two *Jungle Books* and in *Just So Stories for Little Children.* In the most popular of the *Jungle Book* tales, Kipling relates the experiences of Mowgli, a boy abandoned by his parents and raised by wolves to become master of the jungle. Although bearing similarities to other anthropomorphic fiction, Kipling's work was original in its representation of a man living among animals, a conception which spawned numerous derivative tales, among the most popular of which were Edgar Rice Burroughs's *Tarzan* stories. In addition, Kipling portrayed his animal characters with simplicity, humor, and dignity, avoiding much of the patronizing tone associated with many such stories while detailing personalities that are considered ingeniously conceived and remarkably fitting. Demonstrating an exceptional understanding of his young audience and their taste for adventure, drama, and high emotion, Kipling fashioned his *Jungle Book* tales around protagonists who often display cunning skills, stalwart courage, and wise leadership. William Blackburn has written: "Kipling is one of the most influential creators of modern literature for children. Unlike many of his models and contemporaries, he brought a true seriousness to the production of children's literature, a seriousness reflected in his painstaking research and craftsmanship, in the richness and sophistication of his language, and most remarkably, in the seriousness of his subject matter itself."

Biographical Information

Kipling spent the first six years of his life in India, the pampered son of John Lockwood Kipling, an artist and designer who was the principal of a new school of art in Bombay. After the sudden death of Rudyard's infant brother, Kipling's parents sent the young boy and his sister to England to protect them from the intense heat and disease of India. For five years Kipling lived with unsympathetic guardians in a foster home in Southsea that he later called the "House of Desolation"; at the age of twelve, he was sent to the United Services School in Devon. Kipling was relatively happy at this boarding school and his literary talents flourished. His first book, *Schoolboy Lyrics,* a collection of poems written during this period, was published privately by his parents in 1881. Shortly before his seventeenth birthday, Kipling returned to India, working in Lahore as a reporter for *The Civil and Military Gazette* and later in Allahabad for *The Pioneer.* He conducted interviews with Indians of various castes, English soldiers, and others for his newspaper articles, recording vivid impressions of nineteenth-century India. Later, this copious information about dialects, class distinctions, and characteristics of the native culture, as well as Kipling's observations of the British living in India, were incorporated into the author's fictional writings. Kipling's *Departmental Ditties and Other Verses,* a volume of poems originally written as filler for his newspaper columns, was published in 1886. The book was followed two years later by an early collection of stories, *Plain Tales from the Hills* (1888).

Kipling's poetry and stories, lauded for their colorful, insightful portraits of India, brought him widespread recognition. He returned to England in 1889 and began collaborating with the American publisher and author Wolcott Balestier on *The Naulakha: A Story of East and West,* which was published in 1892. That same year, Kipling married Balestier's sister, Caroline. The couple settled in Vermont, where Kipling drew upon his remembrances of India and of Buddhist tales to create the stories of *The Jungle Book* and *The Second Jungle Book.* Several of his *Jungle Book* stories were first printed in the American children's magazine *St. Nicholas* and later collected with illustrations, some by Kipling's father. The books were immensely popular among readers and well received by critics. In 1896, Kipling returned to England and settled in the Sussex countryside, which figures prominently as the setting for many of his later works. Kipling's *"Captains Courageous",* the story of a wealthy, indulgent young boy who learns empathy, integrity, and self-reliance during a three-month stay aboard a fishing boat, was published in 1897. Kipling's next work for a young audience was *Stalky and Co.,* a novel comprised of rousing fictionalized tales of practical-joking students outsmarting teachers and peers at the United Services College. *Stalky* was followed by the critically acclaimed *Kim,* the tale of a young boy who comes under the tutelage of a lama in India at the same time that he is being trained for the Secret Service. *Just So Stories for Little Children* offers Kipling's popular fables about the origin of things ("pourquoi tales"); included are such classics as "How the Camel Got His Hump" and "How the Leopard Got His Spots." *Puck of Pook's Hill* (1906) and *Rewards and Fairies* (1910), Kipling's last significant works for young readers, were written for the benefit of his own children. These books of historical fiction describe, through a series of entertaining vignettes, England's distant past. Kipling's popularity and fame diminished somewhat later in his life, largely because the imperialist views expounded in many of his works had by this time become dated, and critical attention focused upon the political aspects of his writing almost to the exclusion of his stylistic accomplishments. Kipling died in 1936 after several years of illness, and was interred in Poets' Corner at Westminster Abbey.

Plot and Major Characteristics

The *Jungle Books* comprise well-known stories such as "Rikki-Tikki-Tavi," the tale of a mischievous mongoose, and "The Miracle of Purun Bhagat," in which the protagonist risks his life for the sake of saving the people of the neighboring village from a landslide. Nonetheless, the two volumes of short stories are known primarily as the tale

of Mowgli, a boy raised by wolves in the Seeonee Hills of India. In the first three stories of the collection, Kipling outlines the "Law of the Jungle," a disciplinary code which sets standards that include killing only for food, feeding children before adults, and trying to settle differences without fighting. Mowgli, orphaned as a baby and adopted by the wolf Akela and his wife, grows up with great respect for the Law and its importance. Befriended by Baloo the bear, Bagheera the panther, and Kaa the python, Mowgli becomes master of the jungle, feared and hated by Shere Khan the tiger and, eventually, deserted by the wolf pack who had once considered him one of their own. As Mowgli matures, he learns that he is not a wolf and, especially with the dawn of his sexual yearnings, desires some affinity with the humans of the neighboring village. Kipling had earlier described Mowgli's eventual fate in a short story entitled "In the Rukh," which first appeared in the author's collection *Many Inventions* in 1893. "In the Rukh" depicts the adult Mowgli as a civil servant in the forestry service, married to a young woman of the village. The poignancy of the *Jungle Book* stories, however, lies in Mowgli's difficulty in finding the connection with others that he so desires. As he approaches adolescence, he feels like an outsider in both the human and animal communities. Many critics cite Kipling's boyhood experiences in Southsea as the probable inspiration for his effective treatment of alienation. Although some commentators feel that Kipling's portrayal of the savagery of the jungle is too graphic for a young audience, most affirm that Mowgli's touching emotional journey to manhood and Kipling's masterful storytelling appeal to readers of all ages. The tales continue to be reissued in various forms and have been adapted frequently for film.

Awards

The Jungle Book, illustrated by J. L. Kipling, W. H. Drake, and P. Frenzeny, received the Lewis Carroll Shelf Award in 1960. Kipling declined several major awards and distinctions for his body of work, including England's Poet Laureateship and Order of Merit. However, he accepted the Nobel Prize for Literature in 1907, becoming the first English author to be so honored. He also received the Gold Medal of the Royal Society of Literature in 1926 and several honorary doctorate degrees from universities throughout the world.

REVIEWS

The Spectator

SOURCE: "Mr. Rudyard Kipling's Studies of Animal Life," in *The Spectator,* Vol. 72, No. 3440, June 2, 1894, pp. 747-48.

Mr. Rudyard Kipling has, as everyone knows, a singular genius for the delineation of human character. There we have at least some means of verifying what he tells us.

We have all of us the germs, and some of us the fully developed germs, of the qualities and the passions which he loves to paint,—the futile ambitions, the tenacious vanity, the inexhaustible remorse, the ill-regulated gnawing compassion, the cruel and vindictive selfishness, of which he gives us such vivid pictures. But we are not sure that his highly imaginative pictures of animal life are not even more remarkable, though there he is almost necessarily painting from imagination, or at least imagination stimulated only by the physical expression written on the external organisation of animals, in the interpretation of which he has no clue at all to guide him except the clue afforded by his own active and audacious fancy. In his ***Jungle Book,*** . . . he paints some most effective pictures of the characteristics that he chooses to impute to the various animals he has studied, which any writer since Æsop has drawn, and we think we may safely say far bolder and stronger and more impressive pictures than those of Æsop, because they follow the clue of superficial expression into far more elaborate detail. It is curious, too, to observe how Mr. Rudyard Kipling transforms the traditional characters of some of the inhabitants of the jungle. He is very fond of the wolves, in whose love for acting the foster-parent to human children he evidently believes, and whom he idealises into the most loyal and devoted of friends and followers. He even reaches the full height of the sublime in his picture of the python, of whose chivalry and ghastly fascinations he draws one of the most splendid and lurid pictures which has ever been painted in English literature. Again, he is very hostile to the tiger, on whose meanness, greediness, and cowardice, he is much fonder of dilating, than on his strength and audacity. But the creature of which he is most fiercely contemptuous is the monkey:—

> 'Listen, man-cub,' said the Bear, and his voice rumbled like thunder on a hot night. 'I have taught thee all the Law of the Jungle for all the peoples of the jungle—except the Monkey-Folk who live in the trees. They have no law. They are outcasts. They have no speech of their own, but use the stolen words which they overhear when they listen, and peep, and wait up above in the branches. Their way is not our way. They are without leaders. They have no remembrance. They boast and chatter and pretend that they are a great people about to do great affairs in the jungle, but the falling of a nut turns their minds to laughter and all is forgotten. We of the jungle have no dealings with them. We do not drink where the monkeys drink; we do not go where the monkeys go; we do not hunt where they hunt; we do not die where they die. . . .'

They are depicted as creatures remarkable for utter caprice; they cannot remember their own purposes, but are diverted from them by the most trivial accidents. They are incapable of discipline, have no leaders and no capacity for either leading or being led. They are mere fantastic images of the foul and helpless dreams of the worst of men. Indeed, in his picture of the "Bandar-log," as Hindoos call the monkeys, Mr. Rudyard Kipling lavishes all his gift for the expression of scorn, which is indeed a very remarkable gift. We suspect that he has indulged his disgust for certain tribes of monkeys without any wide experience of what other tribes of them are capable of, and has thereby misled his readers. But nothing is clearer than that both in his idealisations and in his depreciations of particular animals, Mr. Rudyard Kipling has interpreted them rather in the colours which his own vivid imagination has suggested to him, than in any strict keeping with wide and careful observation. Here, again, is an instantaneous photograph, as one may call it, of the timidity and depression of the musk-rat, from whom the rash and lively mongoose takes counsel before he attacks the formidable cobras of his master's bungalow:—

> In the dark he ran up against Chuchundra, the musk-rat, creeping round by the wall. Chuchundra is a broken-hearted little beast. He whimpers and cheeps all the night, trying to make up his mind to run into the middle of the room; but he never gets there.

The mongoose gets impatient with such faint-heartedness, and threatens him with a bite unless he gives him all the information he can of the cobras' movements:—

> Chuchundra sat down and cried till the tears rolled off his whiskers. 'I am a very poor man,' he sobbed. 'I never had spirit enough to run out into the middle of the room. H'sh! I mustn't tell you anything. Can't you hear, Rikki-tikki?'

No picture could be more vivid. Æsop never came near it. But it is obvious that Mr. Rudyard Kipling is one of the romantics, and not predominantly a naturalist. He dwells on the images which the different creatures have made upon him, and elaborates these impressions till they fill his canvas, instead of collecting all the experience he can before he forms an image in his own mind. His pictures of the elephant are almost all idealised, and his pictures of the tiger and snakes, except only the python (which evidently gave him full scope for a grand imaginative picture, and was on that ground reserved for respectful treatment), are too hostile. Mr. Kipling is a sort of Rembrandt to the animal world, and when he finds a promising subject for either admiring or indignant portraiture, he deepens all the lines and brings out a most impressive portrait, not of the creature itself, but of that which the creature suggested most forcibly to his vivid imagination. Mr. Kipling can never deny himself a striking imaginative touch. In the remarkable story in which he narrates the rendezvous of the elephants, tame as well as wild, for what they call the elephant-dance, Mr. Kipling does not miss a touch that lends a certain mystery and grandeur to the scenes which he describes. When Kala Nag slips from his fastenings, he "rolled out of his pickets as slowly and silently as a cloud rolls out of the mouth of a valley." Ruskin himself could not have painted a night landscape more impressively than this:—

> Toomai leaned forward and looked, and he felt that the forest was awake below him—awake and alive and crowded. A big brown fruit-eating bat brushed past his ear; a porcupine's quills rattled in the thicket, and in the darkness between the tree-stems he heard a hog-bear digging hard in the moist warm earth, and snuffing as it digged. Then the branches closed over his head

again, and Kala Nag began to go down into the valley—not quietly this time, but as a runaway gun goes down a steep bank—in one rush. The huge limbs moved as steadily as pistons, eight feet to each stride, and the wrinkled skin of the elbow-points rustled. The undergrowth on either side of him ripped with a noise like torn canvas, and the saplings that he heaved away right and left with his shoulders sprang back again, and banged him on the flank, and great trails of creepers, all matted together, hung from his tusks as he threw his head from side to side and ploughed out his pathway.

But the singular power of graphic description which Mr. Kipling shows diminishes instead of increasing our confidence in his animal portraits. It is obvious that he paints rather for an effect than for scientific accuracy. He wishes to show you what he saw and felt rather than what was actually there. The "man-cub" who is suckled by a wolf, and made free of the jungle, is a fine imaginative conception, steadily carried out; but it is evident that the picture is a very free one, founded on hints rather than on anything like experience. Indeed, the "man-cub" is almost more of an ideal man set down in the world of wild animals, than an ordinary child would be. And the other pictures of animal life are equally romantic. Take, for instance, this splendid and ghastly picture of the fascination exerted by the mighty python over the cowering hosts of monkeys:—

The moon was sinking behind the hills and the lines of trembling monkeys huddled together on the walls and battlements looked like ragged shaky fringes of things. Baloo [the bear] went down to the tank for a drink and Bagheera [the panther] began to put his fur in order, as Kaa [the python] glided out into the centre of the terrace and brought his jaws together with a ringing snap that drew all the monkeys' eyes upon him. "The moon sets," he said. "Is there yet light enough to see?" From the walls came a moan like the wind in the tree-tops—"We see, O Kaa."—"Good. Begins now the dance—the Dance of the Hunger of Kaa. Sit still and watch." He turned twice or thrice in a big circle, weaving his head from right to left. Then he began making loops and figures of eight with his body, and soft oozy triangles that melted into squares and five-sided figures, and coiled mounds, never resting, never hurrying, and never stopping his low humming song. It grew darker and darker, till at last the dragging, shifting coils disappeared, but they could hear the rustle of the scales. Baloo and Bagheera stood still as stone, growling in their throats, their neck-hair bristling, and Mowgli [the boy brought up by the wolves] watched and wondered. "Bandar-log," said the voice of Kaa at last, "can ye stir foot or hand without my order? Speak!"—"Without thy order we cannot stir foot or hand, O Kaa!"—"Good! Come all one pace nearer to me." —The lines of the monkeys swayed forward helplessly, and Baloo and Bagheera took one stiff step forward with them. "Nearer," hissed Kaa, and they all moved again. Mowgli laid his hands on Baloo and Bagheera to get them away, and the two great beasts started as though they had been waked from a dream. "Keep thy hand on my shoulder," Bagheera whispered. "Keep it there, or I must go back—must go back to Kaa. Aah!" —"It is only old

Kaa making circles on the dust," said Mowgli; "let us go"; and the three slipped off through a gap in the walls to the jungle.

That exhibits Mr. Kipling's curious power at its full strength, but it is the power of a visionary imagination, not of a naturalist's keen insight. Indeed, this fascinating little book on the life of the Jungle, seems written to show that the life of the animal world is the true field for allegory, rather than the life of men. Whatever is true of our human world, it is certainly not true that man ever represents the embodiment of a single principle, of one single vice or one single virtue. Man is a complex creature, who is always and at every turn exhibiting the great complexity of the nature of which his actions and feelings are the utterance; but we do not know this of the animal world, and it is almost certain that whether or not allegory be also inapplicable to that world, it is at least less inapplicable than it is to the human world above it. Animals are at least of simpler organisation, and are more like the incarnations of single principles than any human being. Moreover, even where we are wrong in attributing to them a false simplicity of nature, we are so ignorant of the real state of the case that we suffer none of that shock from our mistake which allegory, in its elaborate Spenserian forms, always inflicts upon us. The truth is that the inner world of consciousness which we attribute to the wilder animals, is so much of a terra incognita, of a world of

Kipling, age six.

mystery, that we may fairly deal with it in any fashion which a man of powerful imagination like Mr. Rudyard Kipling can manage to make impressive,—and we can answer for it that in this *Jungle Book* he does manage to make his semi-allegorical treatment of the wildbeasts' nature in the highest degree impressive, and not unfrequently even mystically impressive. Take even the least interesting study in the book,—the imaginary conversation between the horse, the camel, the mule, the elephant, and the ox, after the panic in an Indian camp caused by a stampede of the camels, which closes the book. It would be difficult to over-praise the skill with which the horse's deep personal trust in his own rider and dislike to independent action, the mule's frigid vanity in his complete independence of any human guides, the camel's stupid dismay at unaccustomed alarms, the elephant's nervous dislike to anything like shells, and the ox's apathetic plodding indifference to any sort of danger, so long as he can get his full allowance of food, are drawn out by the author. There we have a very prosaic allegorical representation of loyalty, conceit in mechanical sureness of foot, indefatigable but stupid industry, highly charged nervous susceptibility, and the slow docility of an embodied appetite; but in the other stories we have we know not how much happy invention of the bear's imaginary love of teaching and discipline, the wolf's tenderness of maternal instinct, the mystic magnanimity of an elephant's fatherly strength, and the overpowering fascinations of a mighty serpent's spell. Certainly, Mr. Rudyard Kipling is a master in allegory of a much higher kind than any which Æsop ever produced.

The Athenaeum

SOURCE: A review of *The Jungle Book,* in *The Athenaeum,* No. 3477, June 16, 1894, p. 766.

Mr. Kipling has done many good things in his time, and doubtless some of his former work is stronger than what he gives us in [*The Jungle Book*], but it is questionable whether any of his numerous "inventions" will be more widely popular. . . . For one thing, it is wholly free from a suspicion of those defects in taste which even his warmest admirers (among whom we count ourselves) have occasionally had reason to observe and deprecate in his earlier writings. For another, it treats of the natives and the animals of India in an absolutely novel way, and has the benefit of some excellent illustrations by the author's father Mr. J. L. Kipling, Mr. W. H. Drake, and Mr. P. Frenzeny. Take it altogether, with its queer stories, its clever verses, and its capital pictures, it is in every respect a most desirable possession, alike for children and their elders. The first three tales, **'Mowgli's Brothers,' 'Kaa's Hunting,'** and **'Tiger-Tiger!'** form a trilogy based upon the doings of the "man-cub" Mowgli, whom we fancy we have met before in the pages of another of Mr. Kipling's books. Suckled by a she-wolf, and initiated into all the secrets of the jungle by a bear and a panther called Baloo and Bagheera, Mowgli is an altogether fascinating creation—a woodland personage of singular aptitudes and undeniable charm. How he is carried off over the tree-tops by the ridiculous Bandar-log, or Monkey People; how his two friends, assisted by Kaa, the great rock-python, succeed in effecting his rescue; how he finally leaves the forest and goes to dwell with mankind; and how he slays and skins his old enemy Shere Khan the tiger, our readers must discover for themselves. It is a veritable Odyssey of adventure, with thrilling developments at every turn. . . .

The incidental pictures of Indian native life and habits are drawn with a master hand. We may instance the account Mr. Kipling gives of the buffaloes being driven to graze from the village by the children in the early morning, the long, sleepy, sunshiny days passed by the young herdsmen, and the tramp back again in the evening across the monotonous grey plain. It is worth notice, by the way, that among the occupations he specifies for these "hours of idleness" is that of weaving little baskets of dried grass and putting grasshoppers within them, which vividly recalls the careless watcher of the vineyard in the first Idyll of Theocritus. . . . [The] resemblance between these unsophisticated inhabitants of the "village communities" of the East—with their picturesque yet dignified speech, and old-world courtesy and simplicity—and the men and women of the Greek poets, is often so strong as to make the classical reader start with surprise.

'The White Seal' attracted a good deal of attention when it first appeared, in view of the Behring Sea arbitration, now happily concluded, and was well worth reprinting. **'Rikki-Tikki-Tavi'** is a delicious story of the achievements of a mongoose, which rids a house and compound of snakes in the most business-like manner. But best of all, in imaginative scope and descriptive power, we hold to be **'Toomai of the Elephants.'** The account of the night journey of Kala Nag and his tiny rider to the "Tanz-Platz" of these mysterious quadrupeds is simply stupendous. We tender our sincere thanks to Mr. Kipling for the hour of pure and unadulterated enjoyment which he has given us, and many another reader, by this inimitable *Jungle Book.*

The Saturday Review, London

SOURCE: A review of *The Jungle Book,* in *The Saturday Review,* London, Vol. 77, No. 2016, June 16, 1894, pp. 639-40.

As the wild animals of the world become rarer and fewer, the sentiment of interest in them felt by civilized people grows keener. No book is more certain of a sympathetic welcome from the public than one which tells good and fresh stories about beasts and birds. [*The Jungle Book*] does not precisely supply us with animal anecdotes, but it does something better—it helps us to enter, by the power of the imagination, into the very nature of the creatures. It is a modern variant on the old-fashioned modes in which animals and birds were made to speak to one another in the hearing of man, and so to divulge the secrets of the woodland. In this latest evidence of the versatility of his talent, Mr. Kipling shows us once more how close an observer he is, how little escapes his attention when once he rivets it upon an object, and with what brilliant intuition he creates a plausible and coherent impression. Mr. Kipling, if he had happened to be born a geologist, would have electrified science, for no bone would have been too small for him to base the image of a dragon or a mammoth upon.

Of the various creatures which animate these delightful pages, we like none better than Rikki-Tikki-Tavi, the mongoose. The story of the great war which he fought single-handed through the bath-rooms of the big bungalow in Segowlee cantonment is unsurpassed among epic narratives of its kind. We shall not tell the story, which everybody must read; but we would point out to those who do read it with how delicate an art the sweetness of the mongoose temperament towards all but its native enemies is worked out by Mr. Kipling. Fierce to extinguish Nag, the cobra, and his wicked wife Nagaima, Rikki-Tikki-Tavi is gentleness itself to his human friends, and full of chivalrous comradeship for Darzee, the light-headed tailor-bird, and that dejected object, Chuchundra, the musk-rat. We have ourselves enjoyed the intimacy of a mongoose, and have never forgotten the bold cordiality with which, at first acquaintance, it leaped upon our shoulder, and thrust its chocolate-coloured nose between our collar and our chin. But we did not know, until Mr. Kipling kindly explained, what was the cause of this sudden and almost alarming affability. Its mother, we now learn, had carefully told it how to behave if it ever came across white men. Most true, also, is the biographer's remark that a mongoose is a restless companion on a bed, "because it has to get up and attend to every noise all through the night, and find out what made it." If **"Rikki-Tikki-Tavi"** does not have the effect of making people understand that a mongoose is one of the most lovable and useful of all domestic pets, Mr. Kipling has written in vain.

In **"Servants of the Queen,"** which is more boldly fabulous than the rest, a camel breaks through a man's tent in the night, and so he has to take refuge under a waterproof thrown over the muzzle of a gun on the open camp. In this way he overhears the confidences of a mule, a gun-bullock, a troop-horse, and an elephant, each of whom expresses its own character in a delightful way. The horse, with its noble affection for and confidence in its master, a certain Dick Cunliffe, is perfectly engaging; the others have their little faults, and the camel has nothing else. We do not need to be reminded of Mr. Kipling's inveterate prejudice against the oont, for whom he invents, in the present volume, this delightful parade-song:—

> We haven't a camelty tune of our own
> To help us trollop along,
> But every neck is a hair-trombone
> (*Rtt-ta-ta-ta!* is a hair-trombone!)
> And this our marching-song:—
> *Can't! Don't! Shan't! Won't!*
> Pass it along the line!
> Somebody's pack has slipped from his back,
> 'Wish it were only mine.

> Somebody's load has tipped off in the road—
> Cheer for a halt and a row!
> *Urrr! Yarrh! Grr! Arrh!*
> Somebody's catching it now!

It would be wrong, indeed, to notice this volume without some allusion to its verse, as not fewer than twenty poems and poetical fragments occur in its pages, some very slight, and others—as in particular the beautiful lullaby of **"Shiv and the Grasshopper"**—full of Mr. Kipling's rare magic of plaintive colloquialism. But it is the stories, of course, which constitute the real attraction of *The Jungle Book,* whether their scene is laid in India with Mowgli the wolf-boy and Toomai of the elephants, or on the wild strand of Lukannon with Kotick, the white seal. Mr. Kipling is to be congratulated on a very genuine success in a field where, even for a man of great powers, failure might reasonably have been anticipated.

Percy Addleshaw

SOURCE: A review of *The Jungle Book,* in *The Academy,* Vol. 45, No. 1156, June 30, 1894, p. 530.

Hitherto we have been accustomed to find inequality in Mr. Kipling's work. He has never yet given us a book entirely good: each collection of his stories is a mixture of success and failure. Naturally, this peculiarity has always stirred some annoyance and perplexity in his critics; for at his best he is not easily surpassed, while at his worst he is almost puerile. There is a popular superstition, not without an element of truth in it, that equality and mediocrity are interchangeable terms. But though no author, however gifted, can always be at his best, the inequalities of Mr. Kipling's work offer too startling a contrast. His frequent falls from the heights to the deeps, his dazzling leaps from the mire to the mountain top, cannot be satisfactorily accounted for by any theory however respectable. So we are unable to take up a new volume of his without knowing our hopes are dogged by a most uncomfortable fear. Faith in his ultimate success is founded upon the fact that, the more difficult his task seems, the greater the certainty that he will be successful. Consequently, if he wishes to sustain his reputation, he must refuse resolutely to write on subjects commonplace or indifferent.

The Jungle Book has been cordially welcomed; and it is only just to confess, at once, that it is more carefully designed than anything he has yet given to us. There are no serious blemishes in the style and grammar: as a piece of technique it is quite blameless. But a serious doubt arises as to whether the matter of the book is at all worthy of the labour bestowed on it. Again, it is certain that those flashes of genius that used to dazzle us seldom illumine its pages. In them Mr. Kipling's finest qualities are to seek. We prefer to hear his men and women talk, as only Mulvaney or Mrs. Hawkesby can talk, be Bagheera and Baloo never so ingenious. It is impossible to rid oneself of the conviction, that any author rather more clever than the average could have contrived the greater part of *The*

Jungle Book. There are, indeed, a few pages that no one but the creator of *Soldiers Three* could have written: and one new friendship is cemented, for which we are grateful. Rikki Tikki, though only a mongoose, fights his way gallantly enough into the list of Mr. Kipling's immortals. The history of his war with the cobras is entirely delightful, and refuses to be forgotten.

There are times when plain speaking is necessary; and then the most ardent admirer of an author must, if he be honest, say the truth. The truth is, that *The Jungle Book,* had it been written by a person unknown, might have stirred a languid interest, and a certain reasonable hope of better things to come. As the work of a man of recognised genius, it compels disappointment. It is generally true that to gain a worthy success a writer must toil hard, must choose his words with discrimination. But there is no rule without an exception, and in this case Mr. Kipling would seem to be that exception. His best work achieves itself, apparently, spontaneously. It is a startling, nay dangerous, thing to say of a man that he places failure far from him only when he is most careless. But Mr. Kipling may, at any rate, be advised . . . not to concern himself again with words and phrases, but with the greater truths of destiny and emotion. His last book prompts this reflection: few authors know the human heart so well as he, let him forsake, therefore, Mowglis and mules and monkeys, and remember that his vital phrases have ever been born, not made.

Kipling in the 1880s.

The Bookman, London

SOURCE: A review of *The Jungle Book,* in *The Bookman,* London, Vol. VI, No. 34, July, 1894, p. 116.

The Jungle Book is made up of story and song, both of them rich in vitality and imagination. But every time a verse occurs as the heading of a chapter one is inclined to think that Mr. Kipling should write nothing else, so instinctive is his power over vigorous rhythm, and so vivid are his ballad pictures. This **"Night-Song in the Jungle"** is only meant to tune you up to the pitch of the story that follows:

> Now Chil the Kite brings home the night,
>   That Mang the Bat sets free;
> The herds are shut in byre and hut,
>   For loosed till dawn are we.
> This is the hour of pride and power,
>   Talon and tusk and claw,
> Oh, hear the call! good hunting all
>   That keep the Jungle Law!

But we want more of it, and begin the prose in a depressed condition till we come to the great meeting of the pack at the Council Rock, where the Free People are met to judge if the foundling man-cub Mowgli shall be given up to the terrible Shere Khan the tiger. It is a great scene, the hill-tops covered with stones and boulders, the bright moon shining, and Akela, the gray Lone Wolf, who led the pack, crying from his rock: "Ye know the Law, ye know the Law; look well, O Wolves!" There is another fine scene at the Council Rock years later, when Mowgli has gone back to his own kind, has grown strong enough to kill Shere Khan, and comes back to spread the great tiger's skin on the rock, and pegs it down for Akela to sit on. "Akela lay down upon it, and called the old call to the Council, 'Look, look well, O Wolves!' but the old times have gone, the pack is disorganized, and though they cry to Akela and to the man-cub to lead them again into their former greatness, Bagheera, the wise panther, says it may not be. 'Not for nothing are ye called the Free People. Ye fought for freedom, and it is yours. Eat it, O Wolves!'" There is something sternly grand about all the Mowgli stories. Imaginative children, whether or not they follow the narrative with perfect comprehension, will be impressed and even awe-struck by the solemnity and dignity of jungle life as Mr. Kipling paints it.

Of the habits of the animals, of the scenes amidst which they live, he has a marvellous knowledge. It is this picturesque knowledge, joined to a vigorous interpretation of, not their own character, but the ideal nature he has constructed for them, a nature at once remote and familiar to us, that makes the success and the fascination of the stories. Man, without his intellectual power, but with his natural faculties of sight and hearing infinitely intensified, and without the enfeeblement, the deceit, the pettiness that are the fruits of his civilisation, would be something like this conception of the beast that obeys the Jungle Law. We are grotesquely reminded here and there of the ideals of Rousseau and the natural state idealists. Their primitive man they would have desired to be like Mr. Kipling's loyal beasts.

There are stories in the book where he is not at his highest point of vigour. **"The White Seal"** comes near to being a failure, and so does **"Servants of the Queen."** The adventures of **"Rikki-Tikki-Tavi,"** the mongoose that fought with Nag the cobra and Nagaina his wife, are too deadly to be amusing, and the glamour of imagination does not play round them to turn the terror into fascination. The temperature of one's admiration having been reduced by these, we find several other things to wonder at, not all admiringly. Mr. Kipling cannot resist opportunities of political allusion; indeed invents them. And his love for playing the school-master grows on him. It is this quality that is at the bottom of the imperfect sympathy which runs parallel in many readers' minds with a warm admiration for him. The pedagogue in him hides under free and vigorous and unconventional speech, but he is mostly there. Were he to fall asleep a bit oftener, and let some careless, lawless fellow take his place, if even only for a few minutes, Mr. Kipling's range of understanding of human nature would be greatly widened.

But grumbling at Mr. Kipling's temperament is not very relevant here. It does not greatly offend in *The Jungle Book*. More to the purpose is it to point to the feats of imagination in these beast stories. Next to the three Mowgli tales, for great qualities, comes **"Toomai of the Elephants."** Toomai is a little boy who saw what few believed in, and none had seen, the great "dance of the elephants at night and alone in the heart of the Garo hills." He was on the back of the tame elephant Kala Nag that he tended, and when Kala Nag got the signal for the dance the boy was borne away, up the wooded hill, through the thick underwood, through the bed of a river to a space of three or four acres, where the grass was trampled and hard. The assembling elephants crashed through the trees and entered the dance-place, and rolled their eyes, and tossed their trunks, and clicked their tusks, and flicked their great tails. "Then an elephant trumpeted, and they all took it up for five or ten terrible seconds. The dew from the trees above spattered down like rain on the unseen backs, and a dull booming noise began, not very loud at first, and little Toomai could not tell what it was; but it grew and grew, and Kala Nag lifted up one fore-foot and then the other, and brought them down on the ground, one-two, one-two, as steadily as trip-hammers. The elephants were stamping altogether now, and it sounded like a war-drum beaten at the mouth of a cave. The dew fell from the trees till there was no more left to fall, and the booming went on, and the ground rocked and shivered, and Little Toomai put his hands up to his ears to shut out the sound. But it was all one gigantic jar that ran through him—this stamp of hundreds of heavy feet on the raw earth. . . . The morning broke in one sheet of pale yellow behind the green hills, and the booming stopped with the first ray, as though the light had been an order." It is a magnificent sight that Toomai saw that night when the favour of the elephant-folk and of the gods of the jungle was with him. Mr. Kipling has some splendid visions. For all his love of discipline and order, it is when his spirit gets away into the wilder paths of nature and human nature that he touches real greatness.

The Critic, New York

SOURCE: A review of *The Jungle Book,* in *The Critic,* New York, Vol. XXII, No. 648, July 21, 1894, pp. 37-8.

To say that Mr. Rudyard Kipling has scored another success is to chronicle the inevitable. So it is with whetted appetite that we open the fresh-cut leaves of *The Jungle Book,* settling comfortably in our veranda chair, prepared for many a real sensation. And what a "bully" book it is, as what small boy would not say? We are transported into the depths of the Indian jungle, there to dwell through a term of adventure with Mowgli the "Frog," a young werewolf boy. Old Baloo, the fat brown bear, who knows the law of the forest and teaches it to the young wolves, is Mowgli's living preceptor in those things man cannot know. Bagheera, the black, beautiful panther who went surety for Mowgli's life when the Council Pack had determined to kill him, a helpless babe, and was forever his devoted friend thereafter; old Kaa, the terrible python; the careless Bandarlog; the monkey people whom the jungle folk despise, but who are always intending to do great things if only they can remember to carry out their schemes; Akela, the great, gray, lone wolf—these, among others, are the new friends the magician conjures up for us and endows with throbbing, healthful life.

Heartily yielding to the potency of its charm, we acknowledge a real addition to the library in this book, though it is confessedly written for children. But Mr. Kipling has not to look to it for his first success in reeling yarns for the "father of the man." We have known and rejoiced in excellent essays in juvenile exercitation among the earliest of those famous *Plain tales from the Hills,* but we believe that a higher success is here achieved. Who can analyse the charm of this young genius? We have read the learned reviews of his work, but we have not found the secret of that charm. All we know is that our attention is riveted from the first word. That the calm traditions of the novel are boisterously disturbed we confess, for there are no somnolent wanderings through lawns and sunsets before we dare confess expectation to be lessened in realized interest. No aphorism of introduction is exploded on an astonished public, but the "painted veil which those who live call life" is split in twain, and Mr. Kipling shows us real things as suddenly and as vividly as a flash of lightning. In *The Jungle Book* is to be found as close an observation of brute life, as quaint a humor, as splendid a portrayal of the nobler animal passions—gratitude and love,—as spirited battle scenes as in any page of Sir Samuel Baker; but over it all, to make it unique, the artist casts the heavy, mysterious, sombre shadows of the Indian forest, which he knows so well, with its own population of outlandish beasts, familiar to us only in the cooped dejection of the menagerie, or made ridiculous by *dompteurs,*—in forced imitation of the puny habits of the ancestral enemy—Man. But Mr. Kipling knows them as they are, free and magnificent, from the very elephants to the crawling snakes, and like Van Amberg in the song, he "tells us all he knows."

Joel Chandler Harris

SOURCE: "Another Jungle Book," in *The Book Buyer,* Vol. XII, No. 10, November, 1895, pp. 656-57.

Rudyard Kipling follows his first volume of Jungle Stories with another collection called *The Second Jungle Book.* If such a thing were possible, this second collection of tales goes closer to the core of things than the first. The first story of Mowgli was a happy accident; but those that have followed it are not accidents at all, but belong to the natural order of things as the jungle knows them, and present with serene veracity the various incidents that befell the little man-wolf.

The tales take hold of the imagination with a strength that is as rare in modern literature as jungle books are. They go to the source of things without prelude or preliminary flourish, and there is no resisting the force that gives them vitality.

Men whose culture has left no sort of instrument for their imagination to perform on doubtless say, under their breath, that there is a taste or a twang of the savage in these tales of the jungle. And yet there is no animal more elemental than man. We have in these stories the simplicity, and—I dare to say—the refinement that belongs to elemental things. Does the roar of the cataract become courteous and affable in the presence of civilization and culture? Does the crack of the thunder subdue itself to meet the needs of the mental dyspeptics of our day and time? Do the cyclone, the tornado and the hurricane fold their terrific wings and become dove-like when they enter the domain of man?

Now, as of old, the cataract, the thunder, and the tornado perform, each after its own fashion. Now, as of old, the elemental in man rhymes with the elemental in all things else, and Mr. Kipling's genius touches the centre of it all with a swing, a vigor, and a fearlessness that cannot be matched in modern literature. There is no mincing here. A swish and a slash, and the stroke goes home.

Since the days of Uncle Æsop the animals have been parading about and making speeches, sometimes feebly and sometimes to good purpose; but never have they been caught in the act, as it were, by a more facile or a stronger hand than in these jungle tales. And each plays his part after his own manner and according to the law of his own nature.

The first of these stories, **"How Fear Came,"** has for its background the elemental in folk-lore, and it is told with a vigorous simplicity that is inimitable. The wild sweep of the narrative is inimitable, and perhaps, more than any other story in the book, with one exception, is typical of this new order of tale-telling. The myths that belong to India sometimes drag along and, for the most part, have

the desultory vagueness of stories that are preserved only by passing from mouth to mouth; but in this resetting or rebuilding of a myth that is hazy and without purpose, Mr. Kipling has made it entirely his own by transforming that which was without life into a living, breathing, moving piece of literature that lifts itself above and beyond the reach of imitation.

The exception to be noted is the story of the "good hunting," which tells of the rush through the jungle of the hunting-pack of the red dog of the Dekkan, moving to kill. It is a story that takes one's breath away—the race of Mowgli ahead of the fierce hunting-dogs of the Dekkan, to the cliffs where dwell the "Little People"—the Bees— his leap into the sinuous folds of Kaa, the python, who lies floating in the water below—the air swarming with the angry Little People—the red dogs rushing through them, covered with the bees—the fighting in the water— and the final killing of the red dogs. The narrative is so powerful and original in its manner that hardly a hint can be given of its strength and quality.

The Second Jungle Book is a feast for those who admire literature that is vital. Out of these tales surely truth walks naked—the truth that is native to life and experience.

The Dial

SOURCE: A review of *The Second Jungle Book,* in *The Dial,* Chicago, Vol. XIX, No. 227, December 1, 1895, p. 339.

[No] year can be called barren which brings to light a masterpiece like Mr. Kipling's *Second Jungle Book.* Nothing could be of more absorbing interest to children; and yet so artistic a book should not be confined to them alone. When one encounters work as original, as imaginative, as masterly as this, no words can convey an idea of the thing itself. Mr. Kipling takes all nature for his province; he seems as familiar with the flowers of the field as with the beasts of the jungle. And the truth of his statements is never doubted for an instant. His creatures are alive in every muscle, and they are not human beings masquerading in hair and claws. They are beasts, with the instincts and desires of beasts, but with emotions enough like our own to make us shudder now and then. An imagination which can make such creatures live for us, which can give us a breathless interest in their sufferings and triumphs, seems beyond the human. From the superb description of the drought in the jungle, with which the book opens, to the last tale, in which the irreconcilable, eternal difference between man and beast is borne in upon us, the book is a series of magnificent pictures. It is never still, though, but the rush of its movement has a certain stately dignity which makes one respect the Law of the Jungle. Each story is introduced and ended with a little poem, and these rhythmical songs are the work of a true poet, one of the truest poets who is writing in English to-day. Certainly no other could have conceived **"Mowgli's Song against People," "Child's Song,"** and **"The Song of the Little Hunter."** They cling in the mind, like the

Kipling at his Vermont home.

great fight with Red Dog in the Place of Death where lived the "busy, furious Little People of the Rocks." There is a vivid directness about all these descriptions which brings them straight home.

The Athenaeum

SOURCE: A review of *The Second Jungle Book,* in *The Athenaeum,* No. 3565, February 22, 1896, p. 278.

The *"Jungle Books"* rank among Mr. Kipling's best productions. Large ideas inform them, and something of that epic imagination to which we have before referred as Mr. Kipling's most precious gift. What score of pages unveils more of Isis than that which tells of Sir Purun Dass, K.C.I.E., D.C.L., Ph.D., and of the strange ending of his days in Kali's shrine under the deodars? Put so, we understand things that false prophets have darkened. Surely this new manner has gripped Mr. Kipling unawares. Always these Jungle Tales were partly child's book and partly allegory; but while in the first series the child's book, in the last one the allegory—or, let us say, poetry—prevails. That insistence on the Jungle Law had clearly its

intention. Out of the mouths of Bagheera and Baloo Mr. Kipling would teach a wisdom that should profit the human child also, who has not literally to hold his own among wolves. But upon the way, though the fierce delights of **'Red Dog'** must hit at any boyish heart, certain thronging themes and visions have inwoven themselves, which are a bit beyond the child's ken. That fine poem of **'Letting in the Jungle,'** the blotting out of the human habitation, the reassertion by *karela* and bamboo of their ancient sway—is it not a drama of secular antagonism of nature and of man? Stevenson, you remember, tells us how that antagonism weighed upon his imagination as he fought his planter's fight with *liana* and *tuitui* in the clearings of Vailima. Mowgli, again—and the history of Mowgli is the soul of the book—in these later chapters the little man-cub, whom Bagheera saved, has developed into the adolescent wood god. Like the Melampus, of whom one of our poets sings, he has learnt the master-words of beast, and bird, and snake:

> —the things
> That glide in grasses and rubble of woody wreck;
> Or change their perch on a beat of quivering wings
> From branch to branch, only restful to pipe and
> peck.

A beautiful jessamine - crowned figure moves among the Jungle people, waiting for his soul. And when the human soul awakes at last, in the days of the Spring Running, at the sight of a girl, Mr. Kipling rises to the lyrical pitch of the solemn idyl. His manner of writing, victorious throughout these volumes over many of its early defects, answers to his mood. It becomes rich, full-charged, musical:—

> It was a perfect white night, as they call it. All green things seemed to have made a month's growth since the morning. The branch that was yellow-leaved the day before dripped sap when Mowgli broke it. The mosses curled deep and warm over his feet, the young grass had no cutting edges, and all the voices of the jungle boomed like one deep harp-string touched by the moon—the full moon of New Talk, who splashed her light full on rock and pool, slipped it between trunk and creeper, and sifted it through the million leaves. Unhappy as he was, Mowgli sang aloud with pure delight as he settled into his stride.

Very likely Mr. Kipling has never read the 'Pervigilium Veneris'; but, nevertheless, that is what **'The Spring Running'** reminds us of; and a book that provokes comparison with Stevenson and Mr. Meredith and the 'Pervigilium Veneris'—we might add Hawthorne—is surely in the line of good literature.

But it would not have been fair to disappoint the younger people of their fun, and though a second **'Rikki-Tikki-Tavi'** was hardly to be expected, there is much to enchant them in the present volume. Even if the mysticism is not fully understood, it can do no harm. And the illustrations, all by Mr. Kipling's father, are twice as good as those in the earlier book. Of the intercalary verses it is not necessary to say much; they are rugged, but Mr. Kipling often manages to hammer them into a barbaric music.

Margery Fisher

SOURCE: A review of *The Second Jungle Book,* in *Growing Point,* Vol. 1, No. 7, January, 1963, p. 100.

No-one who was brought up on the stories of Mowgli will want to forget the pure excitement of that first tale, when the boy is presented to the wolf-pack, or to miss the gradual unfolding of the characters of Baloo, Kaa and Bagheera; but it is in [*The Second Jungle Book*] that Kipling writes with his full powers. It is in this second cycle that Mowgli, the tough small boy of the earlier stories, becomes vulnerable to awe (in **"The King's Ankus"**) and, in that moving story, **"The Spring Running,"** admits that he is not wolf but man. Here are some of the most vivid scenes Kipling ever described—the pool where the animals observe truce in the drought, the river by which the Mugger reminisces about the Mutiny (not a Mowgli story, **"The Undertakers,"** but a remarkable piece of animal lore), the river ravine where the Seeonee wolf-pack makes a stand against the dreaded Red Dog. With water and jungle ever present, here are animals speaking a human tongue but in all else true to their kind.

Kipling was a journalist, and an unusually observant member of an observant craft. It is not only the dramatic moments in these tales that hold attention, but the artistry and restraint that make each moment of drama more exciting. When Kipling uses an adjective, or a descriptive phrase, he means it. Shere Khan's 'square, frilled head,' the 'heavy-shouldered nilghai,' the treasure at Cold Lairs heaped up, with 'coats of mail, gold inlaid on steel; and fringed with rotten and blackened seed-pearls'—each picture is separate, distinct and complete. **"Letting in the Jungle"** is impressive because of the controlled way Kipling describes elephants deliberately wrecking a village. What could be more simple, or more telling, than this final passage:

> The four pushed side by side; the outer wall bulged, split, and fell, and the villagers, dumb with horror, saw the savage, clay-streaked heads of the wreckers in the ragged gap. Then they fled, houseless and foodless, down the valley, as their village, shredded and tossed and trampled, melted behind them.

Let me suggest that any school child who wants to write should, in the intervals of filling exercise books with derivative poetry or detective stories, pause to study the work of a great technician.

GENERAL COMMENTARY

Charles G. D. Roberts

SOURCE: "The Animal Story," in *The Kindred of the Wild: A Book of Animal Life,* L. C. Page & Company, 1902, pp. 15-29.

Our chief writers of animal stories at the present day may be regarded as explorers of [an] unknown world, absorbed in charting its topography. They work, indeed, upon a substantial foundation of known facts. They are minutely scrupulous as to their natural history, and assiduous contributors to that science. But above all are they diligent in their search for the motive beneath the action. Their care is to catch the varying, elusive personalities which dwell back of the luminous brain windows of the dog, the horse, the deer, or wrap themselves in reserve behind the inscrutable eyes of all the cats, or sit aloof in the gaze of the hawk and the eagle. The animal story at its highest point of development is a psychological romance constructed on a framework of natural science.

The real psychology of the animals, so far as we are able to grope our way toward it by deduction and induction combined, is a very different thing from the psychology of certain stories of animals which paved the way for the present vogue. Of these, such books as *Beautiful Joe* and *Black Beauty* are deservedly conspicuous examples. It is no detraction from the merit of these books, which have done great service in awakening a sympathetic understanding of the animals and sharpening our sense of kinship with all that breathe, to say that their psychology is human. Their animal characters think and feel as human beings would think and feel under like conditions. This marks the stage which these works occupy in the development of the animal story.

The next stage must be regarded as, in literature, a climax indeed, but not the climax in this genre. I refer to the *Mowgli* stories of Mr. Kipling. In these tales the animals are frankly humanised. Their individualisation is distinctly human, as are also their mental and emotional processes, and their highly elaborate powers of expression. Their notions are complex; whereas the motives of real animals, so far as we have hitherto been able to judge them, seem to be essentially simple, in the sense that the motive dominant at a given moment quite obliterates, for the time, all secondary motives. Their reasoning powers and their constructive imagination are far beyond anything which present knowledge justifies us in ascribing to the inarticulate kindreds. To say this is in no way to depreciate such work, but merely to classify it. There are stories being written now which, for interest and artistic value, are not to be mentioned in the same breath with the *Mowgli* tales, but which nevertheless occupy a more advanced stage in the evolution of this genre.

J. M. S. Tompkins

SOURCE: "Tales for Children," in *The Art of Rudyard Kipling,* University of Nebraska Press, 1965, pp. 55-84.

[The following essay was originally published in 1959.]

The two *Jungle Books* had been on the dining-room shelves for some years before my father began to read to my brother and me every evening. I do not know how many times we worked through them, or quite how old I was when we began—about eight, I think. We made no difficulty over the humanized animals; they followed on nicely after Beatrix Potter, and, being town children, we much preferred Mowgli's wolves to natural history. But it was not the playful and domestic passages in these tales that impressed me most, but the notes of elevation and melancholy. The description of Cold Lairs, the crashing salute of the elephants to Little Toomai, the secret beach where Kotick led the seals—it was certainly a happy ending; *why* did I feel so sad?—and the fighting death of old Akela moved me to the depths. We did not turn often to *The Second Jungle Book*, **'The Miracle of Purun Bhagat'** was beyond me—I did not understand what was happening; **'The Undertakers'** perturbed my brother in bed; I fancy the end of **'Kaa's Hunting'** had to be shortened, though it was certainly read in full sometimes, the memory is so deep and clear and awesome. I cannot read **'Red Dog'** now without hearing my father—he had a magnificent voice and no distaste at all for rhetoric—giving out with tragic scorn the cry: 'Howl, dogs! A wolf has died tonight', while the tears with which, when we are young, we recognize nobility, poured down my face.

Won-tolla, however, meant nothing to me; I had quite forgotten him when I came back to the books in middle life; nor did I ever follow Mowgli's manoeuvres clearly, here or in **"'Tiger-Tiger!'"** The grip of the stories was extraordinary, and a sense of something wild and deep and old infected me as I listened. I knew most of the songs by heart, and know parts of them still. 'What of the hunting, hunter bold?' had on me the effect that I now recognize to be that of a heroic lyric. . . .

Kipling did not describe these two collections, as he did the *Puck* books, as tales for children to read until their elders had learnt that they were written for them, too, but he was as ready to stretch the young imagination as to invite the adult to play. He was, however, considerate of his childish audience and often carefully explanatory to them. He used familiar idioms in the earlier tales—'he lay as still as still'—and cut down his descriptions to the minimum—'the moon rose over the plain, making it look all milky'; in the second book the childish idioms are fewer and the descriptions expand—that of the drought-smitten jungle in **'How Fear Came'**, for instance; and at no time did he hold back from his young listeners the momentary glimpse of things sad and grim.

The peculiar quality of *The Jungle Books* consists in the fusion of three worlds. First of all, there is the child's play-world, where all is really subject to his pastime. It is essentially a homely world, and the good beasts have prototypes in the child's daily life. The identification of the similarity in the difference is part of the pleasure. Baloo is the conscientious, solicitous, elderly schoolmaster; but what enchanting lessons he teaches! From him Mowgli learns the master words of all the tribes in the jungle. Mother and Father Wolf live in recognizable domesticity with their four cubs—who, apparently, like grown-up Victorian sons, remain under the family roof for years—but their delightful home is a cave. The heavy Sea-Catch, with his bristling moustache, and his gentle mate, Matkah, reflect another kind of parental grouping, and it is with warm satisfaction that the child reads how Sea-Catch flings himself into the battle on Kotick's side with the shout: 'Don't tackle your father, my son; he's with you.' To this world belong, in the first instance, the pass-words and taboos of the jungle, which are entirely congenial to a child's imagination. This is the part of the books that grew from the remembered children's stories of Kipling's youth, the Freemason lions and the boy who lived with wolves.

The second world, which it is impossible to distinguish from the first by the material it is built of, is the world of the fable proper. The elements of moral instruction, which are certainly not alien to a child's world, are systematized. The beasts, without discarding pleasingly incongruous habits of their own, are plainly representative of human traits and conditions, and we are never oblivious of their counterparts in the world of men. They are grouped into arrangements that point a moral, and the moral may extend beyond a child's comprehension, though it should not lie wholly outside it. In *The Jungle Books* the fable comes and goes, and sometimes lies like a transparent glaze over the adventures. The examples are best found in the Mowgli tales, where we move, most of the time, in a self-consistent animal world; where human beings play a large part in the story, as in "'**Rikki-tikki-tavi**'", the conditions for fable are less good. In '**Kaa's Hunting**', however, the fable and the play-world are inextricably fused. The Bandar-log, the monkey-peoples, who sympathize with Mowgli when he is under punishment and abduct him into the tree-tops, are primarily figures in a thrilling and grim story. The green roads through the trees, along which they take Mowgli, his presence of mind when he gives the master-word to Chil the Kite and bids him mark his trail—this is the stuff of the play-world, raised to an exciting pitch by wonder. But very early and easily, before the adventures begin, the Bandar-log—irresponsible, chattering, without law or shame or memory—are seen as the antithesis to jungle-righteousness, and their dangerous futility is brought out by their doings at Cold Lairs. The adult reader can find the Bandar-log elsewhere in Kipling's writings and read how Frankwell Midmore was saved from one tribe of them. He has a clue in their self-comforting cry: 'What the Bandar-log think now the Jungle will think to-morrow'; but this, in its immediate meaning, is not beyond the child, and at no time does the allegory press too hard. Baloo and Bagheera, fighting for their lives in the moonlight at Cold Lairs, are the beloved beasts in peril, the companions of the man-cub in the play-world; when they become the mouthpieces of the Law, and Mowgli has to learn that sorrow never turns aside punishment, it seems to the child a suitable law in this sort of world; the types and morals are fully absorbed into the story. In '**The King's Ankus**' Kipling takes a version of a wide-spread moral apologue, which Chaucer had used for his *Pardoner's Tale,* and combines it with a tale of hidden treasure and the following of a trail. The failure of Mowgli, the fosterling of wolves, to comprehend the value of the cumbrous jewelled ankus, for which men kill each other, serves the same purpose as the Pardoner's sermon. The power of the ancient tale sends a cold breath of awe through the narrative. In "'**Tiger-Tiger!**'" the fable-elements are more insistent. The young wolves desert their old leader to accept Shere Khan's demoralizing advice, and, at the end, when Shere Khan's skin is pegged out on the Council Rock, they illustrate a Wordsworthian moral—'Me this uncharted freedom tires'. At times, especially near the beginning of the series, before the jungle world has grown into full imaginative authority, the human counterparts of the doings of the pack show too clearly. In the matter of the taboo against killing man the wolves are human enough to give an idealistic reason for what is a measure of plain self-interest.

More important than these two worlds, however, is what I can only call the world of the wild and strange, the ancient and the far. It includes myth, but extends beyond it. There are not very many pages of strictly mythological imagination in *The Jungle Books.* There is Hathi's tradition of how Fear came, a more mysterious *Just So* story, told in the setting of the Water-Truce; there is Kotick's search for the shore where man has never come to destroy the seals—a combination of Leif Eriksson's Wonder-Strands with the Islands of the Blest; and there is, in the

later Mowgli tales, the majestic shadow of Adam, King of the Jungle. It is, however, only a shadow; for Mowgli moves in place and time, suffers the ill-temper of Buldeo and the stones of the man-pack, lets Messua comb his hair, and speeds her to the unknown English at Kanhiwara. He has drawn the milk of a woman and a wolf. Messua thinks him a wood-god; but to children he is more like a boy who is helped by kindly beasts in a fairy-tale. He has a fairy-tale extension of power, and his communion with his foster-brothers, which makes old Muller of '**In the Rukh**' describe him as before the Stone Age, is to the child another magic power.

The Mowgli of '**In the Rukh**' does not quite tally with the Mowgli of *The Jungle Books.* Professor Carrington tells us that the tale was written after '**Mowgli's Brothers**', the first of that series; otherwise we should have guessed that it was written before, and, indeed, that is the impression that Kipling himself conveys in *Something of Myself.* It is not so much that '**In the Rukh**' plays in the Doon, a far cry from the Seeonee Hills, or that this Mowgli's sketch of his history needs some humouring to fit it into what we know of the boy of *The Jungle Books,* but he speaks to Gray Brother as to a dog, in human language, and is 'very mistrustful of the firelight and ready to fly back to the thicket on the least alarm'. Yet the child Mowgli spoke to the beasts in their own tongues, and, in the first tale, showed his superiority to them by nursing the Red Flower in a fire-pot and using it as a weapon against the tiger. It is an odd inconsistency, if Professor Carrington is right; but all it signifies, perhaps, is that it took time for an imaginary world to establish its conditions. Kipling was embarked upon a different kind of creation from the brilliant selections from the known world that had made his name. '**Mowgli's Brothers**' never falls upon my ear with quite the authority of the later tales; nor does '**Weland's Sword**', with the first appearance of Puck; and we know that the author rejected the original tales of the *Puck* series. Muller's talk about paganism and the Stone Age does not point exactly down the road that his Daemon [of inspiration] was to travel.

The realm of wonder extends beyond the limits of myth. The magical distance and strangeness, of which there are hints in the *Just So Stories,* are here all around us. In the midst of the jungle there is a vast ruined city, and under it an abandoned treasure-house, where a sacred white cobra still guards the jewels; there are glades, too, where the axe of the little Gond hunter flies across the clearing like a dragon-fly. Up in the Arctic the pack-ice grinds and roars round the unseen shores, and the sorcerer sings charms in his snow-hut. The wise elephants, tame and wild, in the Assamese hills, meet at night to trample out their dancing ground. A Himalayan mountain-side is loosened by rain, and the animals sense the coming landslide and save the holy man who has shown them hospitality. And in all these places people live with strange skills and strange beliefs. Kotuko buckles himself into his belt for the long watch by the seal's breathing-hole; old Buldeo asserts that the Lame Tiger embodies the spirit of a dead money-lender; the seasonal round of a Himalayan village takes place at a great depth below the shrine where Purun

Bhagat meditates. The refinement of human senses to meet special conditions and the intuitive knowledge of ancestral habit are often brought to notice. In the jungle Mowgli weaves little huts with sticks and creeper, like his forefathers the woodcutters, and knowledge comes to him, as to the beasts his brothers, though not so unerringly, by a taint in the air, a falling shadow, a movement of the grass, the faintest of sounds. All this wonder comes with vivid concrete detail. The world unfolds, unspeakably various and wild and old; and everywhere the family group keeps the child in touch with its own reality. Toomai's mother and Matkah the seal sing their lullabies; Big Toomai and Sea-Catch grumble; and Kotuko's little brother gnaws a nice nutty strip of blubber.

But the true *utile dulci* of the children's book is not attained unless it conveys intimations of obligations and passions outside the reach of a child's experience. *The Jungle Books* do this again and again. Sometimes, though not always, a clue may be laid in his hand, or a violent action may be attenuated for his behoof. When Mowgli's bitterness against the man-pack, who have stoned him, doubles his bitterness against the young wolves, who hate him because he has taken thorns out of their feet, he resolves: 'Now I will hunt alone', and his mood is brought nearer to a child's level by the title of his **'Song against People'**. When in his revenge he lets in the jungle on the village, no human blood is shed. Nevertheless, here and in **'Kaa's Hunting'** and **'The King's Ankus'** and **'Red Dog'**, there is a strong note of the terrible, and the corpse-laden waters of the Mutiny in **'The Undertakers'** are horrible enough, even when reduced by distance in the relishing memory of the gluttonous old crocodile. Here the note is macabre, but in **'Red Dog'** it is heroic. The hunting-grounds of Mowgli's pack are over-run by the inferior but vastly more numerous pack of the Dholes from the Deccan, and the wolves fight to the death for their lairs and their cubs. Only the confidence that comes from moving for a long time in a powerful and coherent world of the imagination could have enabled Kipling to write this tale at this pitch. It is extraordinarily—almost blindly—bold, and courts every disaster; and yet I do not think it can be read without emotion by any except such as are unable to read these tales at all. We are presented with the ancient patterns of desperate valour—the threat of the barbarian horde, the sacrificial exploit, the fight in the narrow place, the death of the old leader—in terms which, if we stop to think, are wholly artificial. But we do not stop to think, because the patterns are too strong. The same thing happens in Professor Tolkien's *Lord of the Rings*. The spells work. It is very odd that they do, and a strong note of surprise was perceptible in the reviews of Professor Tolkien's great imaginative story. In **'Red Dog'**, Won-Tolla, the maimed Outlier, whose mate and cubs have been killed by the horde and who asks only to fight them and die, runs three-legged along the river bank, as his enemies come downstream, taunting them and playing 'his horrible sport'. Considering what parallels such an episode must recall, it is odd that Won-Tolla holds his place as an adequate symbol. The language of the battle is wolf-metaphor. 'The bone is cracked', says Phaon, as the Dholes give back. There is no attempt to obscure the

growling, biting, worrying pack, and the tale ends with the cold requiem of Chil the Kite as his hosts drop to their feast. But before that Won-Tolla has died on his slain enemy, and Mowgli has held up Akela to sing his death-song. It is carried through with astonishing conviction and intensity, and with an elevation that does not flag. The laws of life and death have their way with Mowgli's brethren, and the child learns all this from the shelter of a fairy-tale.

The last tale, **'The Spring Running'**, where Mowgli goes back to his human kindred, is written with a delicate mixture of humour and pathos. At last the Time of New Talk, which sends the wild creatures singing and roving through the jungle and incites even Bagheera to undignified antics, touches the young man. **'Red Dog'** could be told through bare facts; but to convey the compulsion that is driving Mowgli, which neither he nor the child who reads about him understands, Kipling has to move indirectly. Mowgli wonders if he has eaten poison; his unhappiness covers him as water covers a log, and the tears that Raksha, his wolf-mother, has told him are the signs of manhood, come to his eyes, for 'It is hard to cast the skin', says Kaa. But he has seen the young girl walk through the crops, and he goes with the favour of the jungle and—such is the reconciling nature of the fairy-tale—with the company of his four-footed foster-brothers. The young child accepts his departure as he accepts Hiawatha's, as another obscure necessity of the strange life of men, and responds to the high mournfulness of the farewell; and the acceptance of uncomprehended necessity is no bad preparation for life.

Rosemary Sutcliff

SOURCE: "Two Worlds" and "Kipling Today," in *Rudyard Kipling*, 1960. Reprint by Henry Z. Walck, 1961, pp. 32-9, 53-7.

[The *Jungle Books*] were my own first introduction to Kipling. I was not more than five or six at the time, but I possessed a mother who read aloud most beautifully, and found great joy in doing it, and so from the first, I was able to enjoy books far in advance of those I could have coped with myself. From our earliest acquaintance I loved the Mowgli stories with a rather special love, not necessarily stronger, but different in kind from the love I had for any other book. I loved them for their strangeness, their 'otherness' which was somehow kept from ever getting out of bounds or becoming frightening by the familiar pattern of Mowgli's own relationships, for instance with the cosy close-drawn family life of Father and Mother Wolf and the four cubs. My feeling for the stories has of course changed with the years, without weakening; and in a way the stories themselves seem to have changed, too, for like nearly all the really great children's books, they are written on many levels, and for me they have become a following-out of divided life and divided loyalties, the unbearable choice that has to be made and has to be borne. Now also, having come to be a writer myself, I can stand back a little and appreciate, amongst sundry other matters, the superb craftsmanship that has gone into creating the Jungle Folk, each one a perfectly rounded individual (save of course for the Monkey People, whose whole essence is that they are not individuals at all, but merely a gibbering mob) and each one perfectly within the bounds of his own animal nature. These are not human beings in animal skins, as even *Black Beauty,* another love of my childhood, tends to be; nothing so undignified. They are animals lordly in their own right, with the innate dignity of the wild animal who has never been taught to ride a bicycle in a circus.

I realised, of course, precisely nothing of all that when I was five, but I accepted the Jungle Dwellers as dear and deeply satisfying friends, and they were so real to me, especially Bagheera with the voice as soft as wild honey dripping from a tree, that remembering those early readings with my mother, I can still recapture the physical sensation of the living, sensuous, velvet-over-fire-and-steel-springs warmth of his skin, as though I had in actual fact once been on stroking terms with a black panther. I was aware also of Kipling's extraordinary power of getting under the skin of man or beast, time or place or situation, which has seemed to me ever since to be one of his greatest gifts; and I remember trying to explain to my mother what I felt about this: 'Well you see, other people write about things from the outside in, but Kipling writes about them from the inside out.' And therein lies a world of difference.

As a child I loved **The Jungle Book** best, because I knew that all would go well with the people I loved in it; I knew that even when Mowgli was turned out of the pack, he would come back to spread Shere Khan's hide on the Council Rock. But as soon as **The Second Jungle Book** was begun (my mother and I always read straight through from one to the other) I began to smell desolation in store, and even across that most wonderful story of **"The King's Ankus"** lay the shadow of **"Red Dog"** and **"The Spring Running."** I could scarcely bear to listen to either of those two stories; the first battered me and tore at my heart strings with the tremendous sorrows of tragic saga, the second made my whole world ache with griefs and longings that I could not yet understand. But I am inclined to think that it does a child no harm to have its heart wrung occasionally. It broadens the mind and deepens the compassion.

At any mention of the *Jungle Books,* it is always the Mowgli stories that spring to mind; but there are of course many other stories beside. In my young days I particularly loved those of **"Rikki-Tikki-Tavi"** and **"The White Seal"** (why did the story of Kotik always seem so sad? When one comes to think of it, it had a perfectly good happy ending) which now I would exchange, both of them together, for that most lovely and strong and fragile story, **"The Miracle of Purun Baghat,"** which in those days was beyond my reach, as I think it would be beyond the reach of most children. But what is beyond his reach, the child will come back and reach up for again, when once his imagination has been captured; and there is in the *Jungle Books* plenty to catch at the imagination. . . .

Kipling has so much to give to children still, of the things that do not date at all; worthwhile values to set against those of the horror comic; a rich and evocative use of language; stories, never ordinary, in which, because of that gift of his for writing about all things and people from the inside out instead of from the outside in, it is especially easy for the reader or read-to to perform the minor miracle of self-identification which so much helps a small growing mind to stretch itself and open out.

By no means every child will like Kipling, even his *Jungle Books* and **Just So Stories;** and those for whom the penny does not drop and the bell does not ring, will probably dislike him very much indeed, for he is one of those writers about whom there can be no half measures. But every child should have a chance, by having one or other of the books put into his hands at the right moment, to discover for himself whether he likes Kipling or not. Because the child who has never run with Mowgli's wolfpack, or stood with Parnesius and Pertinax to defend the Northern Wall, or thrust a very dead cat under the floor of a rival dormitory to the full length of his arm and Beetle's brolly, has missed something that he will not get from any other writer.

Roger Lancelyn Green

SOURCE: "Letting in the Jungle," in *Kipling and the Children,* Elek Books Ltd., 1965, pp. 108-30.

[Kipling] learnt something from [Ernest Thompson] Seton's early animal sketches which were appearing in *St. Nicholas' Magazine,* but one has only to compare 'Lobo, the King of Currumpaw' with **'Mowgli's Brothers'**—both stories of wolves, and both published in American magazines in 1894—to see the absolute difference of approach. Though it is not fair to compare stories with such completely different intentions, the comparison shows how immeasurably greater Kipling's achievement was than that of Seton—or of any of those writers whose works had inspired the creation of Mowgli's Jungle. Seton wrote brilliant and absorbing studies of wild animals—but nothing more, while Kipling ventured into 'the world's fourth dimension' and brought back an echo, a reflection from that which cannot be heard or seen—by the ears or eyes of the body though we are for ever reaching out after it.

In Kipling's case this is not quite the touch of the numinous which we feel in the stories of George MacDonald or C. S. Lewis—but the Law of the Jungle is as much a part of the 'Tao'—the basic Knowledge of Good and Evil, of Right and Wrong conduct implanted in Mankind—as the more consciously recognised duty of Curdie to the King and of the dwellers in Narnia to Aslan.

Little of this kind of message can be pinned down in *The Jungle Books,* none is realized by the young reader. To him the conscious joy is in the story of Mowgli, his adventures with Shere Khan, with the Bandarlog, with the Man Pack, the Dholes, and only finally in **'The Spring Running'** with something that cannot be visualized or described. But the lasting joy, and one already making itself felt at a deeper level than mere excitement or entertainment, is the immediate identification of himself with Mowgli. For Mowgli's adventures are both of the body and of the spirit—and the spiritual adventures are his also and will be his again and, if passed, will not be recognized yet though they have been felt and experienced.

As in all writings that capture something of the mythopaeic, the meaning cannot be interpreted as in the case of a direct allegory such as *Pilgrim's Progress*. Mowgli may be 'young life conscious of itself and its extraordinarily stimulating world' in both the personal and the general sense, but we must each read our own environment and aspect of the Great Predicament into his adventures. In whatever outward form it comes to each of us the inward experience is the same as Mowgli's, with the emphasis on different facets perhaps, but the whole recognizably universal. We can say, if we like to be more particular, that the home-bred boy goes out into the rough world of school as Mowgli goes to the Man Pack—or that the youth has his first temptation to ally himself with the Teddy Boys, as Mowgli is tempted to join the Bandarlog: but neither of these is the full meaning or indeed more than the actual meaning re-dressed in a form that at once disguises it even more than the form does which Kipling gave it. Or, with a wider vision and so a little nearer to a real interpretation, we may see the Jungle as the Never-Never Land of childhood from which 'Mowgli casts out Mowgli' as he ventures into the adult world of accepted responsibility—the antithesis of Peter Pan, 'the tragic boy' who runs back into childhood instead of forward into manhood. 'The Spring Running' is, indeed, the most haunting and provocative of all the Mowgli stories and exerts its magic even on the child who can interpret none of its meaning and holds that it is not so exciting as an adventure like 'Red Dog'—and we find new echoes and new meanings in it, as indeed in the majority of the Mowgli stories, whenever we re-read and at whatever age.

Roger Lancelyn Green

SOURCE: "Rudyard Kipling and the World of School," in *Tellers of Tales,* revised edition, 1965, pp. 225-37. Reprint by Kaye & Ward, Ltd., 1969.

Kipling had many imitators for most of his children's books—'My Jungle Books begat Zoos of them,' he recorded. His own two volumes, published in 1894 and 1895, are still his most popular works—particularly those stories telling of Mowgli. They became at once and have ever since continued to be the happy hunting ground of children seeking a new world of make-believe: 'We'll play Jungle,' says Oswald in the first story of [E. Nesbit's] *The Would-be-Goods*—which had appeared in *The Pall Mall Magazine* in August 1900, 'and I shall be Mowgli. The rest of you can be what you like—Mowgli's father and mother, or any of the beasts.' Even so have we all played ever since—particularly those of us who are lucky enough to have had the stories read to us so early that we grew up with them as part of our very being. 'I have no

recollection of that first introduction,' wrote Rosemary Sutcliff in 1963, 'it seems to me rather that Mowgli and old wise Baloo and, above all, Bagheera the black panther, with a voice as soft as wild honey, dripping from a tree, were part of my world from the beginning.'

The Jungle Books grow with reading; the skill and the deeper meanings dawn slowly on us as we increase in years, and the eternal allegory of **'The Spring Running,'** poignant even to tears, reveals its true meaning as we too pass from childhood to the responsibilities and disillusion of the adult world.

J. I. M. Stewart

SOURCE: "From *The Jungle Books* to *Rewards and Fairies,*" in *Rudyard Kipling,* Dodd, Mead & Company, 1966, pp. 136-51.

The fame of **The Jungle Book** and **The Second Jungle Book**—the most widely popular of all Kipling's writings—is owing to their central figure, Mowgli, the child nurtured by wolves, who survives and grows to manhood as Master of the Jungle. Mowgli's origin (as a literary creation, that is) is attended by some obscurity, and it is best to begin with the last that we hear about him. This is in **"In the Rukh"** (*Many Inventions*), a story designed to be entirely realistic, and quite certainly not written for young readers. Gisborne, an officer of the Indian Department of Woods and Forests, encounters on the fringes of the jungle a beautiful youth, "naked except for the loincloth, but crowned with a wreath of the tasselled blossoms of the white convolvulus creeper," and with a voice "clear and bell-like, utterly different from the usual whine of the native." He is like an angel, we are told—or, better, like a Greek god: one of "the illustrations in the Classical Dictionary," as Gisborne puts it to himself. His name is Mowgli, and he proves to have an amazing command over all the animals of the rukh. He takes service with Gisborne; and later Gisborne's superior, a German called Muller who has immense experience of the ways of the jungle, understands his case:

> "I tell you dot only once in my service, and dot is thirty years, haf I met a boy dot began as this man began. Und he died. Sometimes you hear of dem in der census reports, but dey all die. Dis man haf lived, and he is an anachronism, for he is before der Iron Age, and der Stone Age. Look here, he is at der beginnings of der history of man—Adam in der Garden, und now we want only an Eva!"

Mowgli gains an Eva, in the person of the ill-treated daughter of Gisborne's native butler: it is the speed with which he not only woos her but wins her that makes it certain that Kipling was not writing for children here. We overhear Mowgli's explaining himself to his bride. Reared by wolves and with wolf-cubs as his foster brothers, he had grown up among the beasts until a time came when the beasts told him to go. He had then become a herder of cattle among men, but had been driven out by them when the old woman who looked after him had seen him playing with his "brethren" by night. Since then he had been a wanderer—but now as an employee of the Department of Woods and Forests he will receive a wage and a pension. At the end of the story we have a glimpse of Mowgli's first child, guarded by a wolf.

What is interesting about **"In the Rukh"** is the entire absence of the magic which the *Jungle Books* were going to create. Kipling has not yet glimpsed what material he has under his hand; this Mowgli is an implausible mixture of Noble Savage, Indian native properly respectful of the raj, and a godling strayed out of Greek mythology in a manner rather reminiscent of some of the more whimsical short stories of Mr. E. M. Forster. Mowgli plays a flute, "as it might have been the song of some wandering wood-god." This last association is emphasized; "the hint of the wood-god was not to be mistaken," we are told a few pages later.

"In the Rukh" was almost certainly written before Kipling had conceived the Mowgli stories proper, but in its published form it may embody revisions designed to make

it fit in with the evolving series. As it is, Mowgli's story seems to have been developed without much planning. Taking the two *Jungle Books* together, he appears in eight out of fifteen stories—including the first, which begins with his being adopted by wolf parents, and the last, which tells of his final departure from the world of the beasts. That there is true imaginative coherence between the Mowgli stories proper appears as soon as we try to set this last of them, **"The Spring Running,"** in any relationship with **"In the Rukh."** The Mowgli of **"In the Rukh"** walks into the story with nothing much behind him except (with an obvious effect of paradox) certain unusual educational advantages. "Hard exercise, the best of good eating, and baths whenever he felt in the least hot or dusty, had given him strength and growth far beyond his age." He is a cross between a Wordsworthian child of nature and a boy scout. He walks out of the story at the other end in the company of a nice girl and with the intention of settling down. He knows all the answers—just as the uninspired Kipling always did. The Mowgli of **"The Spring Running,"** on the contrary, knows neither his world nor himself with any certainty, because he is a human spirit in the throes of some painful and mysterious

From The Jungle Book, *by Rudyard Kipling. Illustrated by Fritz Eichenberg.*

process of growth. It is Spring. "The year turns," Bagheera the Black Panther tells him. "The Jungle goes forward. The Time of New Talk is near." Mowgli must have heard this before. But now he is on the verge of manhood, and there faces him a hard truth, obscurely seen. A boy may run with the Jungle People, but "Man goes to Man." His old companions do not reject him, but—this Spring, he notices it—they come tardily at his summons, having concerns which can be none of his. Yet all this, and the mere surface solution of his problem in the last pages of the story, make too finite and identifiable the occasion of the unhappiness that has come to Mowgli. Something else is elusively present.

This is a characteristic of all the Mowgli stories. All are moral fables—even to the extent of sometimes making us feel that Mowgli is over-lavishly provided with tutors, and is rather constantly having to put up with what the hymn calls Instruction's warning Voice. But this is not, in fact, oppressive—perhaps because there is always some hinted further significance which we have to strain to catch. Take, for example, the monkey-folk, the *Bandar-log*. They stand for something outside themselves, answer to something in our own experience which we are not proud of. But just what? Here, and in some other places, the fable beckons us to territory where we must think for ourselves. And there is one puzzle bigger than all the others. It is what the books mean when they talk about "the Law."

In the *Second Jungle Book* there is a poem called **"The Law of the Jungle."** A schoolmaster might call this title an oxymoron—"a rhetorical figure by which contradictory terms are conjoined." For the jungle is, almost by definition, lawless; we call this, that or the other human activity a "jungle" when we are thinking of some area of savage competition in which no holds are barred. But Kipling's poem turns out to be a set of rules for wolves. Some of them are again of the boy-scout order: "Wash daily from nose-tip to tail-tip." But in general they provide a sensible code for conducting the necessarily predatory and lethal routine of a wolf pack on lines which will preserve the pack's social cohesion—and also in terms of what we must think of as fair play. This conception will not impress us in itself. Children, who feel no impassible gulf between the animal world and the nursery, expect the idea of "what is fair" to obtain in the one as in the other; and they are reassured when they find it so represented to them. Hence hosts of juvenile beast-fables designed for edification. Kipling designs edification, and in this interest contrives to give his Law almost crushing force:

> Now these are the Laws of the Jungle, and many
>   and mighty are they;
> But the head and the hoof of the Law and the
>   haunch and the hump is—Obey!

If we wish to criticize the whole conception we shall probably say that, here in the context of the *Jungle Books,* Kipling is casting the impressive disguise of authentic moral law over certain aspects of animal behaviour instinctively evolved to secure the survival of a species. To test the validity of this criticism we should have to enter deeply into Kipling's theory of society. He certainly believed that moral ideas can be derived only from experience, but that as there is much that is common and universal in all human experience so is there a common and universal law lying beneath all the variations of racial and national cultures. It is a law codified in custom, and its recognition and preservation is the distinguishing principle of civilization. Peoples or societies or individuals ignoring "the Law" thereby diminish themselves—becoming (in the famous and unfortunately ambiguous phrase in **"Recessional"**) "lesser breeds." To show a wolf pack as within "the Law," and a chatter of monkeys as outside it, is simply to use the method of fable to enforce the depth and reach of the idea. But to account for the appeal of the *Jungle Books* we have to go back to Kipling's almost unexampled command of the sense of wonder; his power to bring, as from very far away, reports which validate themselves in the telling, so that our disbelief is suspended in the face of whole new ranges of experience.

Elizabeth Nesbitt

SOURCE: "The Great Originator," in *A Critical History of Children's Literature by Cornelia Meigs and Others,* edited by Cornelia Meigs, revised edition, Macmillan Publishing Company, 1969, pp. 310-17.

In the eighties and nineties, while Howard Pyle was writing and illustrating his fairy tales, retold romances and historic fiction in America, and Stevenson was giving new impetus to the tale of romantic adventure in England, the writings of a new and original genius startled the "precious" era, which was an aftermath of Pre-Raphaelitism and the aesthetic movement.

In 1889, at the age of twenty-four, Rudyard Kipling (1865-1936) came to London from India, already an object of wonder, an exciting and controversial figure because of the fame of his short stories. It is little wonder that he had so spectacular an effect upon that period. Even now it is hardly possible to analyze his genius, compounded of so many things—of inheritance and environment, of natural endowment and temperament, of training and experience.

His mother was Alice Macdonald, one of whose sisters married Sir Edward Burne-Jones. It was in their home that Kipling, as a small boy, found escape and relief from the bitter, unhappy experience of the years when he was committed to the care of a woman incredibly unsuited to assume responsibility for a child. His father was John Lockwood Kipling, a man of culture, architectural sculptor in the Bombay School of Art.

Rudyard Kipling was born in Bombay on December 30, 1865. As a child, he learned to speak Hindustani; indeed it must have seemed to him his natural language, since it is recorded that he had to be urged to speak English to his parents. From babyhood he was steeped in the legends and folk tales of a country which is a cradle of folk literature. All his life he was to keep the love of imagery and metaphor gained in his early years. At the age of six, after five years of normal, happy child life, he was sent home to England to live in the house of a woman who, together with her son, reminds one inevitably of some of Dickens' more fantastic character creations. The terrible unhappiness of his life at this time, so vividly remembered in *Something of Myself,* was relieved only by the holidays spent in the normal, happy and gracious home of his uncle, Sir Edward Burne-Jones. That he returned from these vacations with a tragic submissiveness to the indignities suffered at the hands of the woman to whose care his parents had unwittingly given him, and that he maintained silence about his ill-treatment, are facts not so unnatural as they may seem. His behavior in this respect is indicative of the pitiful helplessness a child may feel, in greater or lesser degree, under the domination of an adult world. It is possible also that this experience deepened the innate tenderness and sympathy he felt for children all his life. Fortunately his school life in the United Services College at Westward Ho! North Devon, where he was sent at the age of thirteen, was more normal.

On leaving this school at seventeen, Kipling returned to India and took a position on the staff of the Lahore *Civil and Military Gazette.* The next several years were the most important and influential of his life. Inherently, he was a great literary journalist, and his experience, first on the *Gazette* and later on the *Pioneer* at Allahabad, sharpened and developed his natural talents—his power of observation, his insatiable curiosity, his acute sensitivity to the romantic, the dramatic, and the actual, his quick response to humor and to pathos, his great sense of fact and at the same time of the truth and significance underlying fact, his human interest in all classes of society and in all kinds of people. The discipline of his daily work, which had to be carried on in spite of tropical heat and consequent illness, taught him compression and the art of vigorous re-creation of experience, situation, and character made colorful and vital by highly selective wording and phrasing. His experiences as a reporter convinced him of the truth of Edmund Gosse's principle that there is nothing in life itself that is not fit material for literature.

His experience and his genius bore fruit in the shape of short stories, some of them written while he was still in his teens, collected in *Plain Tales From the Hills* (1888). It is little wonder that these stories, reaching England before Kipling did, made people aware of a new note in literature. They combined a new kind of realism and a new kind of romanticism. On the one hand, they dealt with the color, the mystery, the exotic quality of the East; and on the other hand, they did not scruple to introduce sordid realities. Through the power of imagination and of style, they rendered the commonplace significant. They were disconcerting, but they could not be ignored.

It is inevitable that so original and experimental a writer should cause controversy. Contemporary criticism accused him of vulgarity, later criticism of imperialism. In the opinion of many, these accusations reflect upon the validity of the criticism, rather than upon Kipling. To him, to

paraphrase a line of his own, there was nothing common in all God's earth. The blemish of imperialism, if it exists at all, is unimportant in relation to the profound and universal morality which underlies his writing. Fortunately, unless exaggeration and distortion enter, such arguments have little relevance to the present discussion concerned with Kipling's books for children. Here, the point of supreme importance is that, with the possible exception of Lewis Carroll, Kipling is the most original, the least derivative of writers for children up to his time and, in these respects, unexcelled since.

In 1892 Kipling married an American, Caroline Balestier. From 1892 to 1896 they lived in Brattleboro, Vermont, where *The Jungle Books* were written (1894, 1895). Not without significance is the fact that critiques of Kipling's work by those not personally nor professionally concerned with children's literature include discussion of his books for children. Still more important is the fact that these books are described frequently as something more than new childhood classics, since such comment indicates growing realization that literature for children may be, and often is, valuable in the study of an author's work and in the study of literature as a whole.

As has been pointed out by [Frederick Joseph Harvey] Darton among others, in *Children's Books in England,* the initial idea of *The Jungle Books* has precedent in legend and history. Nowhere, however, in traditional or sophisticated literature, has the theme of a human boy reared and nurtured by animals had so unique or meaningful a treatment. No doubt the beast-tale was known to Kipling, acquainted as he was in childhood with the folk literature of India. *Stalky & Co.* (1899) gives evidence of the impression made upon him and his boyhood friends by Joel Chandler Harris' classic Uncle Remus stories. But Kipling's treatment of animals in *The Jungle Books* is, as always with him, an innovation. His literary work stems not from other literature, but from life itself, and from the experience of life, whether animal or human.

Of the fifteen stories in the two books, eight are concerned with Mowgli and the jungle. The world Kipling has created in these stories has an impelling reality. Once known it exists in our minds forever, vivid and familiar as an actual experience. It is an elemental world, and it deals with elemental and eternal things—love and hate, fear and courage, loyalty and treachery, honor and dishonor, honesty and deceit, struggle for existence and the survival of the fittest. Its deepest compulsion is toward obedience to the law, a law which is not an arbitrary thing imposed by authority, but rather a code evolving inevitably from fundamentals of living. It follows that the chief quality of these stories is that of a high ethic, a morality transmuted by imagination into something both functional and inspirational. The basic idea is that of responsibility; from a sense of responsibility comes willing obedience to the law, which is made for the good of all. It is the old, old idea of the obligation owed by the one to the many and by the many to the one. It is the concept of true freedom, for only those who are truly free can discipline themselves so that liberty does not become license.

Vitalized by Kipling's great power as a writer, this moral code transcends didacticism and becomes something immensely convincing and unquestionably acceptable. The stories have a gripping quality, drawing one into themselves, necessitating no effort at acclimatization on the part of the reader. The mingled humor and pathos, so frequently made up of little things—it is in little touches that Kipling most excels—make the strange setting of the jungle, the weirdness of the Cold Lairs, the primitive quality of some of the incidents, familiar and even intimate. In contrast are the majesty and grandeur of the moments of drama, many of which have epic quality—for a supreme instance, the moment when Akela, his leadership challenged, faces the Pack with dignity and reserve, holding to the Law of the Jungle. Indeed, it is Akela and his kind who dominate the stories, and rightly so, since it is they who have hewn out the Law of the Jungle. True to their types, they are yet individuals—Baloo the bear, Bagheera the panther, and Kaa the serpent. The monkeys are the essence of monkeyishness and still the prototypes of all who are outside the law, because they have no ability to persist, to progress, no sense of responsibility. In the center of it all is Mowgli, nurtured, loved, and educated in the law by the leaders of the jungle, but innately and irrevocably man, so that even those who love him cannot look into his eyes for long. Story, emotion, drama, and character are interpreted for the reader by Kipling's style, by its simple dignity and formality, its lovely cadence and haunting phrase.

The incidental stories are the equals of Kipling's best short stories, especially **"Rikki-Tikki-Tavi," "The White Seal,"** and **"Toomai of the Elephants."** Many of the poems, which, in accordance with his frequent custom, open and close the stories, may be numbered among his finest poetry. **"Seal Lullaby"** is a perfect exemplification of its kind, with its slow, swinging rhythm, and the recurring, drowsy "s" and "l" sounds. **"Mowgli's Song,"** recited over the body of Shere Khan, is reminiscent of the ancient epics in its repetitive quality, its defiance and triumph, its measured chant. . . .

To deal with Kipling's gift to children's literature is to deal inevitably in superlatives. He was one of the greatest of storytellers, one of those who narrate with authority, as one who has seen or heard these things. His intense interest in all sorts and conditions of men, his acute sensitivity to the drama implicit in human and animal life, his universality of interpretation, his imaginative power, endow his stories with a vitality that makes them living entities in their own right. The strength of his belief in the imperishable decencies lends them lasting significance. His masterly command of the English language, his ear for cadence and rhythm, his gift for creating mood, emotion, and atmosphere through sheer use of words, give his style an almost magic quality. His originality of mind, his utter lack of dependence upon past or existent patterns, make him the great innovator of form and type. The vigor of his mind, the keenness of his insight, the breadth of his knowledge, enrich his stories with freedom and profundity of thought.

By the end of the first decade of the twentieth century, Howard Pyle, Robert Louis Stevenson, and Rudyard Ki-

pling had established literature for children as literature in every right sense of the word. What is more important, they had established it as a force to be considered by literary men as an integral part of the development of literature as a whole.

Gillian Avery

SOURCE: "The Children's Writer," in *The Age of Kipling,* edited by John Gross, Simon and Schuster, 1972, pp. 113-18.

Although Kipling's stock has risen enormously over the past generation, his popularity with children appears to have declined. Rosemary Sutcliff, second to none in her admiration, her own writing profoundly influenced by him, sadly admitted this in her monograph on Kipling as a children's writer (1960); my own contact with children had suggested it, and questioning of librarians bore it out. Only the *Just So Stories* survive as a universal favourite. The first *Jungle Book* is borrowed by [Scout] Wolf Cubs, or by those who have seen the Disney film, but is usually returned without enthusiasm, while I have not found anyone now at school who has ever read the Puck stories. Kipling's reputation as a children's writer is 'artificially kept alive'—the phrase is not mine, but a librarian's—by the fact that he is on the reading-list of teachers' training colleges and the Wolf Cub and Brownie movements. . . .

Perhaps the official hand of the Scout movement has helped to deaden [the *Jungle Books*]. All the ritual of the Wolf Cubs is derived from the first *Jungle Book,* and a drab re-telling of 'Mowgli's Brothers' appears in the Wolf Cub Handbook. Cubs weekly stalk and kill Shere Khan the Tiger and Tabaqui the Jackal, so that for many the jungle is overlaid by the thought of a dusty church hall and little boys in green caps chanting 'Akela, we'll do our best'.

Still, Kipling should certainly never be thought of as the type of the official writer to [founder of the Boy Scouts, Sir Robert] Baden Powell. Even his *Land and Sea Tales for Scouts and Guides,* where he is described on the title page as 'Commissioner, Boy Scouts', contains much that is hardly in the spirit of the Scout and Guide laws. There is, for instance, a light-hearted further adventure of Stalky, who gets himself out of a tight corner by locking up a farmer and his men and lobbing stones at the cattle in the farmyard until they are frantic with fear and pain. Most of the stories, except for the fact that they are adventurous, are completely irrelevant to Baden Powell's movement, and **'His Gift'**, which alone does treat of Scouts, shows that the Commissioner has not really grasped all the technicalities of the organization. It also turns on one of his favourite themes, hatred. Here 'raging hate against a too-badged, too virtuous senior' at last stirs the buffoon of the troop out of his torpor.

The Mowgli stories make up only a proportion of the two *Jungle Books;* there are three of them in the first, and five in the second. The remainder are all stories about animals, but they have not that savage enchantment which held the imagination of people who remember loving Mowgli as children. . . .

Considered as an animal story, 'Rikki-Tikki-Tavi' is a better one than any about the jungle. It really does convey the character of the mongoose and the cobras without a touch of the anthropomorphism that lies so heavily over the other. So does the macabre 'Undertakers', a conversation between a crocodile, a jackal, and an adjutant bird concerning various sorts of carrion flesh, with the crocodile wistfully recalling his satiation in the Mutiny days. But the Mowgli stories possess what the others do not, a fantasy and a wonder and a sadness. 'The grip of the stories was extraordinary,' recalls Miss Tompkins, 'and a sense of something wild and deep and old infected me as I listened.' As a child I myself could never understand Mowgli's tactics when he trapped Shere Khan, I was bored by his visits to the Human Pack, and missed most of the point of the superb 'King's Ankus'. But my imagination was seized by the description of the monkey-folk carrying Mowgli between them in their headlong flight through the tree-tops: 'the terrible check and jerk at the end of the swing over nothing but empty air brought his heart between his teeth' (a marvellously convincing detail that). And I went back time and again to the description of Cold Lairs, the lost city in the jungle where the monkeys hold court and where they fight and lose the battle with Kaa the python.

But Baden Powell did not just choose the *Jungle Books* because the fantasy appealed to small boys. They do have something of the primness of the conventional Victorian children's book mingled with the wild strangeness of the jungle. Kipling's wolves are not cowardly and treacherous like other story-book wolves. Their great virtue is their solidarity and loyalty to the Pack, and the family that adopts the infant Mowgli maintains to the end, when he is a grown man, a touching domestic unity, as safe and certain as in one of Charlotte Yonge's families. Kipling also imposes a curious gentlemanly code upon the jungle. He provides Mowgli with two mentors, Baloo the Bear and Bagheera the Panther, disconcertingly like public-school masters, who teach him the Law of the Jungle. There are hints at Kaa's superior moral status to other snakes because as a python he uses his strength to kill and despises poison-snakes as cowards. The inferiority of the Bandar-log is emphasized, the monkey-folk who

> have no law. They are outcasts. They have no speech of their own, but use the stolen words which they overhear when they listen, and peep and wait up above in the branches. Their way is not our way. They are without leaders. They have no remembrances. They boast and chatter and pretend they are a great people about to do great affairs in the jungle, but the falling of a nut turns their minds to laughter and all is forgotten.

The people of the jungle are bound by law, and one of those laws is that they may not eat man—it is *unsportsmanlike.*

Baden Powell made much of the moral patches, and slid over the episodes that were alien to his purpose. Kipling, even when he was writing for children, was still attracted to hatred, here seen at its most ferocious in 'Letting in the Jungle'. Mowgli, offended by the behaviour of the village towards the woman who has sheltered him, lusts for revenge. It is a community that lives 'year in and year out as near to starvation as the Jungle was near to them', but he incites Hathi the elephant to destroy it, knowing that if the crops perish it will be death for the people. Even Hathi demurs: 'We have no quarrel with them, and it needs the red rage of great pain ere we bear down the places where men sleep.' But Mowgli is inexorable:

> I do not wish even their bones to lie on the clean earth. Let them go and find a fresh lair. They cannot stay here. I have seen and smelled the blood of the woman that gave me food—the woman whom they would have killed but for me. Only the smell of the new grass on their door-steps can take away that smell. It burns in my mouth. Let in the Jungle, Hathi!

It is often asserted that the best children's books come from authors who are not writing deliberately with children in mind, but for themselves. It is also said that the best children's authors are those who have their own childhood in mind, or who still retain in some respects a child-like outlook. But when the point is made it is usually assumed that the childhood was a happy one. Kipling's was not. In 'Baa Baa, Black Sheep' the tormented and lonely Punch, alias ten-year-old Rudyard, 'brooded in the shadow that fell about him and cut him off from the world, inventing horrible punishments for "dear Harry", or plotting another line of the tangled web of deception that he wrapped round Aunty Rosa'. The story concludes: 'When young lips have drunk deep of the bitter waters of Hate, Suspicion, and Despair, all the Love in the world will not wholly take away that knowledge; though it may turn darkened eyes for a while to the light, and teach faith where no Faith was.'

This experience left its mark on *Stalky,* and on the *Jungle Books.*

Margaret Blount

SOURCE: "The Tables Turned at the Zoo: Mowgli and Stuart Little," in *Animal Land: The Creatures of Children's Fiction,* William Morrow & Company, Inc., 1975, pp. 226-44.

[In *The Jungle Books*] the Jungle is on one side of the gulf and civilization, such as it is, on the other. Kipling makes the leap in the exploration of the man-joining-animals theme (wish fulfilment in so many of us) by reversing the usual order and making the Jungle the important place, containing an advanced animal society which is difficult to join and in which it is as difficult to live. The humans in the stories are unimportant supernumeraries living uneasy lives on the Jungle's outskirts, or in clearings that seem to be hardly won and easily lost. The

English fade into the background. 'White men' are indeed only mentioned (apart from **'In the Rukh'**) twice, as some distant authority, responsible for Indian welfare but of no relevance to Jungle life.

The Jungle is the real world. It is described as a place of great beauty, delight and variability, with its forests, rivers, pools, hills, rocks and cold lairs, or places in which the humans have been once and are no more. It always seems to be growing larger, as if the victorious animal kingdom were on the advance. No towns or streets eat up this India, for the animal habitations threaten and destroy what man has made. The Indian villages are described as primitive places: the adults are ignorant, priest-ridden, bigoted and cruel; there are a few groves of sugar cane and herds of cattle managed by children. Mowgli himself, the wolf boy, is a figure of powerful, mythical qualities. He represents the very essence of the longing that humans have to experience animal life, to participate and to understand, to go back to the garden of Eden where all animal life was innocent and good and Man was the leader. Narnia is such a place, and so is the Jungle of *Tarzan of the Apes*, where all the 'good' animals come to the Man's aid when he is in danger, or threatened by the 'bad' ones. Here, Peter Pan has a Wendy; Tarzan and Jane live an idyllic life in the Jungle before Tarzan is discovered to be a millionaire, well able to live an idyllic life outside it.

Narnia has rules of its own and, while closely involved with talking, reasoning animals for plots, is not really *about* them in the end, and Tarzan is merely a potent and exciting fairy tale. But *The Jungle Books* have an immense amount of realistic detail that impels the reader to take the situation seriously. One never pauses to think that the situation of a boy, brought up among animals and able to communicate with them, eventually emerging as their leader, is impossible; it has a kind of logical poetry in its triumphant reversal. Mowgli, who grows into an almost godlike figure, is not, in himself, particularly interesting. It is his predicament which holds the fascination, and the nature of the society in which he finds himself, which, by true reversal, turns out to be so much more complicated than that of the Indian village from which he came.

It is a vast society; belonging to it would appear to be almost as difficult as belonging to the whole human race at once, something which humans find impossible, even in part. All the languages and battle cries and passwords of the animals have to be learned and remembered, otherwise peril is ever present. Even so, there is danger from non-conformists and sub-species such as the bees, the wild dogs, monkeys and snakes. The rules and signs and exclusions are endless and the slightest mistake may mean death, for this uneasy world is a serious, dangerous place and though its societies are ordered, they are not civilised. It is as though we are shown a number of armies engaged in skirmishes in a vast, unseen, limitless country; or the largest, yet most exclusive public school imaginable with its rules and prohibitions, head boy, prefects and renegades. Mowgli is in the position of the new boy

who works his way up the school to become head boy, and eventually to leave, with scenes of nostalgia and regret for his youth and parting from his school friends and masters; or of the new recruit who rises steadily through the ranks to become field marshal, and then, in an unlikely fashion, leaves the army for civilian life while still in his prime. . . . The Jungle is essentially a place of rules and order, and *The Jungle Books* are *about* rules and order, and about the outsider who learns to conform and to pass on to a different (and, one feels, lesser) kind of society. It becomes even more obvious that the Mowgli stories are partially disguised school or soldier stories when one thinks of the way the Scout movement took them over. Telling children that they were wolf cubs ruled over by a female Akela was a way of persuading large numbers of little boys to do something useful all at the same time—as if no solitary boy ever did anything useful—which is what the school is supposed to do for bigger boys, and the army for men.

In contrast, human laws are given no place. Humans are poor things who live in sordid dwellings like traps and haven't even the ability to build beautifully any more. Their city and temple are ruined and deserted, whereas the Jungle is organised and powerful, capable of battle and revenge—the animal vengeance theme is very strong and happens overtly in **'Letting in the Jungle'**; it is silently present most of the time. The theme of sin and retribution is only secondary to that of proving the new recruit or new boy, progress from youth to maturity, the leaving behind of the natural, careless, unclothed, unburdened time of childhood. Neither theme really belongs in the animal world. Animals don't, in real life, take revenge; but of course 'nature' occasionally does, or seems to do so. The initiation of the new young creature to the

Kipling's children, Elsie, John, and Josephine

tribe happens only in a minor degree. In linking these themes Kipling has not only shown a boy among animals, but has made his animals more human than the villagers; he has turned his animals into men. Bagheera, Baloo and Kaa are three Colonels, Akela a General, Shere Khan a wayward leader who tries to make malcontents join his mercenary band and so usurp the leadership. The mass of the wolves are the privates in the army into which Mowgli, when a baby, is bought for the price of a bull to the accompanying password, 'Look Well O Wolves'.

This phrase really does sound like the verbal equivalent of a wolf's howl. The wolves' parliament or council rock may be just such a place as wolves will use to congregate on moonlit nights. Packs have a pack leader, as any student of animal behaviour will know. But for the bear, the tiger, the panther to be present at such meetings, and for the python to be on friendly or speaking terms with all of them is not animal behaviour at all, and demonstrates that these animals are something more. The Law of the Jungle—taught and administered by Baloo, the schoolmasterly bear—has a certain relationship with things that really happen and is a kind of externalising of instinct. It expresses as a set of rules the things that animals do anyway:

> The Jackal may follow the Tiger, but, cub, when
>   thy whiskers are grown,
> Remember the Wolf is a hunter — go forth, and get
>   food of thine own. . . .

The Biblical formality of the animal speech—with its 'thees' and 'thous' which approximate to an Urdu idiom, the solemn names and use of the words Little Brother for Mowgli, including him as part of the tribe, not of wolves alone but of all animals—gives every utterance great dignity. All wild animals have this naturally, but to do them justice, the Indian villagers tend to talk in the same manner. They say so little, however, that their speech is of less importance than their actions, whereas the animals make quite long speeches to each other, reinforcing the rules by reiterating them until 'By the bull that bought me' and 'By the broken lock that freed me' become like a solemn poetic refrain. 'We be of one blood, ye and I,' said in the right accent is the password for all the Jungle creatures. They are never slangy and seldom make jokes. The most they do is join in gentle sarcasm: Is there anything in the Jungle too little to be killed? asks Baloo, giving reasons for teaching Mowgli the Jungle Law. 'That is why I teach him these things and that is why I hit him very softly when he forgets.' The ponderous way in which the animals tell each other everything that everyone knew already in the manner of men making afterdinner speeches or statements of policy is a staple ingredient of a certain kind of romantic epic. Some of the solider characters in Tolkien do this; it is similar to a pre-battle exchange of heralds and formal messages, and its use gives a warlike, epic feeling, as well as a hint of remoteness. Even Mowgli learns the trick:

> I go from you to my own people—if they be my own
> people. The Jungle is shut to men and I must forget

your talk and your companionship: but I will be more merciful than ye are. Because I was all but your brother in blood I promise that when I am a man among men I will not betray ye to men as ye have betrayed me.

The Council Rock is the place for this; in pack or army there has to be a place for parliament or trial or court martial at which leaders are chosen, opinions stated and opposition silenced. This meeting place recurs and is often the scene of dramatic action, especially the theme story **'Mowgli's Brothers'** which contains the acceptance, ageing and proving of Mowgli, and his revenge—not so much on Shere Khan personally, as on the untamed, lawless part of the Jungle that he represents. Mowgli's rejection by the wolves, his turning from the Jungle to the village to be accepted as a man, his real revenge on Shere Khan in **'Tiger Tiger'**, are all a matter of Law and logical negotiation, as was Mowgli's original crossing of the man-animal gulf by being 'bought' by a pact between animals. And the same inexorable rules eventually turn him out again. The wolves' parliament is a skilfully dramatic device for externalising laws that, although they seem manlike, are real and natural and can never be broken. The laws are, as animal instincts are, a built-in system, learned and taught without question. Only Mowgli himself ever doubts, or tries to disobey; and he is the man-cub, the outsider, though unwilling. Tabaqui the jackal brings the dawn of unease into his life by suggesting that he is not in the right place, but naked and human. It is the wise, proud, gentle Bagheera who reminds him that men and animals can never really meet, and that in the end, as he returns to the Jungle from his cage in the king's palace, so 'thou must go back to men at last, to the men who are thy brothers'. The tears that come unlooked for when Mowgli leaves the Jungle for the village, seal his fate; no animal can laugh or cry. . . .

The tragedy of *The Jungle Books* . . . is that the gulf cannot be crossed properly or permanently, and that Mowgli as a man is so greatly inferior to the boy-wolf-cub. The situation is made more poignant by turning Mowgli into a semi-godlike figure, or noble savage, and making the men so mean, superstitious and unworthy. The Bandar-Log show the way by demonstrating the contempt that the Jungle has for the human qualities that they display. Perhaps it is not until the work of Walter de la Mare that monkeys are treated with dignity and poetry. Kipling's Bandar-Log alter one's feelings about monkeys—and the human types they represent—for ever. Feckless, irresponsible children, they have all the faults of a bad imitation: they are faithless, tell lies, cannot concentrate or achieve anything, live from hand to mouth, plunder, do nothing with the hands that are so different from other animals' paws except meddle and spoil, and are so conceited that they can find no fault with themselves. Always there is the implication that *this,* in some measure, is what men are like. The monkey tribal system is the opposite of that of the Seeonee in that it has no laws, no rules, no language. The Bandar-Log quarrel and fight, torment other animals, always trying to be in advance of fashion, making absurd speeches to each other to say so. They are neither man nor beast. The story in which Mowgli is carried off by the Bandar-Log to the ruined city represents Mowgli as being sinful and disobedient. He has to be rescued by his three friends, the python, panther and bear, who are as admonitory with Mowgli as the Rat and the Badger are with Toad when he is having one of his more foolish turns. Bear and panther become quite emotional when Mowgli is at last rescued, but that does not stop Bagheera from giving Mowgli a sound beating to remind him not to do it again.

It is inevitable that the Jungle, or corps of superior creatures, should triumph over both Bandar-Log and the Indian village of primitive, lowly men. The tragedy of Mowgli's having to rejoin the men in the end is similar to that of the hero vanquished by weakness (his love for his human mother?). The weakness is his nakedness or manhood; one must, in the end, leave the school or army. On the way, Mowgli's victories are powerful—over Red Dogs, over the bees, Shere Khan and other wolves. Inside the village, his behaviour is that of a rather noble animal trapped in a zoo; or, as the tables are turned by the story, a man trapped by monkeys. The men's tales—particularly those of the boastful Buldeo—are shown to be childish nonsense which Mowgli can understand, see through, and treat as ridiculous. He sits among the village elders like Jesus in the temple, wiser and more mature than they.

Mowgli's contempt for men is complete and vocal: 'Men are blood brothers of the Bandar-Log: all they do is talk and play with their mouths', boasting, making up stories, eating and drinking and blowing smoke, acting in a generally foolish and inexpert way. His vengeance on Buldeo and the villagers is as swift and sure as that on the tiger, but his attitude is inescapably ambivalent.

'Who is Man,' says Bagheera, 'that we should care for him—the naked brown digger, the hairless and toothless, the eater of earth?' but he is silenced by Mowgli's stare, before which his eyes must drop. Mowgli cannot, even in vengeance, kill one of his own kind. But he cannot acknowledge that he *is* a man: threatening Akela with a knife when he is called one, yet turning on the wolves when they offer to attack and kill Buldeo, saying 'Am I to give reasons for all I choose to do?'

'That is Man,' 'There speaks Man,' mutters Bagheera. Mowgli is neither one nor the other. He is fatally divided and will never fit. He has a curious immunity from human beliefs and superstitions and a curious loyalty that takes him towards the human and not the wolf mother in the end. The psychological depression that attacks him in **'The Spring Running'** is something that the animals don't feel and cannot understand, apart from Bagheera's acknowledgement, with great sympathy, that it exists. Even Bagheera fails to understand the depth and imperative urges towards vengeance on the men that compel Mowgli to plot the obliteration of the Indian village—a vengeance that, had Mowgli identified himself completely with the animals, would not have taken place. All the animals, the flesh-eaters and the grazers, join in plundering and spoiling, led and driven by Mowgli and the elephants, until the village is no more and the men have fled. Even Bagheera murders three horses. Though no humans are killed, they see their houses demolished by Hathi the elephant in an orgy of destruction.

This story ends the *Mowgli* cycle; the theme of retribution has come to its close and all that remains is for Mowgli to move on from the hierarchy in which he has been such an apt pupil and at whose head he stands. The unbearably poignant **'The Spring Running'**, 1895, the last *Mowgli* story to be written, tells of Mowgli's goodbye to his friends. Animal-like, they have grown old while Mowgli is still in his prime. With most humans and animals, for this reason alone, the parting is inevitable. The story is almost a poem to the Indian spring, as Mowgli sings, leaps and swings through the jungle of which he is now the master, afraid of nothing that lives except for the inexplicable human shadow that follows him everywhere and cannot be shaken off. In all his alternating rejections and homecomings he himself must make the final choice and part from everything that he loves most. He does not know what he wants, or what he has outgrown, but realises instinctively that he has reached the end of careless happiness and the beginning of adulthood, and that however much he wishes it, man and animal can never meet. However much Mowgli tries to convince himself that he and the wolves are of one blood, they are not so. . . .

The first *Mowgli* story, **'In the Rukh'**, 1890, shows the end before the beginning—Mowgli as a young man, still part of the Jungle, powerful and beautiful, inquisitive about the Englishman into whose piece of forest he has wandered, eventually settling to take a wife, becoming a ranger and accepting the inevitable pension. The effortless ease with which Mowgli appears and disappears, drives animals about, communicates with them and causes them to come to him as if by magic, makes the 'civilised' narrator appear crude and bumbling. Mowgli is perfect, godlike and so obviously superior in intelligence and power that if one does not think of *The Jungle Books* in which his boyish, animal-nature is stressed, he seems both formidable and slightly annoying. Normally, as Muller the head ranger remarks, such animal-reared outcasts die young; but Mowgli is not at all normal. Neither, of course, was Tarzan. These gulf-crossing stories voice a deep and constant human wish and give it mythical form, powerful because it is all taken so seriously. To me, *The Story of Dr Dolittle* and the Warts' adventures with Merlyn are no less powerful because they are lighthearted and there is less blood about; the animals themselves are gently satirised. But it is a theme that never really dies or disappears. It is interesting to see H. H. Munro's inevitably sinister treatment of the Nature Boy idea with its flippant overtones; Gabriel Ernest, lesser than and different from Mowgli, is a conscience-less animal in human form, voicing his thoughts on eating child-flesh with an accuracy that is not of course believed in by his human listener. Like Tobermory, who voices impossible cat's thoughts in human words, he has to disappear. Saki's humour is black. Man and wolf exist in one psyche in his world to terrify and destroy; Mowgli's wolf nature is one of order, love, loyalty and joy.

Margery Fisher

SOURCE: "Who's Who in Children's Books: Mowgli," in *Who's Who in Children's Books: A Treasury of the Familiar Characters of Childhood,* Holt, Rinehart and Winston, 1975, pp. 243-46.

Mowgli, the Frog, is given his name when he is adopted as an infant into a family of wolves, perhaps partly because of his soft hairlessness, certainly in part because the wolves saved him from Shere Khan, the lame tiger whom they deride as frog-eater. Although Mowgli is accepted by the wolf pack and taught the Jungle Law, yet the time comes when old Akela loses his hold over the pack and in the leaderless days the young wolves turn against Mowgli, so that he has to leave the jungle for the village and use human strategies to put an end to Shere Khan.

It is not only on this occasion that Mowgli shows that he is a man and not an animal. He can always outstare his brother wolves and even the formidable panther Bagheera must drop his eyes before him. Moreover, though Mowgli respects the Law which has been knocked into him by Baloo, the bear, he has none the less a sense of fun and happiness, which his mentors cannot know. His reluctant days as a man are few, for the superstition of the villagers, roused by the jealous Brahmin Buldeo, drives him back to the jungle; but in the spring of his eighteenth year a melancholy which seems to him like a sickness drives him to accept, at last, that he needs human love and companionship.

It is significant that at the end of the poignant last story of Mowgli, **"The Spring Running,"** he once more promises that he will never forget his jungle brothers and urges them not to cast him out completely. Mowgli is not Adam in the Garden of Eden, any more than he is the god that his foster-mother timidly calls him; he is not a totally fantastic creature nor the focal point of a satirical comment on human nature (though this is an important element in the stories). He is a human being growing painfully, and sometimes reluctantly, out of one world into another. His progress through the stories, with their emphasis on physical prowess, loyalty to comrades, obedience, has been likened to a boy's progress through the years of public school or his initiation into the discipline of army life. This last analogy has sometimes been carried to absurd lengths, with the various animals, from Colonel Bagheera downwards, being given army rank; but the intricate order of precedence and behaviour in a wolf-pack provides a simpler and more immediate source for the social organization of the jungle as Kipling describes it, and as he could have known it, if only in a very general way.

At a deeper level, Mowgli is a person who really belongs nowhere. Though he lives fully the life of the jungle (far more fully than he lives the life of man, if we can judge by the isolated story, **"In the Rukh,"** which precedes the *Jungle Books*) yet he is not and never can be an animal, however thoroughly he assimilates their code and their idiom. His personality is a divided one. The sensuous-ness, the joyous activity, the colour and movement and the exotic, rhetorical speeches in the stories, are all subordinated, finally, to a pervading sadness. All his life Kipling had a passionate desire to belong—to a place, a group, a belief. We may speculate, but can never know for certain, how much of himself went to make the character of Mowgli.

Roger Sale

SOURCE: "Kipling's Boys," in *Fairy Tales and After: From Snow White to E. B. White,* Cambridge, Mass.: Harvard University Press, 1978, pp. 195-221.

> Now this is the Law of the Jungle—as old and as
>   true as the sky;
> And the Wolf that shall keep it may prosper, but
>   the Wolf that shall break it must die.
> As the creeper that girdles the tree-trunk the Law
>   runneth forward and back—
> For the strength of the Pack is the Wolf, and the
>   strength of the Wolf is the Pack.

These loose, thrilling, and easily memorized couplets, so quickly recognizable as Kipling's, intone values they do not explain and imply that no explanation is necessary. They, and many other snips of poetry, excited two generations with passion, even reverence. It was Kipling's magic that one could thrill to his words, learn and repeat them, without ever seriously asking what they meant. When I saw a movie of *The Jungle Book* in the mid-1940s, full fifty years after the book had been published, advertisements still assumed that the word "Kipling" could be used like the words "Shakespeare" or "Dickens" as a mark of classic greatness. A few years later, my mother told me that my uncle and the father of my best friend had stayed up late the night before reciting Kipling, and I assumed that was a magical way to spend an evening. I had read neither of the *Jungle Books,* not even *Just-So Stories,* but I attributed that to a flaw in myself, and I assumed that most others had read these books, themselves as old and as true as the sky, committed to memory. Just recently, when I mumbled some demurring remarks about the *Just-So Stories,* I was answered on one side with long phrases about the Elephant Child's "'satiable curtiousity'" and about Tegumai and his daughter on the other.

Everyone I knew when growing up did not, of course, know Kipling's famous books for children, though I'm sure many did, and not many derived, as I now see my best friend did, their vocabulary from *Stalky & Co.* My guess is that for most Americans now he is what he was for me, a rumble of distant thunder. He is of course better known in the countries that once made up the British Empire than he is in the United States, but even there his fame seems to be passing as those who knew the Empire itself also pass away. Writers on Kipling used to begin by saying people either adored or hated him, but there are few real adorers now and almost no passionate haters. He has become an academic subject, alas, a figure of uncertain status, better known than H. G. Wells, not as well known as George Bernard Shaw, certainly not as much admired as Hardy or Conrad.

But the implied equation of Kipling with the British Empire is unfortunate, because it is only the lesser Kipling that can be made to stand in that equation. Kipling is rightly best known as a writer about India, but he was never an ardent apologist for the British presence there, and his really unpleasant jingoistic work comes in the years when he was concerned with Africa. The fact that the British in Africa were more truly imperial than they ever were in India made their cause less easy to defend, which made defenders like Kipling more defensive, more shrill and harsh. But the Empire was never more than a manifestation of what really absorbed Kipling, which was not politics and power but authority, systems of order, of which the Law of the Jungle is the most famous and the Great Game and the lama's Way in *Kim* the most interesting; most interesting of all was the India that defied all systems of order by having and obeying so bewilderingly many.

The point can be stated more precisely. Kipling at his best is a writer about the relations between order, and laws, and youthful boyish energies. Like Kenneth Grahame, who was his almost exact contemporary, Kipling never outgrew boyish impulses and desires. Unlike Grahame, Kipling wanted to grow up and indeed thought he had, so he never offers his stories and poems frankly as the literature of escape. The loose, thrilling, and easily memorized couplets in which the Law of the Jungle is stated are in form escapist, because they imply one can learn a formula and thereby forget life with it. The law they announce, however, is offered seriously, as a grim, wise statement of the sort that Grahame would never have written. He wanted to run from such statements.

Fortunately for us the Kipling that seeks status as adult literature need not concern us here. Even at its best, it seems to me, the adult Kipling is minor stuff, clever and polished, memorable for a few exciting gestures and scenes, but narrow and thin. Kipling's poems, for instance, have lots of lines one remembers when one needs a formulaic way to state a mood or an argument:

> From down to Gaehenna and up to the throne,
> He travels the fastest who travels alone.

> If you can make one heap of all your winnings, and
>   bet it on one turn of pitch and toss—
> And lose, and start again at your beginnings, and
>   never breathe a word about your loss.

> For the sin that ye do by two and two ye must pay
>   for one by one. . . .

I quote these easily from memory, as anyone can who has once fallen under their spell. For just that reason Kipling's poetry won't ever die, though fewer and fewer will stay up late at night reciting it. George Orwell calls it very good bad poetry; T. S. Eliot says it isn't poetry at all, but verse; no matter the best definition. As for the stories, it seems enough to say that only at his best does he earn the title of being the British de Maupassant; the tales are neatly turned, pathetic or shocking, situationally precise but humanly shallow, innocent of what Chekhov or D. H. Lawrence could make short fiction be.

The Kipling that has always been the most popular, and that will last longer than any of the rest, is the work done for children and growing boys.

Kingsley Amis has said of the Mowgli stories that they are paraded wisdom, the sort of stories adults like to give children more than children really enjoy reading. The judgment seems at best partly true of the *Jungle Books,* but perfect for the *Just-So Stories.* Unlike the *Jungle Books* or *Kim,* they were not written out of the need to satisfy anything deep or personal for Kipling, but out of the desire to tell stories to his eldest daughter Josephine, and as we have seen more than once, when an adult works hard to satisfy a child, the results are seldom that adult's best stories.

The Jungle Books reveal no such crippling concern with audience. They were written when Josephine was too young to hear them, they were not told with anyone in particular in mind, and they are also and perhaps therefore much better. One sees what Kingsley Amis means when he accuses them of offering paraded wisdom, but that does not really get to the heart of the matter. Let me quote again the lines with which I began—they come at the end of **"How Fear Came"**:

> Now this is the Law of the Jungle—as old and as
>   true as the sky;
> And the Wolf that shall keep it may prosper, but
>   the Wolf that shall break it must die.
> As the creeper that girdles the tree-trunk the Law
>   runneth forward and back—
> For the strength of the Pack is the Wolf, and the
>   strength of the Wolf is the Pack.

I take these lines out of context, as many others have done, and the effect is to make this one law into The Law, when actually the poem that follows lists all kinds of rules for wolves, and the story which precedes the poem is not much concerned with wolves but with the one night in which man fears the tiger. But even if the lines are taken from context and even if they are then given to Wolf Cub Scouts, aged nine, as though they spoke the only law, even then they seem to me thrilling and harmless, paraded wisdom, but much truer concerning wolves and nine-year-olds than the *Just-So Stories* are about leopards and kangaroos. Kipling's wolves are not Ernest Thompson Seton's, or Farley Mowat's, but neither are they terrible distortions. Lone wolves, almost unknown in Kipling, are also almost unknown in the wild. The law which demands mutual dependence among wolves is also the law which makes them what they are usually called in *The Jungle Books,* the Free People. The wolves are anthropomorphic, and the wisdom is paraded, but it isn't ignorant or patronizing.

From The Jungle Book, *by Rudyard Kipling.*
Illustrated by Fritz Eichenberg.

The basic texture of *The Jungle Books* is like these couplets, and the result is a happy but not complacent picture of the jungle as a place that is obedient to a wide range of laws, habits, and instincts, so that it becomes humanly habitable, as most jungles are not. Kaa, Baloo, Bagheera, Akela, the Bander-log, and Hahti are all easily described because each has only one or two salient qualities, each derived from stereotyped but observable qualities in pythons, bears, panthers, wolves, monkeys, and elephants. They make excellent background figures because, once typed, their traits become as laws, and this takes them out of the category of creatures that can be turned into a hero or a villain. The Bander-log are annoying, but not bad or evil. Even in the non-Mowgli story of Rikki-Tikki-Tavi, where we are intended to want Rikki to win, the antagonists, the cobras, are only being obedient to their natures. There is nothing profound in Kipling's rendering of any of these characters, but nothing is distorted either, except perhaps for those who might wish to complain that Kipling's jungle is not a real jungle.

Far from being real, Kipling's jungle is an ideal as much as Grahame's river and woods, and a brief glance at Kip-

ling in his early years can show how it came to be. He was born and spent his first six years in India, lovingly surrounded by servants with whom he could have relations that were at once secure and dynamic. The servants could treat young Ruddy as an inferior, because he was a child; as an equal because servants and children both lived apart from adults; as a superior because he was British and they were native. At six he was abruptly removed from India and sent to England, where no such surroundings existed. Worse, his foster parents were vengeful and narrow-minded Methodists who, out of duty and desire, made life miserable for young Kipling. In his strongly worded autobiographical story, **"Baa Baa Black Sheep,"** Kipling says near the end: "When young lips have drunk deep of the bitter waters of Hate, Suspicion, and Despair, all the Love in the world will not wholly take away that knowledge, though it may turn darkened eyes for a while to the light, and teach Faith where no Faith was." A terrible and pathetic utterance, surely. Furthermore, after he left his foster family and went to public school, he was given anything but "all the love in the world." If he achieved "Faith where no Faith was," it was what Philip Mason has tellingly called faith in the higher power of the headmaster at the expense of subordinate housemasters (see **Stalky & Co.**).

Then, at seventeen, Kipling returned to India where he found himself "moving among sights and smells that made me deliver in the vernacular sentences whose meaning I knew not." Had this been Kipling's first stay in India, he might have done as he did, work seven years as a reporter, editor, and contributor of stories to provincial newspapers, which laid the groundwork for the literary success that was to follow him back to England when he returned there at age twenty-four. *Plain Tales from the Hills, Departmental Ditties,* and *Soldiers Three* would all be exactly as they are, the work of a young man trying to act more knowing and adult than he feels or is, eagerly and excitedly observing the whole Indian scene, from beggar to halfcaste, from native prince to British viceroy, from Mohammedan mistress to memsahib. But this India Kipling left for good when he left India for the second and last time, and very little of his "adult" writing after he left reveals distinctive traces that he had ever gone.

But that leaves *The Jungle Books* and, a few years later, *Kim,* and these differ from the rest of Kipling's work, for adults or children, about India or elsewhere. They are happy books about ideal worlds, worlds that are not so much versions of the India Kipling knew between seventeen and twenty-four as derived from the world of his first five years. Mowgli and Kim are not Kipling, of course, but versions of the boy he might have been, or imagined he could have become, had he stayed in India. Each is thrust out of the nursery and into the world when very young, and each finds in the world versions of those servants who had surrounded Kipling when he was very young.

Of course Kaa, Baloo, Bagheera, Akela, Hathi, and the others are not Mowgli's servants, because both they and he are better than that name implies, but Mowgli is never alone, either. Even at the end of **"Tiger! Tiger!"** when Mowgli ends up saying, "Man-Pack and Wolf-Pack have cast me out . . . Now I will hunt alone in the Jungle," the next line is "'And we will hunt with thee,' said the four cubs." Mowgli is never more than a few sentences away from the animals who mean most to him. Yet what Mowgli forms with Kaa, Baloo, Bagheera, and Akela is not a pack relation either. For the nameless wolf it may be true and enough that his strength is in the pack and its strength is in him, but Mowgli's relation with those animals closest to him is better, and different from anything the Law of the Jungle could say. It is what C. S. Lewis rightly sees as an essential feature in Kipling, the Inner Ring, the group banded together by ties not of blood but of comradeship, mutual dependence, and higher wisdom. Being distinctly different in kind one from another, Mowgli and his comrades often pursue separate ways, but given a challenge, especially from the outside, suddenly they are all together.

It is, of course, understood without its ever being said that Mowgli is at the center of the stories. "We'll play Jungle Book, and I shall be Mowgli," says Oswald Bastable at the opening of Edith Nesbit's *The Wouldbegoods,* written just five years after the first *Jungle Book.* Of course he wanted to be Mowgli, who is able to be free, to understand wild animals, to sleep by day and hunt by night, to be competent in the jungle, to enact punishment but never recrimination, to be indifferent to the value of money or treasure. These are undoubtedly the major ingredients in the fantasy, but fortunately Kipling needed Mowgli to be more than a boy at one with the jungle, a younger Tarzan. He also had to enact the varied relations Kipling had had with the servants. Thus, being a boy, Mowgli had to be taught, and so we have **"Kaa's Hunting,"** where Mowgli foolishly goes off with the Bander-log because his teacher, Baloo, has been hard on him and the monkeys have been kind to him, or so he thinks. The result is a story of the fun of being wrong when the teachers of the lesson are wise and kind.

A much more important element in the best stories derives from Mowgli's special status as a human being. Kipling's servants had had to treat him as something special too, because one day he would be taken away since he was, finally, not of their world. Kipling learned in England what Mowgli learns in his brief stay in the village: there is nothing happy about this specialness. If there is a law that says he must leave the wolf pack and live among human beings, the law must be obeyed, but with doubt as to its goodness and regret as to its power. Thus Kipling spends little time describing Mowgli in the village, but what he does more often, and with excellent results, is to tug Mowgli between the various laws he must obey and the various roles his relations with animals and people thrust upon him. There is no finer moment in either *Jungle Book* than the scene at the Council Rock in **"Mowgli's Brothers,"** where the wolves, Baloo, Bagheera, and Mowgli all struggle to say who they think Mowgli is.

The crisis in this scene arises because Akela and the other wolves who originally agreed to let Mowgli grow up with the pack, and who have kept Shere Khan the tiger from attacking him, have all grown old. The younger wolves do not want Mowgli living with them. Bagheera gives Mowgli the law: you are a man; Mowgli protests: "'I was born in the Jungle. I have obeyed the Law of the Jungle, and there is no wolf of ours from whose paws I have not pulled a thorn. Surely they are my brothers.'" But no, and Mowgli's ability to pull thorns from paws shows he is not a wolf, as Bagheera tells him. Also, none of the animals can look Mowgli in the eye, and "the others they hate thee because their eyes cannot meet thine." Heredity is stronger than environment; get human weapons before you fight Shere Khan, get fire.

Shere Khan comes to claim Mowgli as his rightful prey, and in the debate that follows the various laws keep pulling various animals in different ways. Some wolves argue they must protect Mowgli because he has kept their law, others that he is a man cub; Shere Khan insists he became his prey years ago; Bagheera answers he paid the price of a killed bull to save Mowgli's life. Mowgli, having been told he is unredeemably a man, rises to the challenge: "'Ye have told me so often tonight that I am a man (and indeed I would have been a wolf with you to my life's end) that I feel your words are true. So I do not call ye my brothers any more, but sags (dogs), as a man should. What ye will do, and what ye will not do, is not yours to say. That matter is with *me;* and that we may see the matter more plainly I have brought here a little of the Red Flower which ye, dogs, fear.'" This is what Ruddy Kipling, aged six, could not imagine saying when he was cast out of his pack and sent off to England. Yet it wasn't the servants he wanted to punish, and we can notice that the wolves he attacks remain nameless, while a loyal group remains: "At least there were Akela, Bagheera, and perhaps ten wolves that had taken Mowgli's part." That would be enough, except Mowgli must leave them all: "Then something began to hurt Mowgli inside him, as he had never been hurt in his life before, and he caught his breath and sobbed, and the tears ran down his face. 'What is it? What is it?' he said. 'I do not wish to leave the Jungle, and I do not know what this is. Am I dying, Baghera?'" "No," says Bagheera, it is only tears, "such as men use." Mowgli has set himself apart from the wolves and has managed to become the Mowgli that young Kipling or Oswald Bastable wanted to be, but in his revenge on the wolves he also seems a rather unpleasant *übermensch.* That leads only to this, though; animals are not given to revenge, and they do not cry either. Mowgli, obeying the laws that make him human, is softer and more pathetic than any of the others.

Mowgli, in this and in the other stories, is seldom allowed to be king of the castle for very long, because he had to be etched with deeper longings than the simple desire for power and mastery. He had to belong somewhere, but the place where he belonged could not be, like Grahame's river and woods, created simply by ruling out all that Kipling disliked. He could belong only when he could feel all those tugs that Kipling felt with his servants because he was their inferior, their equal, and their superior. In a different writer, these tugs could have been made to come into conflict with each other, so that Mowgli could have become doubtful, confused, tormented. Kipling wanted none of that—that was what he had been in England—and so he lets the tugs pull one after the other, but none is so strong that another cannot just pull back. After Mowgli learns his tears are human, he dries them quickly and leaves the jungle. But then comes another story, about his life before he left, and another, in which he kills Shere Khan and comes back to the jungle. The fantasy is rich but not complex. The young lips that had drunk deeply of the bitter waters of hate, suspicion, and despair are not Mowgli's, and Kipling had to protect him from whatever might lead in that direction.

On the other hand, Mowgli's ambivalent status in the forest keeps him unsettled, and this keeps him and Kipling from the smugness of the *Just-So Stories.* The great longings that animated the *Jungle Books* were too strong for Kipling to want to blemish them with easy nostalgia or the easier desire for revenge. The flaw in these books lies elsewhere: the stories are not very good stories. When Mowgli is being tugged to stay or to leave or to return to the jungle, as in **"Mowgli's Brothers," "Tiger! Tiger,"** and **"Spring Running,"** all is well. But when Mowgli's role is more settled, the result tends to be a simple adventure story. In this respect Kipling here resembles a contemporary of his, Arthur Conan Doyle. Mowgli and Sherlock Holmes are fantasy figures of such richness that they become quasimythical and seem able to exist almost independently of the stories told about them. But the stories themselves tend to be casually done, as if by someone who does not know it is difficult to sustain a good tale. By Kipling's own statement, the killing of Shere Khan, the climax of **"Tiger! Tiger!,"** is accomplished with absurd ease. **"Red Dog,"** a story that has been lavishly praised, is good as long as Kaa is using the bees to attack the dogs, but the dogs themselves, like the tiger, are too gullible to be challenging enemies. **"How Fear Came"** is like a good Just-So story, neatly enough told but with nothing to mottle or densify its paraded wisdom. **"Letting in the Jungle"** starts out very well, but Mowgli's plan for the evacuation of the village takes so long that the punishment seems much in excess of the crime. As with the Sherlock Holmes stories, these failings are not strong enough to destroy our sense of the power of the central figure, but strong enough so that the stories are more powerful as a residue in the memory than they are when reread.

Nicholas Tucker

SOURCE: "Literature for Older Children (Ages 11-14): *The Jungle Book*," in *The Child and the Book: A Psychological and Literary Exploration,* Cambridge University Press, 1981, p. 160.

Since Anna Sewell's time, the humanised animal story has become less generally didactic in tone, with Kipling, for example, using animal life in *The Jungle Book* to symbolise a type of order, rather than to make any particular social points. His Law of the jungle stands for a universal acceptance of certain moral standards, binding upon all animals except the degraded monkey society, the Bandar-Log. This vision of the perfect, logical balance of animal societies, where inhabitants follow the Law, also has its attractions for children who still like to see their own universe in similarly moral terms, where rules should be obeyed in a somehow pre-ordained, natural order of things. If they can manage Kipling's rather stately and over-ornate prose style, they may also warm to the loving relationship between Mowgli and his animal protectors, and appreciate the lively adventures and ever-present sense of danger in these tales.

Robert F. Moss

SOURCE: "Between Two Worlds: The Divided Self in Kipling's Adolescents," in *Rudyard Kipling and the Fiction of Adolescence,* St. Martin's Press, 1982, pp. 107-27.

[In the Mowgli stories, the] creatures of the jungle—at least those who are not lesser breeds without the Law—live in harmony with their surroundings. The wilderness provides for them so long as they respect its customs and do not violate its taboos. The virtues they represent are primitive, yet Kipling invests them with a noble simplicity. Hunting well, fighting valiantly, respecting the jungle codes, demonstrating fidelity to friends and fearlessness in the face of one's enemies—these are the things that matter. By contrast, the villagers choose to scratch out a living from the soil and from their livestock. They live in perpetual fear of the jungle, sensing a precariousness in even their moments of greatest tranquillity and prosperity. Moreover, their way of life is distinctly unheroic compared to the four-footed huntsmen who surround them. . . .

Given the clear-cut, black-and-white contrasts Kipling has constructed, one would not expect much conflict in choosing between animal and human society. But in this conflict, which, oddly enough, has not attracted much critical attention, is the psychological foundation on which the stories are built. It is illustrated by the obscure pain that afflicts Mowgli at various points of emotional stress, a pain that, in Tompkins' words, "neither he [Mowgli] nor the child who reads about him understands". When he prepares to abandon the jungle life in **"Mowgli's Brothers"** we are told: "Then something began to hurt Mowgli inside him, as he had never been hurt in his life before, and he caught his breath and sobbed, and the tears ran down his face." Later, in **"Letting in the Jungle"** he returns to the village in preparation for his revenge, but the huts induce an unanticipated response: "Angry as he was at the whole breed and community of Man, something jumped up in his throat and made him catch his breath when he looked at the village roofs." This sensation is followed by the even stronger human tie he feels with his natural mother: "Up to that time Mowgli had been perfectly steady, but here he began to tremble all over, and that surprised him immensely."

The boy's painful ambivalence reaches its climax in **"The Spring Running"**, where "the words choked between his teeth, and a feeling came over him that began at his toes and ended in his hair—a feeling of pure unhappiness—and he looked himself over to be sure that he had not trodden on a thorn". Kipling's strategy of merely *suggesting* Mowgli's confused feelings elicits from Tompkins the comment that "to convey the compulsion that is driving Mowgli . . . Kipling has to move indirectly". At the same time, though, the tactic allows Kipling to avoid any thoroughgoing analysis of these emotions—a task he might not be up to. But the strategy is quite acceptable, since the genre Kipling is working in does not call for psychological complexity.

Mowgli's conflict over his true identity expresses itself in less direct fashions as well. Clearly it is the source—along with an interdiction in the Law—of his refusal to slay any human beings (**"Letting in the Jungle"**), though their plans for dealing with *him* contain no such scruples. It is perhaps also significant that Mowgli insists on assuming an invisible role during the extravagant vengeance he wreaks in **"Letting in the Jungle"**: "The man pack shall not know what share I have in the sport." In spite of his announced hatred of men he apparently does not wish to be incriminated in his revenge against them.

How is it, then, that creatures as despicable as men can exert so much attraction for Mowgli and eventually draw him away from his beloved jungle? The answer seems to be, quite simply, blood ties. In the universe of the *Jungle Books,* like calls to like and each tribe claims its own. In the first of the Mowgli stories, **"Mowgli's Brothers"**—the title is somewhat ironic, since the wolves are not completely fraternal toward Mowgli—Bagheera prophesies the boy's eventual departure: "Thou art a man cub and even as I returned to my jungle so thou must go back to men at last." Another irony takes shape in this story: Mowgli's superiority is based on the fact that he is sprung from the apparently inferior man pack. He is able to stare down each of the animals and demonstrates a budding shrewdness that ultimately makes him master of the jungle. Kipling is perceptive in recognizing that a successful leader must be capable of inducing fear in his followers. When Mowgli exerts his influence over Akela, Bagheera and the others "they trembled in every limb" (**"Letting in the Jungle"**). In a more positive vein, we can also endorse Angus Wilson's notion that Mowgli "wins mastery in the animal world" through his "superior human intelligence and compassion".

But the origins of Mowgli's exceptional abilities constitute an even more arresting facet of these stories than the gifts themselves—indeed, herein lies the central paradox of the works. Had Mowgli grown up as a boy of the village he would presumably have become as insubstantial as the children who tease him in **"'Tiger-Tiger!'"** Yet he dominates the beasts of the jungle because he is a man and declares this fact openly, telling Hathi that the re-enactment of the elephant's revenge on Bhurtpore (**"Letting in the Jungle"**) will be preferable to the original "for the reason that there is a man to direct". Yet the other men in the stories display no such cunning and bravery. The boy's alienation from his own society ac-

counts for both his unhappiness and his spectacular successes.

Celia Catlett Anderson

SOURCE: "Kipling's Mowgli and Just So Stories: The Vine of Fact and Fantasy," in *Touchstones: Reflections on the Best in Children's Literature,* Vol. 1, edited by Perry Nodelman, Children's Literature Association, 1985, pp. 113-23.

[Kipling's] books for juveniles cover a wide range. Most solidly in the tradition of realism is *Stalky & Co.* (1899), a story of a brash trio of schoolboys which is based on Kipling's stay at Westward Ho! Both *Captains Courageous* (1896) and *Kim* (1901), though adventure stories, are also vividly realistic in their settings and characters. The first is an account of a rich and spoiled young boy's developing maturity after he is rescued aboard a fishing vessel off the Grand Banks, and the second a story of Kim's education into the British secret service and his travels through India with a holy man. *Kim* is the acknowledged masterpiece among these three young adult books, perhaps because *Kim* borders on mysticism and therefore approaches the world of myth and legend and fantasy. Kipling is at his best when he is combining worlds, whether of animal and man, spiritual and material, or past and present.

Two of his books for young people that bring together history and fantasy are *Puck of Pook's Hill* (1906) and *Rewards and Fairies* (1910). In both of these, two English children, Dan and Una, are magically transported to crucial moments of Englands' history. J. M. S. Tompkins, in *The Art of Rudyard Kipling,* says of the Puck stories that certain "glowing spots" in them dispelled mists for her and "So I was led, and many children of my generation were led, by intimations of the imagination into a sort of tactual familiarity with what the intellect could not yet clearly see." These Puck books have not, however, had the same following among contemporary children that *Kim* and the *Just So Stories* (1902) and *The Jungle Books* (1893 and 1895) have. These last two have remained accessible to children of several generations, and, for their originality, their varied and precisely crafted style, and their convincing detail amid exotic settings, well deserve a place of honor as touchstones of children's literature.

It is the interplay of varied language and precise detail that gives the *Just So Stories* much of their humor and charm, and makes them less austere than the ancient creation myths they are imitating. Kipling plays on his fancy and captures ours by using catalogs and word play to recount how certain animals and human customs came to be as they are.

[The] *Just So Stories* involve a wide range of readers. Small children have their ears and minds tickled by the playful language, older children gain a sense of the diversity of both language and creatures, and mature readers can appreciate the overarching view of creation, of High and Far-Off Times when the world was still playing at becoming itself.

The Mowgli stories share some of these characteristics, but *The Jungle Books* are written in the language of romantic epic, and in them we move from myths proper to legends of a hero, and from the consideration of the relationship between primeval nature and its inhabitants to the complex interrelations among men. *The Jungle Books,* in spite of their title, are about civilization.

They are also in an unusual format. Spread over two volumes, eight of the stories are about Mowgli, a child raised by wolves, and form a novel of sorts. But these Mowgli stories are interlaced with seven other disparate tales, held together mainly by an emphasis on animals and natural settings. While the mixture may satisfy an adult and even enrich our sense of Mowgli as a mythical hero, described in the midst of tales of animals, most children better enjoy the Mowgli stories themselves. Read together as a group they have a good deal of unity. Kipling has often been reproached for failing to write major sustained narratives, but the three-decker novel against which he was being judged is not the only form of serious fiction, and, if carefully examined, the grouping of the Mowgli stories can be seen to anticipate the sliding panel narrative that Lawrence Durrell used in his Alexandria Quartet and that is admired in our century.

The opening tale, **"Mowgli's Brothers,"** encapsulates much of the entire action and of the thematic structure. Mowgli comes to the wolf's den as a year-old baby, and at the end of the first story is driven out of the pack and towards the village as a twelve-year-old boy. In the course of this introductory tale, Mother Wolf has predicted that Mowgli will someday kill the tiger Shere Khan, and Kipling has hinted at "the wonderful life that Mowgli led among the wolves" which "would fill ever so many books." It should be noted that there is an earlier "adult" tale about Mowgli in his manhood called **"In the Rukh"** (1890), so the hero's future as a ranger in the Indian jungle is known before the account of his childhood begins.

The second tale, **"Kaa's Hunting,"** is a flashback that reveals how Mowgli's training was accomplished. In it his three knightly attendants, Baloo the bear, Bagheera the black panther, and Kaa the boa constrictor, help him through a misadventure with the monkey people (or Bandar Log). In the third story, **"Tiger-Tiger,"** Mowgli, living in exile as a herd boy for the village, manages to kill Shere Khan, but again is cast out, this time by the man pack. He returns to the jungle with Shere Khan's skin but hunts henceforth as a loner. This is the last story of Mowgli in Book I and leaves him as an adolescent in transition between the two worlds of jungle and man, of childhood and adulthood.

The opening story of Book II, **"How Fear Came,"** is a mythic interlude showing the imperfection of the animal world. During a drought when the animals are gathered around a pool, Hathi the elephant relates the fall from grace that occurred when a tiger first killed a man. The next tale, **"Letting in the Jungle,"** the fifth in the Mowgli Series, brings us back to the ending of **"Tiger-Tiger"** and recounts Mowgli's revenge against the villagers who banished him. He harnesses the awesome powers of both beasts and jungle growth to destroy and swallow up the village. **"The King's Ankus,"** a jungle version of Chaucer's "Pardoner's Tale," takes us to Cold Lairs, the abandoned city that was the setting of **"Kaa's Hunting."** Various men's reactions to the jewelled ankus (elephant probe) that Mowgli takes from the treasure trove should have taught the boy about greed and why the villagers behaved as they did, but he remains innocent of its evil.

In the seventh tale, **"Red Dog,"** Mowgli, though still outside the wolf pack, saves them from invasion by the Dholes. The death of the leader Akela in the battle breaks one more of Mowgli's ties with the jungle. In **"Spring Running,"** the final story, Mowgli, now seventeen years old, returns to men for once and all. Bagheera, the other character who has crossed cultures (he was born in the king's palace at Oodeypore but escaped from his cage), releases Mowgli by slaying a bull to buy the boy out of the jungle, out of wolfhood, out of childhood. "From now, we follow new trails," Grey Brother says at the book's end.

If this seems complex for a child's book, remember that while an analysis of the Mowgli stories reveals many intricately woven strands, they are first and foremost a marvelous read. They are also profoundly psychologically satisfying to the young, for they portray a triumphant orphan who is able to move cleverly in the world of both animals and men. Tompkins reminds us that Mowgli is "like a boy who is helped by kindly beasts in a fairy-tale. He has a fairy-tale extension of power." But whether prince or wood god, Mowgli is a figure of enormous appeal.

In addition to their elements of legend, myth, and fairytale, *The Jungle Books* are filled with convincing, closely observed detail. Whether it is a precise touch like the "splash of sunlight . . . on the brass clamps of the old Tower musket" that Buldeo the hunter carries or the graphic description of the drought-stricken jungle, Kipling presents it vividly. He describes the emaciated Mowgli: "His naked skin made him look more lean and wretched than any of his fellows. . . . His ribs stood out like the ribs of a basket, and the lumps on his knees and elbows, where he was used to track on all fours, gave his shrunken limbs the look of knotted grass-stems." The unfortunate children of a current Ethiopian drought come to mind. Tompkins comments that Kipling at no time held "back from his young listeners the momentary glimpse of things sad and grim," and she recalls that as a child, "It was not the playful and domestic passages in these tales that impressed me most, but the notes of elevation and melancholy."

Domestic passages, however, are important in *The Jungle Books*—and one more appealing element for children. Mowgli's world may have all the satisfying perils of fictional adventure, but, while wild, it is ultimately secure. As Tompkins herself says, "The world unfolds, unspeakably various and wild and old; and everywhere the family group keeps the child in touch with its own reality." Mowgli's family group is an extended and exotic one. Apparently orphaned when the tiger Shere Khan attacked his parents' campsite, Mowgli, in the course of the stories, is raised in a wolf den (and is Mother Wolf's favorite cub), has a symbolic father in the head wolf Akela, and fond uncles in Baloo, Bagheera, and Kaa. He finds a human mother (maybe his real mother) in Messua in the village. And all of these regard him as the most wonderful child they have ever known. Consider that most satisfying opening of the head story **"Mowgli's Brothers."** A vulnerable but bold infant is saved from the threat of the villainous tiger by the fierce protectiveness of Mother Wolf. That wolf cave clearly represents the family haven in a hostile universe. Fittingly, it is Mother Wolf who comes to escort Messua to safety when the village is destroyed. Well are we warned by the Maxims of Baloo:

> Oppress not the cubs of the stranger, but hail them as Sister and Brother, For though they are little and fubsy, it may be the bear in their mother.

Or, as in Mowgli's case, a wolf!

In her book *Animal Land,* Margaret Blount sums up the circle of protection which surrounds Mowgli. "Why," she

Kipling with King George V of Great Britain, 1922.

asks, "was not Mowgli suckled by a bear, an antelope, or an animal of solitary habit? There is a precedent for the wolf-boy, but any solitary parent would have spoiled the central idea of *The Jungle Books,* which are about joining and belonging." She notes that central refrain (and Mowgli's password in the jungle), "We be of one blood ye and I."

The power of the family circle and jungle community does not become oppressive because of Mowgli's ability to revenge himself on those who misuse power. For instance, not only does Mowgli fulfill Mother Wolf's Prediction that he, a naked cub, will hunt and kill Shere Khan, but while skinning the slain tiger, he humiliates the hunter Buldeo (archetypal pompous adult) by ordering Grey Brother to stand on the old man's chest. And what a satisfying moment it is when Mowgli waves his flaming stick and scatters the ungrateful wolves, thereby saving both himself and the pack leader Akela. This theme of vengeance, which many critics have deplored in Kipling's work, is one with which most children, powerless and sometimes treated unfairly, can identify.

Balancing these acts of individual assertion is the all pervasive Law of the Jungle. "As the creeper that girdles the tree-trunk the Law runneth forward and back," intones Baloo as endsong for the story **"How Fear Came."** Mowgli is schooled most carefully in the laws, which are presented as of internal necessity rather than outward imposition. When the pack begs Akela to lead them again, they cry, "We be sick of this lawlessness, and we would be the Free People once more." For Kipling, freedom implies order. Though not overtly political, *The Jungle Books* convey his belief in a hierarchial world where men are judged good or evil according to their willingness to submit to a legitimate community. There is a clear hierarchy in Mowgli's jungle. We have Hathi the elephant as king, Bagheera the panther, Kaa the snake, and Akela the wolf as warrior aristocrats; Baloo the bear, a scholarly gentleman, and under them the wolf pack, respectable citizens. The red dogs are a lesser society, the jackals despicable hangers-on and the Bandar Log (the monkeys) the lawless, easily swayed mob. Further, there are good and bad characters of similar species defined by their relationship to some society. Bagheera respects the law of the jungle and of the wolf pack, but Shere Khan, the tiger, is a demagogic leader, outside the law and therefore evil. Kaa is a good snake, the white cobra a bad one, no longer poison himself but poisoned by a misguided devotion to a dead, materialistic society. The jungle is a microcosm of human society. This is what I meant in saying that *The Jungle Books* are really about civilization.

In fact, Kipling is questioning the nineteenth-century romantic view of natural man and the individual. The jungle is presented as post-Edenic. It is superior to the village, but the animals share man's faults. On the surface, Mowgli is the Noble Savage, the child of nature untainted by society, and indeed he is nobly innocent of the power of money. But he does not fit in the jungle any more than he does in the village. In **"Mowgli's Song"** he laments that both man and wolf have rejected him: "As Mang [the bat] flies between the beasts and the birds so fly I between the village and the jungle." In the second-to-last story Mowgli muses over the many roles he has assumed,

> "Mowgli the Frog have I been," said he to himself;
> "Mowgli the Wolf have I said that I am. Now Mowgli
> the Ape must I be before I am Mowgli the Buck. At
> the end I shall be Mowgli the Man."

He, like the creatures in the *Just So Stories,* has to play at becoming. But in *The Jungle Books* the evolutionary theme has taken on a new dimension. Kipling, critical of the Romantic cult of the individual, seems to have recognized the same flaw in the Social Darwinism of the age preceding him. We do not survive singly, but as a species—"For the strength of the pack is the wolf, and the strength of the wolf is the pack." The Mowgli has not found a society of which he is truly part. We are touched by his dilemma because we share it. Our place in nature as a species and our development as a successful community are also unresolved.

Truly did Kipling say, in *Something of Myself,* "My Daemon was with me in the *Jungle Books.*" Lord Birkenhead said of them, "into the *Jungle Books* are poured the full glory of his imaginative genius, untainted by bitterness, and unalloyed by special pleading. Had he written nothing else, these inspired stories would have made a powerful claim to immortality." Kipling's stories for children teach adults and children alike how to cross cultures and species, how to step out of the shell of self. Randall Jarrell said of him, "Knowing what the peoples, animals, plants, weathers of the world look like, sound like, smell like, was Kipling's *metier,* and so was knowing the words that could make someone else know." A child who wanders in the mythic jungles and deserts of the Mowgli stories and the *Just So Stories* is a fortunate traveler.

Margery Fisher

SOURCE: "The Hero," in *The Bright Face of Danger,* The Horn Book, Inc., 1986, pp. 181-227.

Every adventure turns on a test, a challenge offered to its central character. In junior stories the element of *rite de passage* enters, sometimes so strongly that there is a danger that the exploration of emotion and personality may overbalance the plot, taking a book out of the adventure-story genre into the genre of the analytical problem novel. Two of Kipling's young heroes seem relevant here—Mowgli, whose adventures are described in eight stories in *The Jungle Book* and *The Second Jungle Book,* of 1894 and 1895, and *Kim,* a novel of India and the **'Great Game',** first published in 1901, in which the Irish boy Kimball O'Hara is the central character. Both of these young heroes serve as focal points for a whole philosophy of education, for studies of the training of a young person both like and unlike the experiences of Kipling himself in English schools. The effect of the 'schools' (the school of the jungle and the flexible but strict training for a Secret Service) is to sharpen and increase an innate intelligence without destroying individuality: for the purposes of fiction Kipling has used two boys to explore certain aspects of moral and emotional growth but has through craftsmanship developed them as believable, identifiable individuals.

The Law of the Jungle into which Mowgli is gradually initiated is, as Kipling developed it, a combination of observable animal behaviour and the codes of conduct obtaining in society at the time when he wrote the stories. There is no need to assume in him an understanding of jungle animals ahead of his time. The social behaviour within a wolf-pack, the sanctions that applied at any waterhole in a time of drought—these and other points which Mowgli learnt, by precept or by experience, were a matter of common knowledge, as were the natural habitats of the animals and the cycles of predation or territorial aggression, though in Kipling's day they were not yet a matter of behavioural science.

To link human with animal behaviour, Kipling humanised the individual animals contributing to Mowgli's education in a straightforward and appropriate way, developing them as characters from one or two natural points. So, Baloo the lazy brown bear and the black panther Bagheera with his leashed energy became teachers of different types: the monkeys, restless and disorganised, named the Bandar-log, represented certain raffish elements in human society seen from an Establishment point of view; the lame, embittered man-eating tiger Shere Khan and his hanger-on, the sycophantic jackal Tabaqui, fall easily into the shape of human types; while the internal hierarchies of the wolf-pack corresponded so closely to the group-patterns of middle-class education that Kipling's humanisation of Akela was quickly translated back again into the pattern of Cub-Scout packs.

When Mowgli is adopted by the wolf-pack, as an infant found wandering in the jungle after the destruction of his home and parents, he learns to live by the wolf code of family obligations and observances, while Baloo and Bagheera instruct him in the rules by which the jungle animals exist in a shifting pattern evolved for survival, and extract from each species the master words by which he can communicate with every jungle inhabitant. Certain human attributes grow alongside the animal-lore he absorbs from his tutors; in this respect Kipling's wolf-reared boy is obviously romanticised in contrast to the unhappy children taken in real life from a wild environment. Mowgli learns from his animal friends that there is a colony of wild bees in a certain gorge, at the same time as he learns that the occasional irruption of wild dogs into their part of the jungle is one of the greatest dangers they have to face. It is by human reason that he puts the two facts together and works out a way of destroying the ravening pack, his courage and intelligence being equally beyond the animals whose life he shares. Kipling works out his fantasy from two firm bases, of animal and human fact, and uses a writer's technique, in pace, colour and tension, to make the fantasy work.

It is never easy for a reader to define his reactions to a

particular book and with the young, whether they are suggestible or anti-suggestible, the chance of reaching an honest and clean-cut opinion is pretty remote. Obviously, the stories about Mowgli will be read differently at different reading stages. Kipling shared with certain of his contemporaries who wrote for children (notably, Edith Nesbit, Mrs Molesworth and Frances Hodgson Burnett) a breadth in the emotional content of his tales which was to go underground, to a great extent, to surface only in the last two decades. Boys and girls who read, or listen to, the *Jungle Books* when they are eight or nine will probably think of Mowgli mainly in terms of his exotic and exciting life in the jungle. His character, for them, is likely to be that of a wolf-boy, to be envied by those in more staid situations. To the thoughtful older reader the stories present, through jungle-adventures of the most specific and believable kind, a cumulative picture of 'growing up'.

This is not a simple picture nor is the educational process that moulds Mowgli a single one. The instruction he receives from the animals teaches him how to coexist with them; as baby, child and young boy, he is virtually a wolf, though of slower growth than theirs. Kipling jumps from the introductory narrative, in which the feud with Shere Khan is established (the tiger, having killed Mowgli's parents, asserts his right to the boy and is only temporarily bought off by contract with the wolves), to Mowgli's twelfth year, when a second phase of learning begins. Now he must learn to know himself and, in the end, must decide whether he is man or animal.

When he shrugs off Bagheera's warning that the wolves may turn against him, the panther tells the boy to look him straight in the eyes, and quickly turns his head away:

> '*That* is why,' he said, shifting his paw on the leaves. 'Not even I can look thee between the eyes, and I was born among men, and I love thee, Little Brother. The others they hate thee because their eyes cannot meet thine—because thou art wise—because thou hast pulled out thorns from their feet—because thou art a man.'

The panther's predictions are true. The wolves drive Mowgli out; weeping for the first time in his life, he goes down the hillside 'to meet those mysterious things that are called men'.

Some of his difficulties as he tries to adapt himself to life in the village are practical. Helped by an affectionate foster-mother, for whose dead son he is a substitute, he learns to endure sleeping under a roof, to wear clothes, to use money, to discipline his unusual strength. Trained to recognise gradations in the wolf-pack, he ignores the caste system of his fellow men:

> When the potter's donkey slipped in the clay-pit, Mowgli hauled it out by the tail, and helped to stack the pots for their journey to the market at Khanhiwara. That was very shocking, too, for the porter is a low-caste man, and his donkey is worse. When the priest scolded him Mowgli threatened to put him on the donkey, too, and the priest told Messua's husband that Mowgli had better be set to work as soon as possible.

The job of herding buffaloes, a congenial one, leads first to a boyish fit of mischief, when he sets out to expose the beasts of Buldeo the hunter with the help of his pack brothers who are still loyal to him, and then to a well-devised plot by which he brings about the death of Shere Khan. But success turns against him. The villagers, far from being grateful to him for destroying the dangerous man-eater, stone him as a wizard, in unlawful alliance with wolves and perhaps with spirits, and he returns to the jungle—but to hunt alone, for 'Man-Pack and Wolf-Pack have cast me out'. In his song of triumph, as he casts Shere Khan's hide on the council rock of the wolves, he expresses a painful new knowledge of himself:

> 'My mouth is cut and wounded with the stones from the village, but my heart is very light because I have come back to the Jungle. Why?
> These two things fight together in me as the snakes fight in the spring.
> The water comes out of my eyes; yet I laugh while it falls. Why?
> I am two Mowglis, but the hide of Shere Khan is under my feet.
> All the Jungle knows that I have killed Shere Khan. Look—look well, O wolves!
> *Ahae!* My heart is heavy with the things that I do not understand.

Accepting these new, puzzling obligations of humanity, Mowgli sets about rescuing his foster-parents, who have been condemned to death by their fellow villagers for giving a home to a dangerous wizard. Mowgli's revenge is conducted in animal terms. He arranges for Buldeo and his associates to be hazed through the jungle by Bagheera and the wolves and persuades Hathi the elephant and his family to break down the village huts and trample the crops. **'Letting in the Jungle'** is a story of the most telling, vivid and pictorial adventure, but the undercurrent of sadness, perplexity, mixed motives in Mowgli is very strong.

For a year or two longer Mowgli is able to live in reasonable comfort of mind in the jungle, using his human skills (in the defeat of the wild red dogs, for example) or learning at second-hand about the frailties of his kind—as when he steals the King's Ankus from its guardian, the blind white snake, and observes the effect of its ancient curse as it works on human greed. He is surprised and scornful at Bagheera's definition of the Time of New Talk, the spring, and its effect on the animals he hunts with, until he begins to feel at odds with them and with himself. Has he been poisoned, he asks his seventeen-year-old self; why is he hot and cold by turns, weak and strong, sad and excited? He visits the village, to see how it has changed, and finds in his foster-mother a new respect and affection which tempts him, while the sight of a girl going to the well disturbs him. Most of all he is tormented by the thought that he has lost the friendship of his fellow animals. He has lost, in effect, his childhood:

> 'Why did I not die under Red Dog?' the boy moaned.

'My strength is gone from me, and it is not any poison. By night and by day I hear a double step upon my trail. When I turn my head it is as though one had hidden himself from me that instant. I go to look behind the trees and he is not there. I call and none cry again; but it is as though one listened and kept back the answer. I lie down, but I do not rest. I run the spring running, but I am not made still. I bathe, but I am not made cool. The kill sickens me, but I have no heart to fight except I kill. The Red Flower is in my body, my bones are water—and—I know not what I know.'

Kaa the snake has the answer. 'Man goes to Man at the last, though the Jungle does not cast him out.'

The theme that binds the Mowgli tales together, the idea of learning and growing up, has given them a more than merely contemporary significance. This in itself would be enough to attract readers from one generation to another, by inviting them to see something of themselves in Mowgli. This hero has the opacity, the general shape which makes it possible for that inexplicable process of 'identification' to take place; and yet, by the atmosphere, the detail, the dialogue and ultimately by the sheer magic compulsion of the tales, Mowgli is created as an individual.

Margery Fisher

SOURCE: "Animals as Characters: *The Jungle Book*," in *Margery Fisher Recommends Classics for Children & Young People,* edited by Nancy Chambers, Thimble Press, 1986, p. 34.

Did the tales of Mowgli originate in resentment against the people who made Kipling's youth a misery? Whether or not this is the case, most children brought up on the Jungle Books realize sooner or later how much sadness, disappointment, loss and disillusion there is behind the glorious pretence that a child could really live and flourish in community with animals on their own terms. No children's book can last as a classic without a firm basis of mature thought and feeling, and the Mowgli tales will always be read in two ways. As the adventures of a boy in a jungle world (instructed in animal lore but keeping, against probability, a human intellect and heart) the stories exploit young energy and curiosity in scenes where the jungle comes to life sensuously and pictorially. To adult readers the progress of Mowgli's education, his painful adjustment to maturity with an experience of human greed (in **'The King's Ankus'**), of natural disaster (in **'How Fear Came'**) and of social unrest (in the doings of the Bandar-Log) convey a great deal about Kipling's outlook as well as about his ardent response to the Indian way of life. There are other tales in the two books besides the Mowgli cycle, of course—the electrifying **'Toomai of the Elephants'**, the affectionate **'Rikki-Tikki-Tavi'** and **'His Majesty's Servants'**, a story in Kipling's most oblique manner. But it is in the growing up of the wolf-reared human boy that young readers will find the deepest emotional experience.

Dieter Petzold

SOURCE: "Fantasy out of Myth and Fable: Animal Stories in Rudyard Kipling and Richard Adams," in *Children's Literature Association Quarterly,* Vol. 12, No. 1, Spring, 1987, pp. 15-19.

Next to human beings, animals are probably the most common protagonists in children's stories, far more common than fairies, giants, or dragons. Considering the interest children take in all living creatures around them, this is hardly surprising. Slightly more surprising, perhaps, is the fact that in almost all cases animals in children's stories are to a greater or lesser degree anthropomorphized. Even in "realistic" stories animals usually enter into such a close emotional relationship with human beings that they will invariably be described in metaphors suggesting human thought and behavior. . . .

[In some texts] the protagonists are animals which are humanized to such a degree that they can talk and reason like human beings. In a broad sense, texts like these are obviously fantasy fiction in that they create a secondary world which is (at least in this important aspect) radically different from empirical reality, even if many features of that reality, including some observable animal behavior, are faithfully copied. . . .

In their depiction of animals [the *Jungle Book* stories] range from the nearly realistic (**"Toomai of the Elephants"**) to the explicit fantasy of extensively humanized animals. Except for the imperialist parable of military discipline, **"Her Majesty's Servants,"** we have full-fledged stories rather than mere legends, with individualized characters, intricate plots, and plenty of action and suspense. However, traces of the animal fable and of myth are still quite clearly discernible.

The Mowgli stories are probably the most complex in this respect. We may note, first of all, that the fable element is much weaker here than in the *Just So Stories.* Accordingly, the animals are, as a rule, much more individualized, although we do have conventional character stereotypes in the Bandar-log (here the typical simplifications of the fable are made to serve a satirical purpose) and in some side-characters like Tabaqui, the jackal. Most significantly, the relation between Mowgli's jungle world and the world of the reader's experience cannot be described as simply allegorical (which would be typical of the didactic fable); rather, the relation between the two worlds is complex and ambiguous, as is typical of fantasy literature. It is based on myth just as much as on accurate observation of reality, and it contains a good deal of wish-fulfillment.

Mowgli's peculiar upbringing is, of course, a widespread mythical motif. The parallel that comes immediately to mind is the story of Romulus and Remus, but similar tales can be found all over the world. But while in the classical myth the motif serves to underline the exceptional qualities of the hero (his extensive rapport with the forces of nature), here it is part of a pervasive dream of childhood innocence within a world whose order is both natural and rational. As has frequently been pointed out, Mowgli's jungle world incorporates the utopian dream of Eden, but we must not overlook the fact that this paradisaical vision is precarious. It is threatened by man's encroachment from outside as well as by corruption from within.

What we have, then, is a political-utopian myth of a world in which the primitive laws of nature (eat and be eaten) are precariously reconciled with the complex artificiality of The Law (an elaborate code of civilized behavior). To make matters even more complex, this is overlaid by the motif of the passage from innocence to experience, which is essentially private in character. Seen from this angle, Mowgli is an Everyman (or rather Everybody), his story being the universal tragedy of growing up, of passing from the sheltered world of simplicity and innocence to the outside world of complexity and guilt.

There is no direct communication between humans and animals in **"Rikki-Tikki-Tavi,"** but the story is hardly less fantastic because of this, since all animals are thoroughly humanized and individualized. The story is very simple in that there is not the slightest doubt as to who the hero is and who the villains are. Within the conventional moral framework of good and bad (derived, we may note in passing, from the humans' point of view), Rikki's deed is a personal triumph (as a mongoose, he is a natural enemy of the snakes) and at the same time an act of social significance. He is a hero because he is, like any knight, protector of the innocent and the weak. . . . Essentially, this is a small-scale version of the dragon-slayer myth, transposed into the animal kingdom and reduced in scale for the homely setting of an Anglo-Indian's bungalow backyard.

In contrast, the deed of Kotick, the White Seal, has a profound political significance. Kotick is the born leader whose outstanding qualities (stamina, willpower, charisma) enable him to guide his sluggish people to a Promised Land of security and plenty. This is an obvious (and, I should guess, deliberate) version of the biblical Exodus myth, which, we are reminded by Northrop Frye, is itself only a type of the apocalyptic Christian redemption myth. Unlike Christ, however, Kotick is not above bullying when it comes to persuading his obtuse people to accept new ideas. It is precisely through recognizing deep-structure similarities that the importance of such differences becomes manifest.

The transposition of these myths into a slightly humanized animal kingdom—in other words, the use of fantasy—enables Kipling to present them in a form that is comparatively little displaced and therefore fresh and emotionally satisfying, unencumbered by the complexities of real life. One might object to these stories because they celebrate rather a crude hero worship (with some concomitant simplified dichotomy of enlightened leader and stupid masses). On the other hand, it could be argued that they, after all, propagate social responsibility and give shape to dreams which are not only normal but probably necessary for the development of every child who is trying to define, not his position, but his goal in life. . . .

There are a great many things that these animal stories. . . teach, albeit in an unobtrusive way: that every action has consequences; that true communication involves an acceptance of common nature, and respect for the otherness of one's partner; that being a hero means, first and foremost, serving the community selflessly; that true leadership requires qualities like humility, compassion, and self-denial. At the basis of our enjoyment of animal stories founded in myth, however, lies our deep if rarely conscious desire—whether in child or in adult—for a world which is intelligible because in it humans and animals are subject to the same simple order, so that there is no real distinction between our all-too-human cousins and our all-too-beastly selves.

Charles Frey and John Griffith

SOURCE: "Rudyard Kipling: The Mowgli Stories," in *The Literary Heritage of Childhood: An Appraisal of Children's Classics in the Western Tradition,* Greenwood Press, 1987, pp. 189-99.

The Mowgli stories in *The Jungle Books* by Rudyard Kipling (1865-1936) do what many classics of children's literature do: They begin with a psychological dilemma that lies near the heart of the author's sense of his own childhood—an unfulfilled yearning, an old frustration, a wrong unrighted—and generate from it a fantasy which fulfills that yearning, releases that frustration, rectifies that injustice. It is a mark of literary genius when such fantasies reach outside the author's private grievance and touch universal feelings which millions of readers can share. And it is a very high order of genius when the author can not only bring his fantasy to the world, but also bring the world into his fantasy, incorporating in the fiction itself the truths of human life which are the wise corrective to his own wishful thinking. The Mowgli stories achieve that high order of genius.

The essential dilemma underlying these stories is the theme of the song Mowgli sings at the end of **"'Tiger-Tiger!'"** Here Mowgli, having been denied membership in either the society of wolves or the society of men, has killed Shere Khan, the reprobate tiger who has been his most conspicuous enemy.

> Waters of the Wainganga, the man pack have cast
> me out. I did them no harm, but they were afraid
> of me. Why?
> Wolf pack, ye have cast me out too. The jungle is
> shut to me and the village gates are shut. Why?
> As Mang flies between the beasts and birds so fly I
> between the village and the jungle. Why?
>
> I dance on the hide of Shere Khan, but my heart is
> very heavy.
> My mouth is cut and wounded with the stones
> from the village, but my heart is very light,
> because I have come back to the jungle. Why?
> These two things fight together in me as the snakes
> fight in the spring. The water comes out of my
> eyes, yet I laugh while it falls. Why?

I am two Mowglis, but the hide of Shere Khan is
    under my feet.
All the jungle knows that I have killed Shere Khan.
    Look, look well, O wolves!
Ahae! My heart is heavy with the things that I do
    not understand.

To understand the mysteries that Mowgli struggles with
here—to understand why men and wolves have turned
against him when he did them no harm, and why he finds
himself "two Mowglis," laughing and crying, with heart
both light and heavy; to understand why he dances on the
hide of Shere Khan before the watching eyes of the wolf
pack; and to understand why his moment of triumph leaves
him with a heart "heavy with the things that I do not
understand"—is to understand the root-situation of the
Mowgli stories, and to fathom their urgency and depth of
meaning, for Kipling first, and next for his readers.

Classic children's literature contains a number of memorable outsiders, characters who stand significantly beyond
the pale of the culture upon which their lives are a comment: Huckleberry Finn, St.-Exupéry's little prince, Peter
Pan, the child in Hans Christian Andersen's story who
announces that the emperor has nothing on. Mowgli is, in
a general sense, one of them. But he is different, too, in
that he is not simply outside a culture looking in; he is
specifically between two cultures. An outcast from the
society of both men and wolves but in some sense a prod-

From The Jungle Book, *by Rudyard Kipling.*
Illustrated by P. Frenzeny.

uct of both of them, Mowgli thinks and acts very differently from someone who, like Huck Finn, simply has no
place in ordered society anywhere, or someone who, like
Peter Pan, has looked on society and rejected it. That
Mowgli flies "between the village and the jungle" as
"Mang [the bat] flies between the beasts and birds" is
essential to the drama of his life, and makes of the Mowgli
stories something very different from the tense personal
fantasy of *Peter Pan* on the one hand, or the social satire
of *Huckleberry Finn* on the other. In these tales, Kipling
bridges the gap between solipsistic personal dream and
detached, impersonal social comedy. He was well qualified to do so.

Mowgli, as the boy between two cultures, is in an important sense Kipling himself, whose whole life was spent in
odd and excited suspension between and among various
societies. Born in India of English parents, he was very
early made aware that he was neither entirely English nor
Indian. He was raised by a native Indian nurse and spoke
Hindi before he spoke English; at the age of six, like
many Anglo-Indian children, he was sent back to England, away from his parents, to learn to be English. The
experience as he recalls it in his memoirs and in the short
story **"Baa, Baa, Black Sheep"** was profoundly traumatic; dropped from a world where, as the little *sahib,* his
every whim had been honored, into a foster home which
he came to call "The House of Desolation," where a strict
and Puritanical woman set about breaking his spirit, Kipling experienced a dislocation that was virtually absolute.
Later, when he was twelve, he was sent to the United
Services College, a public school established by a group
of army officers to prepare their sons for the responsibilities of army commissions. But Kipling's father was not
an army officer—he was an architect, a man of letters,
and a museum curator, with no intention that his son should
become a military man. Between the ages of twelve and
seventeen, Kipling lived in unreconciled tension between
two styles of life, which one of his biographers describes
this way:

> The holidays he spent with his Burne-Jones and Poynter
> aunts, meeting the Pre-Raphaelite Brotherhood and their
> friends. He looked at pictures of delicate dream women
> set against backgrounds of hard bright detail. At
> school—and it must be repeated that it was a boarding-
> school with no week-ends away, an interminable
> thirteen or fourteen weeks at a stretch—he lived among
> budding subalterns under a headmaster he admired but
> assistant masters whom he regarded as enemies and in
> some cases disliked or despised.

He returned to India in his eighteenth year and took up
the trade of newspaper journalist and, later, local-color
short-story writer, vocations which set him psychologically apart from the officers and civil servants among
whom he lived and whom he observed as material for his
writing. Finally, having escaped India on the strength of
a prodigious early reputation as a writer of fiction and
verse, he settled temporarily in Vermont, where he carried on a polite cold war with neighboring Vermonters,
who did not know what to make of the celebrated and

unsociable foreigner camping in their territory. It was here, in Vermont, that Kipling wrote the Mowgli stories, about a boy who yearns for membership in two social worlds but finds himself ill-suited to either of them. Kipling knew firsthand the dilemma he was writing about.

Part of what he accomplished in the Mowgli stories was a piece of wish-fulfillment, a consoling fantasy akin to Hans Christian Andersen's self-vindication in "The Ugly Duckling." Both Kipling and Andersen made up stories in which heroes are rejected by society not simply because they are different from ordinary people, but because they are better. In both stories, rejection is pictured not as the mark of inadequacy which it seems to be in real life, but as a badge of superiority. In the ironically titled story **"Mowgli's Brothers,"** which tells of Mowgli's first dealings with the Seeonee Wolf Pack, the innocent, good-hearted little boy is at first nominally accepted in membership. He assumes that he really belongs. "I was born in the jungle," he says. "I have obeyed the Law of the Jungle, and there is no wolf of ours from whose paws I have not pulled a thorn. Surely they are my brothers." But he is wrong, as Bagheera the panther explains to him:

> Not even I can look thee between the eyes, and I was born among men, and I love thee, Little Brother. The others hate thee because their eyes cannot meet thine; because thou art wise; because thou hast pulled out thorns from their feet—because thou art a man.

They hate him, in short, because he can do things they can't. Later, the humans' reaction against him will be the same; they fear him because he is stronger, more sensible, and wiser in the ways of the jungle than they are. "Sorcerer!" they cry. "Wolf's brat! Jungle-demon! Go away!"

Rejected by two packs of mediocrities, Mowgli (something like Andersen's swan) joins instead an elite society which is much nobler than the societies from which he has been excluded. Baloo the wise old teacher-bear, Bagheera the model of masculine independence and power, Akela the statesman-leader of the wolf pack, and Kaa the ancient, mysterious and mighty python make up this lordly society, the preferable substitute for the societies that have denied Mowgli. Baloo, Bagheera, and Kaa are all loners, living apart from their own species; Akela, seeing the faithlessness of the wolf pack, virtually renounces his membership in it. "In truth, I have lived too long," he says. "I know ye to be cowards, and it is to cowards that I speak." All four are physically imposing, strong, and dangerous fighters; all are creatures of honor and high principle; all are indisputably expert, the best at what they do. Bagheera is "as cunning as Tabaqui, as bold as the wild buffalo, and as reckless as the wounded elephant." Akela is the embodiment of principled legality. Baloo is the sage of the Law of the Jungle, the scholar of civilized wisdom. Kaa knows more primal stuff, the distillation of age and sheer massive experience:

> Kaa, his head motionless on the ground, thought of all that he had seen and known since the day he came

from the egg. The light seemed to go out of his eyes and leave them like stale opals, and now and again he made little stiff passes with his head to right and left, as though he were hunting in his sleep.

Just to be accepted by this exotic elite would be a great distinction; but Mowgli, even better, creates this heroic brotherhood, for it is only through their love of Mowgli that the four constitute a society at all.

Membership in that brotherhood is dependent on strength, cunning, charisma, personal merit; membership in the various packs that roam Mowgli's jungle—wolf pack, monkey pack, man pack, dog pack—is the merest accident of birth. Pack-thinking and pack-behavior are consistently vulgar, undiscriminating, mean, and petty. Ordinary membership in such groups is equivalent to personal mediocrity. To be purely logical, Mowgli should feel relieved that he has escaped the downward-leveling of wolf pack and man pack.

But of course the matter is not one of pure logic. We can readily understand why Mowgli seeks entry into such groups, inferior as they are; we can see that the Mowgli stories, unlike Andersen's one-dimensional little fable, are something larger than an extended version of the compensatory thought, "Who wants to belong to that crowd, anyway." Being rejected doesn't do much of anything to Andersen's swan; he simply undergoes the ordeal, grows up a little, finds a flock of swans to join, and prospers. Kipling knows, and the Mowgli stories show, that being rejected is not only a painful process but a deeply formative one, crucially affecting a person's sense of self, values, and habitual stance before the world.

The pattern of Mowgli's personality is simple and consistent: In the beginning, innocently, he wants and expects to be loved. The mother wolf, whose instincts are right, adopts him and loves him, and Mowgli assumes that everyone else will, too. But the wolf pack turns on him. By a plain and direct process of substituting an objective which can be reached for one which cannot, Mowgli becomes infatuated with power and dominance. In effect he says to the world, "You have shown you do not love me; very well, I cannot force you to love me. But I can force you to fear and respect me, and that will be good enough." Mowgli becomes preoccupied with revenge— with killing Shere Khan who has insulted him, with destroying the man village that has insulted him, with destroying the red-dog pack that has presumed to enter his jungle. The destruction of his enemies becomes a primary pleasure. When Kaa asks him, "So the jungle gives thee all that thou hast ever desired, Little Brother?" Mowgli answers, "Not all, else there would be a new and strong Shere Khan to kill once a moon."

On this vindictive energy Mowgli rises to be master of the jungle. "It was after the letting in of the jungle [where the native village had been] that the pleasantest part of Mowgli's life began," Kipling writes. "He had the good conscience that comes from paying a just debt [of vengeance], and all the jungle was his friend, for all the jungle was afraid of him."

Honor has become the great ideal in Mowgli's eyes: good reputation, the unsullied name; he values it because society has treated him as if he were not honorable. "They have cast me out from the man pack, Mother," he announces in "**'Tiger-Tiger!'**" "but I come with the hide of Shere Khan to keep my word . . . Look well, O wolves. Have I kept my word?" Making and keeping personal oaths—particularly oaths of vengeance—are one of the clearest ways of demonstrating one's honor in these stories. He declaims in "**Red Dog**":

> I say that when the dholes come, and if the dholes come, Mowgli and the Free People are of one skin for that hunting. And I say, by the bull that bought me, by the bull Bagheera paid for me in the old days which ye of the pack do not remember, *I* say, that the trees and the river may hear and hold fast if I forget. *I* say that this my knife shall be as a tooth to the pack—and I do not think it is so blunt. This is my word which has gone from me.

The whole system of manly virtues follows from this idea of honor: pride, courage, discipline, loyalty, cunning, and physical strength.

The high style in which Mowgli speaks is intrinsic to the stance of defiant self-assertion that he has developed. We see this style most clearly in all the rhetorical occasions of chivalric combat: the taunt, the challenge, the boast; but its characteristics pervade virtually all the speech and manners of Mowgli and his circle: stately, ceremonious, self-conscious, designed to remind one's listeners of one's status and prowess. "A brave heart and a courteous tongue" says Kaa to Mowgli. "They will carry thee far in the jungle." And Kaa is exactly right; courtesy is itself a demonstration of bravery, a formal notice that one takes oneself seriously and demands respect from others.

The very Law of the Jungle itself, which embodies much that is basic to Kipling's attitude on many social subjects, is among other things a construction of principles and values ideal for the pursuit of power and dominion to which Mowgli is driven. Kipling does not present it primarily as that, of course. He presents the Law as the basic rule of survival, growing out of real-life natural history. It is "by far the oldest law in the world," he says; it "has arranged for almost every kind of accident that may befall the Jungle-People, till now its code is as perfect as time and custom can make it." The myth which the elephant Hathi relates in "**How Fear Came**" suggests that the Law has certain moral benefits, as a corrective to natural failings like laziness, petulance and irresponsibility—but that its primal foundation is the fear of death. "The first of your masters has brought Death into the jungle, and the second Shame. Now it is time there was a Law, and a Law that ye may not break. Now ye shall know Fear."

From what Kipling shows us of the maxims that grow out of this beginning, one sees clearly enough that they are mostly concerned with species-survival. The law provides rules within which death can be controlled, and the ani-mals can release their impulses of hunger, ferocity and hostility without exterminating whole species. The occasion on which Hathi tells the story gives a clear example of what this means: He tells it to the animals—predators and grass-eaters together—assembled under "the Water Truce" which goes into effect during drought. The Water Truce forbids killing at the drinking-place, since if killing were permitted there the grazers would stay away from water and die quickly, of thirst, and the predators would then die, too, of starvation.

To a large extent, Kipling's Law prescribes behavior which we would call instinctive. It specifies, for example, that the jackal may scavenge after other hunters but that the wolves should hunt for themselves, and that the wolf should hunt at night and sleep during the day. But Kipling does not leave the matter at that; his Law ultimately is not just a description of the way animals are, but also a moral suggestion of how they ought to be. It is entirely possible in these stories (indeed, it is entirely *common*) for animals to fail to live up the Law—which wouldn't make sense if the Law represented only instinct. Shere Khan is a gross and chronic violator, he kills humans promiscuously and pollutes drinking water with their blood. The wolf pack reneges on its promise to Mowgli and breaks the Law. The monkey people have so little regard for principle that they are said not even to have a Law.

As a moral system, the Law generally urges restraint and responsibility and the long view, as over against ungoverned selfish impulse. It is deeply conservative, making no provision for democratic improvement, and strictly observing the ideal of hierarchy. "Keep peace with the lords of the jungle," it urges at one point; at another, "Because of his age and his cunning, because of his gripe and his paw, / In all that the Law leaveth open, the word of your head wolf is Law." It shows comparatively little concern for helping or protecting the weak; what little there is in that way comes under the heading of ensuring the perpetuation of species (e.g., taking care of mothers with new-born offspring) rather than the heading of compassion. It is, in short, a system within which those thrive best who are strong, suspicious, purposeful, and proud.

In this hybrid concept of Law—neither purely amoral instinct nor purely moral injunction, but something of both—Kipling has an idea of great value in Mowgli's quest for honor and status. What the Law provides is an ideal of behavior both honorable and practical, which stands apart from mere mob-conformity. If Mowgli is to be vindicated in his war with societies both wolf and human, it is important to have a system of absolutes by which he is right and society is wrong. Kipling separates the ideas of *law* and *society,* rather than treating them as two aspects of social order as most social theorists do. In the Mowgli stories, one chooses between ordinary social life—which is sloppy, unintelligent, and irrational—and life under the Law—which is rigorous, disciplined, and sensible. That he so thoroughly understands the Law of the Jungle and observes it so faithfully proves that Mowgli is stronger, wiser and more honorable than those who rejected him, and proves it, moreover, not according to some eccentric, visionary ideal of his own but according to the very time-perfected principles of life in the jungle. Keeping the Law, in these stories, is a little like obeying the Bible as an unimpeachable authority of rectitude (indeed, the nearest model for the maxims of the Law is the book of Proverbs in the Old Testament); furthermore, this Law is worldly and practical, not at all "religious."

If we were to read all but the last of the Mowgli stories, and stop with **"Red Dog,"** the account of Mowgli's destruction of the barbarous dog pack that invades his domain, we would in some ways have a complete story. **"Red Dog"** details an apocalyptic blood-feast, the orgiastic climax of Mowgli's need to dominate, and completes the grim story of his rise to power. If the stories stopped here, one fundamental drive—the drive to react against the pain of rejection—could be seen to color the entire value-system and philosophy of the stories, and to help create their characters and shape their plots. With **"Red Dog,"** the demonstration is complete that the world of Kipling's jungle is not just the place of Mowgli's ostracism but the ideal place for avenging it.

Kipling with his wife, Caroline, in 1928.

But the note of triumph in **"Red Dog"** is discordant, because of another note in the story, a tone of repletion without satisfaction and the passing of the conditions under which such bloody victories make good emotional sense. The inner circle of Mowgli's friends is in decay in this story.

> Father and Mother Wolf died . . . and Baloo grew very old and stiff, and even Bagheera, whose nerves were steel and whose muscles were iron, seemed slower at the kill. Akela turned from grey to milky white with pure age.

Mowgli mounts his epic battle against the dog pack more out of memory than present inspiration. "Listen now," he says, "there was a wolf, my father, and there was a wolf, my mother, and there was an old grey wolf (not too wise: he is white now) was my father and my mother. Therefore I—" and he makes his oath to fight this one last fight for and with the wolf pack. When it is over, and the most graphic, brutal bloodletting of Mowgli's career has been done, Akela tells him, "All debts are paid now. go to thine own people." Mowgli protests in terms he has used since the humans rejected him years before. "I will never go. I will hunt alone in the jungle." But Akela insists. "After the summer come the rains, and after the rains comes the spring. . . . Mowgli will drive Mowgli. Go back to thy people. Go to Man."

And thus the stage is set for the last story in the series, **"The Spring Running,"** which takes the argument one painful, honest, inevitable step further, and faces Mowgli's need for love and acceptance in a new and necessary form. **"The Spring Running"** is an odd story, somewhat mysterious to many readers whether child or adult. It is, in more ways than one, "the last of the Mowgli stories," as Kipling says, for it announces, in effect, the finish of Mowgli as we know him; it precisely refutes the whole basis on which Mowgli has built his personality—the fond belief that a soul can survive on an emotional diet of power and dominance alone. . . .

"The Spring Running" is the story of, really, two big crises in Mowgli's life, and the transition into which they impel him. The first of these, and the most obvious, is the crisis of Mowgli's sexual awakening. At the age of seventeen he feels yearnings and excitements which he has never felt before, even though he has witnessed the spring mating season every year, and has been to some extent aware of a change that comes over all creatures at that time. His sexual hunger sends him running through the jungle, a forty-mile lope which takes him, almost involuntarily, into a village of people. "Mowgli," he says to himself, "what hast thou to do any more with the lairs of the man pack?" The answer comes soon enough—he needs women. Messua, the woman who mothered him once before and who may or may not be his real mother, now takes him in again. Her husband is dead, and she has a two-year-old baby. She feeds Mowgli, caresses him, praises his good looks ("Have any told thee that thou art beautiful beyond all men?" she says). Mowgli rests and dandles the baby on his lap and sleeps. The sickness he has felt inside him is momentarily allayed. As he leaves the woman's hut to return to the jungle, he sees a girl walking down a path.

In one way, then, the story is about the place of sex and reproduction in the scheme of life. The Law of the Jungle, preoccupied as it is with the survival of species, would of course require that creatures go forth and multiply; in this respect **"The Spring Running"** simply shows that Mowgli is not above that feature of the Law.

But the story is also about love, or the need for love, and that is not exactly the same thing. The feelings Kipling writes about here ultimately transcend the simply physical release of mating. Mowgli cannot do as the animals in the story do—disappear into the bushes for brief, intense courtship and mating and then return to the all-male company of Mowgli's circle. Mowgli's fever is sexual, but it is more broadly psychological, too, and finally even philosophical, for it forces Mowgli to question the authenticity of his values. It requires that he leave the jungle and return to human society more or less permanently.

On consideration, one can see rather exactly the nature of the second crisis Mowgli is undergoing. As to the first crisis, the emergence of sexual appetites, we may grant Kipling's notion that this is a natural occurrence for a seventeen-year-old. But the second crisis is more appropriate, perhaps, to a man about the age of Kipling himself when he wrote the story—thirty years. Mowgli, the story tells us, has for some time been the undisputed master of the jungle. "The Jungle-People, who used to fear him for his wits, feared him now for his mere strength, and when he moved quietly on his own affairs the whisper of his coming cleared the wood-path." He is like a man who has made a great success in his career and found that his success is unsatisfying. (Kipling, when he wrote these stories, had already risen to world renown as a brilliant young writer—had known the feeling of being held in almost superstitious awe by the literary world.) The very idea of defining oneself entirely through the power and respect he commands does not sit easily in Mowgli's mind any longer.

He has started to sense that the dignity of his position is not unimpeachable, and that there might be viewpoints from which his eminence could look hollow.

Mowgli tries in half a dozen ways to describe the new feeling that has invaded him. He says:

> It must be I have carelessly eaten poison. By night and by day I hear a double step upon my trail. When I turn my head it is as though one had hidden himself from me that instant. . . . The Red Flower is in my body, my bones are water—and—I know not what I know.

He finds himself washed with gentle, uncontrollable emotion. "A large warm tear splashed down on his knee, and, miserable as he was, Mowgli felt happy that he was so miserable. . . . "

Clearly, Mowgli is not in the grip of snorting animal lust;

he feels rather a mellow, languid desire for gentleness and love and nourishment. His new feeling is tied to all the warm, yielding, lonely, softening feelings which, in his proud and defiant rise to power, he has learned to deny himself. What Mowgli needs is not release of physical tension but a change in his essential life. He has "a new stomach in him," as he thinks; he has "changed his skin," as Kaa puts it, and "having cast the skin, we may not creep into it afresh." Mowgli is realizing the conflict between his past delight in exerting his will over the animals and his new yearning for love. The sexual impulse which transforms the animals in the mating season represents, for him, a counter-principle to his exertion of power, a rebuke to that power, a force more urgent than the desire to dominate which has been the basis of his whole identity. Mowgli wishes, in short, to break out of that enclosed, defiant, paranoid circle of force and self-assertion which his early sorrows have taught him to build and fortify.

The old pride and proofs of self-worth are not immediately forgotten, of course. There is pain in Mowgli's dim new realization, because submission to the demands of love is, in some very serious respects, a betrayal of the old heroic code by which Mowgli has learned to live. To feel as Mowgli feels—lonely and sorry for himself and in need of warmth and caresses—is, by the old code, to feel a loss of dignity and honor. Mowgli must reconcile himself to this as best he can. As he takes his leave of his warrior-friends, they assure him that this new departure is no shame, no repetition of the humiliating exclusions he suffered years before. "Man goes to Man at the last, *though the jungle does not cast him out,*" Kaa says. "The jungle does not cast me out then?" asks Mowgli. "Nay, look up, Little Brother," says Baloo. "There is no shame in this hunting." Shame there may not be, but there is a comedown, an unsettling sense of vulnerability and of mortality, of letting down the barriers which Mowgli has learned to maintain.

"The Spring Running" is a story more about an ending than a beginning. It leaves us with only the loosest idea of what will become of Mowgli when he reaches the man-village. We expect that he will get married—and Kipling says elsewhere that he does, both in **"In the Rukh"** and at the end of **"'Tiger-Tiger!'"** Presumably he will make some accommodations, temper the stern and critical view of humanity which he brought to the village years before in **"Mowgli's Brother"**. (Pitched in its different key, **"In the Rukh"** shows that Mowgli will continue to run afoul of human superstitions and will still be skeptical of human values and customs, but he will acknowledge the legitimacy of society's claims on him anyway.) He comes now not in flight from something—the faithlessness of the wolves—but in search of something—the love of a woman. We know that Mowgli has reached an end to the life lived entirely in reaction to the ostracism suffered in his boyhood. His days of proving his manhood to those who would deny it are coming to a close.

"Four things greater than all things are,—/Women and Horses and Power and War," Kipling wrote elsewhere, with the bravado one finds in much of his fiction and verse. **"The Spring Running"** is one story where the heroic fantasy comes down to earth, and the claims of Women are felt to outweigh those of Horses and Power and War. Here Kipling tests the mystique of honor and defiance against the claims of love and domesticity, and it is honor that has to yield. The deep message here is that hostility and resentment can make a personality formidable and strong in certain ways, but vulnerable, too, and incomplete. The larger values of love and home and generation lie outside its boundaries. It may be surprising to find such an idea advanced by Kipling the notorious drumbanger and saber-rattler, but there it is.

The Mowgli stories are, then, something larger and more conscientious than an outsider's fantasy about the glories of being outside. Kipling and Mowgli fabricate and achieve their dream of proving the insiders wrong—but then, in the end, face the fact that such proofs are made at the cost of important feelings. **"The Spring Running"** is not some half-intended afterthought to the Mowgli saga; it is its inevitable culmination. Mowgli began his days seeking love and acceptance, and he returns to the village in the end, still seeking.

Carole Scott

SOURCE: "Kipling's Combat Zones: Training Grounds in the Mowgli Stories, *Captains Courageous,* and *Stalky & Co.*," in *Children's Literature: Annual of the Modern Language Association Group on Children's Literature and The Children's Literature Association,* Vol. 20, 1992, pp. 52-68.

Kipling's obsession with the mastery of rules, laws, and codes of behavior dominates his work as it did his life. He wrote a charter for his children that identified in detail their "rights" to the Dudwell River near Bateman's; he created a Jungle society with a code "as perfect as time and custom can make it" (*The Second Jungle Book*); and he knew how to manipulate the rules to hasten his son's classification into active military service in World War I. Anyone at all familiar with Kipling's childhood will readily understand these concerns. The shock of being moved at the age of five from a pampered life with his family in India to the care of a harsh foster mother in Southsea, England, must have been traumatic enough. To be rescued after five long years from this "House of Desolation" only to be sent away again in less than a year to public school, a place of strict, often physical, discipline and institutionalized bullying, reinforced Kipling's sense that the world was a dangerous and uncertain place. These early experiences shaped his vision of the world and taught him how to survive: one must understand the system of order, master its code of rules, and apply them relentlessly.

Many writers, especially writers for children, have created unforgettable imaginary realms with their own sometimes fantastic rules; the entrances to such "otherworlds" are often surprising—a mirror, a wardrobe, a rabbit hole— dramatizing the borders of these magical realms and emphasizing their distinctness from the "real" world from which the children have come. It is not surprising, considering the drastic and painful changes to which little Rudyard had been subjected, that the grown Kipling would similarly plunge his young fictional protagonists into parallel worlds with new rules and new modes of survival, and that these otherworlds would be decidedly nonutopian. To Kipling, life was brutal, and his books for young people express this clearly, too clearly perhaps for modern tastes. For just as we find it hard to understand why a proud and loving father would push a seventeen-year-old into battle long before it was necessary, we wonder at his fascination with rules and laws, and why they are associated with such a high degree of violence. We are concerned that he expresses not only casual tolerance, but even encouragement, of behavior and attitudes that we consider unnecessarily brutal and cruel, even sadistic, especially in books for young people. Kipling exalts the harshest side of the manly code, especially the enthusiastic approval of physical punishment and violence and the stalwart indifference to pain, while encouraging the suppression of softer "feminine" feelings that he thought made men vulnerable. Published within a span of five years (1894-99) . . . , the Mowgli stories . . . , *Captains Courageous,* and *Stalky & Co.*, features a testing ground for the protagonist, a combat zone with its own set of laws, code of behavior, mode of being, and appropriate style of language.

The sense that Kipling's harsh code goes too far is not just a modern reaction. Despite his many admirers, there has always been an undercurrent of criticism, even revulsion (particularly in the period between the two World Wars) against the sentiments he expresses. When Martin Seymour-Smith in 1989 describes Kipling's publicly expressed philosophy of life as "cheap, shoddy, unworthy and impractical" and his public utterances revealing of a man "grotesque, merciless and insensitive," he follows in the tradition of Richard Buchanan who, in 1900, declared that Kipling was "on the side of all that is ignorant, selfish, base and brutal in the instincts of humanity" and that "the vulgarity, the brutality, the savagery, reeks on every page." Max Beerbohm's well-known caricatures of Kipling, which began in 1901 and continued for almost thirty years, express a similar opinion.

However, in spite of the criticism, there is no doubt that Kipling's exaltation of the ideals of warfare and its opportunities for manly conduct and heroism was widely shared in his time; it is not often that a new writer achieves popularity as fast as he did. Indeed, his successful expression of the exultant warrior mentality in his books for young people makes them of special cultural significance, for they helped to shape the minds of the young men who were later to die in the mud of Flanders fields. The books teach the ways to achieve success and self-esteem in later life, creating a picture of manliness, courage, and obedience to a clearly enunciated code of behavior from which one may not deviate for any reason. It is not surprising that the young men encouraged to display these traits would advance cheerfully to be mown down by the relentless German machine guns, and would even show their gallant sportsmanship by kicking footballs before them as they went, steadfastly "playing the game." John Kipling naturally falls into this metaphor when he writes his father from the war zone, "Remember our C.O. was 7 months on a 'Brigade' staff & what he doesn't know about the game isn't worth knowing."

The rules of war are very different from the rules of games, but Kipling and his contemporaries were not at all clear on this issue; tragically, it took the Great War and its spokesmen, Wilfred Owen, Siegfried Sassoon, and Rupert Brooke, to change the popular vision of the time. . . .

In *The Great War and Modern Memory,* Paul Fussell discusses in detail the common attitude to war in the decades prior to 1914. He particularly notes the sense that when ordinary men moved into battle they took on the dimension of heroes, and points out how the elevated diction of warfare, very different from the language of everyday life, contributed to this perception. Thus the enemy is "the foe," the dead on the battlefield are "the fallen," to die is to "perish," warfare is "strife," and a soldier is a "warrior". . . .

In this context, Kipling's fictional realms, the "other-worlds" he created as arenas of conflict or combat zones, are more understandable. They are definitely men's worlds; most of the players are male, and the few women we encounter are, like Harvey's mother or the fishermen's womenfolk in *Captains Courageous,* safe on land outside the field of combat. At home the women are soft, nurturing, and emotional. They fear, they weep, they suffer vicariously for their menfolk. Harvey's mother breaks down completely, incapable of any kind of action, when she thinks he is drowned; the passion with which Kipling describes how the entire railroad system conspires to speed her to her recovered son is sentimental to the point of excess. Messua, too, is pictured as vulnerable, suffering for her maternal love and kindness to Mowgli when the villagers stone her; incapable of self-preservation, she must depend on her adopted son for protection. The only self-sufficient female is Raksha, but of course she is a wolf! The men, on the other hand, display no such soft emotions; they are fierce, courageous, hard, even cruel; they exult in pain and they exult in winning. But to escape from the female world and female feelings, they must move over the boundary into another world.

In both the Mowgli stories and *Captains Courageous* we find the main character clearly crossing over from his ordinary world into a completely different one. Mowgli has somehow strayed from the sphere of humankind, and when he walks into Raksha's lair he has entered the Jungle world where animals talk and have created a social structure and history, and where he must learn to survive on their terms. . . .

The Law of the Jungle in the Mowgli stories is described by Kipling as preeminent and "as old and as true as the sky" with a code that is absolute, seemingly immutable, and unquestionable. The reader is never told how or by

whom it was established, or how it might be changed. Driven by a supposedly ageless and eternal vision imbued with a rational wisdom that accepts and incorporates the apparent vagaries of animal behavior and provides a clear pattern fair to each, the law defines each creature's hierarchy, its rights and obligations, and the rules of interaction with its own kind and with other species. Thus the tiger can claim one night of the year when he is entitled to kill Man; a mother wolf has the right to a portion of any wolf's kill for her litter; the jackal may run with the tiger and take what he leaves; and the elephant who lives a hundred years and more has the responsibility to proclaim the Water Truce. Only the Bandar-log, the Yahoos of the Jungle, are outside the law and are consequently viewed with contempt by all of the other animals. While time moves on and the players change, the principles and rules remain; the law has "arranged for almost every kind of accident that may befall the Jungle People, till now its code is as perfect as time and custom can make it." Because it is clearly understandable and dependable, it governs even out-of-the-ordinary situations, like the time of drought, or Mowgli's kidnapping by the Bandar-log and his incarceration among the snakes of the ruined city, when the Master-words of the Jungle ensure safe passage.

The notion of the supremacy of the law, driven by a Darwinian belief in the perfectibility that "time and custom" will unquestionably bring about, suggests a supreme power whose vision is realized in this exact code. Whether this supreme power is divine, or a reflection of the Victorian imperialistic sense of responsibility for bringing light and civilization to benighted areas of the world, is not important here; in fact, the sense of mission characteristic of both is clearly expressed in Mowgli's need to "let in the Jungle" in an attempt to cleanse the nearby village where superstition and greed has led to behavior that violates the morals of the Jungle Law. Because he is so clever and learns the Jungle Law better than the animals, Mowgli becomes invincible. He achieves individual power by following the law and interpreting it with human intelligence, illustrating that the individual is the expression of this deeper power rather than a free agent who can operate outside it.

Those of us who were introduced to the Mowgli stories in childhood probably accept without question that the Jungle in this context is an appropriate source of values. We still delight in Mother Wolf's claiming of the naked man cub, protecting him against the villainous Shere Khan, and watching benignly as he suckles with her own brood. Like Mowgli we feel the joys of companionship with the other wolves and his sense of belonging as he learns to claim, "We be of one blood, ye and I"; and we know his loneliness when he is thrust out of this idyllic existence because of his growing manhood. We share his sense of increasing competence as he learns the rules and becomes Master of the Jungle, and his distaste for the moral turpitude of the village.

When we think a little more objectively, however, the notion of finding codes of behavior in the Jungle, a place usually used as a metaphor for savagery and lawlessness,

Tailpiece for The Second Jungle Book, *drawn by the author's father, John Lockwood Kipling.*

seems contradictory and strange. And when we analyze these codes more carefully, we find that a great many of them regulate the ordered hierarchy of power, particularly power over killing and ownership of the kill. When you wish someone well you wish him "good hunting," and Chil the Kite's function as the scavenger of the dead is cheerfully acknowledged: "almost everybody in the Jungle comes to [Chil] in the end." Moments of great accomplishment are similarly violent: Mowgli laughs when he sets fire to Shere Khan's coat, and later, having killed him, dances in triumph upon his skin pegged out on the Council Rock. **"Letting in the Jungle"** features Mowgli's relentless revenge against humankind, and the story is followed by "Mowgli's Song Against People," which celebrates the obliteration of a village. The nature of the language as well as the splendid rhythms of the death chants and songs gives a legendary quality to this long tale of hunting, killing, and revenge. The violence is continuous, but the everyday tone encourages us to accept it as the way things are, where winning means survival. "'When tomorrow comes we will kill for tomorrow,' said Mowgli, quoting a Jungle saying; and again 'When I am dead it is time to sing the Death Song. Good

Hunting Kaa!'" There are really only two occasions where death seems frightening. The first is in **"Kaa's Hunting,"** where Kaa tells Mowgli "what follows is not well that thou shouldst see" and we are left with the image of the mesmeric Dance of the Hunger of Kaa that will lead to the death of many of the Bandar-log, unable to resist in their hypnotized state; the second is in **"The King's Ankus"** where men kill not for food, but for greed. Somehow the killing on these two occasions seems unsporting and not played by the appropriate rules.

Where rules are broken, they must be mended, and this, it appears, can only be accomplished with violent action. The more uncertain the rules, the harsher the violence that is needed to reestablish the necessary order. While Kipling portrays the duel between order and disorder in social terms, clearly this must also be a metaphor for the surge of personal desires and inappropriate motivation, and the necessity to restrain or redirect them into acceptable channels. Kipling's writings suggest that he held within him serious unresolved conflicts that find expression in the obsession with rules and with the violence necessary to keep order dominant. With equal violence, he disciplines and divides emotions and feelings appropriate for men from those fit only for women. This macho vision of masculinity is hard to sustain for someone like Kipling, whose ambivalence toward the first important woman in his life, who petted and then abandoned him, is depicted so well in **"Baa Baa, Black Sheep,"** where the young boy throws up his arm to defend himself against his mother's caress. By attempting to deny that part of his personality he identifies as "feminine," Kipling is forced to exaggerate the "masculine" characteristics that become, as one would expect in this dichotomy, stereotypically expressed in the bravado, indifference to pain, and brutality of the manly code he proposed.

Kipling was clearly a sensitive man camouflaged by brave words and an assertive, even brash personality. His ongoing attempt to master and to hide his vulnerability, to guard the tender self within, reveals itself in the need to dedicate himself to something greater, a more powerful authority structure whose preservation, whatever the cost, must be ensured. Mowgli's commitment to the Law of the Jungle, Harvey's involvement in the survival of the *We're Here,* and Stalky and his friends' collusion in maintaining the authority of USC's headmaster all illustrate Kipling's belief in an ordered, all-male structure whose shaping power turns boys into men.

Many cultures celebrate rites of passage to dramatize that boys are now grown and ready to take their place in adult society. Frequently the rituals involve isolating the young men from the community and subjecting them to tests by which they must prove their worth, tests which in many cases challenge the youths' ability to endure pain, humiliation, and even physical mutilation in their quest for a new adult wisdom. By plunging his young protagonists into "otherworlds" with clearly delineated codes, rules, and powerful authority structures that hone the boys' potential into strength and self-reliance, Kipling creates his own ritualized arenas in which the boys can prove themselves. The willing, even joyful submission to pain is associated with the need to suppress aspects of the feminine, which Kipling depicts as soft, fragile, incompetent, and rendering the individual too vulnerable to survive in a demanding world. As the need to reject the female self becomes increasingly insistent, the ideal of self-sacrifice grows stronger, so that the giving and acceptance of pain becomes an exercise in power, acknowledging both the strength of the authority figure and the strength of the individual who, by enduring pain, shows himself worthy.

In real life, the self thus divided is in danger. Kipling's public self, the brash jingoist who continued to laud the increasingly anachronistic ideals of manhood and empire, appears to have flourished at the expense of a vulnerable private self that suffered not only from the early loss of his "best beloved" daughter, but from the death of his son in combat, sacrificed to the ideals and code that Kipling espoused. He spent his later years immured in the gloomy Bateman's, protected by his wife from the demands of a too-insistent world; access to his works after death was similarly controlled by his wife and later his daughter, who appear to have decided which of his unpublished writings were appropriate for release to the public.

In his fictional realms, however, Kipling's boys relish their tough, strict training in the combat zones he has created for them, and cheerfully endure and enjoy their preparation for a challenging world where their success seems assured. In each case the "otherworld" Kipling has delineated seems tailor-made as a training ground for the "real" world to which the boys must return; their mastery of the rules and codes, whether they be Jungle Law, sea lore, or military school regulations, promises them mastery not only of the self, achieved by a code-based self-discipline, but of the world in which they will take their rightful place.

Additional coverage of Kipling's life and career is contained in the following sources published by Gale Research: *Concise Dictionary of British Literary Biography, 1890-1914*; *Contemporary Authors New Revision Series,* Vol. 33; *Dictionary of Literary Biography,* Vols. 19, 34, 141; *Major Authors and Illustrators for Children and Young Adults*; *Major 20th-Century Writers*; *Poetry Criticism,* Vol. 3; *Short Story Criticism,* Vol. 5; *Twentieth-Century Literary Criticism,* Vols. 8, 17; *World Literature Criticism*; and *Yesterday's Authors of Books for Children,* Vol. 2.

Astrid Lindgren

1907-

(Born Astrid Ericsson) Swedish author of fiction, picture books, drama, and screenplays.

Major works include *Pippi Longstocking* (1950), *Mio, My Son* (1956), *Happy Times in Noisy Village* (1963), *The Brothers Lionheart* (1975), *Ronia, the Robber's Daughter* (1983).

INTRODUCTION

An internationally renowned writer of children's literature, Lindgren has created works that have been translated into more than sixty languages, selling millions of copies worldwide. Her stories, often set in the region of her childhood home in rural Sweden, are applauded for their sensitive portrayal of the intimacy between parents and children. In Lindgren's books, children revel in being young, playing endlessly and imaginatively. Lindgren takes delight in her characters' feisty independence and their rollicking misbehavior, and young readers have responded with enthusiasm: her books, many of which were written several decades ago, continue to enjoy considerable popularity. At the time of their publication, however, some of Lindgren's books were judged harshly; *Pippi Longstocking*, for example, featured a character so uniquely resourceful, mischievous, and self-reliant that adults were concerned about the effect this tale might have on young readers. Several of Lindgren's later works explore more complex subjects with a tone of hope and compassion. The author believes that children have a much greater capacity to comprehend than they have traditionally been credited with; thus, while she writes in a simple style, her stories are marked by an intensity of feeling. Eva-Maria Metcalf writes: "[Memories] of childhood's intense perceptions and desires, paired with Lindgren's ability to record these feelings with sensitivity and exactitude in the fictional children she has created, distinguish her stories." Lindgren peppers her text with exclamatory words and punctuation, and repeats words and phrases for emphasis, stylistic traits that are unfortunately missing from some translations of her works; as a result, certain versions of her books fail to reveal the spirited quality of her prose. Nevertheless, throughout her lengthy career, Lindgren has offered young readers captivating tales and characters, portraying with sincerity and joy lively children enjoying enviable domestic security. Her success is obvious from the scope of her readership; as Johanna Hurwitz wrote in her juvenile biography *Astrid Lindgren, Storyteller to the World:* "With her books available in every modern language in the world, there is always a place on the globe where it is daytime. There is always a place where children are reading the books of Astrid Lindgren."

Biographical Information

Lindgren was born and raised on a farm near the small town of Vimmerby in Smaland, a rural area in southeastern Sweden which serves as the setting for many of her books. Although her friends and teachers all thought Lindgren would become a writer, she did not quickly embrace the idea, moving to Stockholm to train as a secretary. Years later, she wrote stories for her own children and entered one in a contest for which she won second prize. The tales of "Pippi Langstrump" ("Pippi Longstocking" in English) originated as bedtime tales told to Lindgren's daughter, who had invented the name on a whim. Three years later, while bedridden with a sprained ankle, Lindgren wrote down the story of Pippi and entered it in the same contest she had won before. The tales of Pippilotta Delicatessa Windowshade Mackrelmint Efraim's Daughter Longstocking—Lindgren's eventual name for her heroine—won first prize and, upon publication, became so popular that they were translated into dozens of languages, including Serbo-Croatian, Hebrew, Icelandic, and Swahili. Lindgren has since become one of Sweden's most prominent figures; she has received acclaim as a children's editor and writer, and was a major force in instituting new legislature for animal protection in her country. Many streets in Vimmerby are named after her books and a series of Swedish postage stamps, printed to commemorate her eightieth birthday, feature drawings of characters from her works, executed by major illustrators.

Major Works

Pippi Longstocking is Lindgren's best-known work, considered by many to be a classic. It tells the tale of orphaned Pippi, whose mother is "an angel in heaven" and whose father is lost at sea (although the girl is convinced he landed on an island where he is "king of the cannibals"). Nine-year-old Pippi enjoys complete independence; she lives with her horse, her monkey, and a suitcase full of gold coins, a gift from her father's sailor friends. She shows her young neighbors Tommy and Annika an alternate, sometimes wacky, lifestyle of lighthearted play. Pippi has immense physical strength and tells outrageous, but never meanspirited, stories. Lindgren has said that Pippi "has power, but she never misuses that power." Lindgren's story portrays many common situations from the classroom to a tea party, where Pippi behaves outlandishly, spoofing rigid traditionalism with an abundance of enthusiasm and imagination. Pippi is featured in two sequels to the original book and the stories have been made into several films and television productions. Smaland, the region of Lindgren's childhood, functions loosely as the setting for the "Pippi" stories, but plays a far more significant role in subsequent books, especially those titles written about six children living in "Bullerby" or "Noisy Village." In these books, Lindgren celebrates Swedish traditions and the enjoyment of seasonal activities. Another group of tales set in Smaland concern Emil, whose adventures were drawn from the experiences of Lindgren's father. Like the "Noisy Village" tales, the "Emil" books humorously depict Sweden at the turn of the century, a time which Lindgren believes offered children freedom to explore, coupled with the security of a close family.

Several of Lindgren's later works, most notably *The Brothers Lionheart* and *Ronia, the Robber's Daughter*, are considered more thought-provoking. In *The Brothers Lionheart,* Karl is a seriously ill boy whose older brother, Jonathan, dies while saving him from a fire. After Karl's subsequent death, the siblings reunite in an afterworld named Nangiyala, in which they fight forces which threaten the freedom of the inhabitants of the land. When Jonathan is fatally wounded in battle, the brothers commit double suicide so that they can live together in another afterworld, Nangilima. Both the ending and the unorthodox depiction of life after death were found to be problematic by some commentators, but Lindgren received several letters indicating that she gave young readers—some facing their own death or the death of a loved one—hope and courage. In *Ronia, the Robber's Daughter*, the title character, daughter of the leader of a band of thieves, is a strong, independent heroine who appeals to readers especially through her intense love of nature and her struggle to determine her own future.

Awards

Lindgren won the first Nils Holgersson Plaque in 1950 for *Nils Karlsson-Pyssling:Sagor.* She also received the first Deutscher Jugendbuchpreis, Sonderpreis (German Prize for Children's Books, Special Award) in 1956 for *Mio, My Son.* Lindgren was the first children's author to be given the Swedish State Award for Writers of High Literary Standard in 1957. She won the Lewis Carroll Shelf Award for *The Tomten* in 1970 and for *Pippi Longstocking* in 1973. The first International Janusz Korczak Prize was awarded to Lindgren in 1979 for *The Brothers Lionheart. Ronia, the Robber's Daughter* earned Lindgren's publisher, Viking Press, the Mildred L. Batchelder Award in 1984. For her body of work, Lindgren received the Hans Christian Andersen Medal in 1958; the Swedish Academy's Gold Medal in 1971; the Litteris et artibus plaque from the king of Sweden in 1975; the 1978 Peace Prize of the German Book Trade; the Dag Hammarskjold Award in 1984, and the Illis Quorum—a gold medal awarded by the Swedish government—the following year; and the Selma Lagerlof Award in 1986. In addition, Lindgren received honorary doctorates from Linköping University, Sweden, in 1973, Leicester University, England, in 1978, and the University of Warsaw in 1989. The Astrid Lindgren Translation Prize, given for excellence in children's book translation, was created in Lindgren's name in 1981.

AUTHOR'S COMMENTARY

Astrid Lindgren

SOURCE: "A Short Talk with a Prospective Children's Writer," translated by Roger C. Tanner, in *The Horn Book Magazine,* Vol. XLIX, No. 3, June, 1973, pp. 248-52.

[*The following excerpt is taken from an essay originally published in Swedish in 1970.*]

So, you're going to write a children's book? You're not the only one. Plenty of people who can hold a pen—and more than a few who can't—get it into their heads every now and again that now is the time to set about writing something for children. What could be easier? All you have to do is make a start, and the rest follows automatically—all that childish stuff that the silly little things get so much fun out of. Let's see now, what would be a good beginning? "Once upon a time there was an old kitchen boiler who went out walking with Great Aunt Euphemia Cauliflower"—why, that's just right. Just tie them up together, and keep them at it page after page, and that's it.

Is that what you thought? No, of course not. Your standards are higher than that, so high, in fact, that before you even put pen to paper you keep asking yourself: What should a good children's book be like? If you were to ask me, then—no matter how hard I might rack my brains—

I would only be able to say: It ought to be good. I assure you that I have given the matter some thought for a considerable length of time, but still I can only say: It ought to be good.

What makes a good anthology of poetry? What makes a good novel? Why has nobody ever asked either of those questions? Is it because there is no recipe for a good poem or a good novel, so that it is confidently left to the poet and the novelist to extract their creations from the innermost recesses of their souls without any guidance from outside?

Yes, of course; but you may object when it's just a case of a short book for children, hoping the while for a miracle-working recipe. Oh, but, of course, there are recipes.

Take a bunch of jolly urchins, mix with a few villains, add a stupid policeman, and a nagging mother; carefully stir in an uncomprehending father; spice well with quarrelsome dialogues and a spot of rough stuff; and then, hey ho, for the publisher's table!

Or again, whisk together Cyril the Squirrel, wise old Mother Owl, and Little Boy Blue, a touch of zany and umpteen jolly little quips; and there you are again. Serve cool. Of course, you could try a hash-up of the loveliest, liveliest little whirlie-curlies on the world's loveliest horses, sitting in the world's surest saddles, and bounding over the world's highest and most formidable obstacles. Oh, yes, there are plenty of recipes. But since you are about to embark on your career as a writer in this year of grace 1970, it may have come to your notice that all this business of recipes, heaven be praised, is completely and utterly washed-up. The hashes and puddings of today are made up of completely different ingredients.

Take one divorced mother—plumber if possible, otherwise an atomic physicist will do quite nicely—the main thing being that she does not fall into the slough of domesticity and maternal devotion; add two parts effluent and two parts air pollution, a few pinches of global starvation, parental repression and teacher terror; carefully insert two dumplings of racial problems, two more of sexual discrimination, and a soupçon of Vietnam; sprinkle generously with copulation and drugs; and you have a good and durable concoction which serves any purpose.

All right, I'm being unfair. You didn't want that kind of recipe. No sensible person expects to produce a good children's book simply by following a recipe, and no doubt you fully realize that what goes for poetry also applies to children's books—if there is to be any point in them— and to any other kind of literature.

Seriously, then, you wanted to know how to be a good children's writer—didn't you? Nobody can teach you how to write a good book for children. For heaven's sake, don't go thinking that I am sitting here glorying in my own books and posing as your guide, philosopher, and friend simply because of them. Far from it, but I have spent almost a quarter of a century as a children's pub-

lisher, watching manuscripts of all kinds floating through, so that, one way and another, I think I have learned a few lessons which could be useful to you as well. Just a few basic rules—the rest is up to you and your innate creativity.

First, language. I think this is perhaps the most important thing—for the language and content of a book to harmonize. If you write about Cyril the Squirrel (but you won't, will you?), in other words if you're writing for five-year-olds as being the age group most susceptible to squirrels, then you must not use words and expressions that cannot be comprehended by anyone under ten.

Now I've made you cross. Fancy having the nerve to sit here feeding you such platitudes! Fair enough. But tell me, why does one come across so many children's books that have to be translated into simpler language before they can be understood by the children their subjects are intended for? Not long ago I read a book for linguistically advanced five-year-olds. It was an infantile thing about little trolls, so it can hardly have been meant for older children. I read it straight off, without translating anything, just stopping every now and then to ask my five-year-old listener: What does *rectify abuses* mean? What does *good council* mean? What does *abide together* mean? And every time the five-year-old answered, "How should I know?"

One very good author I know put it this way: "I have found that the best way of writing is to practice a style which even a child could understand." And yet, he was writing for intellectual adults. It is even more vital for people actually writing for children to write so that children can understand them. There is no shame in writing lucidly even above the five-year-old level; simplicity need not necessarily imply banality and emptiness. Often a poet will speak of life, death, and love, and all the most profound aspects of human existence in such simple words that even a child can understand: Have you ever stopped to think of that?

On the other hand, some writers take umbrage if you criticize their language and ask whether they realize that they are writing for children. One should never underestimate children, they say, never talk down to them, for they understand far more than we imagine. Granted. In my view one can and should talk to children about most things. But there still remains the question of *how* to talk to them, if they are to understand what is being said to them; nor can one altogether disregard the limitations of their frame of reference. If, to take one example, a children's book is made to include an extremely funny skit on the minutes of a board meeting—and this in fact has been done—then, as I see it, the writer's efforts have been in vain. To appreciate a parody you have to be *au fait* with the thing that is being mocked, and I know very few children who have ever read the minutes of a board meeting. This, then, is one rule worth bearing in mind when you start writing. By all means, write things that *only* children will find amusing; and by all means, write things that both children *and* adults will find amusing;

but never include in your children's book anything which your own common sense ought to tell you can *only* be amusing to adults. You are not writing in order for the critics to eulogize your ready wit and your neat turn of a phrase—and don't you forget it! Many people ostensibly writing for children are prone to sly winks over the children's heads at an imaginary adult reader, so that the children are left out of their own book. Please don't do anything of the kind.

The best of luck, then. And enjoy yourself. Believe me, writing for children is fun. At least, I hope you think so; otherwise you might as well give up before you start. And I hope you will not be unduly oppressed by that business about "What makes a good children's book?"—today, tomorrow, and thereafter. Don't bother about it too much. Write freely and write as you please. I wish you and all other children's writers freedom, the self-evident freedom of an adult writer to write as he pleases about what he pleases. If you want to write a disturbing book for children about how difficult and impossible it is to be human in the world today, then you are perfectly entitled to do so. If you want to write about racial discrimination, then again you are perfectly within your right. And if you want to write about a verdant islet in a coral sea, then you are perfectly entitled to do that as well. Yes, even in this year of grace 1970, you are still entitled to write about a verdant isle without necessarily having to stop and think: What rhymes with *sewage* and *oil slick*? In a word: Liberty! For without liberty the flower of poetry withers and dies, no matter where it may grow.

GENERAL COMMENTARY

Sten Hagliden

SOURCE: "Astrid Lindgren, the Swedish Writer of Children's Books," in *The Junior Bookshelf,* Vol. 23, No. 3, July, 1959, pp. 113-21.

In 1944, fairly late in life, Astrid Lindgren published her first book which was entitled *Britt-Mari lättar sitt hjärta (Britt-Mari Opens Her Heart)*. With its acute understanding of a child's mind and the breezy freshness of its style this book gave promise of a future attractive writer of children's books.

This promise was amply fulfilled in her second book entitled *Pippi Langstrump (Pippi Longstocking)* which, it is interesting to note, was the first attempt made by the author to write a book for children. The moderate success of *Britt-Mari lättar sitt hjärta* persuaded her publisher to produce *Pippi Longstocking* which, some time before the publication of *Britt-Mari,* had been rejected by another publisher.

It would be unfair to judge the quality of Astrid Lindgren's writing by the fantastic and often nonsensical actions performed by Pippi, who is the central figure in three of the writer's most popular books. The success of this trilogy demonstrates how much children appreciate nonsense and, by the reactions of adults towards Pippi's every day antics and bravado, how little many grown up people appreciate the unreality and immaturity of the child's world.

In Sweden some parents and teachers have criticised Pippi's unconventional behaviour and language. Here opinion stands against opinion and it would be hard for one side to convince the other regarding what is right and wrong about child behavior. There can be few adults, however, who would deny the uncommonly fresh humour, the wealth of bright ideas and genuine hearty character of Pippi Longstocking.

Pippi, a little girl with red pigtails, does all manner of strange, impossible and unconventional things. She sleeps on her bed with her feet where her head should be. She is so strong that she can lift her horse on to the veranda of her house, and as a "turn up stuffer"—a characteristic that can only be understood by reading her adventures—she is perfectly ruthless and yet so tender and careful of a small wounded bird. Clearly, therefore, Pippi leads a fantastic yet real and free life in her house, Villa Villekulla, and also in the South Sea where her later adventures are laid.

In the South Seas Pippi reveals her giant strength. When Tommy, her native play-mate, falls into the sea where a shark rushes to get a fine morsel, Pippi without hesitation jumps into the water. She takes the bloodthirsty beast by both her hands and keeps him above water.

"'Aren't you ashamed of yourself?' she cries. The shark looked around, surprised and very ill at ease by bad conscience and lack of water for his lungs. 'Promise never to do such a cruel thing again and I will let you go.' Then with all her strength she throws the shark far into the sea." Such unusual and vivacious actions ensure the character of Pippi Longstocking a place amongst the classic figures in Swedish children's books.

If funny incidents bubble up in the three books about Pippi, Astrid Lindgren's humour is more subdued in the stories about the Bullerby children. The quality of her humour is, however, none the worse for that, rather the opposite. The question is whether Astrid Lindgren in the Bullerby books does not reach furthest as an entertaining story teller, since she shows in these three volumes what a fine and deep child psychologist she is. Listen, for instance, to Lisa at Bullerby, telling about her beloved grandpa. "In summertime he usually sits underneath the big elm tree that grows on the lawn just outside the North Farm. There he sits and lets the sun shine on him and then suddenly he says: 'Well, well, well!' We asked him why he says 'Well, well, well!' and then Grandpa told us that he speaks like that because he thinks of his youth. That must have been a long time ago, I think. But imagine that there is such a nice Grandpa as ours! I like him so much. I would much rather have him than a dog."

Comic incidents—so common in *Pippi Longstocking*—appear here too. They flower also in *Kajsa Kavat (Kate Courageous)*—read, for instance, the story **"Hoppa Högst"** ("To Jump Highest")—a collection of short stories for children, often characterized by vivid realism.

That Astrid Lindgren understands and also can write about adolescent youth with its unrest, its sudden movements between sentimental affection and aggressive opposition, and its longing for love, is well demonstrated in such books as *Kerstin och jag (Kerstin and I)* and in the Kati books—*Kati i Amerika, Kati vid Kaptensgatan* and *Kati i Paris (Kati in America, Kati at Captain Street* and *Kati in Paris)*. Here the author also shows at frequent intervals her sparkling wittiness.

She has also written picture books of undoubted value for small children. Another type of book is the *Bill Bergson* series. What fine powers of descriptive writing the author shows in the three books about this remarkable detective. It is not only her invention of the story and the concentration of suspense that fascinates the reader. The whole gallery of characters and the summer atmosphere of the small town are given with unusual clarity. Sometimes the summer atmosphere assumes a dark, threatening, almost frightening aspect, as when Eva-Lotta during a thunder storm meets the old man Gren's murderer and flees in wild panic. This episode in *Mästerdetektiven Blomkvist lever farligt (Bill Bergson lives dangerously)* has an etched realism, worthy of any great artist.

Astrid Lindgren has let the events of the Bill Bergson books take place at Vimmerby, her native town on the Swedish East coast, which to some extent she has romanticized. If these books are read aloud to children they listen with fascinated attention.

It is not easy to judge how Astrid Lindgren's work would stand the test of time if she had not written *Nils Karlsson Pyssling (Niels, The Midget)* and *Mio, Min Mio (Mio, My Son)*. These two books which have much in common, have in a way crowned all her books. The former includes the story **"Allra käraste syster"** ("Most Dear Sister"), the most gentle and the tenderest semi-fairy tale written in the Swedish language. These tales confirm that Astrid Lindgren is not only an entertaining writer but that in her nature she also possesses a deeper quality, an affinity with and tenderness towards the unhappy and downtrodden. This is especially revealed in *Mio, My Son,* where in a finely woven web of symbolic writing she shows her sensitive and optimistic attitude to life.

Rasmus på Luffen (Rasmus and The Vagabond) is a most lively book. The story is about Rasmus, the orphan boy, who lived at the beginning of the twentieth century. Rasmus leaves the orphanage and walks out on to the highways and byways. There he encounters Oskar, the tramp, who is so warmhearted and quiet. Oskar has a home, but in summer time his urge compels him to leave hearth and home for the open road. Oskar and Rasmus certainly have a number of varying experiences, both humdrum and mysterious. The latter culminate when Oskar

and Rasmus meet Lif and Liander, two suspect characters, who are capable of the most unworthy deeds. By Rasmus' ingenuity and with Oskar's help the two criminals are handed over to the police. In the end Rasmus finds a home with Oskar and his wife, Martina. "He stopped on the porch and waited for Oskar. There was his kitten lying, asleep in the sunshine. Yes, it was a miraculous day. He had a lake, a cat, a father, and a mother. He had a home!"

With a singularly strong intuition Astrid Lindgren interprets a lonely, unwanted child with personal troubles, shyness and need of care and love. The story is enriched by realistic pictures of the beautiful Swedish "roadside summer" and of the unlimited freedom enjoyed by tramps on highroads now so rapidly being superseded by the tarred motor roads of our time. Although *Rasmus and The Vagabond* is written for children, the present writer feels that the young man of twenty and the old lady of eighty could read the story with the same interest and enthusiasm.

It should be noted that the Rasmus who appears in the author's next work, *Rasmus, Pontus och Toker (Rasmus, Pontus and Toker),* is not the same as the character in her previous book. The surname of this Rasmus is Persson and he is the son of a kindhearted policeman who, like many of his kind, is shrewd and quick. Pontus is one of Rasmus' school-fellows and "Toker" is the faithful dog. Through the temptations of a circus the trio fall in with Alfredo, a man who in spite of his bulk is both wily and smart. Ernst, his assistant, is no better. They both covet a nobleman's treasure of silver which they succeed in stealing. That is, however, not the worst that happens; they steal and capture "Toker," the best and finest dog of all centuries. Children's strong feeling for animals is the new element in this book.

Finally, a few words about Astrid Lindgren's latest book *Barnen på Bråkmakaregatan* (1958) (*The Children in Trouble Maker Street*), which is related to the "Bullerby" books. Jonas and his two sisters, Maria and Lotta at Pottery Street lead a life just as pleasant and nice as that of the Bullerby children. Lotta enjoys herself and is the most enjoyable of the three characters. Once when Lotta had a cold in her head she walked into a shop, she sniffled and sniffled and finally there was a lady in the shop who said to her: "I say, haven't you got a hanky?"—"Certainly, but I don't lend it to people I don't know."

Astrid Lindgren has won a great deal of recognition for her work. The first time that the Swedish Nils Holgersson Plaque was awarded—it is the finest mark of distinction for any writer of books for children and young people—it went to Astrid Lindgren. She has been given several other awards, and in the summer of 1958 she received—at the Fifth Conference of the International Board on Books for Young People in Florence—the Hans Christian Andersen Medal.

It can be said without exaggeration that in Sweden she is looked upon as ranking amongst the finest contemporary writers of children's books.

In expressing her thanks at Florence she said amongst other things: "Sometimes people ask me: 'Couldn't you write a book for adults?' as if they meant that now I have written so many children's books it is about time I did something better. The truth is I do not want to write for adults! I want to write for readers who can create miracles, and you know children do this when they read."

Allow me to conclude this article by quoting a few words from the same speech: "Children in our day view films, listen in, look at T.V., read comics—it may be interesting but it has not very much to do with imagination. A child alone with its book creates in the secret room of its mind its own pictures which surpass everything else. Such pictures are necessary for all mankind. The day when children's imagination no longer can create those pictures, will be a day of loss to our race."

Ralph Slayton

SOURCE: "The Love Story of Astrid Lindgren," in *Scandinavian Review,* Vol. 63, No. 4, December, 1975, pp. 44-53.

Last spring, Astrid Lindgren, the great Swedish writer for children and the most widely read Swedish author in the world today, published a short volume of biographical essays. She described the work in a letter to me in these words: "The main item is the love story of my parents which was most unusual in the meaning of length and strength. My father loved my mother from the time when she was nine and during a whole long life. They were farmers, and the unusual thing was that my father, most unlike all other farmers I have met, every day told her his love so wonderfully." It is this same strong and enduring love and the warmth and affection with which it is told that one remembers best, I believe, as one thinks back over all the Lindgren books and plays read and reread: the Pippi books; *Mio, My Son* (that brilliant fantasy with its beautiful lyric poetry that came as such a surprise from the author); *Christmas in the Stable* (a retelling of the first Christmas that is an absolutely perfect gem); the Noisy Village books and the skerry books that present such a happy idea of childhood (Astrid Lindgren once received a letter in which a child asked if Noisy Village really existed—"If it does," she said, "I don't want to live in Vienna any longer"); *Rasmus and the Vagabond* (for which she was awarded the highly prized H. C. Andersen Medal); the texts that accompany the child photography of Anna Riwkin-Brick; and all the others. It is this which provides the best key to an understanding of her entire work, even of Pippi Longstocking, Astrid Lindgren's miraculous creation and much misrepresented character. Conceived in 1945, Pippi is quite possibly the best-known character in children's literature in the world today. But critics and teachers who describe her as "the model of the liberated child" or as a child who simply does whatever she pleases, mislead their listeners, I believe. It has always seemed to me that *Pippi Longstocking* is a serious probing into the longing for love of a very lonely child and is a rather sad book.

Astrid Lindgren has created quite a number of lonely children: Ann of "Under the Cherry Trees"; Bertil, Nils-Karlsson Pyssling's little friend; Eric, who is visited by Karlsson-on-the-Roof and who tells his mother: "You, Mommy, you've got Daddy; and Bobby and Betty always stick together; but me—I've got nobody"; and, Mio, to name just a few. Of her own experience with loneliness Astrid Lindgren has said that "to be alone is best. There is no loneliness that frightens me. Deep down we all remain alone. Without loneliness and poetry I believe I could hardly survive." And this is an attitude that is also present in her works and which make the sad books very beautiful books, because a lonely child like Pippi is still able to say: "Isn't it glorious just to be alive!"

Pippi Longstocking is quite alone when we meet her and when she meets Tommy and Annika, the children who live next door. They are probably the only children she has ever had any contact with. Her eight or nine years have been spent aboard her father's boat, the *Hoptoad.* Her mother, we know, died when Pippi was a very young child, and now she is "an angel in heaven." Pippi's father, Captain Efraim Longstocking, was blown into the sea the day a great storm came up. We accept the death of Pippi's father and so do Tommy and Annika—at first. But Pippi has refused to acknowledge this last great loss and has invented the desperate notion that he did not drown (because he was too fat) but floated to shore on an island and became the king of a lot of cannibals. Tommy and Annika sympathetically go along with Pippi's fabrication.

Reminders of her own loneliness—the coming too close to the pain of it—seem to prompt Pippi to behave eccentrically. Pippi's loneliness is made even clearer in Mrs. Lindgren's dramatization of the novels when, in a brief moment alone as Pippi goes to bed, she sits quietly and says to her monkey, Mr. Nilsson: "We really are rather lonely, you and me, don't you think?" Her immediate response is to lie down with her feet on the pillow because "that's the way they sleep in Guatemala." At another point, Pippi has just been telling her new-found friends how she manages to live all alone, pretending to them (and to herself) that she is happy without adults around, when she suddenly remembers that she has to lift her horse up onto the porch because "he'd be in the way in the kitchen, and he doesn't like the drawing room." Nowhere is Pippi's loneliness made more poignantly clear than at the end of the third novel: when Tommy and Annika are getting ready for bed and see Pippi, all alone in Villa Villekulla, sitting quietly by the light of a candle. Then Pippi blows out the candle and goes to bed.

Some of Pippi's difficulties in certain situations stem, of course, from the simple fact that she has spent all her life at sea. She has never been to school, and she has certainly never been invited to an afternoon coffee party with "a couple of nice old ladies." Her responses to such encounters might remind us of how absurdly we sometimes behave in our expectations of children. Astrid Lindgren has said that "many people act stupidly toward children . . . tactlessly. They say to a child, for example, 'Now blow your nose' and things like that even though there are other adults present and the child can be embarrassed." Perhaps her most fervent appeal for an understanding of children is contained in *Emil's Pranks,* in which everything that Emil does wrong, like dropping a bowl of blood pudding on his father's head or laying the rat trap in which his father gets his toe caught, arises out of his good intentions. Some excellent advice about adults relating to children is given by one of the youngsters in *Happy Times in Noisy Village* when she says: "It's really easy to take care of children. All you have to do is remember to speak softly and kindly to them. Then they mind you. I read that in the newspaper the other day."

Pippi Longstocking is about the way many adults abuse their power over children. Pippi, Mrs. Lindgren points out, is not a revolutionary—she is not at war with grown-ups. (One of the remarkable characteristics of the whole body of work, in fact, is the presence of adults who are kind and have very good relations with the children around them, like the kindly old grandfather of Noisy Village or Emil and his father, who are "excellent friends.") Pippi is simply a person who is ready and able to defend herself when her freedom is infringed upon. Pippi herself is a person with great power, and she does not misuse it. There is nothing the author more abhors, she says, than an abuse of power, whatever form it may take—the adult with the child, the boss with the employee, or the ruler of a nation with its people.

The values prized in the Pippi books are ones that any sensible person would want to inculcate in a child: resourcefulness, generosity, humor, kindness, inventiveness (put a can over your head and it's midnight), self-control (Pippi tells herself when to go to bed, and she's quite strict with herself when she misbehaves), and readiness to defend the underdog. Yet, she always remains a child. Astrid Lindgren once said something that applies to Pippi Longstocking and all the other children she has created: "That our Lord let children be children before they grew up was one of his better ideas."

Mrs. Lindgren's most recent novel, *The Brothers Lionheart,* has provoked heated controversy in children's literature circles in Sweden; others urged that she be nominated for the Nobel Prize. The book deals with an eight-year-old boy living under a dictatorship, and with his death. Long before she wrote *The Brothers Lionheart,* Astrid Lindgren told an interviewer: "I don't think it's right to completely ignore death in literature for children. Many children feel real dread of death. So I think it would be wrong to ignore it in all books. When I was little I thought we all died and then we met again in heaven. The only problem was that we wouldn't die at the same time." Nevertheless, many people considered the book inappropriate for children. Indeed, it can be a very frightening book. It can also be a very reassuring book if the adults who help children to understand it regard it in that way.

The Brothers Lionheart tells of the great admiration and affection that eight-year-old Karl feels for his brother, Jonathan, who is three years older. "Now I shall tell you about my brother," the book begins. It is Karl's voice.

His older brother is "as kind a person as I wish we could all be." Karl is dying. "Jonathan knew I was going to die soon. I think that everybody knew it except me. They knew it at school because I just stayed home and coughed and was sick all the time and last term I couldn't go to school at all." Jonathan comforts his little brother, telling him that they will meet by and by in the land of Nangijala—a land beyond the stars—where they will be happy together again.

But Jonathan dies before Karl. There is a fire in the house. Jonathan takes his little brother on his shoulders and leaps out of the window to save him, but he himself is killed in the fall. Karl is left alone, and he longs for his brother: "No one could miss a person as much as I missed him." Two months later Karl dies, and the two brothers are reunited, as Jonathan had promised, in Nangijala. They have everything they need: a house to live in, two horses to ride, and—a grownup to look after them. The people of that part of Nangijala in which they live—called Cherry Valley—are friendly and kind. But on the other side of the mountains, in the Valley of the Briars, reigns the cruel tyrant Tengil, called "The Liberator." A fire-spewing dragon called Katla helps Tengil maintain his terrible order. Tengil's slaves have built a wall around the valley, and it is guarded by well-armed and well-mounted police. Karl and Jonathan share a moment of bliss in the shadow of evil:

> Jonathan sat on the grass with his arms around his knees and gazed down at the valley. He sat there so peacefully that one might think he meant to stay there all evening no matter how many of Tengil's men came riding along the wall behind him.
>
> "Why are you sitting here?" I asked.
>
> "Because I love to," said Jonathan. "Because I love the valley in the twilight. I love the cool breeze against my face, too, and the pink roses that smell of summer."
>
> "I shall sit here with you," I said.
>
> "And I love the flowers and the grass and the trees and the meadows and the forests and the pretty little lakes," said Jonathan. "And I love it when the sun comes up and when it goes down and when the moon shines and the stars glitter and some other things, too, that I just don't remember right now."
>
> "I love them, too," I said.
>
> "Everybody loves them," said Jonathan. "And if there is nothing more they desire, you might ask, why can't they enjoy them in peace without some Tengil coming and bothering them?"

Orvar, a fighter for freedom, who is condemned to death, is imprisoned in a cage in Katla's cave. It falls to the brothers' lot to rescue him, and they succeed, but only after a bitter struggle. The dragon is slain, but as it is dying its flame wounds Jonathan, and he is slowly paralyzed. He knows that he will die again. Jonathan comforts Karl by telling of yet another land—Nangilima—where there is no fear. Here, one day, they will meet again. Karl knows what he must do. Now it is his turn to take his older brother on his back and leap from the precipice. This time there will be no separation. They will die together. Karl jumps, and his final words are: "Yes, Jonathan, yes! I see the light! *I see the light!*"

A group of specialists in children's literature at the University of Gothenburg strongly criticized *The Brothers Lionheart,* insisting that a book that depicts the struggle between good and evil should carefully and honestly examine the roots of that evil. Tengil, they point out, is evil for no apparent reason. He is a powerful figure who, according to the story, must be "crushed like a louse." These critics hold that this is a dangerous oversimplification. More importantly, they maintain, the solution Astrid Lindgren has chosen at the conclusion of her book is "frightening." They see the choice of death as an escape, a way for the children to flee from their problems. These critics also ask: If there was evil in Nangijala, how can

From Pippi Longstocking, *written by Astrid Lindgren. Illustrated by Louis S. Glanzman.*

the reader be sure that there will not be evil in Nangilima as well? One runs the risk, they say, of being so captivated by the story of the helpless child and the struggle against evil that one fails to carefully weigh the solutions the author has chosen. Even if it is "only a story," they say, we adults must be aware of these solutions before we put the book in the hands of a child.

In nineteenth-century Scandinavian children's literature, death was a common motif. The most famous death in children's literature anywhere is probably Danish—in H. C. Andersen's "The Little Matchgirl." But from 1910 to 1960 the subject was virtually taboo. Since then it has made a cautious reentry into the literature. Astrid Lindgren was one of the pioneers: In her *Sunnanäng* (1959), two children wander through the portals of death into paradise, and the girl, Malin from the poorhouse, gives her life so that a tree might be nourished and grow. In *The Brothers Lionheart* we have not only death as a principal motif but also what can be taken as suicide, a rejection of life.

Astrid Lindgren worked on *The Brothers Lionheart* for sixteen months, longer than on any of her other books, and she says that she struggled for a long time with the ending. In an interview, she gave some ideas about the book that might help us to understand it in a way that could make it not only an acceptable book for children but a very valuable one. She said that Karl does not really die until the last page. Nangijala is Karl's fantasy through which he is able to be with his brother after he is killed in saving him from the fire, and Karl's leap at the conclusion is also only imagined. The book's ending, she insisted, is a happy one. Karl can go to any kind of death whatsoever so long as he has his brother Jonathan with him, and that is the light that he sees at the end of the novel.

To critics' complaints that the roots of the evil presented in the novel are not explained, the author replies that the evil is representative of all evil from primitive times to the present and is depicted in the broadest terms. In *Mio, My Son,* the author also depicted good and evil in glaring contrast. It is the old folk-tale device that makes good and evil easily distinguishable, and it is as much as most children can comfortably cope with at that stage of their moral development.

The author says that the book was inspired by two things especially—a brilliant rose-colored sunrise over the snow that she saw one morning as she was traveling through Sweden by train, and by gravestones in a churchyard that marked the resting places of children. She was reminded, she says, that not only is death a fearsome thought with which children are occupied but that for some children it can be a preoccupation. She tells of a letter from a physician who spends a large part of his time with children who are dying of leukemia; they know that they are going to die, and they need to be comforted.

We know that children think about death. Once we were able to give them an idea of heaven that provided them with a certain sense of security. Many of us are no longer able to do this with ease. We feel that we are being insincere, and many of us evade the children's questions. Unanswered, they can become a source of considerable anxiety. We need new ideas of death with which we can honestly and reassuringly respond. Astrid Lindgren has provided an answer that many of us and our children will find satisfying: the book can be understood to present two ideas of death. One, in Nangijala, resembles the life we know—it has its problems to be faced, its difficulties to be overcome. The other, in Nangilima, is a utopia, a perfect peace. Perhaps death is like Nangijala, perhaps it is like Nangilima, perhaps it is something else. Whatever it is, the important thing is that with the giving and receiving of love it can be accepted when it comes.

A Swedish critic has compared the book to Tolkien's *Ring Cycle*. There is a more meaningful comparison to be pointed to, I believe, namely, another contemporary Swedish artist, Ingmar Bergman, and his inquiries into the nature of death and his response in an evocation of love. If *The Brothers Lionheart* can be understood as an acceptance of death with an assurance of love, it may become one of the most valuable books for children that we have.

Eva-Maria Metcalf

SOURCE: "Courage and Compassion: Ethical Dimensions in Lindgren's Work," in *Astrid Lindgren,* Twayne Publishers, 1995, pp. 123-39.

Especially in her fantasy tales, but to a degree in her realistic stories, Astrid Lindgren takes her readers to a better place and a better way of life. Villa Villekulla, Farawayland, and Ronia's forest let readers escape into a dreamworld of wish fulfillment, and in a sense they do the same for the adult author. These fictional places are projections of Lindgren's visions of a better society and a more humane life for both children and adults. As such they serve not only as an escape but as an inspiration for her readers. . . .

A constant in Lindgren's character and her fiction is her abhorrence of violence and abuse. Hitler's and Stalin's reigns of terror were as unbearable to her as are the neglect and abuse of children, domestic animals, and the environment—in general, the disrespect of people and things considered inferior. Her horror of all these manifestations of cruelty and insensitivity have found expression in her stories, for never does Lindgren present a scene of neglect or cruelty unbalanced by a projection or a promise of better times. Specific issues and concerns vary from book to book depending on topic and genre and on changing social conditions, to which Lindgren has responded with the artist's sensitivity. The life conditions and the status of children have changed dramatically since Lindgren's childhood. Her work reflects these changes, but despite her sensitive and acute responses to shifts in social and political conditions the tenor of her writing has remained the same. Extending over almost half a century, Lindgren's work displays a rare cohesion through her

ringing indictment of abuse and her appeal to her readers to find the courage and compassion to change the world.

Jonathan Lionheart's maxim that there are things that you just have to do if you want to be called a human being and not just a bit of filth and Pippi Longstocking's declaration that people with great power also have the greatest obligation to be good and responsible not only function as leitmotifs in their respective novels but are also guiding ethical principles for all of Lindgren's writing. These two adages are emblematic of Lindgren's deep devotion to humanity and her commitment to civility in her work and her life.

In her desire to reinforce and foster courage and compassion in her readers, the precondition for a more peaceful, just, and humane world, Lindgren uses a two-pronged approach, addressing those in control and those being controlled. Attaining a better world requires the concerted effort of both. The powerless are called upon to stand up against oppression and abusive treatment, while those in power are reminded of the fact that power can corrupt. Both are urged to respect the dignity of all life and love all living creatures on earth, starting with themselves. Pippi, who is in the remarkable position of belonging to both sides—she is a child, yet eminently powerful—bases both ethical principles on supreme self-confidence. Although Lindgren writes stories for children, her ethical appeals reach beyond the scope of the child audience. Clearly, Pippi's declaration is aimed at those who have the power to oppress and abuse because of their strength and position—be they children or adults—and adults are always in a position of power in their function as parents and educators.

When asked what she would have liked to be, given another chance in life, Lindgren responded that she would have loved to be an activist in the early days of the social democratic movement in Sweden, fighting for the rights of the underprivileged. This statement not only satiates our curiosity about Lindgren's alternative career choices; it is symptomatic of the humanism and social commitment that form the backbone of her entire work. Lindgren has in a sense become just that, an activist for the powerless and underprivileged. In her fiction, she fought for social justice and the pursuit of happiness—and against the abuse of power—in the name of children long before the relatively bland codification of children's rights by the United Nations in 1959 and the more radical demands of children's rights activists in the 1970s. With her crusade for peace and her animal rights campaign in the late 1980s, Lindgren pursued her activist career further by becoming publicly engaged.

Lindgren, like wise women and men of time immemorial, has taken refuge in storytelling to solve riddles and teach lessons. The length of her stories can range from a novel to a short anecdote or tale; their function remains the same, that is, to touch the innermost core of our beings and to provide an inspiring and consoling narrative for a world in need of improvement. "I don't consciously try to educate or influence the children who read my books,"

Lindgren observes. "The only thing I would dare to hope for is that my books might make some small contribution towards a more caring, humane, and democratic attitude in the children who read them." This is a cautious statement, and few authors today dare attribute more influence to their writing. In addition, Lindgren's remark undercuts any implied assumption of didacticism in her work. Her stories are not cautionary tales or moralizing fables, but carry within them the complexity and inscrutability of folktales—hence her preference for this genre. Even more to the point, Lindgren's humanism, in the broadest sense of the word, and her social activism are so much a part of herself that they could never constitute a pose. Lindgren's attempt to improve life on earth by instilling human kindness and empathy in her readers and by making life a little more bearable has remained a constant, from *Pippi Longstocking* to *Ronia, the Robber's Daughter*.

Lindgren strongly believes that how we educate children will greatly influence the world of the future and that what children need most is love and trust. She contends that children who are treated lovingly by their parents and caretakers will in turn love their parents. This mutual love and trust will help them establish a "loving" relationship with their environment that they will retain during their entire life. "And this is good," Lindgren continues, "even if the child does not become one of those who govern the fate of the world. But if one day, contrary to expectations, the child should belong to those powerful people, then it is a joy for all of us if its attitude has been determined by love and not violence, for even the character of statesmen and politicians is formed before they are five years old—this is a horrifying fact, but it is true."

Her message seems simple: if we want to make the world a kinder place, we have to treat children with kindness, gentleness, and respect, since they will shape future societies in the spirit in which they themselves have been shaped. If we teach children violence or treat them with violence and disrespect, the world will continue to be filled with violence. Violence begets violence. That is why we who have the power over children as parents or educators should refrain from violence and model peaceful behavior.

Corporal punishment is one form of violence many parents have committed unwittingly or even with good conscience, since it was the commonly accepted practice. By refashioning an old tale, **"The Old Man and His Grandson,"** in the Brothers Grimm collection, Lindgren contributes to breaking the vicious circle of abuse. . . . By modeling ways of peaceful conflict resolution and conviviality, Lindgren has surely helped raise the level of sensitivity to abusive treatment of children in Sweden, where corporal punishment was allowed in school until the late 1950s and where a law was passed in the 1980s forbidding parents to strike their children. The message of nonviolence is most forcefully expressed in the books that most openly deal with violence and destruction, such as *Mio, My Son* and *The Brothers Lionheart*. In *The Brothers Lionheart* Lindgren moved one step further away from the traditional dragon-killer quest on which both

books are based. Whereas Mio hated the idea of having to take the sword in his hand and kill evil Sir Kato to break the spell—and relieve Sir Kato himself from the pain and suffering of a heart of stone—Jonathan flatly refuses to arm himself and kill Tengil or Katla. Both heroes show no signs of the heroic-aggressive behavior that is commonplace in traditional quests and nineteenth-century retellings of fairy tales. Still, Lindgren placates her readers' fear, satisfies their hunger for excitement, and instills in them hope and courage.

Courage assumes center stage in *The Brothers Lionheart*. As their name suggests, the brothers have ample courage and big hearts. Jonathan represents these qualities in an idealized form, whereas Rusky's long struggle against fear—following his ideal as he follows his brother—is a more realistic portrayal of the human condition. Jonathan differs from his namesake, King Richard I Lion-Heart, in at least one important respect. He is a champion of nonviolence. Jonathan, who dares to confront the dragon, is neither the valiant dragon-slayer of traditional fairy tales and sagas nor a powerful and ruthless ruler. Instead of killing the dragon, he averts the danger by trickery. All in all, this new hero does not yearn for power; instead he is a warm, tender, and caring person who would neither hurt nor kill anybody—not for lack of daring, but out of conviction.

Courage in *The Brothers Lionheart* is not synonymous with bravery and definitely not with ostentatious fearlessness. This becomes evident when a Tengil soldier named Park, bragging about his strength, foolhardily forces his horse into the swift rapids of the river of the Ancient Rivers to prove his courage. Only with Jonathan's help—and at the risk of Jonathan's life—do horse and rider survive, yet Park has not even a word of thanks. Not only is Park called a fool, but a coward as well. By frivolously gambling his life on a bet he displays the same disregard for human life that is characteristic of the despotic Tengil regime as a whole. Courage in this book about death and suicide is synonymous with love and a high esteem for life.

By raising the question of pacifism, Lindgren lends considerable complexity to the struggle of good versus evil, especially because it does not remain uncontradicted. There are heroic and caring figures in this novel who do not shrink from using violence to combat oppression and abusive cruelty. Among them are Antonia, who is prepared to avenge the murder of her husband ordered by Tengil, and particularly Orvar, the intrepid rebel and freedom fighter. Orvar sees no other recourse but to use violence to liberate his country from the forces of evil. While he plans for the decisive battle, he and Rusky begin to argue. Orvar's prediction that if everyone were like Jonathan evil would forever reign in the world is contradicted by Rusky, who gets the last word: "if everyone were like Jonathan, there wouldn't be any evil." Since this poetic tale of human brotherhood is written to console children, including the child within the adult, love, the remedy against all evil, wins out over hatred, indifference, and death. Wild Rose Valley is freed from evil through Jonathan's nonviolent courage, although—and here Lindgren makes a concession—Orvar's spirit of resistance proves to be a key part of the effort.

A composite of adventure and robber's tale, *Ronia, the Robber's Daughter,* like *The Brothers Lionheart,* can be classified as quest narrative. Like its predecessor, *Ronia* departs from the traditional path of the heroic narrative in which a solitary male leader perpetuates the paternal order by removing and killing obstacles to his ascent to power. Ronia, too, is born into a world of conflict and ambiguity—in her case, during a raging thunderstorm in which the castle is split in two, leaving Hell's Gap between. Initially, there are two sets of conflicting values, one reigning inside the family and the other in the world "outside." While caring, love, and understanding guide life inside the castle under the auspices of Lovis (modeled on the bourgeois family myth), the professional code of the robbers is based on conflict and exploitation. Neither of the two behavioral patterns is impervious to the influence of the other, however, and conflict invades the family while the two bands' reconciliation is based not only on pragmatic concerns of survival but on love and understanding as well.

Much like Romeo and Juliet's, Ronia and Birk's relationship eventually brings the fighting to an end, with the one difference that Ronia and Birk do not have to pay with their lives for it. With her courageous leaps, Ronia at first playfully bridges Hell's Gap, which symbolizes the senseless conflict between the two robber bands. Later, at a more mature stage of her childhood, there is little playfulness left in her effort to connect the two parts of the castle by building a pathway through the rubble and debris, a feat she accomplishes with much physical and psychological suffering. She feels torn between opposing values and incompatible demands, as when she decides to steal food from her mother's larder to keep Birk and the enemy camp alive during the winter, and when she is forced to choose between Birk and her father. One lesson that Ronia (and the reader) learns is that there are no easy solutions, but solutions can be found if one works hard at it.

Through her actions Ronia offers a model for conflict resolution based on give and take and caring enough about others to learn to understand them. This model runs counter to the magical solutions and the rigid patriarchal hierarchy encountered in classical fairy tales, where the underdog hero prevails thanks to magical helpers and where dissenters either perish or have to find their way back into existing structures of society. The dream in the classical fairy tale, which emerged out of a rigid, authoritarian culture with stable hierarchies, had been to get to the very top through luck or cleverness and to stay there. It is replaced by a very different dream of success in a dynamic, late capitalist society based on the laws of Social Darwinism. This dream, which constitutes the subtext of all three Lindgren novels—*Mio, My Son, The Brothers Lionheart,* and *Ronia*—expresses the need for peaceful cooperation and a life that does not depend on the exploitation of nature or people.

Superheroes like Pippi, Mio, Jonathan, and Ronia belong to the utopian world of fantasy, but there is plenty of everyday heroism in children who stand up for their rights and protest abuse of power in Lindgren's realistic fiction as well. Tjorven in *Seacrow Island* defiantly stands up to the materialism of the rich real estate speculator just as Pippi does, and Emil reveals the true meaning of Christmas when he invites the most wretched and desolate people in Lönneberga to the big feast. Like Jonathan, Emil, too, shows courage of heart when he saves Alfred's life.

Lindgren's social commitment and her call for courage of the heart permeates her realistic books as much as her fantastic tales, though the choice of genre somewhat alters the way it is expressed. Typically, this call is reflected in the protagonists' open or underhanded revolt against presumptive behavior and the abuse of authority. Pippi's and Emil's wild and joyous parodies of pretentiousness are toned down in the books about Madicken (Mardie to the British reader, Meg to the American), but this protagonist also chastises others for such vices as conceit and arrogance. Especially in the second book about her, *Mardie to the Rescue,* the heroine's sense of justice underscores the problems of human inequity and social inequality. Sometimes the protagonist's—and by extension Lindgren's—ethics are at odds with public morality, as in the episode about Mia's theft at school. Having found the headmaster's purse, Mia does not return it but instead buys chocolates and angel bookmarks, which she distributes freely to her class to gain a little recognition. To Mardie's comment, "It was terrible of Mia to take the purse as well. It's wrong to steal," her father replies, "Yes, but little children do it sometimes, and it's not right to try to knock it out of them with a cane." For that is what the headmaster does in front of the whole class. It is indicative of Lindgren's ethics of compassion that Mardie's father does not get half as upset over Mia's theft as he does over the punishment she has to endure from the headmaster. Throughout the episode the narrator's sympathy is with Mia.

The issue of abusive treatment is closely linked to institutionalized abuse in the form of socially sanctioned discrimination and social disparity. Mia, called Louse-Mia by the other children because her hair is full of lice and her clothes are dirty and torn, clearly belongs to the lowest social class and feels the effects of discrimination daily. She is a fighter who stands up for her rights, which makes her into a renegade in the eyes of authority. The disgruntled head teacher can finally vent his anger after having found her guilty, and he employs the then-accepted practice of combining physical with psychological pain to break the offender's will. Mia must first confess, then ask for forgiveness, and finally she must be beaten as well. "You will thank me for it one day," is the righteous comment of the head teacher. This torture in the name of education, or "poisonous pedagogy," as Alice Miller calls it, is portrayed with equal disdain by Ingmar Bergman in his film *Fanny and Alexander,* through the character of the bishop/stepfather. Lindgren and Bergman belong to the same generation, and although their childhood experiences were diametrically opposed, both vehemently condemn the repression and hypocrisy of the bourgeois authoritarian educational ethic.

While Alexander's will is broken—he will never be free of fear, and memories of his stepfather will haunt him for the rest of his life—Mia's remains unbroken in spite of the fact that "there was no child he [the head teacher] could not break." Mia stubbornly refuses to ask for forgiveness. Lindgren, who writes to console and inspire children, lets Mia keep her pride. Fearlessly and triumphantly she leaves the scene. Instead of delivering the expected excuse with downcast eyes, Mia stands up to the head teacher, looks straight into his eyes and says loudly and clearly "Pisspot!" before she leaves. Again, it is not Mia's expletive or her action that Mardie's father calls the most indecent thing he's ever heard but rather the headmaster's action. Lindgren's opinion about those who abuse their power over the weak can hardly be stated in more drastic terms.

The powerless and disadvantaged, often members of the working class and children, stand up for their rights in Lindgren's books, and alliances between the two are often formed on the basis of mutual understanding and common interest. Lindgren, who has always taken pride in being a farmer's daughter, empathizes with working people and uses a sharp pen to highlight the conceit of people who look down on the working class. She condemns the rigid class barriers that were prominent between masters and servants in the middle-class family at the beginning of the century, and she saves much mockery and ridicule for pretentious small-town society ladies and pompous politicians. Emil regularly gets the better of society ladies and the mayor, but a more pronounced criticism of the propensity to look down on simple folk can again be found in *Mardie to the Rescue*.

There Alma, the maid in Mardie's household, speaks up for herself if need be. Alma's insistence on having the last salmon from a fishmonger evidences Lindgren's reproof against preferential treatment on the basis of social status and title. Unfortunately for the mayor's wife, Alma is the first to claim the last piece of salmon in the shop, but the mayor's wife does not give up that easily. She uses her status to pressure Alma into relinquishing her claim: "Do you know who I am, young woman? I am the mayoress of this town!" But Alma's retort, "Well, I am the one who is going to have this salmon," leaves her speechless. In the end, Alma makes off with the salmon.

Alma dares speak up because she has some backing from Mardie's father, the town's newspaper editor, who is also called the "gentleman-socialist." He takes Alma along to the great charity ball organized by the mayor's wife, which constitutes an affront to the hostess and to many other townspeople. Cutting off the mayor's wife, who is remarking that servants are not invited to the ball, he asserts, "Then it is about time that there will be a change." And he is savagely pleased—as is the reader—when the chimney sweep crashes the party and asks Alma, who had been frozen out, to dance. Like Cinderella and the prince, these two take over the dance floor. For Mardie, through whose eyes the reader observes the incident, this is a fairy tale come true: "They danced and danced and sang and laughed and danced as Mardie had never seen people dance before. It was beautiful, oh, how beautiful it was! For Alma was beautiful and white and the sweep was handsome and black." The fairy tale's sense of justice prevails here as well, with the difference that Alma does not get her prince, for he is already married and has five children. Lindgren adapts the fairy-tale motif for her own purpose. The dream she communicates to her readers is the victory of the truly human over hollow pretense.

Many critics have found Mardie to be utterly bourgeois in behavior and values. She certainly grows up in a bourgeois household, but the cultural patterns she experiences are far from uniform. *Mardie to the Rescue* presents a cross-section of social classes, with heavy sympathies for those at the lower end of the scale, but Lindgren does not uncritically sing their praises. The mentally disturbed Lindson is outright dangerous as he walks through town snatching small children, and Mia and her little sister, Mattis, are definite cases of child neglect—dirty and full of lice and aggression as they are. Mr. Nilsson, the neighbor, is a good-for-nothing drunk with a flair for self-aggrandizement and a love of words who leaves his wife and son to fend for themselves. He is a considerably more problematic version of Paradise-Oscar in *Rasmus and the Vagabond*. Oscar only gives in to his need for freedom in the spring, when he has the urge to hit the road, in effect taking a vacation from farming, but otherwise shoulders his responsibilities; Mr. Nilsson, however, has taken a permanent leave of absence from his responsibilities.

In *Mardie to the Rescue* Lindgren allots more room to the shady sides of life than she does in most of her realistic books. A more pronounced focus on social injustice may have been Lindgren's answer to the strong movement of social realism that pervaded children's literature in the 1970s in Sweden, Europe, and the United States. Lindgren's tendency to harmonize is not carried quite as far in this book. Mr. Nilsson does not change. Lindson is finally locked up in a home to make the small town a safer place again. Mia and Mattis are deloused by Mardie's mother, but, as her father points out, this is a temporary measure that changes little in the real-life conditions under which the two girls have to live. Yet even in this book Lindgren cannot deny herself. Happiness wins out over sorrow, fear, and pain, as it does in the Alma-as-Cinderella episode. The shady side of life gives Mardie an opportunity to reflect, but it does not permanently alter her cheerful and positive disposition, for she has "a healthy young person's ability to forget anything disagreeable almost from one day to the next." Mardie's unencumbered joy of life also sets the tone for this book. With the cast of characters in the Mardie books Lindgren has created a multivoiced discourse in which the only common denominator is a basic democratic humanism. Despite her clean aprons, Mardie is much too strong-minded, high-spirited, and unconventional to fit the mold of the bourgeois female heroine. As a matter of fact, Mardie, like Emil, is but a more realistically drawn version of Pippi—full of ideas, energy, *joie de vivre,* curiosity, and cunning.

Something provocative and liberating is part of their playful experimentation with the physical, emotional, and intellectual realities of life, and this playfulness no doubt resonates in the reader.

Pippi and Ronia, the two strong female protagonists that demarcate the beginning and end of Astrid Lindgren's career as a children's book author, exemplify not only the growth and development of Lindgren as a writer but also developments in children's and women's life experience. This life experience has changed considerably thanks to the struggles for children's and women's rights in the Western world during the latter part of the twentieth century. Pippi's refusal to be part of the adult world she ridicules in Dadaist deconstructive fashion in 1945 is superseded thirty-six years later by Ronia's resolve to do her part to rebuild the world.

In the world of twentieth-century children's literature Lindgren is not categorized by herself or by others as a feminist author. Her prime concern remains that of children's rights; yet in her effort to give a voice to the voiceless she has often touched on feminist issues. Obvious parallels exist between the struggle for women's rights and the struggle for children's rights. A short glance at the history of childhood, motherhood, and family life, as told by Philippe Aries, Elisabeth Badinter, John Boswell, and Lloyd deMause, among others, suffices to confirm the double victimization—both as child and as female—that girls have experienced throughout the ages. In the case of girls and their fictional representation both struggles are compounded. Girl protagonists in children's literature, after all, offer models of identification for the purpose of socialization of female readers. The debilitating or emancipatory influences these protagonists exert may last a lifetime.

Despite obvious systemic differences, the movements for women's and children's rights employ similar rhetorical strategies. That is why it may be difficult at times to define Lindgren's emancipatory rhetoric as specifically feminist, counter-cultural, or child-oriented. These voices converge in Lindgren's high regard for personal integrity, community, caring, and sharing, which runs like a red thread through her entire writing. Which of these tendencies readers will bring to the fore in their analysis will depend on their focus as well as on the narrative itself. A gender-based reading of Lindgren's work would scarcely be able to bypass the two strong and self-assertive characters that flank it—Pippi and Ronia—for they invite such a reading.

Pippi's emancipatory voice reached the public four years before the publication of Simone de Beauvoir's *The Second Sex,* and I would like to argue that within its genre it became equally influential. Pippi set the stage for future female heroes who will not let themselves be confined to the domestic sphere. In Pippi Longstocking girls encountered an active and self-assertive female protagonist with whom they could identify. Her playful subversion of authority was followed cautiously in the 1960s and more vigorously in the 1970s by a whole wave of antiauthoritarian children's literature questioning traditional roles and conventional values.

Pippi's emancipatory subversion and aggressive nonviolence belong wholly to the realm of fantasy and wishful thinking, as does she herself. The liberating potential in **Pippi Longstocking** largely remains an expression of the playfulness and exuberance of childhood, a familiar romantic trope. Outwardly, the effect of Pippi's actions on social reality within the narrative seems as limited as it must have been on the immediate everyday life experiences of her readers. Nothing much seems to change in Tommy and Annika's life when Pippi is not around, nor can we trace any important changes in their attitudes. In both behavior and reasoning these two remain model children who prefer the security and comfort of the conventional. Nonetheless, as they swallow Pippi's magic chililug pills, which promise eternal happy childhood, they imbibe a permanent spark of revolt and regeneration, just as many readers must have in reading Pippi's books.

In **Ronia, the Robber's Daughter** Lindgren presents her readers with a female hero who bears much resemblance to Pippi, yet readers are confronted with two distinct concepts of childhood and femininity framed in different narratives. Both female heroes are curious, caring, courageous, and strong-willed, but while Pippi, the fantastic character in a realistic setting, represents only one side of childhood—the boundless playfulness, neglectful of time and place—Ronia, the realistic character in a timeless fairytale setting, is an altogether believable and complex individual.

The reader of **Ronia, the Robber's Daughter** delves into the magic world of fairy tale and adventure in which Ronia resides and follows her growth and development through the stages of childhood and beyond in a female bildungsroman. The theme of growth and responsibility, which is added to the free and adventurous childhood spirit reigning in **Pippi Longstocking,** lends this last novel its depth and importance. In both books readers follow the adventures of female heroes whose fathers have taken the law into their own hands (Pippi's father is a pirate captain and Ronia's is the chief of a robber band). Each daughter revolts in her own, unpredictable fashion. Pippi, the playful supergirl, ridicules and exposes untenable conditions with zest and courage in the realm of fantasy. Still, the concrete results of her subversive tactics remain untold. Ronia, on the other hand, needs no superhuman strength to undo her foes. She uses her muscles, acts on her convictions, and achieves concrete goals. While Pippi abrogates her growth voluntarily, Ronia accepts the challenge of the future and of adulthood. Unlike Tommy and Annika, she is not compelled to shed fantasy and playfulness like an old snake skin upon entry into the adult world; her imagination gradually loses its childish qualities but remains an important source for Ronia's vision and ambition. This portrayal of Ronia would not have been possible without the concomitant developments in society. Without the breakdown of barriers between manhood and womanhood, and between adulthood and childhood, and without the growing importance of the idea of the inner child, *Ronia, the Robber's Daughter* might not have been written, at least not in its present form.

The impact of recent social change, which has affected both the feminist and the children's rights movements, has opened up possibilities for new literary discourses that support parallel changes in women's and children's social realities. *Ronia, the Robber's Daughter* is an example of the books that regenerate the genre by regendering it. This regendering goes beyond the superficial gender change of the quest hero from male to female. Feminine values and modes of expression have infiltrated the traditionally male discourse of the quest, leading to its feminization, which I see manifested in this novel. From playfully deconstructing patriarchal standards and values in *Pippi Longstocking*, Lindgren moves on to reconstruction by means of feminist myth building in *Ronia, the Robber's Daughter*. No longer is the feminist discourse deferred to fantasy and hidden in parody and trickster tale, revealing the strategy of resistance against an overwhelming force. At a time when a greater number of women are working their ways into positions of influence and power, Ronia has become a natural role model for young readers.

A feminine discourse of peaceful, nurturing coexistence and a sense of community pervade Lindgren's robber's tale. Ronia balances her autonomy and independence with an acute sensitivity to her environment and a sustained connectedness to family and community unknown in traditional quest stories. The heroic tale starts conventionally enough with Ronia's ominous birth during a thunderstorm and continues with a series of daring feats performed by Ronia, who, like Pippi, claims her right to journey into the world as a matter of course. Since Ronia is clearly at the center of the story, her counterpart, Birk, despite his virtues, pales in comparison.

In this female bildungsroman, which traces Ronia's gradual maturation to full independence within the framework of communal interdependence, the two female protagonists, Ronia and her mother, Lovis, are, by and large, stronger and wiser than their male counterparts. Lovis, whose wolf song exudes strength as well as nurturing qualities, is full of wisdom and profound affection. Nothing but a vague sense of adventure remains of the glorification of male might and power, of the feuds and open violence in traditional robber's and adventure stories. In fact, these attributes are even ridiculed when they surface. Big, tough, bragging Matt, who is also colorful and endearing, receives a fair share of ridicule, for example, when he whimpers about the bruises he has sustained during the "heroic" duel between the two chieftains. Ultimately, both women prove to be stronger and more enduring than the men. No robbers dare contradict Lovis when she chases them out into the snow stark naked for the castle's early spring cleaning. This surely is a complete reversal of values attributed to the sexes in the classical quest, where men were active, daring, and strong and women suffering, supportive, and good-looking.

Ronia's leap across Hell's Gap, the chasm separating the two parts of the castle and symbolizing the split between the two robber bands, sets her off on her as yet unconscious and undefined quest to change the world. In the traditional manner, this quest takes her away from her family and clan and out into uncharted territories in the forest, where she will spend the summer in a cave together with Birk. Her separation from her family, however, is not complete. Moreover, family ties define her attempts to gain independence and to chart her own course. Her father's unreasonably stubborn grief at having "lost" his daughter as well as her own guilt at having betrayed her parents weigh heavily on her conscience. Her inner struggle to overcome separation anxiety and to redefine her interpersonal relationships, as well as her role in society and nature, are portrayed as tasks that are just as difficult, if not more so, than any of her more flamboyant, action-oriented—and traditionally male—feats of courage. Her mental courage demands empathy, integrity, and farsightedness above and beyond daring and forcefulness. Hence, Ronia's most heroic act lies not in her attempt to save Birk's life at the risk of her own but in her attempt to reunite the warring bands and in her refusal during the bands' reconciliation celebration to become a robber's chieftain as her father desires.

All by herself and with singular persistence, Ronia changes the conditions for everyone concerned. Her bridge-building effort brings about the reconciliation of the robber bands and the rewriting of their history, erasing old dualisms, as does Lindgren with her novel. But, most important, the refusal of Ronia and Birk to continue in their fathers' footsteps will do away with the old robber ways and eventually change society fundamentally. Matt has to grin and bear Ronia's decision not to become the robber chieftain he had always wanted her to be. The ways and values of the founding fathers are overthrown and give way to change. Patriarchal authority and traditional male values of aggression and competition belong to the past and have to be replaced by a sense of community if the future is to be any brighter. The narrator tells us that this is a change for the better. Matt and Borka look forward to theft and plunder again as spring approaches, but Ronia and Birk, the narrator tells us, are "much wiser. They delighted in quite different things."

Ronia picks up where Pippi leaves off. Despite her professed eagerness to follow in his footsteps, Pippi never becomes a pirate like her father. She eventually chooses a very different career. Seeing no other solution to her dilemma of retaining her wildness and freedom in a society bent on domesticating and institutionalizing her, she reverts to eternal childhood. Ronia also looks up to her father and envisions herself as a robber chieftain when she is small, but consciously chooses another path once she has reached the age of reason, realizing the cruelty and lack of social responsibility inherent in a robber's life. Ronia's father, although successful as a robber and much loved by his daughter, cannot ultimately remain her role model. Neither can her mother, who is strong and independent but nevertheless supports the robber ways. Ronia is forced to chart her own course together with Birk. Trusting their intuition, she and Birk will become the founders of a new, and, as Lindgren calls it, "wiser" world order, where the quest for possession and power is tempered by caring and nurturing and a joyful openness toward life that is expressed in Ronia's primal scream at the conclusion of the novel. In this female bildungsroman Lindgren takes her readers beyond dualism and difference to a relatively open ending and visions of a better future.

Sisterhood and brotherhood are the guiding principles of the novel **Ronia, the Robber's Daughter**. Besides the special closeness Ronia and Birk feel for each other, the idea that both belong to one big family of human beings on this planet, symbolized by the robbers' forest, also resonates in their calling each other "Sister" and "Brother." Ronia and Birk change and develop as they grow up, and their fathers, who are grown men, are forced to change as well. Admittedly, they still go on in their old robber ways. They are steeped in these ways and don't know any better, but their relationship with the younger generation changes. The absolute authority of the older generation gives way to greater tolerance and understanding. Ronia does not, like the prodigal son, return begging for forgiveness following her decision to move away from home; her father has to meet her half-way and has to ask her forgiveness.

The destructive versus nurturing attitude and male versus female voice do not simply run along gender lines; likewise, the division between the more primitive life-style of the parents and the "wiser" and more advanced choice of their children is not an exclusively generational one. The vision for change originates with the oldest and wisest of the robbers, Noddle-Pete. He influences Ronia's decision to give up robbery through his underhanded and witty criticisms of the old way of life. His role very much resembles that of Astrid Lindgren, the author who writes books for children in order to entertain, console, and inspire. His voice prevails, and the optimistic message of progress, defined not in material terms but as a shift in mindset toward a more peaceful, humane society, resonates throughout the novel as it does throughout Lindgren's work. Only the future will show whether her voice will be heard and whether it will prevail.

TITLE COMMENTARY

 *PIPPI LONGSTOCKING* (1950)

New York Herald Tribune Book Review

SOURCE: A review of *Pippi Longstocking*, in *New York Herald Tribune Book Review*, November 12, 1950, p. 12.

The list of books about rambunctious, funny, almost-bad boys has grown apace; those about girls to match them come along more slowly. This Pippi is a prize. Quiet little girls of eight to ten will join those who are tomboys by nature, in uproarious glee at her absurd doings. She lives alone with her horse and monkey, and foils all attempts of police, schools, and polite neighbors to make her conform to the accepted social pattern. Her wild doings are shared by a very "nice," normal little boy and girl who live next door. Her rare conversation includes tall tales of her life in many lands, with her father, a ship's captain. Sometimes Pippi admits she invents, but her hoards of gifts and of gold pieces are real.

All this good fun comes to us from Sweden, invented by a storytelling mother for her children and their friends. . . .

Welcome to Pippi, once met, never to be forgotten!

Marian Rayburn Brown

SOURCE: "The Amazing Pippi," in *The New York Times Book Review*, November 12, 1950, p. 28.

In the amazing Pippi, Mrs. Lindgren has created an unusual character. This 9-year-old has escaped from all adult supervision and restriction. Her sole companions in the old house at the edge of the Swedish village are a monkey and a horse. The children next door are fascinated by her carrot-colored hair, tremendous freckles, strange clothes and great strength. They watch her lift her horse off the porch; carry two policemen down the path when they try to take her to a children's home; successfully wrestle the Mighty Adolph, and subdue two robbers who want her chest of gold. Pippi's fantastic stories and humorous escapades exemplify many of the frustrations of normal children. They will, therefore, delight young readers.

Bettina Hürlimann

SOURCE: "Fantasy and Reality: *Pippi Longstocking,*" in *Three Centuries of Children's Books in Europe,* edited and translated by Brian W. Alderson, 1967, pp. 81-3.

[There was] a special event in modern children's literature, which raised a lot of dust among the grown-ups and brought a lot of pleasure to the children. This [was] Astrid Lindgren's **Pippi Langstrump** [published in English as **Pippi Longstocking**] (1945), a unique arrival among the heroes of children's literature.

Many famous characters who have today become classics found their way into the hearts of children straight from the books on the adult bookshelf. Leatherstocking, Robinson Crusoe, David Copperfield, and many others have done this, thereby avoiding the round-about route via the pundits. On the other hand, others, like Heidi, Pinocchio, or Nils Holgersson, had all the textbook qualities which the pundits require but nevertheless still found their way to a long-lasting popularity. There can be no doubt that children fell in love with Pippi Longstocking from the first moment, while the well-meaning adult world just as violently repudiated her. It must, however, be said in favour of those who abide by the textbook that in this case they have by and large allowed themselves to be converted.

Astrid Lindgren was born in Sweden in 1907 and she created this character at the bedside of her sick daughter, who was herself responsible for inventing Pippi's name. Gradually Pippi was furnished with such improbable attributes that the stories about her present no difficulty in being categorized with other fantasies for children. Astrid Lindgren has written over twenty books and has successfully turned her hand to writing such things as fairy stories, detective stories for boys, career stories, and stories for young girls, but she has never bettered her first book in spite of the exceptional merit which has distinguished her work in these other fields.

Pippi Longstocking probably had much the same appearance in the sickroom where she started life as in the books which came later—hair the colour of carrots, a nose the shape of a small potato, dotted with freckles, a large mouth, a home-made dress by no means long enough, one black stocking and one brown and two shoes like rowing-boats. This nine-year-old has a strength greater than anyone else in the town. She can pick up a couple of policemen or her own horse with one arm, and since she has no parents this comical creature can do as she likes. The necessary base for her operations is provided by her own cottage and a suitcase full of gold pieces.

Roughly speaking, that is the child's 'police-description'— a figure to strike terror to grown-ups in a way that the most exaggerated comics can scarcely surpass. Astrid Lindgren put it all into a book at the behest of her daughter in 1944, when she was herself confined to bed. With some difficulty she also found a publisher, although he considered that a wild little girl who does what she likes was hardly a good example to set before the public. Similarly, teachers found it impossible to accept Pippi's non-attendance at school, her preference instead to take ship for the South Seas or else wander around the town with her pet monkey Mr. Nilsson, looking for treasures. But police descriptions can deceive. Even though Pippi Longstocking fulfilled all the dreams suppressed in children's hearts, she also possessed other qualities which must have an almost therapeutic effect on the children of today. Her pranks are neither stupid nor damaging; she is full of a good-hearted willingness to help people weaker than herself; she is indescribably open-handed and, above all, never boring. And that is probably her finest quality, making her more invincible than all her superhuman powers and turning her into the best friend in the world for her companions Thomas and Annika.

It has now been generally accepted that the three books published in England as **Pippi Longstocking, Pippi goes on board,** and **Pippi in the South Seas** are full of the most splendid and comical nonsense, which also fascinates those grown-ups who have not grown too old for it. In spite of their exciting plots the books are written extensively in a dialogue which packs plenty of punch (a feature which they share with the English nonsense stories) and even fifteen- or sixteen-year-olds, who are otherwise inclined to treat their children's books with scorn, cannot help chuckling when they inadvertently get hold of a Pippi Longstocking volume which eight or nine years previously may have set them free from Mickey Mouse or Noddy.

In contrast to Peter Pan, the first fantastic character in modern children's literature, and one who can be described as 'child eternal', Pippi Longstocking is a kind of 'super-child', setting free kindly impulses in the children who read about her, as respectable teachers throughout the world now admit. Pippi and her two friends find that, thanks to her extraordinary powers, being a child is a glorious experience and they therefore decide that they do not ever want to grow up. The 'superchild' has an excellent medicine which will deal with that little problem. In a situation like this one can see the connexion across the sea with that English 'superchild' Alice—a more civilized and perhaps somewhat more intellectual sister to the little Swedish girl.

In Sweden, Astrid Lindgren is a kind of children's idol. Such is the fame of her heroine that schoolchildren are allowed to call themselves 'Little Pippis' after doing some particularly good turn; moreover, Astrid Lindgren's other books, not mentioned in detail here, have also brought in some badly needed fresh air, particularly where fairy stories are concerned and in the rather difficult category of books for young adolescents.

Though she may be an idol in the children's pantheon, Astrid Lindgren is a very straightforward person who has not allowed her enormous success in almost every country of the world to go to her head. Like her English contemporary, P. L. Travers, she is a poetess. Humour, reverie, and sadness are reflected equally in her fine-featured nordic face—that restrained sadness which runs through the work of Andersen and which gives the true finish to the fantasy and humour of this genuinely poetic writer for children. No receptive child and no adult can read without emotion the closing pages about Pippi as she sits dreamily beside a candle in the middle of a children's paradise which has never been lost.

Laura Hoffeld

SOURCE: "*Pippi Longstocking:* The Comedy of the Natural Girl," in *The Lion and the Unicorn,* Vol. 1, No. 1, Spring, 1977, pp. 47-53.

Outrageous, delightful Pippi Longstocking is a character who comes to us in translation from a Scandinavian culture, but is as familiar to us as the little girls who live in our midst. Her most striking characteristic is her great capacity for joy, which we adults recognize from afar, but which has more immediacy for children. The primacy of enjoyment in her life is the key to her deliciousness and her shock value. Pippi does exactly as she wishes, and says so.

That the nature of the comedy is related to the gratification of Pippi's desires is indicated by the episodic structure of the Pippi books. Breaking up a narrative into episodes happens to suit the concentration span of children, but the structure of *Pippi* is organically generated as well. As in a Rabelaisian fantasy in miniature, Pippi moves from one situation to the next, taking from each everything it offers her wild imagination, and incidentally giving the other participants either wonderful bolts of surprise or horrible moments of shock.

A sense of outrage, in fact, is built into the adroit combination of fantasy and reality that Astrid Lindgren gives us. Pippi is a fabulous superheroine who inhabits a real Swedish village. She may be familiar, but that is because we recognize in her our own unfettered impulses; no one we know has her powers or lives the way she does. The life she leads is pure fantasy, placed in the context of the real world. I say "real world" advisedly, for it is sketched in cartoon fashion, and from a child's point of view. Nevertheless, it retains the moralistic strictures which make it identifiable as reality. And the more moralistic the society drawn becomes, the more outrageous Pippi is.

The very circumstances of her life are fantastic. She is exceedingly rich, has no parents to bother her, and lives, moreover, with only a horse and a monkey in a dirty and exciting house. We are surprised to come upon an independent, self-sufficient child, and more surprised because the child is female. A little girl without parents to protect her and represent her to the world would ordinarily have the lowest status, be the least powerful member of her society. But Pippi can both romp and manipulate the people around her with utmost nonchalance. Her super strength is emblematic of her ability to make other people do as she wishes. Moreover, our sense of outrage derives from the mixture of fantasy and reality in her characterization. By being a *natural* female child she belies most of our expectations about central characters in books for children. She is a girl, and many girl protagonists are pretty, but Lindgren allows her to be at best comical looking, at worst ugly. And her behavior can be as ridiculous as her appearance. Her naturalness entails selfishness, ignorance, and a marked propensity to lie; but she is simultaneously generous, quick and wise, and true to herself and others (like real children, she is complex). It is astounding that she is a girl with super powers, and without the culturally imposed inhibitions to prevent her from using those powers. There is nothing demure about Pippi. Thus, the comedy stems from two sources: the undercutting of our own attitudes about little girls in stories and in life, and the undercutting of the conventional expectations held by those characters who represent society in the book. In effect, we are laughing at ourselves as well as at the satire of social conventions.

The way Lindgren treats Pippi's lies is typical of the humor of the story. It is startling that Pippi brags and tells tall tales the way male figures in folklore are wont to do, and funnier that her bragging—"Don't you worry about me. I'll always come out on top"—proves true. Her tall tales involve exotic places and relay hints of a style of life that

From Pippi Longstocking, *written by Astrid Lindgren. Illustrated by Louis S. Glanzman.*

feels fuller and more real than the narrowly confined existence of her two conventional friends, Tommy and Annika. And Pippi lies with a sense of honesty, freely admitting that she is lying when she's challenged. Lying, if that is what her imaginative storytelling and teasing must be called, makes her happy, while the dull truth makes her sad. For readers schooled on moralistic stories like *Pinocchio,* Pippi provides a refreshing shock.

It is funny and shocking, too, that so many of the episodes entail Pippi's victories over boys and men. Lindgren clearly intends this to be part of the humor. And it is not the kind of sophisticated war-between-the-sexes humor one finds in some books supposedly written for children. When Pippi vigorously bests the five boys who are bullying little Willie, she calls herself a "helpless little girl." Wrapping Bengt, who has teased her about her appearance, over a high tree branch, she says "I don't think you have a very nice way with ladies." She herself can get up and down trees with agility, and has fun in the process. Her pleasure in climbing all over her house and jumping from roof to tree top, while two clumsy policemen try to chase and capture her, provides a portion of the reader's enjoyment in that episode. Not only can Pippi make two preservers of law and order lose all dignity and look like helpless children themselves, but she takes delight in doing so. As Annika puts it, after Pippi helps her overcome her fear of horseback riding, "it's lots more fun with Pippi around, I think."

It is Pippi's will to enjoy herself that involves her in the funniest overpowering of a man. Never having seen or heard of a "surkus" before, she assumes, to the chagrin of both male and female circus performers, that paying the price of admission entitles her to join in the stunts. When The Mighty Adolph, incarnation of male strength, conceit, and pomposity, seeks a challenger, Pippi is willing. Annika warns her that Adolph is the strongest man in the world, and Pippi responds, "*Man,* yes . . . but I am the strongest *girl* in the world, remember that."

Women come in for their share of the fun in **Pippi,** too. The schoolteacher is one of the best-intentioned and most ridiculous representatives of the dictates of society. In her schoolhouse, Pippi amuses herself by drawing a huge horse directly on the floor, while the other children scribble obediently on paper. More comical, though, is the mock morality with which she answers the teacher's questions. Not only doesn't she know the "right" answers, she clearly doesn't need to know them when she can fabricate such wonderful responses. The purposes of the classroom are held up for ridicule when we realize that it is the teacher's own Puritanical morality (and thus the morality of the society) that Pippi is aping in her responses:

> "Gustav was with his schoolmates on a picnic. He had a quarter when he started out and seven cents when he got home. How much did he spend?"

> "Yes, indeed," said Pippi, "and I also want to know why he was so extravagant, and if it was pop he bought, and if he washed his ears properly before he left home."

Her vision of an ideal school where children eat caramels all day might strike us as merely foolish and hedonistic, if it were not for the fact that her criticism of the conventional school strikes home: "'So long, kids,' she cried gaily. 'Now you won't see me for a while. But always remember how many apples Axel had or you'll be sorry.'" With her characteristic offhand generosity, Pippi gives the teacher a beautiful gold watch before she goes, a gesture which seems to offend the conventional woman as much as Pippi's derisive verbal play.

Puritanical morality is combined with platitudinous thinking in the women at the coffee party Pippi attends. They represent domestic convention in the book. Pippi destroys their pious peace by eating everything she wants, without the pretense of lack of interest in the food which characterizes our behavior at parties, and without proper table manners. Her chatter is funnier still; nothing could be more amazing than a bourgeois aphorism coming out of Pippi's mouth. After she eats all the cream pie, she solaces the ladies with "The main thing is that we have our health. And at a coffee party you should have fun." When the women begin to speak of their servant problems, Pip-

pi interrupts with a most ludicrous tale about a barking, biting, filthy, china-breaking, idiot servant named Malin—a "jewel of a maid"! One might hope that the women never had the nerve to criticize their servants again.

Pippi is capable of eating all the cake because she would just as soon give it all away. In fact, as one might expect, her notions about material possessions are far from conventional; she is always giving away things that are more valuable than she knows. But the joke is not on the untutored girl. After she forces the thieves who tried to rob her to pass a hard night dancing the schottische with her, she gives them each a gold piece and says, "These you have honestly earned." What is being parodied is not Pippi's innocence so much as the society's moralism about honest wages. The chaos in financial transactions in **Pippi Longstocking** is related to the general chaos of things in Pippi's world: cups are forever breaking, eggs are broken into hair instead of frying pans, monkeys sleep in beds and horses on porches. This chaos, of course, is also in tune with the transcending of physical laws that the working of Pippi's superhuman powers entails. What is most exciting for adults and children alike, in this topsy-turvy world, is the undercutting of childhood taboos related to self-protection. When Tommy cuts his thumb with a dagger Pippi gives him to play with, it does not matter. Pippi tries to fly, to the consternation of Tommy and Annika, falls, and jokes about her failure. More horrifying, and therefore funnier, Pippi actually picks a wild mushroom and eats it. Later, she plays with loaded pistols. The others accept guns from her on the understanding that they aren't loaded, but we know they are. While she shoots holes in the ceiling, Pippi recites, "Never let children handle firearms. . . . Otherwise some accident can easily happen."

She has no care for her own safety. During the episode in which she rescues two children from a burning house, she actually enjoys the fire, is excited when sparks fall on her, and does not understand the endangered children's fear. At the end of the fire scene we get a glimpse of the true Pippi, perhaps not so comical, but certainly enjoyable and enviable in her anti-conventionality. Dancing on a precariously placed board high above the street, in the light of the flames, she is a wild child, pagan in her joy in the fire and the night sky. She sings a wonderful, primitive song about the fire burning for all who are, like her, dancing, cheers loudest for herself, and shows us the nature emblematized by her flaming red hair.

Pippi in tableau at the end of the book, illuminated strangely, with her red hair uncontrolled, a pistol in one hand and a sword in the other, is a fierce figure, mocking societal prohibitions. She cries out, "I'm going to be a pirate when I grow up," and the laugh is on the reader, for expecting less of the little girl.

Pippi is funny and moving because her wild and generous impulses and excitement are uncontrolled, and because we spend so much time and energy refining those impulses in ourselves and our own children. As an unrefined female child with superhuman powers she is unique in children's literature; the only figures we can compare her to are witches, and she is not one of that number. We sense the ways in which she is a real child, and we love her, as Lindgren seems to, for her wildness and her appetites.

Michele Landsberg

SOURCE: "First Novels: *Pippi Longstocking*," in *Reading for the Love of It: Best Books for Young Readers*, Prentice Hall Press, 1986, pp. 66-7.

The "wish to be an orphan" is in part a wish for joyful anarchy, and the quintessential orphan of modern fiction is surely Pippi Longstocking, the nine-year-old girl who lives alone, climbs on the furniture, and scrubs floors by tying brushes on to her shoes—though not always before rolling out her cookie dough on the linoleum. I have noticed that children's eyes light up when they remember reading Astrid Lindgren's Pippi books: The playful wish fulfillment is so strong that the glee lingers on in memory.

Pippi is the strongest girl in the world; her mother is an angel in heaven (far more liberating, as any Victorian daughter could have testified, than an Angel in the House) and her father is a marooned cannibal king on a desert island. She lives in her own secluded house with a horse on the porch, a monkey called Mr. Nilsson, and a suitcase full of gold coins. Pippi's marvelously breezy style ("So long, boys," she says to the sailors who have brought her home after her father was lost at sea) is a bracing antidote to the sentimentality with which children's vulnerability is so often treated. Leaving the sailors, she strides into her new life without looking back . . . and it's clear that her physical strength is a metaphor for her emotional indomitability.

But Pippi offers more than just a fantasy of omnipotence. Even more wonderful than her physical power is the freeing of imagination she brings to play with the rather conventional and stereotyped children who live next door. Pippi is a namer. She delights in explosively expansive language ("My name is Pippilotta Delicatessa Windowshade Mackrelmint Efraim's Daughter Longstocking, daughter of Captain Efraim Longstocking, formerly the Terror of the Sea, now a cannibal king"); linguistic ridicule ("I have got along without any pluttifikation tables for nine years," she says in a dreary math class); and the creation of magic through words. One of her favorite games is finding things: An old rusty can becomes a delightful JAR WITH COOKIES if you put cookies in it, or JAR WITHOUT COOKIES if you don't.

There is an enriching dimension of poignancy to the Pippi story. Headstrong Pippi, in her willful defiance of convention, does not have it all her way. She may sabotage her neighbor's well-meaning tea party by her unrestrained greed and her *reductio ad absurdum* of adult chitchat, but there is a price to pay for anarchy. Pippi is left out in the cold, socially and at school.

Not too much is made of Pippi's isolation. The tone of the story, after all, is not emotional realism but liberating tomfoolery. Nevertheless, this slight shading of the book's high spirits tends to deepen its color and integrity. To see how fresh, how inspiriting a book *Pippi Longstocking* is, compare it to any one of a thousand mass-circulation books for young children in which wayward choo-choo trains or discontented flowers who want to be butterflies finally learn to accept their fate and buckle under to conformity. Pippi never buckles; she may wilt momentarily in the cold draught of society's disapproval, but, more characteristically, she bounces away to a new, ever more outrageously naive plan of adventure.

Ulla Lundqvist

SOURCE: "The Child of the Century: The Phenomenon of Pippi Longstocking and its Premises," in *The Lion and the Unicorn*, Vol. 13, No. 2, December, 1989, pp. 97-102.

My motives for choosing to write about the three volumes about Pippi Longstocking—*Pippi Longstocking* (1945), *Pippi Goes on Board* (1946) and *Pippi in the South Seas* (1948)—are very personal. I was seven when the first book appeared, and it was a revolutionary experience to me, and very likely to most of my generation. We were brought up in a strict, conventional way, so the meeting with this strong, self-reliant *and* kind-hearted little superchild provided both relief and fresh courage. Pippi has been my constant companion. I have read about her for my younger sisters, for my own and other children, and am convinced that she still functions in the same manner. She has now been spread over the world in 52 languages. It seems that children's need for Pippi is universal.

From about 1930 onwards a new conception of child care and education gained ground in Sweden. It arose from a growing interest in and knowledge of child psychology, fertilized not least by psychoanalytical theories about the origin of neuroses. Freud and his disciples, especially Alfred Adler, gave new impulses to the discussion about education. The Adlerian ideas concerning the inferiority complex, need for compensation and lust for power in children ran counter to the old way of bringing up children by threatening and punishing them, crushing their wills. It probably seldom occurred to the educators—parents as well as teachers—that flogging and other forms of chastisement would do more harm than good. . . . [Many] progressive educators visited Sweden, gave interviews and lectures, and thus intensified the discussion about psychology and education. In Sweden, these discussions concentrate to a large extent on one crucial point: the question of corporeal punishment. During the period 1931–45, many efforts were made to abolish the right of schoolteachers to hit their pupils, but in vain. The teachers protested loudly each time—not until 1958 was corporeal punishment forbidden in the Swedish "folkskola" (public elementary school). Belief in this type of chastisement has, as the documents show, been hard to dispel. Children were injured physically—*and* mentally—to an extent that far exceeds the evidence of maltreatment which was brought to public attention. . . .

Children's books were also discussed, and reviewed. It is striking how moral and pedagogic criteria dominate assessments of literature for children. The moral tendency in children's books is equally striking. Among the books (36 out of 145 Swedish original titles in 1945) I have found only a handful that run counter to this pattern—and none so totally as Pippi Longstocking.

In many respects the Second World War arrested progressive social and educational development and in some respects it even involved a reaction against the radical educational ideas of the early thirties. Food was rationed. The war winters were very severe. Refugees, not least children, entered the country. The news bulletins on the radio were ominous and children certainly often found them frightening. Children in the north of Sweden did not get enough to eat. Clothes and shoes were also rationed. Sweden was not at war, but Swedish children were well aware that war was being waged.

Such was the time that the first generation of Pippi-readers received their early impressions of the world around them. And Pippi herself appeared on the stage in the very year when peace heralded a brighter future.

Pippi Longstocking came into being in 1941 when Astrid Lindgren's daughter Karin was ill in bed and asked her mother to tell her about Pippi Longstocking—thereby inventing the name. During the following years the Lindgren bedside stories about Pippi and her deeds also became popular with the playmates of the Lindgren children, and in 1944 Astrid Lindgren wrote them down and gave the manuscript to Karin on her tenth birthday. She sent a copy to a publisher (Bonnier), enclosing a letter in which she describes Pippi as a little "Uebermensch" incarnating children's instinctive desire for power, a thought that she ascribes to Bertrand Russell. After some discussion the publisher returned the manuscript, accompanied by a rather conventional letter of refusal. In the meantime, however, Mrs. Lindgren wrote a girls' book which won second prize in a literary contest arranged by another publisher, Rabén & Sjögren. Thus encouraged, she revised Pippi Longstocking, submitted it the following year to the contest for children's books at Rabén & Sjögren—and on this occasion won the first prize. The book was an immediate success.

The revision of the manuscript affects approximately one third of the text. The author has cut out passages that are either not as good as the rest (some clumsy jokes, writing that is alien to a child's mind, nonsense rigmaroles and verses), or too daring and provocative. She has also tidied up Pippi herself: her speech is made less intricate, she acquires a new modesty and tenderness, and also a slight touch of melancholy. In place of the rejected material there are new episodes that fit in better with the rest. These changes have made the style and vocabulary more uniform and better adapted to children's reading. And the

figure of Pippi Longstocking has become both more humble and more superior.

In her new appearance, Pippi Longstocking incarnates several ideas that were discussed in the field of education during the thirties and forties. Firstly, she is a completely *free child,* nobody brings her up, leads her, confines her, punishes her. Her mother is an angel in heaven, and her father, so she believes (this turns out to be true) is a Native King on a South Sea island, where he floated ashore after a terrible storm that wrecked the ship whose captain he was. Pippi's independent life in her wonderful old cottage in a small country town is made possible by her strength and her fabulous riches. But her relationship to her physical strength and to her bag of gold coins is entirely relaxed: her strength she uses only when challenged, and only to defend herself or others (and sometimes to make a funny show), and having money is just practical. It is important here that the children around Pippi share her indifference towards her wealth—only grown-ups are impressed and become ingratiating at the sight of the gold.

Pippi also symbolizes children's desire for power, or, more accurately, superiority. She is not only stronger and richer than the adults, she is also more clever, and thanks to her sharp wit she wins every verbal dispute—sometimes by means of a very special kind of logic. But her power is not the kind that makes her rule others. She just defends her rights, and demands respect from people. The right of children to be respected is a leading theme in Astrid Lindgren's writing for children—and this has been so, as we see in Pippi Longstocking, right from the start.

By means of her freedom, her strength and independence, Pippi is also the sure protector of the children around her. She is warm-hearted, generous and solicitous. In her company nobody has anything to fear. She is revolutionary only in the children's world. She is not interested in society—in fact she is not even a part of it. She does not attend school; knowing all she has to know, there is no need. She plays all day; for her, work is play and play work. She eats what she wants to eat; no delicacy is rationed in her house.

Thus Pippi represents most children's dreams. Astrid Lindgren often stresses this quality; it was never the author's intention to create a pattern or model for her readers. She is aware of the frustrations and confinements of a child's existence, and she has provided consolation and amusement in the figure of Pippi.

The books about Pippi Longstocking are not nearly so sophisticated in style and structure as Astrid Lindgren's more mature works. Nor are the stories extraordinary: Astrid Lindgren writes about parties and picnics, circus shows and school lessons, Christmases and birthdays—motives that are so common in children's books as to verge on becoming clichés. But they have been given new life thanks to the fantastic Pippi, who acts so unexpectedly and turns the most everyday occurrence into a dazzling adventure. She acts with wondrous speed, there is not a moment's dull silence in the world where Pippi leads the way. And the stories are told in a tone of intimacy, even conspiracy, that serves two purposes: it makes the young reader trustful, and lends the appearance of truth to the most fanciful elements of the adventures.

The most important and most striking feature in the books about Pippi Longstocking, however, is their humor and wit.

Pippi herself is a comical figure, representing two frequent archetypes in (comic) art: the *senex puer* motive (i.e., the wonder child) and the *mundus inversus* motive (the topsy-turvy world). Her strength and wisdom makes her wondrous—she is only nine—and her behavior and speech defy the tenets of normal logic.

The comic qualities of the Pippi stories are principally of a verbal kind. Even when Pippi's actions are farcical, they are accompanied, and emphasized, by her witty volubility.

Large sections of the stories consist of Pippi's yarns, which she often commences in order to justify her peculiar behavior. In China, or farthest India it is quite normal to sleep with one's feet on the pillow, or to walk home backwards. She is often carried away by her inventiveness and at times clearly believes what she is saying. When her friends make disbelieving comments, she is ready to admit that she is lying, but only to make her story take an opposite turning that is still more absurd.

Her repartee, moreover, is often excellent, especially in discussions with grown-ups. Her vocabulary is a peculiar mixture of standard phrases, archaisms, slang and sophist turns of phrase. She is irreverent and frank—but in an apparently innocent way. This and her actions serve the obvious purpose of making the normal, conventional way of thinking and acting seem narrow and ridiculous. Sometimes the author sharpens her tools and writes what can be classified as real satire. The objects of her scorn are the same as in satire throughout history: human vices like conceit, arrogance, bullying manners, meanness and deceit—phenomena that are common in the grown-up world. Pippi represents the opposite of these abominable qualities: she is honest, modest and kind-hearted.

Pippi of course has "relatives" in literature. The books about her have often been described as nonsense stories and/or rogue's stories, and they certainly contain elements from both types. She has been compared to Alice in Wonderland, Peter Pan, Tom Sawyer, Huck Finn and Richmal Crompton's William—to mention a few. The Swedish researcher and critic of children's literature, Göte Klingberg, has presented a sophisticated discussion of genres. Applying his criteria, one would place Pippi in the line of "alien children," a term that originates from E. T. A. Hoffmann's story *Das Fremde Kind* and implies a figure that arrives from a strange world to visit the ordinary one. But though there is indeed much of the alien in Pippi, she cannot be classified that easily. She is fantastic—but at the same time she is very real, and the world around her, the children, the little town, the native

island are likewise real, though also conventionalized, stereotyped.

The most fruitful of comparative studies is between Pippi and Carroll's Alice. They are both alien in the worlds in which we meet them—but in totally opposite ways: Alice is a neat, well-behaved, intelligent visitor to a world where normal logical laws are suspended, whereas Pippi is a mischievous, uneducated and irreverant visitor to a conventional, "normal" world, which is mocked by Pippi's own nonsensical way of reasoning. Pippi is an inverted Alice—and Alice was a popular figure with the Lindgren family by the time the Pippi stories were invented.

In any case, it is more accurate to see a highly original work like **Pippi Longstocking** as the starting point of a new tradition rather than as the continuation of some old one. This is all the more applicable to the Pippi stories in that they often start from conventional patterns and motives, but turn them upside down—just as Pippi herself turns everything upside down, both literally and metaphorically.

Eva-Maria Metcalf

SOURCE: "Tall Tale and Spectacle in *Pippi Longstocking*," in *Children's Literature Association Quarterly*, Vol. 15, No. 3, Fall, 1990, pp. 130-35.

Pippilotta Delicatessa Windowshade Mackrelmint Efraimsdaughter Longstocking, or Pippi Longstocking for short, is fully as outrageous as her name promises. She is without doubt one of the funniest and most beloved characters in children's literature in the industrial world. Since the publication of **Pippi Longstocking** (1945), **Pippi Goes on Board** (1945), and **Pippi in the South Seas** (1948), Astrid Lindgren's story of Pippi has become a touchstone in children's literature. Much of the story's popularity and enduring quality rests on its special kind of humor. . . .

The humor in the *Pippi Longstocking* books is a humor of extravagance and excess. It seems especially appropriate for children, who can and do laugh more often and sometimes at different things than do adults. Lindgren herself has noted that, while reading parts of her books to mostly adult audiences, she has more than once heard the high ringing of laughter of a child among a crowd of hundreds of seriously attentive adults. Lindgren knows that there is a humor which adults seem to have outgrown and forgotten. She has not. Somehow, she has been able to keep the child within her alive. Her remarkable memory has permitted her to recall not only events from childhood but also its emotional states. Over and over again, Lindgren has asserted that she only writes for the child within her and only in a way that this child can understand. As far as humor is concerned, she seems more partial to children than to adults. If not all adults laugh at everything that children find funny in her books, it is perhaps deplorable, but unavoidable; when the adults laugh, children should be able to laugh too. After all, these are children's books. As she advises young authors:

Go ahead and write things that are *only* funny for children and not at all for adults; go ahead and write things that are funny for both children and adults, too; but never write anything in a children's book that your common sense tells you is only funny for adults. You're not writing so that reviewers will think you are clever and express yourself in a spiritual way, remember that! Many children's writers wink cleverly right over the heads of their young readers to an imagined adult reader, wink in agreement with the adults and leave the child aside. Please don't ever do it! It's an insult to the child who is to buy and read your book.

This fundamental attitude sets her apart from those authors whose stories can be read on quite different levels by well-educated adults and by children unable to understand all the references and associations—literary or otherwise—that make the text interesting for adults. The extent and level of difficulty of the secondary literature on *Alice's Adventures in Wonderland* is just one case in point. Admittedly, as reader response theory has taught us, no one reception of a certain text is like another in view of the different cognitive and emotional experiences which each reader brings to the text. And there is no one *Pippi Longstocking* for children, either. What can be said, however, is that Lindgren has succeeded in keeping her narrative emotionally and cognitively appealing to both young and old. Because she is well aware of the fact that the pleasure derived from humor stems from the distortion (in fantasy) of previously acquired knowledge and experience, Lindgren limits references and allusions to the cognitive and experiential horizon of children. Doing that she can run the whole gamut of humorous expression from the simplest word play through inversion of letters to highly sophisticated self-parodies. Clever puns, parody, and gallow's humor are all presented in a manner to which children can relate. All these humoristic rhetorical devices are based on a fundamental emotional situation that is especially strong in childhood, but that lingers on into adult life, namely, the desire to be strong, clever, and independent. Indeed, the argument can be made that all parody and satire belong to the powerless and suppressed who find in parody an underhanded way to set up a new discourse against the dominant one. As I will show, Pippi is no exception. Pippi certainly has both the brawn and the brains to come out on top in every situation and to remain her own "master." And she possesses another necessary precondition for total independence; she is "as rich as a troll." Her independence, an independence that normal children can only dream about, is aptly illustrated in the exchange that the 10-year-old Pippi has with her father shortly before he departs on his ship *Hoptoad* to ravage the seas:

> "You're right, as always, my daughter," answered Captain Longstocking. "It is certain that you live a more orderly life in Villa Villekulla, and that is probably best for little children."
>
> "Just so," said Pippi. "It's surely best for little children to live an orderly life, especially if they can order it themselves."

By the end of *Pippi Goes on Board,* no reader/listener will have missed the fact that Pippi is more than merely a "little child," since she is the strongest girl—indeed, the strongest human being—in the world, and since she outsmarts everybody. Moreover, she does not lead an "orderly life" in Villa Villekulla, where she lives all alone with her monkey and her horse, and where everything is in great disarray. There she sleeps with her feet on her pillow, "the way they sleep in Guatemala." The way she makes herself go to bed at night is equally unorthodox: "First I tell myself in a nice friendly way; and then, if I don't mind, I tell myself again more sharply; and if I still don't mind, then I'm in for a spanking—see?" Well, Tommy and Annika, to whom she has offered this explanation, do not see at all. Pippi's attempts at self-control are far removed from their own internalized behavioral norms, for she basically does what she pleases when she pleases. But having been sent to bed against his or her will many a night and having felt rebellious at times, the reader/listener understands the irony—especially as we have been told that Pippi always goes to bed extremely late.

A second reason for the wide appeal of Lindgren's humor is her heavy reliance on narrative forms from oral storytelling, which knows no age discrimination. A farmer's daughter born in the Swedish countryside in 1907, Lindgren has deep roots in the vernacular storytelling tradition. She frequently reveals this in short conversations and in public addresses and debates in which she regularly slips in tales and anecdotes to illustrate her points. In *Pippi Longstocking,* influences from the oral storytelling tradition are especially strong. As a matter of fact, the Pippi episodes were even conceived within that tradition as bedside stories for her daughter, Karin, who gave Pippi her name. Pippi's adventures, then, existed for approximately three years before they were ever committed to paper. Lindgren has provided further etiological information about the Pippi stories. She found the heroine's name so wild and crazy, she said, that the stories themselves simply had to turn out the same way.

Each of the three Pippi books can be described as a tall tale that encompasses a great variety of comic expressions, from nonsense and boisterous situation comedy to self-parody and delicate irony. With their deep roots in oral storytelling, tall tales easily lend themselves as paradigms for humor in children's fiction. They provide both satisfaction and a challenge for those who have left a world filled with wonder and entered a world of logic and science. Moreover, the Pippi books show Pippi not only performing tall tales, but telling them, as well. This is especially true when she is carried away—as she frequently is—by an unrestrained abandonment of common sense and by the pure delight of telling a story. Apropos to walking in a gutter full of water, Pippi contends that "In America the gutters are so full of children, that there is no room for the water. They stay there the year round. Of course in the winter they freeze in and their heads stick up through the ice. Their mothers have to carry fruit soup and meatballs to them because they can't come home for dinner."

Pippi introduces herself to Tommy and Annika and to the reader/listener in a fitting manner. The first glimpse they catch of her is when she proceeds down the road with one foot on the sidewalk and one foot in the gutter, unperturbed and seemingly oblivious of her new audience. Her action is child's play, of course, but like her parentage, it characterizes her. Pippi straddles the realm of the conventional, proper, and acceptable and the realm of the unconventional, improper and unacceptable. She lives at the periphery of town, in a no-man's land between the small town and the wide open sea. The daughter of an angel—as Pippi unsentimentally calls her mother, who died while giving birth to her—and a pirate and cannibal king, Pippi has inherited traits from both. She is intangible and invincible, but also down-to-earth and very human; she puts up a good fight, but at the same time she is peace loving and compassionate, and can secretly shed tears about a dead bird that has been kicked out of its nest.

To top off her introductory performance, Pippi retraces her steps backwards "because she didn't want to turn around to get home." This is a perfect fool's trick. By not doing the obvious, and by taking a step beyond the accepted, Pippi reveals the often invisible limits of freedom everybody accepts even in the freest societies. In defense of her action, Pippi argues: "Why did I walk backward? . . . Isn't this a free country? Can't a person walk any way she wants to?" Thanks to her superhuman powers and her wealth of imagination, Pippi can walk as she pleases. Tommy and Annika, who observe the spectacle from their securely fenced in yard, can only look aghast and marvel at a freedom they will never possess.

Through Pippi, Tommy and Annika—and the reader, as well—meet chaos and adventure in the safe and enjoyable form of illusion and spectacle. Pippi's wild imagination, wit, and energy provide an environment which is exhilarating and at times unsettling. Pippi becomes a part of their lives that they do not want to be without. Her performances and stories may be tall, and her presence may be domineering, but she is never dominating. The power she represents is not the static power of domination, which easily gives way to abuse. Pippi is a sworn enemy of all violence and of any abuse of power. Despite her sable swinging and pistol shooting, Pippi practices non-violence. Usually her reprisals take the form of a circus performance. She simply lifts up rogues and bullies and throws them high up in the air a few times; when they come down they are nonplussed and usually not quite the same as before. Pippi's dynamic power appears as an enabling energy which is shared between the powerful and powerless in order to decrease the gap between them. Wit and humor help her in this pursuit.

The incongruity of the tall tale, in which events disguised as facts are taken far beyond the limits of credibility, is reflected and intensified in the language of the Pippa books. In the guise of Pippi, Lindgren subverts society's suppressive forces through the playful manipulation of language. Substitutions and inversions, distortions and exaggerations appear in the smallest building blocks of language, in single words and names. They intrude into the sentence structure and grammatical logic, and they are equally omnipresent on the conceptual level.

Unfortunately, much of the playfulness and wealth of connotations are lost or misrepresented in the English translation. Thus, the word "pippi" means crazy or nuts in Swedish. Multiplication is deformed into "pluttification" by Pippi. The pun unfortunately gets lost in the translation. A correct semantic rendering would be "fartification." The name of Pippi's house, Villa Villekulla, evokes not only a playful mood with its alliterations, but also associations and connotations in Swedish. The Swedish "villa" comes close to beautiful mansion, but Pippi lives in a rather dilapidated old house. Calling it "villa," however, is in line with Pippi's propensity for exaggeration and tall tales. "Ville" can be associated both with "vilja" ("will, desire")—and Pippi definitely has a strong will—and with "villa bort, vilse" ("confuse"), which is Pippi's favorite pastime. "Kulla" makes me think of other closely related words. "Kulle" means hill, "kul" means fun, "spela kull" means to play tag, "omkull" means overturned, toppled.

Overturning rules and conventions and inventing something new is Pippi's favorite pastime. One morning, Pippi, the ever-creative thinker and tinkerer, invents a new word, which she considers—with her characteristic absence of modesty—to be the best word she has ever heard. The word is "spink." Now, after having invented the word, what is she going to do with it? The only thing she knows about it is that it does not mean vacuum cleaner. That sets her off on a search for the meaning of "spink" which is considerably more high-spirited, illustrative and fun than any crash course on Saussure's arbitrariness of the relationship between signifier and signified. In her quest, Pippi manages to embarrass a few townspeople who dare not admit their ignorance (a well-known theme from the emperor's new clothes). But eventually, after many unsatisfactory attempts to find the absent signified, she decides on a whim that a beetle that happens to cross her path is the "spink." By virtue of this act of naming, Pippi undoes the authority of the "bunch of old professors," who, according to her, "decided in the beginning what all words should mean." Pippi also revolts against the tyranny of logic on the level of sentence structure. Pippi and Lindgren keep their audience on their toes with a sentence like: "Even if there aren't any ghosts, they don't need to go round scaring folks out of their wits, I should think." Throughout the story, common sense is turned into un-common sense straddling the narrow line between sense and nonsense.

The most profound and pervasive trait in *Pippi Longstocking* is Pippi's penchant for the extraordinary and her nonchalant approach to the distinction between fact and fiction, between truth and lies. Watching a melodramatic theatre performance, she storms the stage to save the heroine from the brute villain. On the other hand, life for her is just a stage on which she herself performs her stunts and sommersaults.

In Pippi's world of fiction, truth and lies are indiscernably and inseparably interwoven. One can never quite be sure whether Pippi is serious or not. She tells one fib or tall story after another, does everything backwards, and laughs at others and herself. As a matter of fact, neither Tommy and Annika nor the reader/listener can ever be quite sure of her. Pippi eludes total comprehension and so does the story. The heroine's and the story's inner contradiction and ambiguity distance the story from any sort of didacticism. Its playful intermingling of sense and nonsense and its denial of any demarcation between the two makes reading and understanding *Pippi Longstocking* a challenging pleasure in the sense that Roland Barthes has defined the pleasure of reading.

Pippi readily admits to Annika that it is very bad to lie, but at the same time she feels no pangs of conscience about making up tall stories. She is what Ingmar Bergman's Alexander is not allowed to be in the film *Fanny and Alexander*. As a very normal child in a social environment that cannot tolerate blurred lines between fact and fiction or between truth and falsehood, Alexander is severely reprimanded for lying when he makes up stories like the ones Pippi spews forth. Pippi, however, merrily straddles the grey zones between fact and illusion and goes unpunished.

In the chapter "Pippi Sits on the Gate and Climbs a Tree," Pippi tells a girl who happens to pass by an incredible story about Hai Shang from Shanghai, who had more children than he could count. In this story and many others, Lindgren takes little bits and pieces from the narrative tradition for children and combines them into a collage that becomes the new story. Peter, one of Hai Shang's children, is pig-headed and does not want to eat a swallow's nest. The story develops just like the "Suppenkasper" story in Struwwelpeter. Peter dies because he refuses to eat what he is served. The story itself makes fun of the moralistic "Suppenkasper" story and its frightening elements. There are more turns to the tale, however, as Lindgren topicalizes the reception of the story. The girl who listens to the story is first reprimanded for not believing what Pippi tells her. A second later she is reprimanded for believing that a child can live without food from May until October: "To be sure, I know they can get along without food for three or four months all right. But from May to October! It's just foolish to think that. You must know that's a lie. You mustn't let people fool you so easily." The girl leaves utterly confused, and Tommy, Annika, and the reader/listener, too, may be a little dizzy from Pippi's logical sommersaults. But teasing, impish Pippi is also a loving, warm friend, and Tommy and Annika can be sure she will always stand by them and defend them. Pippi is their entertainer, their distorting mirror, and their guiding star, twinkling with wit and irony.

Thanks to her superhuman strength, Pippi not only tells tall tales, she performs them, too. Thus, she subdues various strongmen, saves small children from a burning house, and emerges victorious in fights with a bull, sharks, and a boa constrictor. All these heroic deeds are performed with a flair for theatricality so that the show itself, rather than the deed, becomes the central focal point. Thus, the chapter heading "Pippi Acts as a Lifesaver" is to the point. To Pippi, life is a circus in which she performs continu-

ously. That is why the concepts of circus and theatre are alien to her. Pippi does not need a compensatory entertainment industry that is part of the cultural differentiation in industrialized societies. As a result, she falls asleep during the performances of the "real" circus that has come to town once she is no longer participating herself. But during her performances she keeps the audience spellbound and roaring with laughter in the best tradition of a circus clown. With her potato nose, her shoes twice the size of her feet, her red hair sticking straight out from her head, and her hodge-podge of ill-fitting clothes, Pippi certainly has the looks of a clown.

Her red hair, freckles, and de facto orphanhood also make her remarkably similar to characters such as Anne of Green Gables and numerous other heroines in nineteenth and early twentieth-century girl's books that are familiar to her readers. When *Pippi Longstocking* first appeared in Sweden in 1945, it upset readers' expectations by inverting value patterns, role models, and the stereotypical uniformity and predictability of the traditional girl's book. Just as Pippi had done with Villa Villekulla, Lindgren turned a few things upside down and brought new life to the old, dilapidated house of the girl's book that had once been new and respectable. It is probably no coincidence that Pippi resembles the heroines of some girl's books, but she could not be farther removed from these models in her behavior and her state of mind. She loves her freckles and does not suppress her imagination or her pride in the least. A totally emancipated girl, she can and does mock and parody the narrow-mindedness of bourgeois norms and values and defies all authority with exuberant irreverence.

In part then, *Pippi Longstocking* is a parody of the nineteenth-century girl's book. Pippi feigns ignorance and uses her role as outsider—a world traveller who is unfamiliar with bourgeois behavioral codes—to make fun of society ladies, teachers, and other representatives of law and social order. She imitates them not in order to become accepted into this institution, but to ridicule social games by playing these games to the extreme. In response to a formal invitation to the Settergrens' for coffee and cake, Pippi takes the demands of the social role imposed on her in that situation more than seriously, thereby undermining the social codes. As is the custom, Pippi dresses up for the occasion. She has combed her hair, but it is even more unwieldy than usual; she has painted her face white, used a lot of red lipstick, and dressed in a fancy dress which does not fit her. The final result is that she looks even more like a clown. In accordance with her image, she dives straight into the cream pie, pours sugar on the floor, gets into everybody's way, and is a perfect parody of the assembled ladies both in looks and behavior. When not telling tall tales, she mocks the discourse of this social gathering. By treating the accepted social codes and discourse as a performance, she reveals the artifice of the parodied model and its demands to represent reality and normalcy.

Pippi wears "the popular mask of a bewildered fool" that Bakhtin assigns to Socrates as the central hero of the novelistic, carnivalesque genre. This produces her wise ignorance, which uncovers, familiarizes, and dismembers conventions and the emptiness of small talk. Like all clowns, Pippi is awkwardly graceful or gracefully awkward. She dives into pies and stumbles into puddles, yet she can walk a tightrope with ease and climbs trees and rocks as quickly and nimbly as her monkey. She has one further characteristic of a clown, an inner sadness and solitude that is hidden under a thick layer of merrymaking. The last glimpse the reader catches of Pippi from the warm comfort of Tommy and Annika's home reveals some of the loneliness of the outsider and the sadness of someone whose life reveals a fundamental emptiness. When her two friends see her, she is unaware of being observed and is not performing: "Pippi was sitting at the table with her head propped against her arms. She was staring at the little flickering flame of a candle that was standing in front of her. She seemed to be dreaming. 'She—she looks so alone,' said Annika."

The foremost task of a clown or a storyteller is to entertain and to amuse us. As Freud has demonstrated, however, humor can also be therapeutic; and depending on the need of the reader/listener and the cultural matrix within which it is situated, it can either be affirmative or subversive of the status quo. While Pippi entertains and delights her audience, she also helps them to endure situations of stress, anger, and fear. She helps them assert themselves against various oppressive forces—be they the forces of a threatening unknown looming overhead or the forces of oppressive norms and conventions.

Pippi Longstocking was greeted with a wave of protest in 1946. Critics called it demoralizing and contrived. Moral indignation no longer colors reactions to Pippi, but two opposing views still prevail in the secondary literature and in reviews. Literary critics on the "left" like Eva Adolfsson, Ulf Ericksson, and Birgitta Holm regard Lindgren's books as fundamentally escapist and affirmative of middle class values. Other critics make Pippi into the prototype of an anti-authoritarian, subversive children's novel. Winfried Freund finds emancipatory qualities in Pippi's spontaneity and her caricatures and parodies that can lead to the "dissolution of the solidification of norms."

One of the most controversial questions raised lately about humor is the question whether it is subversive or affirmative. Followers of Bakhtin and his concept of the dialogic and the carnivalesque believe in the former. About laughter as emancipatory force Bakhtin writes: "As it draws an object to itself and makes it familiar, laughter delivers the object into the fearless hands of investigative experiment— both scientific and artistic—and into the hands of free experimental fantasy." Barthes has argued instead that carnivalesque tendencies lose their emancipatory tendencies in a society in which there seems to be an ongoing carnival, a society which is "amusing itself to death," as Neil Postman has put it. For *Pippi Longstocking,* both views are justified. The Pippi books were long ago accepted in school curricula, and the original impetus of revolt against the stuffy and highly regulated bourgeois childhood, found in Pippi, has lost its edge on account of

ongoing social developments. But Pippi's ambiguous, elusive personality, which is full of contradictions and self-irony, cannot very easily be put at the service of any hegemonic cultural or educational apparatus. Not unless the character of Pippi is changed so that Pippi becomes a pastiche of herself. Unfortunately, that happened when the stories about Pippi were translated into a Hollywood film in 1988. There she became a mere shadow of herself, and her original creative spark and exuberance were transformed into flat, stereotyped merrymaking and sentimental show business. In the original (or original translation), I believe, Pippi cannot fall prey to the "dominance of stereotypes" that Barthes tells us are enforced by petit-bourgeois culture, because she attacks these very same stereotypes and reveals the artificiality and arbitrariness of the sense-making process by juggling with established cultural codes in a highly skilled, artistic way.

In the end, it is the reader/listener who will make the humor in *Pippi Longstocking* either affirmative or emancipatory. The reader can laugh both with and at Pippi. Lindgren's humor becomes culturally redundant if it is understood as playful inversion. Pippi's errors in language or logic are funny because the readers/listeners know better. They can laugh at Pippi's "stupidity" when she mispronounces words or assumes that walking backwards is easier than turning around. Pippi's instantaneous and tremendous popularity can probably be traced to the fact that she is a compensatory figure for the readers/listeners, just as she is for Tommy and Annika. But her humor is also subversive because of its fresh, unusual look from the periphery or from the "odd" or "out"-side. Pippi's tendency to equate all school knowledge with "pluttification" (i.e., "fartification") and her outsmarting the teacher at school ridicules the quantification of knowledge and formal learning outside of any practical context. When Pippi refuses to acknowledge the symbol of the letter "i" and calls it "a straight line with a little fly speck over it," she delights the reader/listener who has just accomplished the difficult task of learning to read and write, but she also raises questions about the relationship between signified and signifier for those readers whose relatively stable language skill and knowledge of the semiotic framework enables them to handle the subversion of cultural codes and conventions through parody and irony. She does not even spare her own birthday party, which becomes a parody of the already parodied coffee party at Mrs. Settergren's.

Read in the 1980s in conjunction with debates about postmodernism, Pippi stands out as the post-modern character par excellence. The role model with which the reader identifies is that of the ultimate child and the ultimate grown-up in one person. She is a wise fool who subverts for the sake of subversion and makes life into an endless game. Pippi is a true "Thing-Finder" and tinkerer, misusing utilitarian objects and basically making her environment into one single tinker toy. With her sophisticated and studied imbecility, she reads the world against the grain. Pippi is full of inconsistencies and contradictions, which are enhanced by her refusal to separate neatly between fact and fiction and life and stage. The perspective mediated by Pippi to the reader/listener is that of a child situated in an eternal present. Pippi does not see any ultimate value in growth and development; instead, she seeks it in the play of things. As a consequence, she decides in the end to remain a child and never to grow up.

Children's need to free themselves from constricting conventions may not be quite as strong and as sharply delineated in the 1980s as it was in 1945 when *Pippi* was first published, for a strong wave of anti-authoritarian education has given children greater freedom, independence, and responsibility. As concerns behavioral codes, children have moved a little closer to the state of total freedom Pippi enjoys and they have more choices as consumers than their counterparts thirty or forty years ago, but they are still far enough removed from power to be able to see in Pippi the embodiment of all their desires. On the contrary, one could even argue that today's child is just as removed from Pippi's state of freedom as were the children of the forties and fifties. Today's children live in a highly mediatized and thoroughly structured world in which the opportunities for intense primary experiences and uncontrolled action are fewer than ever. In a society

in which internalized norms and values imposed by the state and consumerism continue to supervise and direct the movement of each citizen in a new form of hidden paternalism, the anarchistic, joyous vitality of Pippi still remains a wonderful and funny device for compensation and inspiration.

📖 *BILL BERGSON, MASTER DETECTIVE* (1952)

Virginia Kirkus' Bookshop Service

SOURCE: A review of *Bill Bergson, Master Detective,* in *Virginia Kirkus' Bookshop Service,* Vol. XX, No. 14, July 15, 1952, p. 411.

Comically styled young sleuthings translated from the Swedish and set in a small town in Sweden. At the beginning of summer Bill and his two friends, Anders Bengsstrom and Eva Lotta Linders—an actively eager trio ready to pounce on suspense at the drop of a hat—encounter a

From The Tomten, *adapted by Astrid Lindgren. Illustrated by Harald Wiberg.*

new element in their lives in the person of mysterious Uncle Einar, itinerant cousin to Mrs. Lisander. Bill's suspicions are aroused at such activities of Uncle Einar's as writing to people in care of the General Delivery in Stockholm, his lock picking in the basement of some old castle ruins in their town. At the end of the summer, the course of which is further highlighted by a home made circus performance, and a crook catching rivalry with three contemporaries, Bill, Anders and Eva Lotta are heroes in a speedy automobile chase that lands Einar, two pals and some stolen jewels. Pleasant thrills.

Lavinia R. Davis

SOURCE: "Busy Summer," in *The New York Times Book Review,* Part II, November 16, 1952, p. 35.

Bill Bergson and his two best friends, Anders and Eva-Lotta, play out this story during a wonderful summer, in which they give an amateur circus, invent war games and chase three jewel thieves. Bill had often thought and dreamed of himself as Master Detective Bergson, but when he actually discovered stolen jewels it was the surprise and shock of his 13-year-old life.

This book comes from Sweden, where the author is probably the most popular writer for children. The characterization and the setting are good, the episodes credible. The book is distinguished by an atmosphere of high good humor which invests every aspect of the story.

📖 *BILL BERGSON LIVES DANGEROUSLY* (1954)

Virginia Kirkus' Bookshop Service

SOURCE: A review of *Bill Bergson Lives Dangerously,* in *Virginia Kirkus' Bookshop Service,* Vol. XXII, No. 15, August 1, 1954, p. 489.

Bill Bergson, the friendly Swedish boy of *Bill Bergson, Master Detective* is on his merrily haphazard way again— with his pals Anders and Eva Lotta. In their small home town (where they caught a jewel thief in the last story), the kids who call themselves the White Roses have a friendly rivalry with another bunch, the Reds, and their town and country skirmishes lead to a mystery. For while hiding near Green, the money lender's house, Eva Lotta finds an I.O.U. It later helps to convict a culprit, anxiety-ridden Claus, of shady dealings to repair his debt with Green. Light mystery-light reading in a jolly Scandanavian setting.

Lavinia R. Davis

SOURCE: "White Rose Knights," in *The New York Times Book Review,* Part II, November 14, 1954, p. 32.

Readers of Astrid Lindgren's earlier *Bill Bergson, Master Detective,* will need no introduction to Bill's habit of combining a day dream of super-detection with active participation in the rough-and-ready affairs of his village gang. Bill, Eva-Lotta and Anders, self-styled Knights of the White Rose, are at their best in this brisk and wholly credible adventure that leads to the capture of a real murderer.

The author is writing about a village in her native Sweden, but her characters are so real and her emotional values so universal that the young reader will feel as though the action of the story had just taken place in his own home town.

John Daniel Stahl

SOURCE: "Imaginative Uses of Secrecy in Children's Literature: *Bill Bergson Lives Dangerously,*" in *Triumphs of the Spirit in Children's Literature,* edited by Francelia Butler and Richard Rotert, Library Professional Publications, 1986, pp. 38-9.

Secrecy is a means for fictional characters to create a meaningful sense of self, frequently in productive, not necessarily hostile, opposition to grown-ups or rivals. One value of such themes lies in children's being encouraged to imagine similar sources of self-awareness in their own lives. In Astrid Lindgren's *Bill Bergson Lives Dangerously* some of the appeals of secret signs, secret languages, and secret organizations are made more explicit than in many books for children, surely one of the reasons for the popularity of Lindgren's work. The book opens with the war of the Red Roses against the White Roses, and it becomes clear that the war and the mystery surrounding it, especially the secrecy about the totemic object called the Great Mumbo, are ways of introducing purpose and entertainment into random, dull experience: "Bill grinned contentedly. The War of the Roses, which with short interruptions had been raging for several years, was nothing one voluntarily denied oneself. It provided excitement and gave real purpose to the summer vacation, which otherwise might have been rather monotonous."

The Whites (with whom the story is primarily concerned) have a secret language, which involves doubling each consonant and placing an "o" in between. The Whites can flaunt their identity with their secret language: "There was no surer way of annoying the Reds. Long and in vain they had tried to decipher this remarkable jargon which the Whites spoke with the greatest facility, chattering at such insane speed that to the uninitiated it sounded like perfect babel." When the Reds capture and interrogate Anders, the leader of the Whites, he does not reveal any secrets under "torture."

Lindgren's narrative perspective does not disguise adult awareness of children's maintenance of secrets. In fact, it acknowledges secrecy as the child's way of creating self-identity; but the open, indulgent attitude of the adult narrator defuses potential conflicts between generations. Eva-

Lotta, a member of the Whites, meets her mother in the market place. When asked where she is going, Eva-Lotta says, "'That I must not tell. . . . I'm on a secret mission. Terribly secret mission!'" Despite Eva-Lotta's refusal to tell, the exchange between mother and daughter is affectionate and amusing:

> Mrs. Lisander smiled at Eva-Lotta.
>
> "I love you," she said.
>
> Eva-Lotta nodded approvingly at this indisputable statement and continued on her way across the square, leaving a trail of cherry stones behind her.

Her mother's acceptance of Eva-Lotta's right to have secrets is a liberating, loving attitude. That the secret mission represents the development of an independent personality is suggested by Mrs. Lisander's concerned thoughts about her daughter: "How thin the girl looked, how small and defenceless somehow! It wasn't very long since that youngster had been eating biscuit porridge, and now she was tearing about on 'secret errands'—was that all right, or ought she to take better care of her?"

But Eva-Lotta's experiences are narrated also from a perspective that implies the child's need and ability to face danger on her own. For a while, a secret box, containing mysterious documents, is the object of an entertaining struggle between the Reds and the Whites. But secrecy only comes into full play in a dangerous situation when Eva-Lotta is alone with a murderer in an abandoned house. The murderer has every reason to kill her: she holds the key to knowledge of his guilt. When Anders and Bill arrive in this frightening situation, she communicates with them through secret signs: with the danger sign, then with a song in secret code that tells the boys that the man is a murderer. The boys respond with another secret sign (pinching the lobes of their ears) which means that they have picked up the information. Here, quite explicitly, children have to protect themselves from harm from the adult world through the code they have created. Secrecy is necessary for self-preservation. . . .

Lindgren, like many other of the best of children's authors, is able to convey the comic incongruities of childhood experiences without diminishing their significance. In the final chapter of **Bill Bergson Lives Dangerously,** after the murderer has been captured, the Whites teach the Reds their secret language. Bill explains why: "'We can't have it on our consciences, letting the Reds walk about in such dreadful ignorance. They'll be absolutely done for if they ever get mixed up with a murderer.'" Though that statement may strike an adult reader as comic, murder is not minimized in the book. Eva-Lotta's reaction to finding the body of the murderer's victim is a state of shock that realistically lasts several days. Despite the implausibilities of the plot, the theme of secrecy is treated with a seriousness that does justice to its importance as a means of achieving identity and as a defense against the danger of harm by powerful adversaries.

MIO, MY SON (1956)

Margaret Sherwood Libby

SOURCE: A review of *Mio, My Son,* in *New York Herald Tribune Book Review,* January 13, 1957, p. 10.

The very chapter headings sing in Astrid Lindgren's new book: He Travels by Day and by Night. Do the Stars Care If You Play to Them? The Well That Whispers at Night. The Deepest Cave in the Blackest Mountain, and finally "Mio, My Son" which is also the title. It is a fairy tale that is beautiful, poetic, and true, with that deepest truth of meaning rather than incident. Little, unloved Andy is magically taken from Stockholm to Farawayland where he is welcomed as Mio, the cherished son of the King. His desperate yearning satisfied, he lives among the roses, silver poplars, white birds and twinkling stars, with a best friend Pompoo, and Miramis, a white horse with a golden mane, the gift of his father. Becoming strong and brave, he fares forth to challenge the wicked Sir Kato, the terrible and mighty enemy of all Farawayland.

The opening paragraph catches the reader's attention immediately: "Did you hear them asking for news of a boy who had disappeared? The Stockholm police are looking for a nine-year-old boy. Karl Anders Nilsson. He disappeared completely. No one knows where. Nobody knows except me, for I am Karl Anders Nilsson." What ten-year-old can fail to read on whether he enjoys fantasies or prefers adventurous naughtiness like Mrs. Lindgren's beloved *Pippi Longstocking?* Indeed young or old will be moved by the deep sense of security and happiness. They will love Andy, share his exciting struggle with the cruel spies and Sir Kato, and rejoice when "all is well with him." Written with beauty and skill, deftly translated [by Marianne Turner] and illustrated in black and white [by Ilon Wikland] with just the right feeling, this is a book to cherish.

Margaret Mahon

SOURCE: A review of *Mio, My Son,* in *The Saturday Review,* New York, Vol. XL, No. 7, February 16, 1957, p. 53.

Andy is in Farawayland. "He's in a place where the silver poplars rustle . . . where the fires glow and warm at night . . . where there is Bread That Satisfies Hunger" . . . where he can ride Miramis, the beautiful white horse with the golden mane, and play with Pompoo, the son of the rose gardener . . . and, "where he has his father, the King who loves him, and whom he loves." But in order to stay here Andy had to fight singlehanded and kill with a "fearsome" sword the cruel Sir Kato. All this is told in *Mio, My Son,* an allegorical fairytale of exquisite and rare beauty with drawings by an artist of the same sensitive mind as the author.

📖 *PIPPI GOES ON BOARD* (1956)

Margaret Sherwood Libby

SOURCE: "Jolly Pippi, Gnomes and a Leprechaun," in *New York Herald Tribune Book Review,* November 17, 1957, p. 24.

"Pippilotta Delicatessa Windowshade Mackrelmint Efraim's Daughter Longstocking, daughter of Captain Efraim Longstocking, formerly the Terror of the Sea, now a cannibal king," is back, and all the girls and quite a few boys in the eight to eleven group are saying, "Oh, good, when can we read it?" Absurd, funny, and tender-hearted as ever, she's still as rich as a troll with a suitcase full of gold coins which enable her to have a most lavish shopping expedition with her friends Annika and Tommy. She has a short, a very short experience at school, because she believes that on fine days the only "shun" one should have is recreation, but she does go on a school picnic and to a fair. The tall tales she tells, of the man in Batavia, for instance, whose eyes were so red that the police refused to let him on the street because people might think he was a stop sign, entranced her friends. Not only does she tell of all the desert islands she has been shipwrecked on, but stages a most convincing shipwreck for them to share. When she was almost ten, however, and had "seen her best days," Captain Longstocking came in his boat, the "Hoptoad," and Pippi went on board. No wonder Annika and Tommy cried bitterly. Nothing ever happens in an ordinary way around Pippi, not even a farewell party or departure for the cannibal isles, though she said she thought it "surely best for little children to lead an orderly life, especially if they order it themselves." Superior nonsense. A book for every child's library, one that gives the most satisfying release to youngsters who are a bit more circumscribed in their everyday lives than the exuberant Pippi.

Lavinia R. Davis

SOURCE: "Gloriously Uninhibited," in *The New York Times Book Review,* Part II, November 17, 1957, p. 36.

Here is another hilarious story about Swedish Pippi Longstocking who is stronger than a horse, rich as a troll and gloriously uninhibited. When Tommy and Annika first met Pippi she was living at Villa Villekulla, with her money for company, awaiting her father's return from the sea. The purchase and consumption of thirty-six pounds of candy; the rescue of an exhausted horse (which Pippi carried home to its stall); a decidedly unconventional day at school; the capture of an escaped tiger and the defeat of the village bully are a few of the things with which Pippi occupied herself and her friends during Captain Longstocking's absence. When he finally arrived at Villa Villakulla, the Captain was determined to take Pippi to the cannibal island of which he had recently been made king. Tommy and Annika were desolated at the prospect

of losing their amazing friend. But the story ends on a happy and uproarious note.

Although this is frankly a slapstick modern tall tale which was primarily intended to entertain, Mrs. Lindgren is far more successful in transmitting the virtues of generosity and loyalty than many more pretentious and moralistic writers.

Louis Glanzman's black-and-white drawings are in excellent keeping with the crisp, unsentimental prose. Warmly recommended.

📖 *PIPPI IN THE SOUTH SEAS* (1957)

Margaret Sherwood Libby

SOURCE: A review of *Pippi in the South Seas,* in *New York Herald Tribune Book Review,* November 1, 1959, p. 5.

In her fine uninhibited way Pippi Longstocking manages, at the beginning of this latest book, to be shockingly rude to a stupid, obtuse man who would have been nasty to the children if he could have managed it, chatters far too much at a coffee party as she tries to cheer up her friends' dear old Aunt Laura and is saucy to an old quizbody who comes to school intending to shame children who cannot answer her questions. This exaggerated rudeness is fun. Eight to ten year olds glow with the consciousness that they *never* behave as badly and yet secretly enjoy the enormity of it all. For as Mrs. Settergren said when she allowed her children to go to the South Seas with Pippi despite her outrageous actions, "Pippi Longstocking's manners may not always be what they ought to. But her heart is in the right place." Warmhearted, crazy Pippi then gives the Settergren children a marvelous time on Kurrekurreduth Island (sharks, pearls and long-distance spitting contests) where her father is King, and even manages an untimely Christmas party back in Sweden when they return. All gorgeously, sensibly absurd, and a sure cure for frustrations. No wonder Pippi is popular all over the world today—she's as prime a favorite with youngsters in the Soviet Union as here and in her native Sweden—for as long as there are serious tasks to be done it is fun to watch Pippi kick over the traces.

Gertrude P. Lancaster

SOURCE: A review of *Pippi in the South Seas,* in *The Christian Science Monitor,* November 5, 1959, p. 6B.

"Sugar and spice and all things nice. That's what little girls are made of." And very charming they are, these demure, starched little girls. But don't forget the spice. Astrid Lindgren hasn't. Her Pippi Longstocking is all spice, and the ginger isn't confined to her hair. Pippi is a tomboy. Pippi can discomfit the bossy, outwit the bullying or, if wit fails, she just happens to be the strongest little girl in the world. A meeting between Pippi and her father is a brave sight. He throws Pippi into the air. Pippi throws him into the air. It is the suddenly unexpected, the hilarious gravely introduced, illogical logic, straightfaced riddles, wild good humor that make this collection of short stories just right for a certain type of 8–12-year-old.

Lavinia R. Davis

SOURCE: "Leaving an Impression," in *The New York Times Book Review,* January 3, 1960, p. 16.

Any reappearance of Astrid Lindgren's irrepressible character, Pippi Longstocking, is cause for celebration. This particular installment in which Pippi takes her friends, Tommy and Annika, to the island of Kurrekurredutt which is ruled by her father, Captain Longstocking, is no exception.

From the moment Pippi walks off the boat carrying her horse over her shoulder, the children of Kurrekurredutt are her admiring devotees. Their admiration grows when she rescues a boy from a man-eating shark by simply holding the great fish in the air and "talking sense to it." By the time Pippi outwits, and it must be added, outmuscles, two thieves who are after the children's pearl marbles they are her willing slaves.

By setting the first and last part of the book in Pippi's home in Sweden, Mrs. Lindgren successfully establishes her characters for readers unfamiliar with her earlier Pippi stories. Also in the Swedish scenes, especially the one in which Pippi uses a spell against growing up, the author demonstrates her gift for creating hilarious fantasy and genuine feeling.

📖 *RASMUS AND THE VAGABOND* (1960; British edition as *Rasmus and the Tramp*)

Virginia Kirkus' Service

SOURCE: A review of *Rasmus and the Vagabond,* in *Virginia Kirkus' Service,* Vol. XXVIII, No. 3, February 1, 1960, p. 90.

Rasmus, within the confines of his Swedish orphanage, dreams of a family which will overlook his stubbornly straight hair, and will love him. When he runs away, he meets Oscar, a carefree vagabond. Together they share many adventures, and when Rasmus finally finds a family which will adopt him, he is too deeply attached to his comrade of the roads to forsake him. The child and man, who now share a deep love for one another, decide to follow the road together permanently, and, to Rasmus' delight, the road leads to a modest, but loving home. Rasmus has all the appeal of the spirited and neglected orphan and his sentimental alliance with a hobo is handled with a winning freshness.

Pamela Marsh

SOURCE: A review of *Rasmus and the Vagabond,* in *The Christian Science Monitor,* May 12, 1960, p. 3B.

Orphans can be dangerous, especially when they are drawn with controlled sweetness, in words as skillful as Mrs. Lindgren's. These children creep into the reader's heart, refusing to stay confined between the covers of the book. Rasmus, the little boy who runs away from an orphanage because no one seems to want a straight-haired boy, is as enchantingly touching as the child in the French movie *The Red Balloon.* Happily the tramp he meets is Oscar, honest, happy, though rather an unconventional guardian. "I've already had a bath . . . last year, in honor of our royal family . . . I don't want to do that over again." An adventure with bandits, more frightening in atmosphere than in deeds, ripens their mutual affection, and just when it seems that there can be no happy ending the unexpected happens naturally, satisfyingly, and rather movingly. This is the kind of book grownups enjoy too, and it may be that books good enough to appeal to them are the only ones fit for our 8–12-year-olds.

The Junior Bookshelf

SOURCE: A review of *Rasmus and the Tramp,* in *The Junior Bookshelf,* Vol. 25, No. 4, October, 1961, p. 227.

This author has already exhibited a rough and unbridled form of expression in some stories but here she has regulated and controlled her writing and ideas so that the finer and more imaginative aspects of her work shine through. This is the story of an orphan who runs away in search of a home and a mother and father of his own and in his search becomes the friend, and ultimately the son, of a tramp. There is some very good characterisation with plenty of depth, shades and overtones. Only the villains bring with them an aura of convention and the stereotyped to mar the freshness and the originality. There is too a certain healthy philosophy of life that seems to grow naturally from the country setting and this gives rise to some poetic writing that adds charm to the book. Only occasionally does the philosophy smack of licence and then the poetry too is disturbed and ruffled. One does wonder if the translator [Gerry Bothmer] has done justice to the original text which won the Hans Christian Andersen Medal. The production is attractive and the illustrations by Eric Palmquist convey both the quiet thoughtfulness and the vivacity of the text.

📖 *KATI IN PARIS* (1961)

Zena Sutherland

SOURCE: A review of *Kati in Paris,* in *Bulletin of the Center for Children's Books,* Vol. XIV, No. 9, May, 1961, p. 146.

First published in Sweden in 1953, a book about a Swedish girl who goes to Paris with her best friend and her fiancé. Kati tells her own story: she and Lennart marry in Paris, and they and Eva explore with relish the delights of Paris. They meet another Swedish visitor, and Peter attaches himself hopefully to Eva. Back in Stockholm, Kati describes the progress of the love affair between Eva and Peter, and she tells of her own joy at becoming a mother. The author presents Kati as a volatile, impetuous, and romantic young girl; as Kati tells the story, she becomes a little wearing in her ingenuous role. The writing is somewhat static, and the ending (Kati's thoughts about and to her newborn son) is quite saccharine.

The Junior Bookshelf

SOURCE: A review of *Kati in Paris,* in *The Junior Bookshelf,* Vol. 29, No. 5, October, 1965, pp. 292-93.

All the magic and mystery of Paris in the Spring forms the background for this happy story of Kati's wedding. Kati and Lennart decide to be married in Paris with Eva as bridesmaid. They all stay at a little student hotel in the Latin Quarter and Kati's romantic heart is overjoyed by the city and its story.

It struck me as rather odd that the actual wedding is not described at all and that the bridesmaid stayed on for the honeymoon but perhaps this will not worry the very young teenage girls for which the story must be intended. Also this triple honeymoon does introduce Eva to her own romance, a rather stormy one but with a happy ending just round the corner.

I hope the author will continue these stories about Kati and her baby; as well as being carefree and very romantic, Kati has some very sound ideas and can do the young nothing but good.

THE TOMTEN (1961)

Virginia Kirkus' Service

SOURCE: A review of *The Tomten,* in *Virginia Kirkus' Service,* Vol. XXIX, No. 21, November 1, 1961, p. 969.

Who is it that wanders the countryside on a snowy peaceful night in winter? It is the Tomten, a kindly whitebearded troll who whispers the promise of spring to all the animals in the farmyard. Too bad only animals, not children, can understand Tomten language, for the little troll cannot communicate his message to the sleeping inhabitants of the farmhouse. That's all there is to it—yet the story's fascination is as surely felt as the secret words whispered by the Tomten, largely because of [illustrator] Harald Wiberg's darkly luminous rendition of a tranquil snowy farm with its one wakeful visitor. A reassuring bedtime treat with room for creative fantasy when the lights are dimmed.

Publishers Weekly

SOURCE: A review of *The Tomten,* in *Publishers Weekly,* Vol. 216, No. 25, December 24, 1979, p. 59.

Wiberg's lovely, full-color paintings convey the hushed atmosphere of night in the Swedish countryside and also the sweet charms of the Tomten. He is a tiny old troll who guards the farmer's house while the humans sleep. Lindgren has caught the spirit of a poem by Viktor Rydberg in her lyrical description of how the Tomten tiptoes about, reassuring cows and horses and cats and dogs and the other farm animals, promising that "Winters come and winters go . . . "; they will rejoice in summer again. The gentle story with its eye-filling scenes is an apt choice for bedtime read-alouds. . . .

M. Crouch

SOURCE: A review of *The Tomten,* in *The Junior Bookshelf,* Vol. 57, No. 1, February, 1993, p. 14.

Astrid Lindgren's story, based on a Swedish poem by Viktor Rydberg, is a little on the long side but is broken up by periodical passages in verse, translated from the secret and silent language in which the Tomten talks to the farm animals. The Tomten is a Scandinavian gnome, a solitary and nocturnal being dedicated to keeping the farm on an even keel. Harald Wiberg, who provides the pictures, is careful to avoid being too specific about the small hero of a gentle story, for each child will wish to create his own image. The soft colours of the snowbound farm in starlight set the scene most satisfactorily. It is a slight book but one which is curiously satisfying.

MISCHIEVOUS MEG (1962; British edition as Madicken)

Virginia Kirkus' Service

SOURCE: A review of *Mischievous Meg,* in *Virginia Kirkus' Service,* Vol. XXX, No. 3, February 1, 1962, p. 111.

Mayhem and merriment combine in equal doses and descend on the quiet little village of June Hill, Sweden, whenever mischievous Meg and her devoted follower, baby-sister-Betsy, decide to exercise their potent imaginations. Playing "Moses in the Bulrushes", creating a convenient scapegoat for all ills in the form of invisible Richard, soaring off into space on an umbrella handle (though alas winding up with a brain concussion) are a few aspects of life in one Swedish household. But even being bed-ridden has its compensations—gifts galore arrive making little Betsy wish she too could have a concussion. The delicious goodness in "bad" little girls comes rollicking through, thanks to the wit and charm of these gleeful episodes.

Alberta Eiseman

SOURCE: A review of *Mischievous Meg,* in *The New York Times Book Review,* May 27, 1962, p. 28.

The author of the ever popular **Pippi Longstocking** has created another entertaining heroine, one not quite as sensational as that appealing redhead, yet zany enough to keep readers chuckling happily.

Unlike Pippi, who lived alone except for a horse, a monkey and a suitcase full of gold pieces, Meg Peterson has a more conventional home life. She lives in a big red house in Sweden, right by a river where she loves to play. Of course the games occasionally get out of hand, like the time when Meg was the Pharaoh's daughter and baby Moses—played by younger sister Betsy—was dunked rather than rescued. Or the day the two sisters decided to have a picnic on the roof of the woodshed, and Meg thought she'd try to fly. Quite a girl, that Meg. She might make some weakhearted parents tremble, but her contemporaries will find her "neat." And both generations will appreciate the humor and warmth of this appealing Swedish family.

Virginia Haviland

SOURCE: A review of *Mischievous Meg,* in *The Horn Book Magazine,* Vol. XXXVIII, No. 3, June, 1962, p. 274.

This story by a favorite Swedish author stands out for its unusual vividness and reality of child emotion. It is not only the story of fourth-grade Meg, but that of five-year-old Betsy, too—of their play together and their perfectly natural sibling relationship, loving each other, but not without short-lived flare-ups of stubborn selfishness and anger. Meg has marked imagination for devising games, acting out stories, and getting herself and sister into danger-filled predicaments—which always have wise settlement by their loving and conscientious parents. Christmas, inspiring reflections of joy and unselfishness, fills one particularly delightful chapter.

Alice Dalgliesh

SOURCE: A review of *Mischievous Meg,* in *The Saturday Review,* New York, Vol. XLV, No. 28, July 21, 1962, p. 36.

The many young admirers of **Pippi Longstocking** will gravitate to this story by the same author; it is well written, cheerful, and occasionally amusing. Meg, not mischievous, but unable to foresee consequences, will appeal to little girls. But won't twelve-year-olds (or even tens) demand more plot and think it foolish that, at ten, Meg would jump off the roof with an umbrella and expect to land unhurt? (From the spirited picture it's a mercy she had only a concussion.) Madcap children are a European tradition, while ours are encouraged, at least in books, to

walk a straighter path, which is probably why they go with Pippi and Meg in imagination.

The Junior Bookshelf

SOURCE: A review of *Madicken,* in *The Junior Bookshelf,* Vol. 27, No. 3, July, 1963, p. 132.

There is warmth and humour in this charming story from Sweden of two little sisters, Madicken and Lisabet. Madicken is a tomboy whose bright ideas for games involve little Lisabet in awkward situations—as Moses in the bulrushes and Joseph down the well, for instance.

Is this story of an earlier generation based on the author's own childhood perhaps? It is obvious that Astrid Lindgren has not forgotten what it is like to be a child when Christmas is ecstasy and there are endless exciting things to do and see.

The relationship between the children and the adults is a warm and tender one and home is a place of security and affection. Little girls of 7 - 10 will enjoy this lively and amusing tale.

📖 **HAPPY TIMES IN NOISY VILLAGE** (1963; British edition as *Happy Days at Bullerby*)

Virginia Kirkus' Service

SOURCE: A review of *Happy Times in Noisy Village,* in *Virginia Kirkus' Service,* Vol. XXXI, No. 13, July 1, 1963, p. 599.

The frolics of six "cardboard" children take place on three adjoining farms, which the author states (in the person of Lisa, the nine year old narrator) make up Noisy Village. The times may be happy, but the events are meager and dull, and the overly intimate, babyish tone of the narrator is annoying—even embarrassing. The well-known Swedish author has slipped here, ending up only with a pot boiler, if that, in this sentimental book. An easy vocabulary for the backward reader.

Colin Field

SOURCE: A review of *Happy Days at Bullerby,* in *The School Librarian and School Library Review,* Vol. 13, No. 2, July, 1965, p. 244.

These brief domestic episodes about six Swedish children are pleasant, chatty and cosy. The book is described on the dust-jacket as 'A read aloud book' and there is certainly nothing in it to disturb even the most-coddled suburban child. But, not surprisingly, there is nothing in it to excite the liveliest intelligence or arouse the insensitive from their slumbers. A sensitive teacher or parent reading aloud these stories might find them down-right embarrassing in spite of their being the fruit of a sympathetic understanding of young children.

Harmless entertainment for seven- and eight-year-olds.

DIRK LIVES IN HOLLAND (1963)

Zena Sutherland

SOURCE: A review of *Dirk Lives in Holland,* in *Bulletin of the Center for Children's Books,* Vol. XVIII, No. 1, September, 1964, p. 14.

A book in which the photographs [by Anna Riwkin-Brick] predominate; they are mildly informative, fairly repetitive, and attractive—since they record the activities of a charming child. The text is slight, leaning heavily on the pictures; the style is simple—occasionally having a note that seems artificially ingenuous. Little about the story gives any flavor of the background of the Netherlands—nicely provided by the photographs—but focuses on Dirk's desire for a bicycle and his attainment of it at the close of the book.

KATI IN AMERICA (1964)

The Junior Bookshelf

SOURCE: A review of *Kati in America,* in *The Junior Bookshelf,* Vol. 28, No. 2, March, 1964, p. 101.

This is a lighthearted story [translated by Marianne Turner] of Kati's visit to America accompanied by her aunt. The aunt is a quite unbelievable character; button boots and ankle length dress seem a little out of place particularly when the aunt is proposed to and about to be married within a few weeks of touching American soil.

Kati is rather too slick; perhaps this may be due to the difficulty of translating idiomatic Swedish into English, but the story which is in the first person is rather jerky and sometimes difficult to follow. The description of what Kati sees and does in America is well done, it is when Kati is speaking her thoughts that the story seems to stumble.

Margery Fisher

SOURCE: A review of *Kati in America,* in *Growing Point,* Vol. 2, No. 9, April, 1964, p. 292.

[The] mood in which Astrid Lindgren has written *Kati in America* [is light hearted]; describing her twenty-one year old heroine, with her engaging interest in young men and her naïve self-criticism, in a gay, causal fashion that might make Kati, for many girls of fifteen or so, an agreeable change from the heroine of magazine stories. Nothing

much happens in the book. Kati goes on a trip with her stern Auntie (who relaxes into marriage at the end); she sees Washington with Bob, New Orleans with John, adores drug-stores, ignores politics, flattens her nose against the windows of Fifth Avenue stores, and returns cheerfully to Sweden and to Jan, her steady, at the end of a light, accomplished and entertaining book. Clearly, the author has remembered pretty successfully what it is like to be a girl footloose in a fascinating world and, as clearly, she has flattered her readers with a portrait they will all believe is of themselves as they might be one day.

THE CHILDREN ON TROUBLEMAKER STREET (1964; British edition as *The Mischievous Martens*)

Virginia Kirkus' Service

SOURCE: A review of *The Children on Troublemaker Street,* in *Virginia Kirkus' Service,* Vol. XXXII, No. 7, April 1, 1964, p. 362.

Jonas, Maria, and Lotta—Big Noise, Little Noise and Little Nut as their father calls them—are the three reasons for the street's name. Maria, second in rank to Jonas, narrates some of the comical accidents and involvements in their everyday lives. The prose is successfully imitative of a child's way of speaking to a degree, but at times becomes annoyingly precious and sing-songy in tone. Each happening is contained in a chapter, and chapters vary from highly to barely amusing. . . .

Superior to the author's recent **Happy Times in Noisy Village.**

Margery Fisher

SOURCE: A review of *The Mischievous Martens,* in *Growing Point,* Vol. 30, No. 3, September, 1991, pp. 5570-71.

[The following excerpt is from a review of the 1991 edition of The Mischievous Martens.*]*

Thirty years ago when these tales of a Swedish family were first published it was permissible to write about mischievous children without any implied social issues or dire suggestions of the deep significance of a tantrum or a disconcerting request from a junior member of a family. Today such considerations are almost obligatory in domestic tales for the middle years even when they are facetious or fanciful and though, happily, cheerfulness keeps breaking in, it is a relief to be able to enjoy wholeheartedly Astrid Lindgren's vigorous, uninhibited and shrewd portraits of the Marten children, personalities jostling for recognition while accepting the sensible rules and routine of everyday.

Lotta takes the lead in both books as she moves from the

age of three to a lively almost-six, exercising a talent for obstruction, a fertile imagination and a tenacity beyond her years as she fights for her right to share everything that the older Jonas and Maria get up to. To be sure of a place in their games she submits to be the patient of an eccentric doctor and nurse, acts the maid in the toyhouse in grandmother's garden and even accepts their insistence that being a pirate involves lying quite still under the bed. The authorial voice is heard in the background in the way her awkwardly direct questions and misunderstandings are expressed but the tone is observant rather than coy both in narrative and in the very natural dialogue. After Lotta has eaten all the pancakes which she had insisted on hanging up as leaves in the tree-house she issues her orders to Jonas and Maria:

> 'The pancake leaves are all gone. Now you have to start eating the green ones!'
>
> She ripped off a whole handful of green leaves and wanted us to eat them. But Jonas and I said that we weren't hungry any more.
>
> 'They taste all right if you put sugar and jam on them,' Lotta told us, and she put some jam and sugar on a green leaf and ate it.
>
> 'You'd better make sure there is no worm on that leaf Jonas said.
>
> 'The worm has to watch out for himself,' said Lotta.
>
> 'That kid has an answer for everything,' as Grandfather would say.

Maria, the narrator of **The Mischievous Martens,** puts Lotta's words and doings into relief by her rather smug side comments while the stable family background is implied in the protective if critical attitude which she and Jonas take to this persistent small sister while they get on with their own energetic lives; their seniority is subtly indicated in Maria's confident behaviour with their kindly neighbour Mrs. Berg and her ready understanding that Lotta ought not to call their cleaning lady by her surname without the correct prefix.

Lotta may be central in every episode but the picture of family life is broad and pertinent. . . .

📖 SPRINGTIME IN NOISY VILLAGE (1966)

Virginia Kirkus' Service

SOURCE: A review of *Springtime in Noisy Village,* in *Virginia Kirkus' Service,* Vol. XXXIV, No. 8, April 15, 1966, pp. 418-19.

The children of Noisy Village (this is their fourth book) may set your teeth on edge with their intense, hyper-wholesome pursuit of happiness, but they have become a staple with pre-schoolers. The springtime activities of the children vary from pastoral activities like picking flowers, sailing paper boats, and watching for baby farm animals to daring ones like jumping off the low roof of the woodshed and riding an immobile bull.

Mary Silva Cosgrave

SOURCE: A review of *Springtime in Noisy Village,* in *The Horn Book Magazine,* Vol. XLII, No. 4, August, 1966, pp. 426-27.

Bursting with merriment and mischief, the seven children of Noisy Village give spring a hale and hearty welcome. Springtime in Sweden, like spring everywhere, is a bounteous season. Calves and piglets and lambs arrive daily, snowdrops and crocuses and tulips bloom profusely, and, instinctively, children build playhouses, sail paper boats, splash through the mud, and invent feats of bravery, all with enviable abandon. With the same picture-book format as **Christmas in Noisy Village,** it may be younger in spirit, but it is just as festive and colorful.

📖 NOY LIVES IN THAILAND (1967)

The Junior Bookshelf

SOURCE: A review of *Noy Lives in Thailand,* in *The Junior Bookshelf,* Vol. 31, No. 6, December, 1967, p. 378.

One of the most attractive volumes by this experienced partnership [Lindgren and photographer Anna Riwkin-Brick] shows well the family life and poverty of the Thai peasants and their work in the ricefields, fishing and selling produce in Bangkok. One sees the characteristic waterways, streetsellers and temples of the capital. Though as usual a child's view of life, there is a better attempt here at a general picture of the people than in some of the earlier books in the series.

Zena Sutherland

SOURCE: A review of *Noy Lives in Thailand,* in *Bulletin of the Center for Children's Books,* Vol. 21, No. 8, April, 1968, pp. 130-31.

As in other books of this series about children the world over, this is a compilation of excellent photographs and an adequate text. The writing occasionally seems contrived to fit the pictures, but this is not omnipresent; the writing has a note of fondness, and often a note of humor. In describing Noy's family life and a trip she makes with her father to the Bangkok market, the book gives a considerable amount of information about Thai customs, foods, religion, et cetera. It also gives, happily, a stronger impression of similarities than it does of differences.

📖 *SEACROW ISLAND* (1968)

Kirkus Reviews

SOURCE: A review of *Seacrow Island,* in *Kirkus Reviews,* Vol. XXXII, No. 17, September 15, 1969, p. 1000.

"Of course it depends on what you like," old man Soderman tells Pelle about Carpenter's Cottage, which the Melkersons have rented for the summer—an assessment that applies to most of the 287 pages about their first two years on Seacrow Island. There will be many, many more: bumbling father Melker ("an author . . . more or less crazy"), Malin, a honey at nineteen, good pals Johan and Niklas, and "dear little animal" lover Pelle have found a home on the island and among the islanders, and, by chance and by charm, they beat our obstreperous parvenus to buy the cottage at the close. The fast action is long-delayed, but a youngster who drifts along through the first summer, marked mainly by father Melker's affectionately indulged incompetence and anxiety and the precocious pushiness of little Tjorven next door, will find that interest freshens when Pelle acquires a rabbit, Tjorven gets a baby seal, and her devoted St. Bernard Bosun gets jealous. The more romantic reader may take heart too when Tjorven and Stina, her rival for Pelle, produce a princely suitor for particular Malin ("before it's too late") by kissing a frog. It could be a sweet Scandinavian bracer if there weren't so much tedium to it.

Susanne Gilles

SOURCE: A review of *Seacrow Island,* in *School Library Journal,* Vol. 16, No. 5, January, 1970, p. 71.

An average, pleasant story about a modern-day Swedish family, showing how the family affects, and is affected by, life on a small island. The Melkersons (father, near-adult daughter Malin, teen sons Johan and Niklas, and seven-year-old son Pelle) have taken Carpenter's Cottage for the summer. Widower Melker, a writer, cares about his children but resembles the kind of bumbling father familiar to viewers of United States television. Malin is the one who really holds the family together, and young Pelle, animal lover, is quite worried when she falls in love, until he gets a puppy from the beau. Tjorven, an island child, is reminiscent of another of the author's characters, Pippi Longstocking, in her take-charge attitude toward life and Pelle. The generally quiet story even features a villain, whose attempt to buy the rented cottage out from under the Melkersons is thwarted by a deus ex machina finish, in which Papa Melker is suddenly given an unexplained grant of 25,000 crowns from the Swedish government. Though he fails to get to the real estate agent before said villain, Pelle and Tjorven have saved the day by contacting the owner and making a down payment of one crown. An introspective, quietly humorous view of a likeable community.

📖 *SKRALLAN AND THE PIRATES* (1969)

Kirkus Reviews

SOURCE: A review of *Skrallan and the Pirates,* in *Kirkus Reviews,* Vol. XXXVII, No. 20, October 15, 1969, p. 1108.

In effect if not intent a trailer for Mrs. Lindgren's latest novel, this photo album shows the assorted Saltcrow Islanders—Melker, Petter, Malin, Pelle, Johan, Niklas, Stina, Old Soderman, Tjorven, Teddy, Freddy, Nisse, Martha—engaged in various antics, the last and longest of which is playing at pirates. Three-year-old Skrallan doesn't understand what's going on, youngsters won't understand who's who, and neither of them will have lost out.

Pamela Marsh

SOURCE: A review of *Skrallan and the Pirates,* in *The Christian Science Monitor,* November 6, 1969, p. B10.

Saltcrow Island is a spot the 10-14's have come to know through Astrid Lindgren's stories about it. Now they can see the island as the cameras of Sven-Eric Deler and Stig Hallgren have recorded it—full of Swedish blues and golds. In fact *Skrallan and the Pirates* is a book for a family to share together.

The attraction of full-page, full-color photographs of children, sea, and the island itself knows no age limit. And the small adventures of three-year-old Skrallan on a summer, sun-drenched day, are simple enough for the youngest listener to understand. The Swedish atmosphere of course, is another bonus.

📖 *KARLSSON-ON-THE-ROOF* (1971; British edition as *Karlson on the Roof)*

Zena Sutherland

SOURCE: A review of *Karlsson-on-the-Roof,* in *Bulletin of the Center for Children's Books,* Vol. 26, No. 2, October, 1972, p. 28.

Karlsson is a wee man who flies and who considers himself better at everything than anybody in the world, a fact he does not hesitate to tell little Eric. Astounded by his visitor, Eric believes all the boasts and falls for every trick the gluttonous Karlsson pulls. Reports to Eric's family bring irritated disbelief, and they are convinced that when Eric gets a long-desired dog for his birthday he will forget Karlsson-on-the-roof—but in a final scene, Eric's astounded parents see that their son's playmate is not imaginary. The story, episodic in structure, has some appeal in its nonsense humor, and the style is yeasty, but the episodes are clogged by a stress on Karlsson's boasting and his appetite to the point where contrivance outweighs comedy.

Sally Emerson

SOURCE: A review of *Karlson on the Roof,* in *Books and Bookmen,* Vol. 20, No. 8, May, 1975, p. 78.

Midge is a young boy who lives in Stockholm and longs for a special friend or a dog to talk to. He and his family are all perfectly ordinary, the only extraordinary person in the house is Karlson on the Roof. Karlson is a pompous and chubby little man who has his own little house on top of the roof and a propeller on his back. He flies into Midge's room like a little helicopter and gets Midge into some trouble but much fun. Karlson on the Roof is a magnificent character given to extreme selfishness and hyperbole: he has to have and be the world's best and he claims he's 'a handsome, intelligent and reasonably stout man in my prime'. He also has a memorable collection of catch phrases such as 'Easy, take it easy' and 'A trifle, a mere trifle' to be employed whenever his mischief has run riot. Finally Midge is given a dog of his own and we suspect that when he returns from his grandmother's Karlson will no longer be up on the roof.

📖　*OF COURSE POLLY CAN RIDE A BIKE*
　　(1972; British edition and later U.S. edition as
　　Lotta's Bike)

Ellen Fader

SOURCE: A review of *Lotta's Bike,* in *The Horn Book Magazine,* Vol. LXVI, No. 1, January-February, 1990, p. 53.

Lotta desperately wants a real bicycle to replace her old tricycle. When she does not receive one on the morning of her fifth birthday, she steals a much-too-large bike from her neighbor, Mrs. Berg. Lotta's inaugural downhill ride leaves her bruised and bleeding in her neighbor's rosebushes; even worse, she has lost her brand-new and greatly treasured bracelet, a birthday gift from Mrs. Berg. Adults may find her father's sudden arrival with a perfectly-sized secondhand bicycle and Mrs. Berg's discovery of Lotta's bracelet coincidental and unrealistic, but young people will relish the gratification of Lotta's wish to have her own bicycle and her triumph in being able to ride it. Children will recognize Lotta as a very real little girl—impulsive, envious, and with a strong sense of what she wants in life.

📖　*THE BROTHERS LIONHEART* (1975)

Sarah Hayes

SOURCE: "Allegorical Action," in *The Times Literary Supplement,* No. 3826, July 11, 1975, p. 767.

This simple tale of good, represented by the brothers, versus evil, in the shape of a red-eyed tyrant, master of a hideous and seemingly sexually frustrated monster, is the author's first venture into fantasy proper, and she seems distinctly uneasy in it. It is surely strange for a classic comic writer to avoid the faintest whiff of humour, and odder still that the writer found it necessary to introduce her half-heroic, half-magical world by gruesomely ending the present-day life of the brothers at the beginning of the saga and then having them die again (in a courageous double suicide master-minded by the younger and feebler of the brothers) in the finale.

The main section of the book, in which the young Lionheart tells of his adventures, terrors and pleasures, and most of all, of his worship for his much older brother, is written in a direct, unadorned style, although many readers may find the ecstasy, the honesty, and the naked emotion very hard to take. Carps about blurbs are rather underhand, but copywriters should beware of using adjectives such as "epic", particularly where Scandinavian writers are concerned. *The Brothers Lionheart* never attains epic stature, but the writing has a certain spare power about it.

Kirkus Reviews

SOURCE: A review of *The Brothers Lionheart,* in *Kirkus Reviews,* Vol. XLII, No. 14, July 15, 1975, pp. 777-78.

Is there a death after death? In Nangiyala there is . . . also tyranny, battles and adventure enough to test the courage of Jonathan Lionheart and his little brother Rusky. You see, both brothers die near the beginning of the story—Rusky from a long illness, Jonathan heroically in a fire—and Jonathan has promised Rusky that they will meet in the kingdom of Nangiyala where "it's still in the days of sagas and campfires. . . . " But Nangiyala turns out to be far from peaceful; it is menaced by the ogre Tengil who commands a horrible dragon, Katla, and a band of oafish soldiers. Jonathan soon becomes a leader of the resistance and Rusky joins him, heeding Jonathan's philosophy ("sometimes you have to do things that are dangerous; otherwise you aren't a human being just a piece of filth"). Both boys infiltrate Tengil's stronghold in Wild Rose Valley, outwit the enemy soldiers (whose stupidity makes their success rather easy) and find their way past Karma Falls to Katla's cave where they rescue the imprisoned leader Orvar. The battle that follows seems destined to bring peace and security to Nangiyala, but Jonathan is paralyzed by Katla's fiery breath. So he tells Rusky about yet another, better kingdom called Nangilima and Rusky carries his brother off the edge of a cliff—into a second world, shouting "I can see the light, *I can see the light!*" The brothers' affinity with extinction and the curious, Nordic innocence of their brand of courage makes us vaguely uneasy; surely even in the realm of myth and legend which Nangiyala vaguely recalls, death was something more than an easy out. But if you can admire Jonathan's princely beauty and bravery as much as Rusky does, this simultaneously grave and playful fantasy will delight you.

Ethel L. Heins

SOURCE: A review of *The Brothers Lionheart,* in *The Horn Book Magazine,* Vol. LI, No. 6, December, 1975, pp. 594-95.

A truly original writer, who refuses to capitalize on popularity and become a stereotype of herself, has written an enigmatic fantasy which asks more questions than it answers. Karl, a timorous, self-effacing invalid, talks about his impending death with his adored older brother Jonathan, an almost saintly thirteen-year-old who is extraordinarily beautiful, strong, kind, brave, and brilliant. But ironically, it is Jonathan who dies first, for he is killed saving Karl's life in a tenement-house fire. The death of the younger boy soon afterwards ends Karl's unbearable loneliness and longing for Jonathan; the two brothers are promptly reunited in Nangiyala, an unspoiled land which is "still in the days of campfires and sagas." For a short time their life is idyllic; then Jonathan tells Karl that a monstrous tyrant, using a hideous, primeval dragon as a weapon, is enslaving the people of Nangiyala. Jonathan, now even more an heroic, god-like figure, leads the people in their desperate struggle for freedom. In the great final battle, "an evil saga of death and death and more death," Jonathan is mortally wounded; and the two boys, seeking yet another place of peace and beauty, commit suicide together. Although the story is brimming with excitement, treachery, hairbreadth escapes, and convincing suspense, it cannot be counted a success. Like many other works of fantasy, it exists on many levels, and it is not necessary that readers perceive the allegorical relationship between the two brothers or the philosophical implications of the apparently infinite struggle against evil. But the subjectively emotional, often ecstatic tone of Karl's first-person narrative may make young readers uneasy; the book's preoccupation with death and its hints about transmigration of souls may be confusing; and the final, cool acceptance of suicide, too shocking.

Penelope Farmer

SOURCE: A review of *The Brothers Lionheart,* in *The New York Times Book Review,* March 21, 1976, p. 10.

Alas, let no one encountering this new book by the creator of Pippi Longstocking expect more of the same. Not that I am against new departures, but the content of *The Brothers Lionheart,* a fantasy about life after death, seems to me dubious.

Brave, beautiful Jonathan dies saving sickly, frightened Karl. But as he has promised, when Karl too dies the brothers meet in Nangiyala, a paradisal land from the days of "sagas and campfires" where, however, they find themselves involved in a classic struggle against the tyrant Tengil and his enslaved, appalling dragon. In the ultimate victory Jonathan is paralyzed by the dragon's breath. He will walk again, he promises, if he can get to yet another land, Nangilima, where dragons are rendered harmless by laughter. Karl, brave at last, takes Jonathan

on his back and leaps over the precipice—to wake, one understands, into that further light.

The conflict itself will do; it's conventional and mostly one-dimensional in human terms, yet powerfully told. My doubts lie in the device of the two stages of eternity, the lands beyond death. Is it meant to make children less afraid of dying? If so, the premise seems to me as suspect as those of the sects, Christian or otherwise, that promise future compensations to their followers in return for enduring danger and privations here.

This is being literal, I know. But children are literal, and on their terms that final leap into joy looks practically like an invitation to suicide, escapist in the worst sense; whereas fantasy, properly, is not escapist at all, but rather sheds light on reality. (And Astrid Lindgren, indeed, outside her main thesis illustrates this precisely, even here, in the way she shows Karl learning to face his darkest fears.)

No, I would not keep this book from my children; but I would certainly discuss it with them afterwards and maybe show them Donne's sonnet on death. Lapsed Christian I may be, yet Donne's final triumphant "death, thou shalt die," still to me rings true, as *The Brothers Lionheart* certainly does not.

Tordis Orjasaeter

SOURCE: "The Handicapped in Literature," in *Bookbird,* Vol. XVIII, No. 1, March 15, 1980, pp. 3-6.

That a handicap is worse than death and that the handicapped person should be allowed to die rather than to live is expressed in Astrid Lindgren's book *The Brothers Lion Heart*: "Do you have to die again now?" Scorpan wept, and then Jonatan said: "No! but that is what I would like to do since I will never be able to move again". And Jonatan explained to his little brother what was so terrible about the fire of Katla. If it did not kill, it did something far worse. It ruined something inside a person, something within, making this person lame. It was not noticeable at first, but it came stealthily, slowly and unstoppably.

But on the other hand—when he is dead and comes to Nangilima, he is not lame any more: "No—then I will be free of everything evil and so happy I should not know what to do!"

Gunnel Enby, Swedish author and children's book critic, herself stricken by polio at the age of seventeen and now permanently in a wheel chair, has written a solidly based criticism of this masterpiece by Astrid Lindgren. I quote from Gunnel Enby:

> It is a fine book. Seductively beautiful. The good and the bad fight the black fight as they have always done in the fairy tales. And then she lets a child become handicapped. Jonatan Lionheart, the brave giant, is struck by a paralyzing flame from the monster Katla—

and he feels his body become paralyzed. After a while he can only move his arms—and then no limb at all. There is only one way of getting rid of the disease: Brother Scorpan must take his big brother Jonatan on his back and jump down from a precipice, and die. In Nangilima, the land of death, eternal happiness reigns. And little timid, frightened Scorpan jumps.

'Oh, Nangilima! Yes, yes, Jonatan, yes I see the light! I see the light.'

Astrid Lindgren has put the bright future of the lame child in the land of death.

Certainly, Astrid Lindgren should be allowed to write the kind of books she wants. Of course it is very far from me to wag my finger in disapproval of her poetic imagination, but I cannot help thinking of how a handicapped child would feel about Jonatan Lionheart's longing for death. Does it paralyze this child's will to do something about his right to live—and not only to live, but to live a life of quality?

I am certain that this will not motivate the child to fight to improve his situation—instead it will tempt him to escape into fantasy.

Somehow—and naturally—I hesitate to criticize this solution of the adventurous story, because we need fantasy and dreams.

But nevertheless I feel we should listen to this criticism from Gunnel Enby: To what prize?

Eric A. Kimmel

SOURCE: "Beyond Death: Children's Books and the Hereafter," in *The Horn Book Magazine,* Vol. LVI, No. 3, June, 1980, pp. 265-73.

Astrid Lindgren in *The Brothers Lionheart* presents [death] as a babushka doll—a series of separate existences, each contained in the other. *The Brothers Lionheart* . . . [puts] forward some interesting ideas. Karl Lion, sickly and shy, adores his kind, brave older brother Jonathan. But Jonathan dies giving his life to save the helpless Karl from a fire in their apartment. With Jonathan's death the joy goes out of Karl's world, and he dies too, going not to heaven but to Nangiyala, the fairy-tale land that Jonathan once told him about—the land of the sagas.

Karl arrives in Nangiyala to find it all he ever dreamed of. There is a pretty farm in a beautiful valley white with cherry blossoms. There are streams to swim in, horses to ride, and pure air to breathe. Furthermore, in Nangiyala Karl isn't sick anymore. He is strong and healthy. And of course, Jonathan is with him. But all is not ideal. There is still danger in this paradise, an evil tyrant and a terrible dragon to overcome. And these battles aren't make-believe. Death is a reality in Nangiyala. Some of their friends are killed. Even worse, Jonathan is badly hurt and

has no hope unless he can get to Nangilima, where the people of Nangiyala go when they die. As Jonathan describes it, "Nangilima was not in the days of cruel sagas but in days that were happy and full of games." But to get there Karl and Jonathan have to die. Jonathan is helpless, so Karl must take the responsibility. Carrying his brother in his arms the way Jonathan once carried him, he leaps off a cliff into—Nangilima.

The Brothers Lionheart is certainly not the best conceived or the most successful of Lindgren's books, but it is worth noting because of the picture of death it presents. Conventional religion is completely ignored even in the sequences that take place in our world. The book harks back to Viking mythology not only for its imagery but particularly for its ethics. Being a helpless invalid is the worst possible fate of all, far worse than death. But to be afraid of dying is the most dreadful of all. Confronted with the final leap into Nangilima Karl thinks to himself, "Well, if you don't dare now . . . then you're a little bit of filth and you'll never be anything else but a little bit of filth." The taboo against suicide, one of the strongest in all western religions, is thus reduced to an adolescent dare. The message coming through is a very disturbing one: Why endure suffering and pain when you can end it with a quick leap and start over again in a new body in a better place? Heroism and tragedy are reduced to a game of musical chairs, or better, musical worlds. But are Karl and Jonathan really going anywhere? Does passage to Nangilima represent spiritual growth, or is it simply running away to another never-never land like Nangiyala? Instead of the birth-rebirth cycle of Karma (a term used rather flippantly as the name of the waterfall where the final battle of Nangiyala takes place), Lindgren substitutes a linear progression through a sequence of different worlds, each not appreciably different from the next. For one concerned with the larger issues of life and death, the result is distinctly unsatisfying.

PIPPI ON THE RUN (1976)

Kirkus Reviews

SOURCE: A review of *Pippi on the Run,* in *Kirkus Reviews,* Vol. XLIV, No. 6, March 15, 1976, p. 323.

[Bo-Erik] Gyberg's oversize technicolor photos of three real children may or may not correspond to a given reader's image of Pippi and her friends Tommy and Annika. For us, the problem is not that he has any of the details wrong but just that the wish-fulfilling life and exploits of the strongest girl in the world go a lot farther on their own. There's not much story here—Tommy and Annika decide to run away and Pippi goes along, ostensibly to watch over them but actually to stir up adventure. With the old bravado, Pippi eats a fish skeleton whole, rides a barrel over a waterfall, and drives into a lake in an old jalopy she's just repaired with glue; but other adventures—especially diverting a bull when the farmer's baby wanders into his reach—seem staged for the kiddie film this looks like. The prose, too, reads like a spin-off, and the format suggests a dime store market.

Barbara Elleman

SOURCE: A review of *Pippi on the Run,* in *The Booklist,* Vol. 72, No. 16, April 15, 1976, p. 1186.

Tommy and Annika live next door to Pippi Longstocking, and when they decide to run away from home, Pippi goes with them. It's true adventure from the start as daring, fun-loving Pippi goes over a waterfall in a barrel, tight-rope-walks above an amazed crowd, and rides downhill in a car with no brakes. Her companions get their fair share of the escapade with train-hopping and losing their clothes to a hungry cow but at the end are glad to be home. Laid out in picture-book format, the story is illustrated with color photographs featuring Inger Nilsson, the star of the motion picture about Pippi Longstocking. The characters unfortunately come out looking posed and stilted, and where live photographs sometimes heighten reality, here they tend to lend an unbelievable air to the story. Pippi fans who get caught up in the story may overlook this—and of course movie viewers will—but Lindgren's heroine did better under the pen of [illustrator] Louis Glanzman.

☐ *KARLSON FLIES AGAIN* (1977)

Gillian Hadley

SOURCE: A review of *Karlson Flies Again,* in *The Times Literary Supplement,* No. 3949, December 2, 1977, p. 1414.

In *Karlson Flies Again* the fantasy of flying becomes a charmingly matter-of-fact reality. Karlson on the roof is, by his own definition, a "handsome, highly intelligent, reasonably stout man in his prime". His egocentric logic is undeniably appealing; he is delightfully self-opinioned and secure in the face of his own incompetence and greed. He is sure that his granny is grannier than Midge's, the boy who lives in the flat under Karlson's roof. He knows he is "the world's best trickster", the authority on bun-fever and the vacuum-cleaning of small boys' ears. The fat little man with a propeller on his back who lives on the roof is accepted by Midge's parents as a nuisance, indisputably real, a potential source of social embarrassment. For Midge, Karlson provides interesting extensions to the normal possibilities of everyday living, especially in the area of "tirritating" home helps who possess "a number of chins and angry eyes".

M. Hobbs

SOURCE: A review of *Karlson Flies Again,* in *The Junior Bookshelf,* Vol. 42, No. 1, February, 1978, p. 28.

Karlson, the fat little man with the propeller on his back, the best in the world at most things in his own estimation, once more flies down from his house, hidden away between the chimney and the wall on Midge's roof, to bully and tyrannise his little friend, and do all the antisocial, selfish, awful things children's fantasies can envisage. Not that Karlson is only in Midge's mind: his parents, brother and sister see him this time, and quickly try to ignore the facts. Poor Miss Black, left to look after Midge as various disasters remove the rest of the family, also sees Karlson, and is reduced from severity almost to humanity by her experiences of a ghost who is not. The secret of Karlson's success is like that of his predecessor Pippi, the matter-of-factness of the exaggeration and fantasy. The little house, with its porch and green window frames, seems quite possible, and Karlson himself, for all his adult status, behaves exactly like any insecure child, not just in his bullying but in his anxiety to outvye everyone in everything. His well-meant know-all destructiveness is very like Paddington's, as is his voracious appetite, but Midge is a sensitive child, and has moments of vivid awareness of seasons and times of day which bring this book into a different class. Midge must also be a very nice child, for he scarcely rebels at Karlson's tyranny! Good catharsis, and funny with it—though sometimes marred by careless proofreading.

☐ *OF COURSE POLLY CAN DO ALMOST EVERYTHING* (1978; British edition and revised U.S. edition as *Lotta's Christmas Surprise)*

Margery Fisher

SOURCE: A review of *Lotta's Christmas Surprise,* in *Growing Point,* Vol. 17, No. 6, March, 1979, p. 3468.

There could be a nostalgic pleasure for a girl of eight or nine in contemplating the exploits of the particularly determined five-year-old in *Lotta's Christmas Surprise.* Astrid Lindgren writes as an adult observing small children rather than reliving her own childhood, but it is obvious that she enjoys and understands the way a child's mind might work and how a little girl will instinctively exploit the grown-ups for her own ends. This particular anecdote about Swedish Lotta shows her as the family saviour, for without her they would never have had a Christmas tree, and if she does lose her precious stuffed pig in the course of her adventures, she seems pretty confident that things will turn out to her advantage in the end. "You were right, Lotta," her brother James says generously, "You really *can* do everything", and it is seen amusingly to be the case.

M. Crouch

SOURCE: A review of *Lotta's Christmas Surprise,* in *The Junior Bookshelf,* Vol. 43, No. 2, April, 1979, pp. 93-4.

Astrid Lindgren is in a class apart. Her new picture story book about Lotta keeps up her highest standard. Lotta sometimes threatens to become intolerably awful, but her creator's infallible instincts always pull her back from the brink. Lotta is a very lively small girl, living in the everyday world and contributing to it her own brand of helpfulness. This time she finds the family a Christmas tree—it happened to fall off a lorry, quite literally!—as well as helping nice Mrs. Berg, who is in bed with her out-of-breathness. Lotta can be maddening at times, but we like her; what is more, I fancy that we should like her in real life too. . . .

Zena Sutherland

SOURCE: A review of *Of Course Polly Can Do Almost Everything,* in *Bulletin of the Center for Children's Books,* Vol. 32, No. 9, May, 1979, pp. 158-59.

Polly, the youngest of three, takes great satisfaction in the number of skills she's acquired and the responsibility she can carry, so she's glad to do errands for Mother. She does make mistakes—like putting a toy and gift into the garbage can and arriving to deliver the gift only to find the remains of a fish. Still, Polly achieves what nobody else in the family can when she produces a Christmas tree

From I Want a Brother or Sister, *written by Astrid Lindgren. Illustrated by Ilon Wikland.*

at a time when the town dealer has sold out. Lindgren's writing is sprightly, her Polly an ingenuous character, and the well-constructed plot has the double appeals of humor and of achievement of a goal.

Carolyn Phelan

SOURCE: A review of *Lotta's Christmas Surprise,* in *Booklist,* Vol. 87, No. 7, December 1, 1990, p. 752.

[*The following excerpt is from a review of the revised edition of* Lotta's Christmas Surprise *published in 1990.*]

Librarians will have a surprise altogether less jolly than Lotta's if they order this book as a new title—only to find it on their shelves under its original English title, *Of Course Polly Can Do Almost Everything*. While the new edition's text is reworded, the changes are so minimal that few would order it on that account. The text is a little longer than that of most picture books, but the story of Lotta's trials and triumphs will please children who are beginning to test their own mettle in a slightly larger sphere than the home. For libraries without the earlier edition, this will be a charming addition to the holiday collection.

📖 *THAT'S MY BABY* (1980)

E. Colwell

SOURCE: A review of *That's My Baby,* in *The Junior Bookshelf,* Vol. 44, No. 3, June, 1980, p. 119.

A familiar theme and family problem is the arrival of a brother or sister who seems to supplant the first-born in the parents' affections. This is dealt with understandingly in a simple text and clear and bright illustrations. A book of this kind can be used with young children by their parents to prepare them for what is going to happen and to encourage them to feel they have a share in the new baby and are still loved as much as ever.

It is possible that the perspective in a few of the pictures may puzzle some children, for the furniture seems to stand on end and children are literal. On the other hand this allows the child to see details that would otherwise remain hidden.

Mary Hoffman

SOURCE: "When the Lap was Theirs Alone," in *The Times Educational Supplement,* No. 3369, January 16, 1981, p. 25.

In *That's My Baby* the parents play the despicable trick of pretending to Peter that they had baby Lena to please him. After he has acted naughtily his mother says: "We had her for you. From now on she's your responsibility.

You look after her yourself." What a wicked lie! Even if not wanting a child to be an "only" comes into parents' calculations, they only ever have children to please themselves and sometimes not even that. If you don't want to turn a reasonably tractable child into a furious demon, don't read him *That's My Baby*.

📖 *THE WORLD'S BEST KARLSON* (1980)

B. Clark

SOURCE: A review of *The World's Best Karlson*, in *The Junior Bookshelf*, Vol. 44, No. 5, October, 1980, pp. 240-41.

The third in the series of stories of the irrepressible and incorrigible young friend of Midge, who is reported in Midge's father's newspaper to be a "mysterious peculiar object flying about the town". The newspaper report is correct as far as it goes, but what it can hardly be expected to notice is that Karlson is a very cheeky little chap who gets Midge into all sorts of awkward situations and comes out triumphant in every case. This story concerns the annual visit of Uncle Julius, and while Midge's family are away, the arrival of Miss Black—"Black Beetle" to Karlson—to look after the house. This gives the extraordinary Karlson with his propeller, by which he winds himself up to fly over the town, ample opportunity to get up to his most ingenious tricks, and Uncle Julius and Miss Black are involved together in a way they never have been before, and are engaged to be married by the end of the story! Young boys—most of whom would love to be Karlson—will love this book.

📖 *I WANT TO GO TO SCHOOL TOO* (1980)

Publishers Weekly

SOURCE: A review of *I Want to Go to School Too*, in *Publishers Weekly*, Vol. 232, No. 18, October 30, 1987, p. 68.

This Scandinavian import by the author of the Pippi Longstocking books depicts a lively day at grammar school. Five-year-old Lena is eager to go to school like her seven-year-old brother Peter. So one day, Peter obliges. Lena is honored when allowed to sit at her own desk, join the children for lunch and go to recess with them. The busy, cheerful illustrations [by Ilon Wikland] fill in the details of Peter's school with satisfying completeness. Although Peter's school is different from an American school in its specifics, its uniqueness gives it personality and substance. The book provides a comforting answer to young children's questions about starting school.

Kirkus Reviews

SOURCE: A review of *I Want to Go to School Too*, in *Kirkus Reviews*, Vol. LV, No. 21, November 1, 1987, p. 1577.

The first American edition of a 1979 publication by the famed Swedish author that, surprisingly, is more memorable for its illustration than for its text.

The routine plot concerns Lena, five, who envies her older brother Peter, seven, going to school. One day he takes her along: they meet friends in the schoolyard for a game of marbles from which Lena is excluded; she is introduced to his classmates, who greet her with equability; there is a schoolyard fight during which Peter defends his right to take Lena to school with him; Lena shines in nature study and Peter doesn't during reading.

The story is hardly distinctive, but the crowded, brightly colored illustrations are entertaining and full of detail that the careful eye can follow from picture to picture. Lena and Peter are full of movement and expression, and the perspectives and antic detail give a believable child's-eye view. A modest effort for older readers of picture books.

Phillis Wilson

SOURCE: A review of *I Want to Go to School Too*, in *Booklist*, Vol. 84, No. 7, December 1, 1987, p. 635.

One day Peter, who is seven, takes Lena, who is five, to school for a visit. The children want to know who Lena is and Peter tells his teacher. "She wants to know exactly what it's like in school." Typical activities of the classroom and school yard are explained, though with a distinctly Swedish flavor, such as the pancakes with lingonberry jam on the menu at lunchtime. At day's end Lena is content with her knowledge of her expanded world. Wikland's depiction of the multitudinous hodgepodge of childhood stuff adds a sense of action and excitement to the story line, and her rendering of the children catches their both charming/awkward and mischievous/natural exuberance. With a text as forthright as the title, Lindgren tells the story from Lena's point of view, adding appeal for readers who share Lena's curiosity. A well-executed version of an ever-popular theme.

📖 *I WANT A BROTHER OR SISTER* (1981)

Betsy Hearne

SOURCE: A review of *I Want a Brother or Sister*, in *Booklist*, Vol. 77, No. 19, June 1, 1981, p. 1300.

Perhaps there has been a plethora of books about sibling arrival, but this one happens to be warm and happy enough to provide another choice, and it goes beyond the usual adjustment period to a family situation in which yet a third infant makes firstborn Peter glad he has his growing sister for company. Lindgren's direct, down-to-earth style is smoothly translated [by Barbara Lucas], while the accompanying full-color illustrations [by Ilon Wikland] are cheerfully chaotic with household detail. Reassuring and more entertaining than the bibliotherapeutic title implies.

Zena Sutherland

SOURCE: A review of *I Want a Brother or Sister,* in *Bulletin of the Center for Children's Books,* Vol. 35, No. 3, November, 1981, p. 49.

Smoothly translated, illustrated with realistic drawings that are weakened occasionally by over-ambitious use of perspective, and written in a guilefully simple style, this is the story of a small boy who discovers that the baby sister he'd wanted isn't all that much fun. Besides, Mama and Papa seem to love Lena more than they love him. Then Mama explains that all babies are lovable and troublesome; and that she needs his help. Having a vested interest proves satisfying; later, there is a third child, and both Peter and Lena see that it's easy to coo at a cuddly infant. Mama is busy, but, that is all right, since Peter and Lena can have uninterrupted pillow fights. No pretense about this one; it's a brisk little tale meant to assuage the pangs of jealousy, and it's very nicely done.

📖 *MARDIE TO THE RESCUE* (1981)

Margery Fisher

SOURCE: A review of *Mardie to the Rescue,* in *Growing Point,* Vol. 20, No. 4, November, 1981, pp. 3964-65.

Sweden in the 1920's seems to have had much the same overlapping of class and custom as it has now, and there are moments in *Mardie to the Rescue* which might be puzzling to an English reader. It could be an instructive exercise, for instance, to translate into English terms the scene where Alma, a devoted servant in Mardie's family, cheerfully delouses the little girl together with 'Lousy Mia', a school-fellow with a very different background. And how about Mardie's playmate Abe, whose alcoholic father provides material for one or two unsavoury incidents? With a mischievous small girl as the centre, Astrid Lindgren has put together scenes in which poverty, bodily functions and family crises are looked at candidly: the candour may belong more to our time than it does to the '20's but the customs, the environment and the behaviour are, I feel sure, as authentic as the author can make them.

A. Thatcher

SOURCE: A review of *Mardie to the Rescue,* in *The Junior Bookshelf,* Vol. 46, No. 1, February, 1982, p. 27.

This story tells of a year in the life of Mardie, a young girl living with her Mama, Papa, five year old sister Lisbeth, and their maid Alma in a country community in Sweden in the 1920's. It starts and ends with a vivid picture of the May Fire celebrations that mark the return of Spring. The seventeen chapters cover many facets of their life—a birthday picnic, the exciting visit of a flying machine, the Autumn Ball, a head-lice cleaning-up session, and the birth and attempted kidnap of baby sister Katie.

Mardie and her sister and friends are very human youngsters. They can be naughty and mischievous, rude, bad-tempered and quarrelsome, but also very resourceful, brave, generous and kind. Poor Mrs. Nilsson had sold her body to the Doctor for research for £25 to pay off her husband's debt. Mardie is so concerned that she gives her most of the £30 prize she won in a raffle.

A happy book, with living characters, the author understands children, and remembers in fascinating detail her own childhood in a happy and united family. There is sorrow, hardship and drunkenness in the community, but Mardie accepts this with compassion as the natural pattern of living.

📖 *RONIA, THE ROBBER'S DAUGHTER* (1983)

Denise M. Wilms

SOURCE: A review of *Ronia, the Robber's Daughter,* in *Booklist,* Vol. 79, No. 16, April 15, 1983, pp. 1095-96.

A special world and a special relationship are at the core of Lindgren's engaging fantasy. Ronia, the vibrant heroine, is the beloved only daughter of robber chief Matt, whose domain is a fearsome wood where harpies threaten tortuous death, and various goblin folk make their way. A spirited, sharp-witted girl, Ronia has made the forest her own and spends much time in its beguiling midst. It's here that she encounters Birk, the son of Matt's arch-rival Borka, whose band is encroaching on Matt's domain. Their relationship blossoms but raises deep problems when both Matt and Borka discover their offspring's affection for each other. In a rage, Matt disowns Ronia. She, the light of her father's and the castle's life, leaves home to live in the forest with Birk, who has forsaken his own angry family as well. They pass a contented summer, and by the onset of autumn, Matt has softened enough to apologize to Ronia and ask her return, with Birk if she wishes. That acceptance inspires another important development, the uniting of Matt's and Borka's bands, who are increasingly harried by the forces of law. Ronia and Birk, meanwhile, are united in their wish not to take on a robber's life. Lindgren's storytelling abilities are strong and she has created vivid characters for her unique setting. Ronia's brave spirit makes her an appealing heroine whose dilemmas will capture the sympathies of young readers.

Kirkus Reviews

SOURCE: A review of *Ronia, the Robber's Daughter,* in *Kirkus Reviews,* Vol. LI, No. 8, April 15, 1983, p. 459.

To his glee and joy, Matt the robber chief has a child: "a robber's daughter," and the next robber chieftain. It would be Lindgren who'd put it into Matt's wild head to have wanted a girl all along, and who'd make Ronia a fit, free-spirited, dauntless robber's daughter—just a little skeptical when she learns what robbers do. But worse is to come: Matt's archrival Borka has moved with *his* band into the unused half of Matt's Fort, on the other side of Hell's Gap, and Borka has also got himself a child: a son, Birk. Once Birk and Ronia have made contact—first, leaping back and forth across the gap; then, saving each other's life—it will of course be Romeo and Juliet. The rivalry between the two robber bands heats up, Matt all the more enraged because he can't figure out how to eject Borka from the fort. And when he captures Birk by chance, intending to imprison him until Borka leaves, Ronia vaults the gap . . . and, in defecting, breaks Matt's heart. Ronia and Birk flee to Bear's Cave for the summer—an idyllic, laughing summer. But, come autumn, Ronia's all-knowing mother Lovis seeks her out, and then Matt himself invites her back—with Birk, if must be. The two unregenerate old robbers, Matt and Borka, will fight hand-to-hand and join up. But their offspring and heirs, without peaching, have another trade in mind. Ronia as the darling of the robber's band is a delight, Snow White and the Seven Dwarfs crossed with *The Beggar's Opera;* and her relationship with Birk, if lyrical/pastoral, is also realistically touchy (and never mawkish). You can see exactly where this is headed, but you do want it to get there.

Ethel L. Heins

SOURCE: A review of *Ronia, the Robber's Daughter,* in *The Horn Book Magazine,* Vol. LIX, No. 3, June, 1983, p. 304.

The famous author's new novel is redolent with the atmosphere of Scandinavian landscape and folklore. In a forest stronghold lived Ronia, the beautiful, adored daughter of Matt, a robber chieftain. Like a spirited animal, the fearless child ran free—clambering on the wooded mountain, swimming in the lake, picking her way along the turbulent river, and making friends with the wild creatures. Ronia was as unafraid of the forest as she was of its "goblinfolk"—the little "rumphobs"; the spiteful gray dwarfs; the eerie, beguiling "Unearthly Ones"; and the ferocious harpies. The hot-tempered Matt was enraged to discover that his archenemy Borka and a rival band of robbers had brazenly installed themselves in another part of Matt's fortress, across a perilous chasm. Unbeknown to their parents, Ronia and Birk, Borka's son, met and became inseparable companions. Lovis, Ronia's mother, a pillar of quiet sanity and strength (and a wonderful foil for the blustering Matt), soon perceived the bond between the peace-loving children; but when Matt realized how deeply they cared for each other, his grandiloquent fury and sorrow knew no bounds. Fluently translated [by Patricia Crompton], the book is full of high adventure, hairsbreadth escapes, droll earthy humor, and passionate emotional energy; and cast over the whole narrative is a primi-

tive, ecstatic response to the changing seasons and the wonders of nature.

Jane Woodley

SOURCE: A review of *Ronia, the Robber's Daughter,* in *The School Librarian,* Vol. 33, No. 2, June, 1985, p. 140.

[This] must be one of the most delightful of the now ageing Astrid Lindgren's many books. Ronia's emotional adventures in relationships, and physical adventures in the cruel winters and primeval springs, are recounted with vigour, humour and tenderness. She is the daughter of the robber Matt, a character of fierce and blustering comedy, and is being brought up in the primitive company of a robber band who pillage and plunder in the dark forests, which are populated too by sinister grey dwarfs, rumphobs and harpies. But Ronia casts gloom on all and brings a predictable flood of parental blame on her head when she befriends Birk, the son of the rival robber band's leader, adopting him as her 'brother'.

It's an exciting tale, with plenty of action, and conveys feelings about parents and growing up which all children will enjoy. Excellent for reading aloud, episode by episode; and deepened by an atmosphere of northern darkness.

📖 *THE RUNAWAY SLEIGH RIDE* (1984)

[*In translations of* The Runaway Sleigh Ride, *the main character is named either Lisbet or Elizabeth.*]

Carol E. Rinzler

SOURCE: A review of *The Runaway Sleigh Ride,* in *The New York Times Book Review,* December 16, 1984, p. 23.

Astrid Lindgren's near-classic children's book, *Pippi Longstocking,* was published in this country in 1950, a little late for my childhood; I also missed it during my reading-to-children years, an omission I happily rectified recently. Pippi proved to be a delightfully naughty 6- or 7-year-old who lives all by herself in a big house. She spends her time outwitting grown-ups who want to provide her with more suitable accommodations, and corrupting two young neighbors, stout-hearted Tommy, who follows Pippi anywhere, e.g., down hol'ow tree trunks, and timid Annika, who glumly tags along.

Miss Lindgren's *Runaway Sleigh Ride* is a nice little book . . . about Elizabeth, a spirited 4- or 5-year old Scandinavian girl who sees a boy hitching a ride on the back of a horse-drawn sleigh and decides to do likewise. Alas, Elizabeth's adventure turns into disaster when the driver heads deep into the snowy forest at too fast a clip for Elizabeth to jump off. Discovering his passenger, the driver summarily dumps her; Elizabeth makes her terrified, tearful way back alone to her distraught family. You can bet she isn't going to hitch any more rides on any more sleighs, let alone climb down any hollow tree trunks. *Sleigh Ride* and Elizabeth are so far a cry from *Pippi* and its determined heroine that a doctoral candidate might usefully examine it as one of the most dramatic turn-arounds in modern fiction since John Dos Passos. I don't even want to think about the implications here for feminism.

A headstrong small child who scoots across streets without looking might benefit by this cautionary tale; most little children and most parents prefer a protagonist who is not so compelling an advertisement for namby-pambyness.

M. Crouch

SOURCE: A review of *The Runaway Sleigh Ride,* in *The Junior Bookshelf,* Vol. 49, No. 2, April, 1985, p. 74.

What an entrancing glimpse of a Scandinavian Christmas, surely a reminiscence of Astrid Lindgren's own childhood.

It is time to go to buy Christmas presents, but Mardie has a temperature after snowballing, so she has to stay home and help Mother make gingerbread men while Alma takes Lisbet shopping. All goes well until Alma leaves Lisbet on her own while she buys secrets, and Lisbet, who is that sort of girl, climbs on the back runners of Farmer Anderson's sleigh for a free ride. Anderson, who has been drinking, has got to the stage of singing improper songs; he doesn't notice his passenger until they are deep in the forest, and then he turns Lisbet off to find her own way home. Lisbet manages—she is that sort of girl too—but not before the whole family and neighbourhood have been put into a panic. It is going to be a lovely Christmas.

Lovely as Ilon Wikland's coloured pictures are—and they are full of snowflakes—it is the words that matter here, and Astrid Lindgren's are perfect for their purpose. No one knows better how to invoke, with the simplest of means, the atmosphere of a happy family and the unpredictability of naughty little girls. She proves conclusively that there is a world of difference between two children and only one. This book will give much pleasure for many Christmases to come.

📖 *MY NIGHTINGALE IS SINGING* (1985)

Myra Barrs

SOURCE: A review of *My Nightingale is Singing,* in *The Times Educational Supplement,* No. 3597, June 7, 1985, p. 55.

Astrid Lindgren's *My Nightingale is Singing* is a potentially grim story about a consumptive child pauper in a nineteenth century Swedish poorhouse. Maria is hungry for any scrap of beauty in her depressing surroundings, but nothing feeds her. All she succeeds in finding is a single line of verse; "My linden plays, my nightingale is singing," and she uses this as an amulet against pain and misery. Eventually she builds a fantasy round it that turns into a miracle when, one day, a linden tree actually does grow in the middle of the paupers' potato field. It is all a bit Pollyannaish with Maria as a little ray of sunshine in the poorhouse, but the understatement of the narration and Svend Otto's sensitive watercolours save the story from an excess of sentimentality.

M. Crouch

SOURCE: A review of *My Nightingale is Singing,* in *The Junior Bookshelf,* Vol. 49, No. 4, August, 1985, p. 175.

My Nightingale is Singing is far removed from the Astrid Lindgren of *Pippi Longstocking*. It is a tender and heart-rending story of a little orphan girl who goes to the poorhouse with her small bundle under her arm. 'Poor me,' thinks Maria, but she is about to transform the lives of the wretched inmates. The 'littlest pauper in Scunton', who sleeps on the floor 'among the dirt and the bugs'—'If I were a bug I'd leave this place,' thinks Maria—goes begging around the village with Poppadella, the ruler of the poorhouse, and at the parsonage, where they are given the bread of charity, Maria hears a story being read to the parson's children. A few words sink 'into her soul like morning dew on the fields of summer.' As she repeats

'My linden plays,
my nightingale is singing'

the wretchedness of the poorhouse is dispelled. In time she decides to make the words come true. She plants a pea, overlooked from a pauper's ration, and believes that it will grow into a linden tree. The paupers mock her, but one morning the linden comes. All the paupers gather, waiting for it to play and for the nightingale to sing, but the tree stands there 'beautiful, silent and dead'. So Maria breathes her life into the tree. In the morning the linden plays and the nightingale sings, but Maria has gone. Only Joey Squint, 'who was not too bright', hears a voice in his head whispering 'This is Maria!'

The little story is told with restrained eloquence and makes its point most powerfully. It is impossible to dissociate the words from Svend Otto's drawings which have the same kind of quiet passion. Here is the rare meeting of two masters and a wonderful blending of their two arts in the making of a most lovely and memorable book.

📖 *THE GHOST OF SKINNY JACK* (1988)

Margery Fisher

SOURCE: A review of *The Ghost of Skinny Jack,* in *Growing Point,* Vol. 27, No. 2, July, 1988, p. 5020.

A grandmother's tale about a farmhand employed by the parson who dressed up as a ghost to scare his enemy the organist but by unfortunate accident was frozen into his disguise and remained propped by the roadside for no less than a century: eventually the new minister and a fearless maid-servent brought the body back to the parsonage and the sad corpse disintegrated after speaking an apology over the organist's grave. The girl who tells the tale as her grandmother told it to her brings it into a third dimension of time; the strange events are recorded in supple, lively prose and pleasing scenes [by illustrator Ilon Wikland] of farmhouse and field, with lively portraits of the characters in the comedy, suit period and plot admirably.

Betsy Hearne

SOURCE: A review of *The Ghost of Skinny Jack,* in *Bulletin of the Center for Children's Books,* Vol. 42, No. 3, November, 1988, p. 78.

A little girl remembers her grandmother's story about a farmhand, Skinny Jack, who pretends to be a ghost and ends up scaring himself stiff and cold. So he remains for a hundred years until, on a dare, the new parson's maid brings his body into the parlor and back out to the graveyard, where. . . . After this story is over, the little girl and her brother have to walk home through the woods, where. . . . The legend of Skinny Jack is pretty good stuff, with a teasing blend of reality and the supernatural. The framework story of the children visiting their grandmother seems to complicate things considerably (the little girl's getting caught by a branch echoes Skinny Jack's getting caught by a church door—both terrifying but natural events) and gives the book a nostalgic air. The text is long for a picture book, but the subject is an attention grabber and will appeal to middle-grade readers as well as primary grade listeners.

Phillis Wilson

SOURCE: A review of *The Ghost of Skinny Jack,* in *Booklist,* Vol. 85, No. 9, January 1, 1989, p. 791.

On the spine-tingling chiller scale, this entry hits the high mark. Two children listen as their grandma tells the age-old tale of Skinny Jack, who despised the church organist. One night, after badly frightening the fellow, Skinny Jack found himself the victim; his blood turned to ice and he became a ghost, left propped up alongside the church. A hundred years later, a brave and feisty parson's maid—on a dare—picks up the ghost (still lying stiff and lifeless) and slings him on her back. Suddenly, old Jack demands she carry him to the organist's grave where, in a ghoulish voice, he begs forgiveness. Following the story, the children start home through the woods, but in the deepening twilight, sense the specter's chilling presence. All's well that ends well as the terrifying element is, in truth, a hazelnut branch, and Dad wondrously appears to take them the rest of the way home. Lindgren's skillfully

crafted text exudes gripping suspense; coupled with the murky, eerie atmosphere of [Ilon] Wikland's church and graveyard scenes, this will leave read-aloud listeners wide-eyed.

I DON'T WANT TO GO TO BED (1988)

Ilene Cooper

SOURCE: A review of *I Don't Want to Go to Bed,* in *Booklist,* Vol. 85, No. 7, December 1, 1988, p. 652.

Five-year-old Larry is adamant—he doesn't want to go to bed—and each night he has a temper tantrum when bedtime rolls around. One evening, Larry visits an old woman named Aunt Lottie, who shows him her magic glasses. Through the glasses, Larry sees wonderful things: a teddy bear tiring himself out in a stream, a rabbit family getting ready for bed, squirrel children who are promised a treat if they fall asleep quickly, and bedtime high jinks at the rat household. Larry gets the message that nighttime is for sleeping and goes quietly home and gets ready for bed all by himself. The story has some internal logic problems. The rambunctious behavior of some of the animal children does not seem to lead to the story's soothing conclusion. Still, there is much to like here—lots of amusing action and well-wrought depictions of the animal clans. . . . While this may not have the desired effect on sleepyheads, it's still a pleasing read.

Patricia Hackbarth

SOURCE: A review of *I Don't Want to Go to Bed,* in *Children's Book Review Service,* Vol. 17, No. 6, Winter, 1989, p. 62.

Larry hates to go to bed and his bedtimes are occasion for a great deal of screaming until a kindly neighbor lets him have a look through her glasses. Through these magical glasses he sees all the animal families in the forest and the assorted events surrounding their bedtimes. Seeing that no one screams at bedtime except him, Larry is reformed. The book has bumpy writing and is not too convincing, but kids may enjoy the animals and their antics.

LOTTA'S EASTER SURPRISE (1991)

Hazel Rochman

SOURCE: A review of *Lotta's Easter Surprise,* in *Booklist,* Vol. 87, No. 14, March 15, 1991, p. 1499.

In another of Swedish author Lindgren's warm family stories about preschooler Lotta, the youngest child switches roles and gets to provide the Easter candy. Fed up with waiting around for her brother and sister to dress up with her as Easter witches, Lotta wanders down to the candy store to see the chocolate-covered eggs. The shelves are empty, the owner is going out of business. She cries with him, but when he offers her the leftover Christmas candy, she knows she's found a special kind of miracle. She hides her hoard, hugs the secret to herself, and then astonishes her family with chocolate Santas and Christmas angels, marzipan pigs and snowmen in the garden on Easter morning. True to the experience of a sensitive, bouncy five-year-old, the book is full of gentle surprise in mood and story.

Zena Sutherland

SOURCE: A review of *Lotta's Easter Surprise,* in *Bulletin of the Center for Children's Books,* Vol. 44, No. 8, April, 1991, p. 199.

In an import that travels well, Andersen medalist Lindgren has created an Easter story that has humor, sweetness, and an understanding treatment of a child's belief in legendary figures. Capably translated from the Swedish [by Barbara Lucas], the story is written with a light, sure touch. . . . The local candy store has closed, and since the Easter bunny has always bought his eggs there (so Mom and Dad say), there can't be an egg hunt. But Lotta knows, as do the readers, that Lotta has arranged a very special candy hunt. At one point, Lotta's older siblings explain that "Dad is the Easter bunny. He is also Santa, if you want to know." Lotta definitely does not want to know this, and she accepts it on one level but keeps right on thinking "What a terrible Easter it would be without the real Easter bunny," thus admitting reality but keeping her faith in the symbol. This is longer than most read-aloud books, but the combination of a light style, the appeals of the holiday, and the protagonist's ingenuity should hold the audience.

THE DAY ADAM GOT MAD (1993)

Kirkus Reviews

SOURCE: A review of *The Day Adam Got Mad,* in *Kirkus Reviews,* Vol. LXI, No. 6, March 15, 1993, p. 374.

Why the prize bull should be in a rage and break out on Easter morning is a mystery; people from miles around gather to see what will happen next. Among them is Karl, seven, who watches while the bull rips his owner's Sunday trousers, listens to the anxious men discuss what should be done, and then—in a tender, persistent little voice—offers to scratch Adam between his horns. Adam accepts, docilely letting Karl lead him back into the barn. In the end, what matters isn't the cause of Adam's outbreak but the pleasurable excitement it causes—pungently described in Lindgren's amusingly precise text—and the peaceful resolution of the barnyard contretemps by the little "Swedish bullfighter." [Marit] Törnqvist visualizes these farm folk in lovely watercolors, recalling Barbara Cooney in their careful attention to design, authentic

detail, and animated characterizations; [Barbara] Lucas's carefully honed translation is unusually felicitous. In every way, a delightful vignette.

M. Crouch

SOURCE: A review of *The Day Adam Got Mad,* in *The Junior Bookshelf,* Vol. 57, No. 2, April, 1993, p. 61.

[This] book is of the very essence of the Scandinavian farm scene, described (and drawn by Marit Tornqvist in rich and gloriously funny pictures) with precision and affection. Adam is a bull, generally good humoured and at ease with the world. One day he 'got mad' and added a share of excitement to the calm of an Easter Day. The problem is resolved, but only after much drama, in a highly satisfactory way—not to be disclosed here! The longish text is relaxed and quietly humorous. The pictures make the most of a wide landscape page by filling it with sharply observed characters human and animal.

Emily Melton

SOURCE: A review of *The Day Adam Got Mad,* in *Booklist,* Vol. 89, No. 15, April 1, 1993, pp. 1440-41.

Adam the bull lives on a farm in Sweden and is usually mild and good-tempered, but he gets mad one Easter day. Roaring out of the barn, he makes his displeasure known not only to the farm hands, the farmer, and the farmer's family, but also to all the villagers for miles around. The villagers are happy to have a distraction on this quiet springtime Easter day, but no one can quite figure out how to calm Adam down, until a runny-nosed urchin named Karl gives Adam lots of loving pats and talks him out of his "mad spell." Adam docilely returns to the barn, the villagers go away entertained but relieved, and the farmer and his family go back to their interrupted Easter day. As a reward for his heroism, Karl is given a basket of eggs and two coins. This is a pleasant enough little tale, but given that Lindgren is a well-known children's author, one expects more. The story is not particularly original or imaginative, and the text is plain and unembellished, with no particular humor, joy, or excitement. The story may not hold the attention of many youngsters for the time it takes to get through the 20-plus pages. . . .

Betsy Hearne

SOURCE: A review of *The Day Adam Got Mad,* in *Bulletin of the Center for Children's Books,* Vol. 46, No. 11, July-August, 1993, p. 351.

"This is the story of the great bull, Adam, who got loose on an Easter day a long time ago. He might still be loose if only—well, here's what happened." What happened is actually pretty climactic, as a whole farming community turns out to watch the standoff in the barnyard, until seven-year-old Karl tames the beast by scratching him between the horns. Although the translation seems smooth, Lindgren has an unfortunate habit of interrupting her story with summaries ("He was a little Swedish farm boy, exactly like a thousand others—blue-eyed, flaxen-haired, runny-nosed") or asides ("What a foolish situation!") that sometimes distract from the action and occasionally sound condescending: "Why did Adam get into such a dangerous mood on that particular day? We may never know. Perhaps one of the calves said something rude to him in calf talk, or perhaps the cows teased him." Törnqvist's watercolors make up for it, however—no authorial interruptions there as the idyllically old-fashioned scenes of rural Sweden unfold with good-humored aplomb.

Additional coverage of Lindgren's life and career is contained in the following sources published by Gale Research: *Contemporary Authors New Revision Series,* Vol. 39; *Major Authors and Illustrators for Children and Young Adults*; and *Something about the Author,* Vols. 2, 38.

Jill Murphy

1949-

(Full name Jill Frances Murphy) English author and illustrator of fiction and picture books.

Major works include *The Worst Witch* (1974), *Peace at Last* (1980), *Five Minutes' Peace* (1986), *Geoffrey Strangeways* (1990).

INTRODUCTION

Murphy is a popular and highly regarded creator of books for young people. Her works, frequently praised as imaginative and engaging, present experiences commonly shared by children with a droll humor that appeals equally to adults. Murphy's stories for middle graders, including those centering on her "Worst Witch" series' heroine Mildred Hubble, are considered especially inventive in their approach to subjects and themes familiar to this audience. Murphy is perhaps best known, however, for her picture books for preschoolers and primary graders, anthropomorphic stories which have been commended for depicting recognizable family situations in a warm and reassuring manner appropriate for young readers. Murphy's illustrations have also garnered a wealth of favorable commentary and are often acknowledged for their central role in setting the tone for her books. Her "Worst Witch" series, for instance, features black-and-white line drawings that have been described as "vigorous" by Margery Fisher and "brisk and tidy" by Zena Sutherland, while her family stories for a younger audience present colorful pictures of soft shapes in lively, full-page spreads. Reviewing *Peace at Last, Publishers Weekly* praised the "exuberant spirit of [Murphy's] remarkable paintings," adding that in this work "big, beautifully colored pictures leap with jovial surprises."

Biographical Information

Murphy was born in London, England. Encouraged artistically by her parents from an early age, she recalls having "drawn and written little books stapled together ever since I can remember." Of her early education, Murphy notes: "I always had a difficult time at school because I never wanted to do anything except write stories and draw pictures, which drove my teachers to distraction." She later attended art schools at Chelsea, Croyden, and Camberwell, and worked in a children's home and as a nanny for parts of six years. Murphy's first published story, *The Worst Witch,* was released in 1974.

Major Works

Murphy's "Worst Witch" books, including *The Worst*

Witch Strikes Again and *A Bad Spell for the Worst Witch,* present a unique twist on an otherwise common motif—the adventures of a somewhat awkward young girl who enrolls in a proper English boarding school. In this case, however, bungling protagonist Mildred Hubble attends Miss Cackle's Academy for Witches, an institution designed to impart the knowledge of spells, potions, cats, broomsticks, and other witching essentials. Murphy's inventive premise allows her to address topics and themes relevant to all children—relations with teachers and classmates, schoolwork, self-esteem—with a freshness and wit that have appealed greatly to readers.

Two other series of Murphy's books, her stories about a family of bears and a family of elephants, are directed toward preschoolers and primary graders, centering on domestic situations involving the very young. *Peace at Last* details Papa Bear's efforts to escape the noises that are keeping him awake. *Whatever Next!* (U.S. edition as *What Next, Baby Bear!*) follows Baby Bear, introduced in the previous book, on his evening picnic trip to the moon in a cardboard rocket. Critics have commended the balance of imagination, adventure, and domestic security in this latter work, which concludes with an exasperated

Mama Bear cleaning up her sooty cub after his return through the chimney and sending him off contentedly to bed. Several reviewers have also noted with approval the quality of each book's illustrations and design; both feature verso pages of text and sharp line drawings that alternate with facing pages of soft, full-color spreads.

Five Minutes' Peace introduces the Larges, an endearing family of elephants who are also featured in several subsequent works. In this first story, Murphy describes the humorously familiar ways in which Mama Large's three young children unwittingly sabotage her efforts to enjoy a few moments of quiet privacy. *All in One Piece,* which *Publishers Weekly* describes as the "continuing saga of the beleaguered Mrs. Large and her boisterous offspring," pictures with Murphy's characteristic wit how difficult it can be for parents to manage an evening out. *A Piece of Cake,* in which Mrs. Large has her family dieting, and *A Quiet Night In* have been popular additions to Murphy's elephant family series.

Awards

Peace at Last was nominated for the Kate Greenaway Award by the British Library Association in 1981, and was named a Children's Choice Book of 1981 by the Children's Book Council and the International Reading Association. *Five Minutes' Peace* received a *Parents* Best Books for Babies award in 1987.

GENERAL COMMENTARY

Margaret Carter

SOURCE: "Jill Murphy," in *Books for Your Children,* Vol. 21, No. 2, Summer, 1986, p. 12.

Jill Murphy's dog, Lottie, seems to approve of Barbara Woodhouse. At least it would appear so, since when Lottie watched that lady on television remarking on the stupidity of humans, Lottie appeared to be crooning in agreement. . . .

So what has that got to do with Jill Murphy, the artist and author of . . . *Five Minutes Peace*? Possibly quite a lot because Lottie is a highly trained dog that, in the days before the success of her mistress's books, earned enough through her TV roles to buy Jill Murphy a car.

People's lives have some tortuous connections. When Lottie was three months old Jill was offered a job as a nanny (to another three month old). The dog could come if she were house-trained "so I had to get on with it. What I do I do thoroughly."

The thorough approach showed itself early. Since the age of three she has been writing and illustrating books: by

the age of six they were "real books—stapled together."

Twelve years later—at eighteen—she had written and illustrated **The Worst Witch,** destined not to find a publisher's list for many years. "I still have the rejection slips and when they accummulated I relegated the script and the pictures to a drawer." Several years later these were to be resurrected and published to immense success. This year brings yet another acknowledgment of the book's appeal—a dramatised version starring Diana Rigg will be televised on Central television on Hallowe'en.

But the intervening years could have been hungry while waiting for the income a success brings, so, interspersed with training at various art schools, there have been several other jobs. "I produced cheap and cheerful book jackets and also colouring books for children." It is obvious that she has always had a rapport with children. "I've heard it said that you can't understand children unless you've had some of your own but I don't think that's true. What matters is if you can remember some bits of what it's like to be a child. I recall very vividly the way little things worried me as a child. Standing outside the headmistress's door, waiting to be 'seen' for instance."

That particular recollection could be significant. Was Jill Murphy often to be found standing outside the headmistress's door? Perhaps. There's an individuality about her approach and her outlook that could, earlier on, have smacked of the non-conformist.

For two years Jill Murphy worked in a children's home— "and that was lovely." *Peace At Last* grew from a story she told a small boy as she was taking him to playgroup. "When I went to collect him he asked if he could have the story again so I wrote it down and illustrated it."

The book—commended in the Kate Greenaway Awards—tells how poor Mr Bear cannot get to sleep. First it's the tap dripping, Mrs Bear snoring, the clock ticking . . . when at last he drops off it's only to be awakened by the alarm going off.

It remains the artist's favourite. "For one thing when I read it to children in libraries it doesn't sound too bad. Usually I'm consumed with embarrassment when I read aloud."

Many so-called children's books today are books for the parents. Jill Murphy's books are rare because although they explore situations familiar to parents they can also be recognised as familiar to children. They allow a child to step outside his body, as it were, and see events objectively.

Five Minutes Peace grew from a real life situation. "A friend and I wanted to have a chat, uninterrupted by her children, so we thought if she had a bath I'd take up a cup of tea and we'd have a bit of time on our own. What happened? Well, they all came up. First one read us a story in that Dalek sort of voice children have when they're first reading, and then the baby kept plonking things in the water."

There is a robustness to her books that could mask their sensitivity. Look at the three elephant children on this page, learning that Mum is off "to have five minutes peace from you lot." Each is reacting in keeping with its age. The eldest is a bit truculent, the middle merely meek, the youngest is near to tears.

Perhaps surprisingly Jill Murphy prefers the writing to the drawing. "The illustrations are very laborious. I use coloured pencil and it takes three or four days to finish one drawing."

"It's all beautiful though—and terrible. I can remember going upstairs on my hands and knees just so that I wouldn't be seen through an open doorway by three small children. Just for once I wanted to go to the lavatory alone. It wasn't to be though."

The only trouble with getting peace at last is that when you've got it you miss the chaos.

TITLE COMMENTARY

📖 *THE WORST WITCH* (1974); *THE WORST WITCH STRIKES AGAIN* (1980)

Leon Garfield

SOURCE: "The Real Thing," in *The Spectator,* Vol. 234, No. 7659, April 12, 1975, pp. 440-41.

The Worst Witch, is for nine or ten year olds—and up. This, perhaps, is more in the nature of a romp, but it comes off beautifully. Miss Murphy has taken all the ingredients of the traditional girls' school story (the girl who's good at everything, the unlucky blunderer and the awful mistress), and turned them to excellent purpose in Miss Cackle's Academy for Witches. This might so easily have gone off the rails, but Miss Murphy's absolute sincerity and enjoyment are fully communicated. In addition, Miss Murphy has enriched her book with charming pen drawings. I particularly liked the one of the inept pupil-witch in her gothic bed, cuddling her equally inept cat and surrounded by friendly bats. Her pointed hat, one notes with especial pleasure, sports the school colours and badge.

Publishers Weekly

SOURCE: A review of *The Worst Witch,* in *Publishers Weekly,* Vol. 217, No. 23, June 13, 1980, p. 73.

During her first year at Miss Cackle's select school for

witches, Mildred Hubble blots her copybook continually, drawing lectures from form-mistress Miss Hardbroom. But the fumbler struggles on, trying to learn until Halloween Eve, when she makes a mess of the broomstick-riding display, a performance attended by the chief wizard, no less. The school meanie has cast a spell on the broom she "kindly" lends Mildred. But even knowing she wasn't at fault for once, the chastised student runs away in her dejection. Then her luck changes, finally. Mildred foils a wicked coven plotting to take over the school and becomes a heroine. Murphy's brisk, tongue-in-cheek version of doings at a British academy for young ladies, with its zippy ink drawings, is a treat. So is the sequel, *The Worst Witch Strikes Again. . . .*

Margery Fisher

SOURCE: A review of *The Worst Witch Strikes Again,* in *Growing Point,* Vol. 19, No. 3, September, 1980, pp. 3744.

Junior stories that centre on a witch are likely to be either comic, with the young reader encouraged to take a light view of the improbable aspect of magic, or sinister, with magic threatening to get out of hand. The kind of metaphor which Helen Cresswell achieved through Lizzie Dripping's sardonic apparition is rare in books for the young—rare, most of all, because of the complete integration of adult and child vision. In *The Worst Witch strikes again* (and its predecessor, *The Worst Witch*) the species witch is, as it were, humanised, and serves the same role as the animated scarecrow Worzel Gummidge in providing an outlet for the anarchic feelings of the young. Mildred, *enfant terrible* of Miss Cackle's Academy for Witches, is put in charge of a new girl in the hope that responsibility will steady her. Unfortunately blonde Enid's demure appearance is deceptive; her behaviour is as subversive as Mildred's but more capably disguised. It is a long time before anyone realises that the monkey who disrupts school discipline is her permitted cat-familiar under enchantment, and the spell which hurls Mildred through a window into a decorous tea-party at the end of her pole-vault is never brought home to Enid. However, Mildred does learn some sense by Enid's mischief, and the young reader learns something about cause and effect in a series of episodes in which teachers (soft, tough or sarcastic) and fellow pupils (loyal, quarrelsome or gullible) approximate with comic effect to the everyday life of any classroom. The racy humour of the book is supported by vigorous drawings that lend personality to the characters in terms of gentle caricature.

Susan Cain

SOURCE: A review of *The Worst Witch* and *The Worst Witch Strikes Again,* in *School Library Journal,* Vol. 27, No. 1, September, 1980, p. 62.

Miss Cackles' Academy is a typical girls' boarding school, with one exception: it is for witches. The curriculum consists of broomstick riding, cat training, spells, potions, chants, etc. The premise is a good one; unfortunately, the execution is not as good. There is no plot or character development, no suspense, and the episodes are only mildly interesting, even when the "goody-goody" is turned into a large pig. Everything about the books are disappointing except the illustrations, which are numerous and humorous.

Zena Sutherland

SOURCE: A review of *The Worst Witch,* in *Bulletin of the Center for Children's Books,* Vol. 34, No. 2, October, 1980, p. 38.

Brisk and tidy line drawings illustrate a story about the least promising scholar at Miss Cackle's Academy for Witches. Harum-scarum Mildred breaks her broomstick, makes the wrong potion, turns a classmate into a pig, and is the despair of the teachers. Mildred runs away, stumbles into a coven of evil witches who are planning to take over the school, turns them into snails, and becomes the school heroine. The writing is competent if not outstanding; what gives the book character is the combination of arcane subjects and the uniforms-and-rules atmosphere of a typical English girls' school; the appeal for readers lies in the humor of that combination and in the small disasters that beset the hapless Mildred's path.

PEACE AT LAST (1980)

Publishers Weekly

SOURCE: A review of *Peace at Last,* in *Publishers Weekly,* Vol. 218, No. 16, October 17, 1980, p. 65.

Mr. and Mrs. Bear and Baby Bear retire after a busy day. Mrs. Bear is soon snoozing peacefully but snoring so explosively that Mr. Bear gives up hope of getting any rest. Searching for a quiet spot, he settles down in Baby's room but the child won't stop pretending he's an airplane—with sound effects. Throughout the endless night, Mr. Bear seeks the silence he needs and finally dozes off just as breakfast is served. Murphy's story is familiar, crisply told and amusing. It is not a patch, however, on the exuberant spirit of her remarkable paintings. Big, beautifully colored pictures leap with jovial surprises like the single fat curler under the net protecting Mrs. Bear's coiffure, the baby's mushroom night-light, his drawing tacked to the wall and other neat touches.

Kristi L. Thomas

SOURCE: A review of *Peace at Last,* in *School Library Journal,* Vol. 27, No. 4, December, 1980, p. 54.

Three bears, Mr., Mrs. and Baby, settle down for a good night's sleep. Unfortunately, while the Mrs. begins to snore the Mr. is left open-eyed, sleepless and searching for quiet. There follows a series of "'Oh NO,' said Mr. Bear, 'I

can't stand THIS.'" as he encounters various noises in Baby Bear's room, the living room, etc. Morning finds him back in bed; Mrs. B. has ceased snoring just in time for sunrise. The lumpish, stolid text contains enough repetitions to make it a storyhour candidate, but it will not hold interest to the end. The subject matter is unfamiliar to most preschoolers (few suffer from insomnia), the format is too babyish for beginning readers and the text is irritatingly littered with UNNECESSARY capitalization. HOWEVER, the illustrations are lovely. Meticulously detailed black-and-white pages containing the text alternate with richly colored scenes glowing with inner lights: the cozy closeness of lamplight, the shadowy wash of moonlight.

Mary James

SOURCE: "New Slants on Old Themes," in *The Times Educational Supplement,* No. 3365, December 19, 1980, p. 21.

The problem of getting to sleep is . . . a common one and, making a teddy bear suffer it in *Peace At Last,* Jill Murphy combines originality with simplicity of storyline, another important ingredient of picture-book success. *Peace At Last* is particularly good for reading aloud, requiring a challenging range of sound effects including Mrs Bear's snores and a dripping tap.

Elaine Moss

SOURCE: "Unsuspected Charms," in *The Times Literary Supplement,* No. 4069, March 27, 1981, p. 342.

Teddy Bear Baker and *Peace At Last* look strangely out of place in the plethora of sophisticated art-picture books (Bayley, Anderson), socially progressive family portraits (the van der Meers) and psychological explorations (Sendak and followers) that are typical of the 1980s scene.

What, one asks oneself, can be said about such simple, basic, unpretentious offerings? Even the youngest child will have no difficulty in following the story, absorbing the detail in the pictures, making each book his own in that special way that almost excludes the adult. It is for this reason, perhaps, that neither book has received due critical attention: such comfortable, unfashionable books needed no intermediary. Perhaps it is embarrassing even to include them among the scintillating internationally beamed art work? But Jill Murphy's *Peace At Last* and Phoebe and Selby Worthington's *Teddy Bear Baker* do deserve mention, special mention. Unashamedly British, totally child-oriented, carefully written and meticulously illustrated they make a restrained bid for a return of innocence to early childhood's picture books.

Peace At Last tells the story of Father Bear who cannot get to sleep anywhere. "Baby Bear . . . was lying in bed pretending to be an aeroplane . . . NYAAOW . . . NYAAOW". Garage, kitchen, garden—all have their night

From The Worst Witch Strikes Again, *written and illustrated by Jill Murphy.*

noises. But with dawn comes "peace at last"—and the alarm bell! Jill Murphy's large framed colour pictures of the bears are full of good old-fashioned domestic humour, and her black-and-white illustrations that mingle with the satisfying text add their own delectable touches.

Zena Sutherland

SOURCE: A review of *Peace at Last,* in *Bulletin of the Center for Children's Books,* Vol. 34, No. 8, April, 1981, p. 157.

An engaging vignette of family life focuses on poor Mr. Bear's efforts to get some sleep. He tries Baby Bear's room because Mrs. Bear is snoring, but his offspring is wide awake and making airplane noises; he moves from room to room getting more and more heavy-eyed, as ticking clocks, dripping faucets, and outdoor night noises keep him awake. Just as he finds peace at last the alarm clock rings. His cheery, rested wife brings a cup of tea and the mail, and the last page shows bleary Papa gazing in resignation at Baby Bear, who has brought himself and toys,

and has affectionately climbed in Papa's bed. The story appears on the verso pages with line drawings; facing pages are in full color; the pictures have warmth and humor and the story is told in brisk, forthright style with an appealing refrain that will probably elicit listener-participation, "Oh, NO! I can't stand THIS."

Frances Ball

SOURCE: A review of *Peace at Last,* in *Books for Your Children,* Vol. 16, No. 1, Spring, 1981, p. 10.

Poor Mr Bear can't sleep. Everywhere he goes there is some kind of noise: Mrs Bear snores in their bedroom, the clock ticks in the living room, a tap drips in the kitchen. At last he returns and falls exhausted into bed only to be woken by the alarm clock.

The story is beautifully simple, beautifully illustrated. Each illustration makes its point clearly but also includes details about the life of the Bear Family. The pages of text have also been treated imaginatively. It is a very satisfying story: partly because of its simplicity, partly because of the feeling of warmth and security conveyed by the colour and detail of the illustrations.

📖 *A BAD SPELL FOR THE WORST WITCH* (1982)

A. Thatcher

SOURCE: A review of *A Bad Spell for the Worst Witch,* in *The Junior Bookshelf,* Vol. 46, No. 5, October, 1982, p. 192.

In an hilarious sequel to **The Worst Witch,** and **The Worst Witch Strikes Again,** Mildred Hubble flies back for her second year at Miss Crackle's Academy for Witches, with her terrified tabby cat spread-eagled on her broomstick. Her friends Enid and Maud are very pleased to see her. But it isn't long before she manages to upset her detested teacher, Miss Hardbroom. A misunderstanding with her old enemy Ethel Hallow ends in Mildred being turned into a frog. However, all ends happily and Mildred is able to help an old frog-enchanted magician she had met in the school pond.

A funny, very original, fast-moving idea, in which an uncomfortable girl's boarding school atmosphere and witch practices are integrated cleverly. There are plenty of amusing black and white cartoon-like illustrations, full of imaginative detail. The scarlet and black front cover is vividly dramatic, contrasting with the tearful appealing green from Mildred on the back. Good fun that girls from 6 to 12 should enjoy.

Rodie Sudbery

SOURCE: A review of *A Bad Spell for the Worst Witch,* in *The School Librarian,* Vol. 30, No. 4, December, 1982, p. 343.

The classic theme of a naughty girl at school is here given an added fillip by the fact that Mildred Hubble is a young witch, and the school she attends is a Witches' Academy. I have not read the first two books about her, but this one is fun, and stands up well on its own. From the first few pages, one knows that one is in for a good read—characters skilfully drawn, both in words and in pictures, and possibilities abounding. Mildred very soon manages to annoy both the fearsome Miss Hardbroom and the sneaky Ethel Hallow; people become frogs, and frogs people; and disappearing potions are opportunely to hand. It is a beautifully cosy book, despite the Spartan school and its iron discipline: 'Let us hope that your feet are in the correct place by the morning, Mildred', says Miss Hardbroom frostily, and Mildred sits there in pyjamas, with her tabby cat warming her toes. The illustrations are just right—endearing young witches in uniform cloaks and pointed hats, grim teachers, and Mildred's cat clamped to her broom because of its terror of flying.

Carolyn O'Grady

SOURCE: "Flights of Fancy," in *The Times Educational Supplement,* No. 3472, January 14, 1983, p. 34.

A Bad Spell for the Worst Witch could do with a little more . . . spice. Ms Murphy's [third] Worst Witch book, it is based on a wonderful idea—an academy for young witches where Mildred Hubble and her friends Maud and Enid learn their craft. But the style and the storyline is essentially English public school all-gels-together. Mildred is the unacademic heroine with her heart in the right place; Ethel is the school creep; Miss Hardbroom is the severe teacher who applauds Ethel and harrows Mildred; Miss Cackle is the too-soft headmistress. The difference, of course, is that they are all witches and, instead of walking, ride on broomsticks and, instead of making apple-pie beds, they turn each other into frogs: the chapters in which Mildred is a frog are the best in the book. But the stories need a pinch more imagination really to take off.

📖 *ON THE WAY HOME* (1982)

M. Hobbs

SOURCE: A review of *On the Way Home,* in *The Junior Bookshelf,* Vol. 46, No. 5, October, 1982, p. 180.

Jill Murphy's **On the Way Home** also uses what is really an element from folktale, this time the tall tale with variations. In lovely clear doublespread strip-scenes, Claire goes slowly home after hurting her knee to tell her mother of her fall, meeting each of her (multiracial) schoolfriends with a different explanation of "how I got my bad knee." Her fantasies, pictured within wavy frames so that you recognise them as such, encompass a wolf, a flying saucer, crocodile, python, dragon, gorilla, giant, ghost and witch—Claire is obviously an avid reader! But to her sympathetic mother she tells the truth. A beautifully designed book, from the endpapers onwards. A whole town's life is subtly built up in the unobtrusive but very detailed backgrounds.

Audrey Laski

SOURCE: A review of *On the Way Home,* in *The Times Educational Supplement,* No. 3566, November 2, 1984, p. 26.

There is a pleasant uncertainty here about whether the visitors are real magic or simply products of his imagination; in **On The Way Home,** we can clearly see the little girl producing dazzling explanation after explanation to explain her wounded knee to her friends, it is only the reassuring presence of her mother that allows her to give up, cry, and tell the less exotic true story: a stunning picture-book.

📖 *WHATEVER NEXT!* (1983; U.S. edition as *What Next, Baby Bear!*)

Margery Fisher

SOURCE: A review of *Whatever Next!* in *Growing Point,* Vol. 22, No. 5, January, 1984, p. 4203.

As a surrogate child, a cosy little bear sets off up the chimney on an imaginary adventure in a box space-ship, with a colander for helmet and Wellingtons for space-boots: he and his chance-met friend, an owl, enjoy a picnic on the Moon; then the voyager comes down to earth and his mother, ignoring his excited tale, submerges his sooty person in the bath. An affectionate softness of shapes and outlines suits the gentle tale, which reconciles domestic security and imagination in a way to suit small children.

Tessa Rose Chester

SOURCE: "Fantastic Creatures," in *The Times Educational Supplement,* No. 3524, January 13, 1984, p. 44.

Play fantasy is the theme of Jill Murphy's *Whatever Next!* Baby Bear flies to the moon in a cardboard box for a rocket and wellingtons for space boots, and comes back down the chimney in time for bed. Here again the security of family life is emphasized by the end ritual of bath-time with a comforting Mother Bear. Though this is not an original theme, being seen at its best in the Minarik/Sendak "Little Bear" stories, the text is inoffensive and concise, with smooth, glowing illustrations.

M. Hobbs

SOURCE: A review of *Whatever Next!* in *The Junior Bookshelf,* Vol. 48, No. 2, April, 1984, p. 62.

Jill Murphy's serene larger-than-life Bear family is back, and Baby Bear at bedtime has a trip, not to the Wild Things but in a gentler and younger way, to look at space in a cardboard-box rocket, with his Teddy and a passing owl. Inevitably, his passage up and down the chimney leaves its traces, but when, in answer to his mother's pained questions, he tells her where he has been, "Whatever next!" she exclaims. The secret of the attractiveness of Jill Murphy's large and comforting shapes and simple colours is above all the similarity in cuddliness between bear and human toddler.

Ilene Cooper

SOURCE: A review of *What Next, Baby Bear!* in *Booklist,* Vol. 80, No. 17, May 1, 1984, p. 1252.

A sprightly, inventive story features Baby Bear, introduced in *Peace at Last*. Baby Bear looks out the window and wonders if he can go to the moon. His mother tells him he can't; it's bath time. Besides, he'd need a rocket. That's okay, Baby Bear reasons, and pulls out a cardboard box to be his spaceship, with a colander as helmet. He pushes the craft to the chimney and whoosh! Out he goes into the night. He meets a companionable owl, waves at the passengers on a jet, has a picnic on the moon, and then goes down through his home chimney—just in time for a bath. The story is simple, yet teases young listeners with the question, was the trip purely imaginary? Baby Bear is, after all, very sooty in the end. But most appealing is the artwork; cleverly wrought black-and-white drawings alternate with charming full-page pictures in jewel-like colors. Little ones will feel an affinity for the whole package; as a bedtime story this should elicit some sweet dreams.

Judith Gloyer

SOURCE: A review of *What Next, Baby Bear!* in *School Library Journal,* Vol. 31, No. 1, September, 1984, pp. 107-08.

In this appealing sequel to *Peace at Last,* Baby Bear takes center stage in a tale well suited for bedtime reading or evening story hour programs. When Baby Bear decides he wants to take a trip to the moon, his mother informs him that he can't go because it is bathtime and he doesn't have a rocket. He finds a rocket (a large carton), a space helmet (a colander) and a pair of space boots (galoshes). Taking provisions and his teddy bear, he blasts off into space via the chimney, returning in time for his now much-needed bath. Sharp pen-and-ink drawings alternate with softly glowing and gently shaded full-color drawings. The action seems frozen, but this technique suits Baby Bear's flight in weightless space. His gestures and expressions ably capture his shifting moods; his arms tucked into the front of his overalls, his obvious guilt when he is completely covered with soot from the chimney and his final yawn when he is dressed for bed are in perfect keeping with gestures and expressions of young children.

Margery Fisher

SOURCE: A review of *Whatever Next!* in *Growing Point,* Vol. 27, No. 5, January, 1989, pp. 5083-84.

Humanising toys, like humanising animals, is most successful (that is, most readily accepted) when writer and artist keep as close as possible to a reality. The stylised shapes of teddy bear and wooden doll can be manipulated into human situations and postures very readily; indeed, some writers (Joan Robinson, for example) have chosen incidents in which the toy in question is totally passive and arranged rather than supposedly free moving. . . .

The baby bear standing in for a child in *Whatever next!* has a toy teddy of his own but there is enough resemblance here in his cartoon-shape to identify him as a toy himself, used as a medium for a familiar example of imagination. Finding accessible objects at home to make a space-ship (a box for the rocket, for instance and a colander for a helmet), the bear takes off up the chimney and reaches the moon, accompanied by a passing owl which shares his picnic; his mother bathing her sooty son on his return predictably comments 'You and your stories. . . . Whatever next?'. The deep colour of the night sky and the toy-tea-party appearance of the lunar picnic make a gently attractive picture-book with a small hero congenial to the very young for more than one reason.

FIVE MINUTES' PEACE (1986)

Publishers Weekly

SOURCE: A review of *Five Minutes' Peace*, in *Publishers Weekly*, Vol. 230, No. 8, August 22, 1986, p. 92.

Mrs. Large just wants five minutes' peace from her three rambunctious elephant children, that's all. But what meets her eyes one morning when she enters the kitchen? "The children were having breakfast. This was not a pleasant sight." Pure understatement for a mealtime mess that includes an overturned cereal box, a dripping jar of honey, crushed soft-boiled eggs and on the littlest one, the wearing of a once-full bowl of corn flakes. So Mrs. Large lumbers off to the bathroom, tea on tray, newspapers in bathrobe pocket. But her bubble bath isn't soothing for long; she's soon joined by three visitors. Lester wants to play a tune for her on the flute. "Must you?" Mrs. Large asks. Laura wishes to read out loud. "Just *one* page," says Mrs. Large. The toddler offers—and he will not be refused—*all* his bathtoys. Then they hop into the tub. Mrs. Large heads for the kitchen and finds exactly three minutes and 45 seconds of peace. This book is pure joy, one that parents, not just children, will want to keep on hand; Murphy's frazzled mom will find a soft spot in every reader.

Gillian Cross

SOURCE: A review of *Five Minutes' Peace*, in *British Book News Children's Books*, Autumn, 1986, p. 10.

Five Minutes' Peace . . . , is all about maternal fantasies. A mother elephant retreats to the bathroom to escape from family breakfast but, inevitably, her children follow her, brandishing toys, reading-books and recorders. The story is very slight, but the pictures are exuberant and full of elephants, and even two-year-olds could probably understand Mrs Large's plight, and appreciate the chaos her children generate.

M. Hobbs

SOURCE: A review of *Five Minutes' Peace*, in *The Junior Bookshelf*, Vol. 50, No. 6, December, 1986, p. 220.

Elephants this time, and as large and placid as Jill Murphy's bear family. Mother tries to breakfast in peace in the bathroom. At first it seems she has succeeded, as she sets up her bath and the tray. Then, one by one, the three children follow her upstairs on various ploys, and they all end up in the bath. Mayhem! Mother retreats to the kitchen and achieves 3 minutes 45 seconds' peace before it all begins again. It is amazing how elephants can reflect expressions we all recognise in such family situations. It is also amazing how many such kep situations Jill Murphy identifies in her books, with their clear, fresh illustrations. This is another really splendid one, for parents as well as for children.

Betsy Hearne

SOURCE: A review of *Five Minutes' Peace*, in *Bulletin of the Center for Children's Books*, Vol. 40, No. 5, January, 1987, p. 93.

Inasmuch as children can laugh at themselves and their parents, this will appeal to young listeners; adults will love every minute of it. Mrs. Large takes one look at her three elephant children wreaking havoc at the breakfast table, makes up a tea tray, and sneaks off to the bathroom for "five minutes' peace." There she is shortly joined by Lester, who plays "Twinkle, Twinkle, Little Star" three and a half times; Laura, who reads four and a half pages of "Little Red Riding Hood"; and the baby, who generously throws all his toys into Mrs. Large's bubble bath. Abandoning the tub to the children, Mrs. Large returns with the newspaper (the children have eaten her breakfast) to the kitchen, where she finally achieves three minutes and forty-five seconds of peace. The fine-grained color pencil drawings are softly textured and funny; and mother elephant's dilemma is a familiar enough one that children may enjoy it even from her perspective.

Graham Nutbrown

SOURCE: A review of *Five Minutes' Peace*, in *The School Librarian*, Vol. 35, No. 1, February, 1987, p. 36.

A picture book with delightful, detailed, whole-page illustrations in which each of the Large family of elephants has individuality and character. Mrs Large is fed up with the usual breakfast-time chaos and escapes with cakes and a newspaper to a lovely bubble bath, only to be pursued by the children. They insist on reading to her, playing their recorders, sharing their bath toys with her, and finally joining her in the bath. The large-print text is economical and understated. Suitable for readers and non-readers of two upwards, it may strike most chords with weary parents.

ALL IN ONE PIECE (1987)

Publishers Weekly

SOURCE: A review of *All in One Piece*, in *Publishers Weekly*, Vol. 232, No. 7, August 14, 1987, p. 101.

Five Minutes' Peace delivered into the hands of readers a near-perfect reflection of a family's typically calamitous morning; now the adult elephants are dressing for an evening out, and their well-meaning but high-spirited children won't leave them alone. They stuff Mrs. Large's hosiery with toys, mess with makeup and clatter around in high heels. She, of course, loses her temper, which has the effect of subduing her children. But she inadvertently sits on a paint box and goes out unaware that her dress is adorned with small bright patches of color. Sharp-eyed readers will spot this development; others will want to go through the story again to find out when it all happened. *Five Minutes' Peace* fans may not find the antics in this followup quite as funny as its predecessor. But with its resemblance to real life, this continuing saga of the beleaguered Mrs. Large and her boisterous offspring is still a delight.

Kate Flint

SOURCE: "Extraordinary and Everyday," in *The Times Literary Supplement,* No. 4416, November 20-26, 1987, p. 1284.

In *All in One Piece* Jill Murphy introduces a large, lively, and socially conventional family of elephants. Mr and Mrs Large prepare to go to the office dinner-dance, deftly using the trunk-tip to knot the striped tie, dangling earrings from the long grey lobes, and painting the toe-nails a delicate pink. Granny comes to look after the young elephants, but she is powerless to prevent them smearing themselves with paint and make-up, and stretching their mother's already voluminous new tights with their collection of toys. They woefully hang their trunks when Mrs Large explodes at them, demanding her one night of freedom in the year: as she and her husband leave the house, however, the neat squares of paint on her bottom, left from where she injudiciously sat down on a paint-box, are brightly conspicuous. Murphy has a deft command of endearing elephant expressions, conveys well the comfortably untidy family home, down to the details of the spreading shaving foam in the bathroom, the elephant's-head door-knocker and the children's first drawings of their own species. None the less, this family, tamed in striped jerseys, starry pyjamas and an evening dress that looks as if it has been borrowed from Miss Piggy, are depressingly trapped within suburbia. Rather than our being taken into an elephant world, they are brought entirely within our own.

Barbara Elleman

SOURCE: A review of *All in One Piece,* in *Booklist,* Vol. 84, No. 7, December 1, 1987, p. 636.

The elephants Mr. and Mrs. Large and their family from *Five Minutes' Peace* are back. An invitation to a dinner party is on the evening's agenda, and Mrs. Large is trying, in vain, to get ready for the big event. Luke plays with his father's shaving cream, Laura clops about in her mother's best shoes, the baby is decorating herself with Mother's makeup, and Lester and Luke are seeing how many toys they can cram into Mother's tights. At last, Mother issues an ultimatum and sends them downstairs. When she joins them the children agree she looks smashing; then, with Granny in charge, the little ones wave off their parents with a minimum of tears. Mrs. Large sighs "All in one piece," to which Mr. Large gallantly replies, "You'd look wonderful to me, even if you were covered in paint." As they walk away, only readers will see the squares of colors that decorate Mrs. Large's skirt—a souvenir of the paintbox she inadvertently sat on while saying good-bye to the children. Adults reading this aloud may be more amused than the children, but all will delight in the rich colors, attention to detail, and marvelous faces that Murphy uses to distinguish her oh-so-human elephants.

M. Crouch

SOURCE: A review of *All in One Piece,* in *The Junior Bookshelf,* Vol. 52, No. 1, February, 1988, p. 24.

Another endearing picture-book from a favourite author-artist. Every parent will sympathize with Mr. and Mrs. Large whose preparations for a night-out are being sabotaged by their unruly offspring. Despite all the efforts of the rowdy and paint-smeared children, Mr. and Mrs. Large are at last able to leave for their dinner-dance, with an unperturbed Granny in charge at home. Mrs. Large is looking 'a smasher', at least from the front!

It somehow sharpens the reality of this familiar domestic situation when all those taking part are elephants.

Judith Sharman

SOURCE: A review of *All in One Piece,* in *Books for Keeps,* No. 58, September, 1989, p. 11.

Jill Murphy has found the winning formula of making her books work just as successfully for both children and adults. Mrs. Large, who struggled so hard to get *Five Minutes' Peace* in the last book, is once again submerged in motherhood, this time trying to get ready to go for her long-awaited evening out and being thwarted by the help and hindrance offered by her children. The appeal to children is immediate with the wonderfully naughty children and brilliantly clever character illustrations. Rueful identification with Mrs Large is inevitable in any adult with experience of young children!

WORLDS APART (1988)

Kirkus Reviews

SOURCE: A review of *Worlds Apart,* in *Kirkus Reviews,* Vol. LVI, No. 23, December 1, 1988, pp. 1742-43.

Susie, an English 12-year-old—who apparently knows she's addressing Americans, since she explains (rather unnecessarily) that "'Mummy' is the word we use for 'Mommy'" and that plays in London's West End are "like Broadway," and even calls the Underground "the subway"—tells how her unknown father turns out to be a famous actor, familiar from a long-running American soap.

Since Susie's mother, Petunia, earns their support by working in a dress shop, money has always been scarce. Susie is naturally curious about her other parent; now, with a bit of detective work—largely limited to asking an old friend of Petunia's the right questions—she discovers that he is the renowned Lloyd Hunter just returning to London to appear in a play, and that her mother turned him out because of his alcoholism. Susie goes to see him and is welcomed with open arms. He's rich, he's reformed, he still loves her mother, they're even still married—and soon back together.

There's not much plot here, just a common fantasy fleshed out. Easily absorbed trivia.

Publishers Weekly

SOURCE: A review of *Worlds Apart,* in *Publishers Weekly,* Vol. 234, No. 24, December 9, 1988, p. 65.

Murphy's first novel is an exercise in adolescent wish-fulfillment. Packed with authorial asides and Americanized slang (which some readers might find jarring, given the London setting), the story tells of Susan, 12, who lives an equable life with her mother Petunia, an actress-turned-retailer. They exist amiably in a flat outside London, with little money, but few real concerns. Susan's problem is that she wants to know more about her father, whom her mother refuses to discuss. He turns out to be matinee idol Lloyd Hunter, a rich, kindly man who is still madly in love with Susan's mother, and longing to know his daughter. Naturally, the three of them are soon together. They move into his wonderfully opulent house and Susan gets the dog she's always wanted by story's end. This is more fairy tale than novel, and therefore, may appeal to those looking for light escape. But readers seeking substance will do better elsewhere.

Bill Boyle

SOURCE: A review of *Worlds Apart,* in *The School Librarian,* Vol. 37, No. 1, February, 1989, p. 22.

Jill Murphy has a proven track record for quality fiction for the middle junior age/interest range (as well as highly successful picture books for the younger end of the market); and *Worlds apart* will do nothing to damage that reputation. The 'broken family' situation is one that an increasing percentage of young readers can identify with, and they also are likely to have developed, like Susan, 'an invisible magic shield', a defence mechanism to repel the taunts of uncharitable peers. Susan has no idea who her father is, but manages by ingenious wheedling not only to discover his identity, but also to manipulate a

reconciliation between her parents. This is not nearly so contrived in the development of the story, of course, though the predictability of events does become obvious a little too early. But that remains the only criticism of this well-written, highly relevant tale, told with the cold factuality necessary in dealing with a highly emotive situation, and relieved with the necessary leavening of fantasy.

Ilene Cooper

SOURCE: A review of *Worlds Apart,* in *Booklist,* Vol. 85, No. 11, February 1, 1989, pp. 940-41.

Twelve-year-old Susan Hunter lives with her mother in a dingy London flat near Hampstead Heath. Although Susan and her mother are close, there is one subject Mrs. Hunter refuses to discuss—Susan's father. One day after Susan's particularly emotional appeal, Mrs. Hunter gives her some of the facts. Susan's father was an actor. At first, the three of them were happy, but when Mr. Hunter couldn't find work, things began to fall apart. His drinking was the final straw, and when he almost injured Susan, Mrs. Hunter took her and left. This information, which her mother thinks will be the final word on the subject, only whets Susan's appetite, and she goes on a "quest" to find her father. At this point, the story deteriorates into a fairy tale. Mr. Hunter, recently in a hit American TV series, has returned to London to star in a West End play. Susan finds him, her parents reconcile, they move into a big house, and she gets a dog. Both the chatty first-person narrative and the uninspired turn of events are problematic. However, the happy-ever-after factor may be just the thing kids will like about the story. Who hasn't wished for a rich daddy to come and make things right?

Zena Sutherland

SOURCE: A review of *Worlds Apart,* in *Bulletin of the Center for Children's Books,* Vol. 42, No. 7, March, 1989, p. 177.

Susan, who tells the story, is an English eleven-year-old whose mother has never talked about the husband from whom she had long been separated, but who agrees to tell her story when Susan pleads for information. Susan then uses guile (in dealing with a family friend) to get the one fact Mother has omitted: the name. Turns out he's a famous actor, turns out he's thrilled when Susan presents herself in his dressing-room, turns out that the flame of love has never died and so Mother and Father are reunited, and everybody is happy, including the puppy that Father gives Susan. Palatable because of the adequate style and appealing because of the romantic plot, but not Murphy at her best.

Trev Jones

SOURCE: A review of *Worlds Apart,* in *School Library Journal,* Vol. 35, No. 7, March, 1989, p. 178.

In a fast-paced, chatty style perfectly suited to the story, 12-year-old Susan meets her father, whom her ex-actress mother had left years before and refuses to discuss. Susan discovers that he is a rich and famous actor living in America, where he stars in a popular television series, *Worlds Apart,* but who is returning to London to star in a new play. Determined to meet him, she sneaks into his dressing room, and from then on events progress satisfyingly smoothly. She gets her mother and father together (they'd never remarried because they were still in love with each other); and they all live happily ever after on his enormous estate instead of the dingy little apartment in which she and her mother lived. It's a light and frothy modern fairy tale, great fun to read, and not meant to be taken seriously. No problems, no heavy message—just enjoyable escape reading, casted with thoroughly likable people.

Linda Taylor

SOURCE: "Parental Worries," in *The Times Literary Supplement,* No. 4497, June 9-15, 1989, p. 648.

Jill Murphy became well known as a children's writer with her Worst Witch series which was directed at a slightly younger age group than *Worlds Apart:* coyly enchanting tales about girls at witch-school, about getting into trouble and the generation gap between adults and children. Though the witch girls do take off on broomsticks, the stories are firmly earthed in domesticity, as are Murphy's books for the under-fives which concern sweetly naughty offspring misbehaving within a comforting family enclave headed by a good, though amusingly harassed, mother.

In *Worlds Apart,* eleven-year-old Susan Hunter's actress-mother is harassed because she is a poor single parent estranged from her drunken actor husband. Petunia Hunter left Lloyd and acting, and she now has a not very well-paid job in a trendy boutique near Hampstead Heath. Susan knows almost nothing about her missing father who, in the interim, has given up drink and become famous in a television series. When she does discover her unlikely relationship with fame, Susan sets out on a quest to find him. In the story, everyone's dreams come true: Petunia and Susan are set up with Prince Daddy in a thick-carpeted house in Hampstead.

The sentimentality of all this is somewhat relieved by Susan's narrative tone: her matter-of-fact view of the world and how ugly she is; her chatty ease—this is me having a bash at writing a book and I'm not much good at it. The self-conscious writer in Susan provides the only bit of provocative thought in the book. Susan deconstructs her text as she goes, with authorial asides, digressions and a discussion about the impossibility of beginnings and endings: "I'll never get the hang of writing books. I mean, how do you *end* the thing when there's always so much more to add?" But aside from this tongue-in-cheek interest in structure, the book's content, characters and general level of conversation ("Oh Susan . . . I can't tell you how thrilled I am to have found you again") is dimly conceived.

A PIECE OF CAKE (1989)

Publishers Weekly

SOURCE: A review of *A Piece of Cake,* in *Publishers Weekly,* Vol. 236, No. 17, October 27, 1989, p. 66.

Mrs. Large, that peerless pachyderm parent last seen in *Five Minutes' Peace,* makes a return engagement. This time, she decides that she's just a tad too elephantine (as her baby succinctly puts it, "Mummy's got wobbly bits"). Accordingly, she dons an enormous orange sweatsuit emblazoned with the word "FIT" and puts her reluctant husband and the four little Larges on a diet. There's watercress soup, grated carrots and other unappetizing fare, as well as lots of jogging. Nothing seems to work, however, and the fitness kick is undermined by the arrival of a cake from Granny. None of the Larges can resist its sugary allure, and in a hilarious climax they unwittingly rendezvous in the kitchen for a midnight snack. Murphy's drawings are both delicate and droll (the sight of Mrs. Large tiptoeing determinedly to the kitchen in nightgown and curlers is particularly memorable), and the tale's message—that it's important to love yourself the way you are—will strike a universal chord in readers.

Kirkus Reviews

SOURCE: A review of *A Piece of Cake,* in *Kirkus Reviews,* Vol. LVII, No. 23, December 1, 1989, p. 1751.

A portly mother elephant, Mrs. Large (of *Five Minutes' Peace,* 1986) decides that she's fat, though her children disagree: "You're our cuddly mommy . . . *just* right." Nevertheless, she puts the whole family on a stern regimen of exercise and healthy food, to no avail: "Perhaps elephants are *meant* to be fat," says little Luke. Joy is restored when Mrs. Large herself sneaks down to the kitchen for a midnight snack—only to find that the rest of the family has saved her the last piece of the forbidden cake sent by Granny. There's a niche ready-made for a book that says it's okay to be fat; this one, with its earnest, anxious elephants dutifully squeezed into running togs, makes the point with winsome good humor. A portrait of the family collapsed in an affectionate heap after their unaccustomed exertions is especially appealing.

Virginia E. Jeschelnig

SOURCE: A review of *A Piece of Cake,* in *School Library Journal,* Vol. 36, No. 1, January, 1990, pp. 86-7.

The elephantine Large family is back! This time they are plagued by pounds, and Mrs. Large is determined to lead them on the quest for fitness. Mr. Large and the four children reluctantly join Mother in jogging and junkfree dining. Although they succeed in resisting old habits for a time, the fatal temptation arrives by mail: a calorie-laden cake from Grandma. Mrs. Large promptly puts it away for guests, but as night falls, so does the family's resolve. Mrs. Large succumbs to the call of the cake, only to arrive in the darkened kitchen to find her husband and children already there—and but a slim slice left for her. Murphy succeeds in giving readers a delightfully candid view of human nature by the trunkful. As in her other vivid looks at family life in *Five Minutes Peace* (1986) and *All in One Piece* (1987), she weaves real behavior into her books. Much like the Berenstains' bear family, the Larges are complete with human frailties. Murphy's skillful illustrations feature rich color, amusing detail, and an engaging blend of elephantine and human characteristics. The pages are filled with wonderful facial expressions complete with dextrous trunks. This book won't win the battle of the bulge, and readers may enjoy it all the more for that reason.

Angela Redfern

SOURCE: A review of *A Piece of Cake,* in *The School Librarian,* Vol. 38, No. 2, May, 1990, p. 60.

I gather this book is selling like proverbial hot cakes and is fast becoming number one favourite with nursery and infant classes. It is the latest saga about the Larges, Jill Murphy's famous family of elephants. Mrs Large faces up to the fact that she is not 'cuddly' but 'fat'. The expressions on the family's faces speak volumes, as she unceremoniously dumps bread, cakes, biscuits and crisps into the dustbin. TV is out. Jogging and exercising are in, along with healthy meals of sardines and carrots. How I felt for Mrs Large, standing, incredulous, on the bathroom scales after all that effort! Temptation (by way of a large sponge cake oozing cream) arrives from Granny and is whisked away to the top shelf of the cupboard. It is too much for Mum. In the dead of night, she tiptoes furtively down to the kitchen. The rest of the family have beaten her to it . . . though there is one last piece of cake left, which Mrs Large promptly eats before anyone else can.

I can vouch for the appeal of this delightful book well beyond the infant school. Myself at fifty and my daughter at twenty-one, we chortled from start to finish. Go treat yourselves to a slice of this cake.

S. Williams

SOURCE: A review of *A Piece of Cake,* in *Books for Your Children,* Vol. 25, No. 2, Summer, 1990, p. 7.

This is a delightful tale about a large family of elephants. Mum has decided she is too fat and feels that they should all go on a diet and also a fitness kick. This touched the giggle spot of Mark (9) and Lucy (7) as their mum has this problem at present. The story is simply told but the

pictures show in detail the expressions of the family when faced with watercress soup. We did wonder about the sardine and carrot supper as we thought all elephants were vegetarian, but it certainly emphasised the point. The gift of a cake brings the family to their senses in an amusing way, and the realisation that elephants are not meant to be thin.

GEOFFREY STRANGEWAYS (1990, U.S. edition as *Jeffrey Strangeways*)

M. Hobbs

SOURCE: A review of *Geoffrey Strangeways,* in *The Junior Bookshelf,* Vol. 55, No. 1, February, 1991, p. 36.

Jill Murphy has written a very funny, not-exactly-historical tale, using a gothic setting modernised—pink wash under the half-timbering, antique filing trays and office girls in wimples, and a host of things not yet invented, from potatoes to post offices: a child's interpretation of the mediaeval. It is a very moral tale: you might subtitle it "The story of a lie". Geoffrey, eleven and fatherless, is sent to the town to find work, since his mother, the breadwinner, has broken her arm. What he wants to be, however, is a knight. On his return home, not really having tried, he encounters Sir Walter of Winterwood, a filmstar hero on an assignment from the town's Freelance Rescue Services Limited, who shares his meal with Geoffrey. To excuse his lateness back, the boy invents a job with the Rescue Services. He has a worrying time avoiding the discovery of his lie, but by chance is the only one present when an urgent plea for help arrives from Sir Walter. Accompanied by an overlarge, overenthusiastic puppy who has already created mayhem in the office, he sets off to tackle a one-eyed giant (more like a huge gorilla) about to devour the knight, and by sheer luck, through the puppy's antics, kills him. As a reward, Sir Walter offers to pay for Geoffrey to be made a knight at his old school, and the dog, who has become firm friends with him, not surprisingly is in need of a home—all very satisfying, and told with great humour, beautifully illustrated with a combination of line-drawings and silhouettes.

Margaret Banerjee

SOURCE: A review of *Geoffrey Strangeways,* in *The School Librarian,* Vol. 39, No. 1, February, 1991, p. 24.

Jill Murphy can only add to her reputation with this hilarious tale of a would-be knight errant. Hoping he might begin as an office boy or a groom, Geoffrey takes himself along to the offices of Freelance Rescue Services Ltd. Overtaken by events, he finds himself setting off (with Lancelot, an overgrown puppy) to rescue the agency's most prestigious knight from the clutches of an evil ogre.

The entertaining mix of ancient and modern, both in style and content, adds to this lively story. It is also greatly enhanced by the author's line drawings, of which the undoubted star is Lancelot the dog. A book to keep children laughing up to around the age of ten.

Michael Cart

SOURCE: A review of *Jeffrey Strangeways,* in *School Library Journal,* Vol. 38, No. 5, May, 1992, pp. 114, 116.

More than anything in the world, 11-year-old Jeffrey Strangeways wants to be a knight. There's only one problem: he's a commoner and a small, scruffy, and clumsy one at that, and in his medieval world commoners commonly aspire to kitchen duty instead of knighthood. But Jeffrey has a dream and he's such a likable kid that readers know *something* good will happen to him—although it takes a real knight, an ogre, and a puppy every bit as scruffy as Jeffrey to make it occur. Murphy has filled her lighthearted tale with cheerful anachronisms (knights with clipboards, local newspapers, paper bags, Earl Grey tea, etc.) and equally good-humored black-and-white line drawings (plus a few snazzy silhouettes).

Kirkus Reviews

SOURCE: A review of *Jeffrey Strangeways,* in *Kirkus Reviews,* Vol. LX, No. 10, May 15, 1992, p. 673.

The author of **The Worst Witch** (1974) tells a funny story about a medieval 11-year-old whose rescue of the local knight-errant is the result of slapstick-style good luck.

Jeffrey's widowed mother has broken both arms (she fell from an ox-cart after too much mead); her present inability to knit leaves them even more destitute than usual. After a friendly chance encounter with the great Sir Walter, Jeffrey goes to the knight's agency, "Free Lance Rescue Services Ltd.," with feeble hopes of a job (peasants aren't normally eligible for errantry). No luck, but while there he intercepts an urgent plea for help: Sir Walter is about to be devoured by an ogre. Jeffrey sets out, armed with his mother's kitchen tools and accompanied by a dog on an overlong leash. After various comical adventures, he finds the ogre; the dog accidentally snares the ogre's feet in the leash, toppling him so that he gets a fatal bump on a convenient rock.

From Five Minutes Peace, *written and illustrated by Jill Murphy.*

This thoroughly British, entirely accessible romp derives much of its humor from creative anachronisms—from the Earl Grey tea the knight fancies to the secretary and office arrangements at his headquarters. In the face of this, it seems even more ludicrous than usual to call Jeffrey's parent "Mom." Still, a witty, wonderfully entertaining spoof/adventure. Murphy's adept pen drawings add a lot to the fun.

Julie Corsaro

SOURCE: A review of *Jeffrey Strangeways,* in *Booklist,* Vol. 88, No. 20, June 15, 1992, p. 1840.

This clever spoof of the epic quest features a clumsy 11-year-old boy of humble circumstances who wants nothing more than to become a knight. When Jeffrey lies to his mother about Sir Walter of Winterwood promising him a job in the (relatively speaking) big city, he sets into motion a comedy of errors that leads to Sir Walter footing Jeffrey's tuition bill for knight school. Together, Jeffrey and the rambunctious pup Lancelot wreck the offices of Free Lance Rescue Services, steal a donkey cart, and accidentally (but, nevertheless, heroically) kill a one-eyed ogre. Jeffrey's medieval England is a place where chivalrous men have celebrity status, work for corporations, and have personal problems ("My poor wife Elaine gets awfully fed up stuck at home with our two youngsters. . . . Still at least she understands, having been a distressed damsel herself"). Murphy's delicate pen-and-ink drawings complement her vigorous, pun-filled prose. A natural read-aloud for primary-grade children who have enjoyed [Clyde] Bulla's *Sword in the Tree* and other simple retellings of Arthurian legends.

Kathryn Jennings

SOURCE: A review of *Jeffrey Strangeways,* in *Bulletin of the Center for Children's Books,* Vol. 46, No. 1, September, 1992, p. 20.

In this medieval comedy, young Jeffrey Strangeways plays an unlikely hero. Ever since Jeffrey's widowed mother has broken both arms and is unable to produce knitting for sale, eleven-year-old Jeffrey has had to earn the family's living. No commoner's job for Jeffrey, nothing less than the path to knighthood will do. He proves he's knight material by bravely charging off to rescue his new friend, Sir Walter, from a giant one-eyed ogre named Grobb. Funny anachronisms pop up throughout the story—Sir Walter drinks Earl Grey tea and works for the "Free Lance Rescue Services Limited," Sir Cedric (the boss knight) gets tipsy from his long lunches at his club, and Jeffrey has to walk five miles to the next village if he wants an evening paper or a bag of groceries. If young readers' knowledge of history isn't sharp enough to catch these jokes, they'll certainly recognize the humor in the many pen-and-ink illustrations that frolic around the text. The happy ending is no surprise in this light-hearted story.

THE WORST WITCH ALL AT SEA (1993)

R. Baines

SOURCE: A review of *The Worst Witch All at Sea,* in *The Junior Bookshelf,* Vol. 58, No. 1, February, 1994, p. 25.

Mildred Hubble is notorious as the worst trainee witch at Miss Cackle's Academy, and is not helped by the ineptitude of her cat, Tabby. Despite this she scored a triumph during the winter term by rescuing and reinstating as a human a magician, Mr. Rowan-Webb, who had been turned into a frog. Now, despite snowstorms, the summer term has begun and the magician has offered a holiday at his seaside home, Gloom Castle of Grim Cove, to a party of second year girls.

Jill Murphy equips her heroine with a heart that leaps first in fright then in joy as she sets out on nocturnal activities, difficulties in coping with the practicalities of using broomsticks, and the knack of making things come right in the end.

This author has the enviable ability to illustrate her own story with lively black and white portraits of the characters involved.

A QUIET NIGHT IN (1994)

Judy Constantinides

SOURCE: A review of *A Quiet Night In,* in *School Library Journal,* Vol. 40, No. 5, May, 1994, pp. 100, 102.

Mr. and Mrs. Large and their four children are back. This time Mrs. Large wants her husband to enjoy a quiet birthday evening at home. Her "helpful" children innocently impede her preparations for a special dinner-for-two, and then beg for a bedtime story as a reward for going to bed early. Finally leaving their exhausted parents dinnerless and sound asleep on the sofa, they trail off to bed quietly, taking Mr. and Mrs. Large's special repast with them. Another hilarious chapter in the elephant family's chronicles, this is a definite winner. The illustrations are first rate; especially priceless are the expressions on the elephants' faces. The text is full of humor and instantly recognizable as true to life; the story is a fine example of a happy, loving family. Not to be missed.

Mary Harris Veeder

SOURCE: A review of *A Quiet Night In,* in *Booklist,* Vol. 90, No. 17, May 1, 1994, p. 1609.

The Larges are back. This time, the pachyderms' parental goal is getting the children to bed early so that Mom and Dad can celebrate Mr. Large's birthday with "a quiet night in." Youth, of course, gently triumphs over age: the parents snooze on the sofa, site of the bedtime story, and the children take off upstairs to enjoy whatever wine, fruit, and bread hasn't spilled from the trays that Mrs. Large had prepared. Murphy's pictures have the same affectionate feel for children's daily lives as her text. The grumpy looks at bath time and the bickering over a storybook about Binky Bus and Micky Milktruck are vintage.

Jo Goodman

SOURCE: A review of *A Quiet Night In,* in *Magpies,* Vol. 9, No. 3, July, 1994, p. 26.

In this, the fourth book about the Large family, it is Mr Large's birthday and Mrs Large wants all the children in bed early so she can enjoy a peaceful celebratory meal. But as usual things are never that simple, and the nitty gritty of family life gets in the way. This is a family of elephants and Murphy is adept at taking advantage of this—a trunk as well as front feet—whilst depicting scenes and characters that elicit an immediate grin of recognition from both parents and children. The book is both for children and a therapeutic laugh for parents.

THE LAST NOO-NOO (1995)

Publishers Weekly

SOURCE: A review of *The Last Noo-Noo,* in *Publishers Weekly,* Vol. 242, No. 41, October 9, 1995, pp. 85-6.

Marion, a crocodile, doesn't need a noo-noo, a pacifier, all the time: "Only at night or if he's a little tired." Unfortunately, his grandmother insists he's too old to have a noo-noo at all. This tale may not be as memorable as Murphy's *Five Minutes' Peace* and subsequent tales about the Large elephant clan, but it ably showcases her droll wit. For example, after Marion's mother throws away all the noo-noo's, Marion hides one in a boot; the accompanying image shows Marion shaking out the hidden object from the footwear as if it were the last M&M in a box. Parents and kids will also nod in recognition at the dialogue ("He looks ridiculous with that stupid big thing stuck in his mouth all the time"). The expressive crayon illustrations humorously portray Marion's insistence on his pacifier despite objections by his parents and grandparents, as well as teasing by his peers. In all, an appropriately lighthearted look at a situation that will hit close to home for many toddlers.

Additional coverage of Murphy's life and career is contained in the following sources published by Gale Research: *Contemporary Authors New Revision Series,* Vol. 44; *Major Authors and Illustrators for Children and Young Adults*; and *Something about the Author,* Vols. 37, 70.

Hilda Simon

1921-

American author and illustrator of nonfiction.

Major works include *Exploring the World of Social Insects* (1962), *The Splendor of Iridescence: Structural Colors in the Animal World* (1971), *Dragonflies* (1972), *The Courtship of Birds* (1977), *Sight and Seeing: A World of Light and Color* (1983).

INTRODUCTION

A highly regarded author and illustrator of science books for young people, Simon is praised for the striking color drawings and clear, straightforward text that commentators have cited as distinguishing features of her work. She examines diverse life forms, including insects, fish, birds, and flowers, with an approach that celebrates the insights of the naturalist, physicist, sociologist, and artist. While the majority of Simon's books are intended to introduce high school students and general readers to the wonders of nature, the author has also published studies of light and color appropriate for middle schoolers. These works include discussions of optics, eyesight, and design, as well as the color separation technique Simon developed to permit a more easily reproduced and inexpensive form of full-color artwork for her books. Simon's illustrations are central to her works, as she begins each new project with a visual conception and then builds the text around the images. Reviewers praise Simon's writing as both scientifically accurate and easily accessible to young people, while her precise, highly detailed artwork is considered an essential factor in each book's overall appeal.

Biographical Information

Simon was born in Santa Ana, California, where her father, an engineer, was a partner in a tool-manufacturing plant. When Simon was eight years old, the family traveled to Germany to visit relatives. During their stay, the U.S. stock market crashed and their business was ruined. They decided to remain in Germany, where Simon's father found work as a science writer and translator. But Hitler was rising to power, and the Simons' anti-Nazi position drew hostility from their community. Rejected by her schoolmates, eleven-year-old Simon befriended a neighbor's dog and a pheasant that was kept in the school yard. She spent her free time sketching and writing stories about these and her own small pets, including a frog named Emily that later appeared in one of her books. Simon left school two years before graduation because the curriculum had become politicized with Nazi ideology; she began attending biology and language classes as an unofficial guest student at the University of Jena in East Germany. Simon was also able to help support her

family by using her skill as an artist to create portraits. After the war, Simon returned to the United States, becoming head of the art department at Hart Publishing Company in New York. At Hart, she published three of her early books, *The Amazing Book of Birds, The Young Pathfinder's Book of Snakes,* and *Hart's Maps of New York City,* in the 1960s.

Major Works

One of Simon's most popular early works, *Exploring the World of Social Insects,* describes the elaborate social system that structures the activities of bees, ants, and other insects. Reviewers have commended the work as scholarly and well documented, while also praising the quality of Simon's illustrations. Another of Simon's best-known works, *The Splendor of Iridescence: Structural Colors in the Animal World* (1971), examines the science of optics in relation to the colorful appearance of birds, butterflies, beetles, fishes, and mollusks. Simon's illustrations for this book offer vibrant examples of iridescence, and her text contains biographical information about many of the scientists who have helped shape our understanding of color. In *Dragonflies,* which has been cited as an especially well-designed and attractively illustrated book, Simon uses simple text and realistic drawings to trace the life cycle and evolutionary history of the dragonfly. The author tackles a more complex subject with *The Courtship of Birds* (1977). In this work, Simon divides numerous species of birds into four major courtship modes, discusses the elaborate posturing and acrobatics some birds exhibit, and adds colorful illustrations of the impressive plumage displays that are often part of the ritual. *Sight and Seeing: A World of Light and Color* (1983) deals with vision in various members of the animal kingdom, from insects to humans. Simon compares the visual organs of different life forms, relates vision to other aspects of life, and includes a survey of color perception in numerous animals.

Awards

Two of Simon's books were exhibited in the Children's Book Showcase: *Dragonflies* in 1973 and *The Racers: Speed in the Animal World* in 1981. *Birds and Flowers of the United States* was selected as an Ambassador Book by the English-Speaking Union in 1980.

GENERAL COMMENTARY

Zena Sutherland and May Hill Arbuthnot

SOURCE: "Informational Books: Hilda Simon," in *Children and Books,* Seventh Edition, Scott, Foresman and Company, 1986, p. 502.

As a student of art and biology, Hilda Simon is well qualified both as author and artist for the books she has written and illustrated in the field of biology. Her drawings are beautifully detailed and accurate, and the same accuracy is evident in her writing, which is informal and lucid. While there are scientific terms used, the writing is not laden with jargon but can be understood by readers with little background. However, since Simon uses neither anthropomorphism nor condescension and since she treats her subjects in some depth, her books are also appropriate for readers who do have background in biology.

In *Living Lanterns* (1971) Simon begins with a brief survey of what has been known about the phenomenon of luminescence in the past, then describes luminescent creatures according to their habitats (land, air, or sea), and concludes with a discussion of the anatomy of luminescence. Observations are validated by citing research, and the text is explicit in stating the fact that not all the questions about bioluminescence have been answered. Simon's books exemplify the best kind of science writing, authoritative and accurate, illustrated with pictures that are carefully placed and informative, and supplied with indexes, bibliographies, and—in some books—maps that show the ranges of species.

Most of her books are for older readers, but Simon's *The Amazing Book of Birds* (1958) is for the middle grades. Written in a light, informal style, it gives many facts about birds, but the random arrangement makes it less cohesive and therefore less useful than her later work. A better book for the middle grades is *The Magic of Color* (1981); color and how it is perceived by human and animal eyes is the subject of *Sight and Seeing* (1983). A study of imitative patterns or adaptations in the insect world, *Insect Masquerades* (1968), is a more typical example of Simon's writing: logically organized, and leading from the discussions of individual creatures to conclusions about the survival potential of insects which have such advantages.

TITLE COMMENTARY

▥ *EXPLORING THE WORLD OF SOCIAL INSECTS* (1962)

Robert E. Roth

SOURCE: A review of *Exploring the World of Social Insects,* in *School Library Journal,* Vol. 9, No. 9, May, 1963, p. 109.

Excellent explanation of the activities of social insects in exhilarating, yet scientific style. The author vividly describes the societal structure and life activities of honeybees, ants, termites, wasps, and certain non-social bees and wasps. Text is well documented with pertinent illustrations of high quality and is aided by a good index and table of contents. List of scientific names and related data about the various insects is valuable and meaningful. First purchase for elementary school and public libraries.

Robert C. Cowen

SOURCE: A review of *Exploring the World of Social Insects,* in *The Christian Science Monitor,* May 9, 1963, p. 7B.

Miss Simon's detailed scientific drawings of insects and their homes are a key to this book, which is essentially a scientific rather than a mere "nature" book. Her study of bees, wasps, ants, and termites deals with their kings and queens and workers, their evident laws and amazing habits, and the ways in which they build their homes. Particularly remarkable is her description of the dance of the bees, how they tell where nectar is to be found. She even charts these dances and interprets the message. It is a book to interest any older elementary schoolchild, but so scholarly a study in its junior field that older children and even adults will particularly like it.

Alice Dalgliesh

SOURCE: A review of *Exploring the World of Social*

Insects, in *The Saturday Review,* New York, Vol. XLVI, No. 19, May 11, 1963, p. 50.

Who says a science book does not have to be handsome? This one, with its detailed yet decorative two-color illustrations, is also, to quote from the introduction by [Alexander B.] Klots, "not only clear, accurate and most interesting but properly values the insects by their own measuring sticks, not by man's." In the author's words, "social insects behave as they do chiefly from instinct . . . rather than because of individual intelligence or learning from experience."

This excellently designed book has pages roomy enough to show the pollen baskets on the legs of bees, the scissor-like jaws of the leaf-cutting or parasol ants, the detail of the bees' brood comb, and the "city" of the carpenter ant. The insects are enlarged, but each kind is carefully given in scale at the end of the book. There is a good index.

WONDERS OF THE BUTTERFLY WORLD (1963)

The Christian Science Monitor

SOURCE: A review of *Wonders of the Butterfly World,* in *The Christian Science Monitor,* January 2, 1964, p. 7.

Beginning with a short chapter on the butterfly in history and superstition this attractive book for the 8-12's gives full basic information about the loveliest of insects, and is illustrated by decorative and accurate sketches of butterflies, caterpillars, various cocoons, and details like antennae, eggs, and the like. The ever-marvelous migration of the Monarch is described, with drawings in color and description of the "butterfly trees." Many kinds of butterflies are identified, interesting "partnerships" and means of defense described and a chapter on how to study butterflies added. Altogether this makes a delightful addition to the "Wonders of" series from this publisher and includes a good index.

Virginia Haviland

SOURCE: A review of *Wonders of the Butterfly World,* in *The Horn Book Magazine,* Vol. XL, No. 1, February, 1964, p. 74.

An absorbing nature subject treated with knowledge and artistry to create maximum interest. The detailed, well-labeled drawings reveal stages of development, anatomical structures, and comparative sizes of a variety of species; and the text considers also such fascinating matters as migration, "Actors and Imitators," "Strange Partnerships," and "Giants and Dwarfs." Finally, the author tells how to raise butterflies in the home. Recommended particularly for its distinctive illustration. For the middle years.

WONDERS OF HUMMINGBIRDS (1964)

Gladys Conklin

SOURCE: A review of *Wonders of Hummingbirds,* in *School Library Journal,* Vol. 11, No. 4, December, 1964, p. 61.

Near the equator in South America, there are more than 150 species of hummingbirds and there are about 15 in the United States. The jungle hummingbirds come in unbelievable shapes and colors, and Hilda Simon successfully catches much of this beauty in her exquisite drawings. Text, with drawings, gives structure and flying patterns and life habits of hummingbirds in general. A short chapter gives some detail about the ruby-throated and rufus hummingbirds, the only two found widely in the United States. Final chapter explains how to attract hummingbirds to your garden. Recommended.

Priscilla L. Moulton

SOURCE: A review of *Wonders of Hummingbirds,* in *The Horn Book Magazine,* Vol. XLI, No. 2, April, 1965, p. 186.

Children who already consider these lovely birds as favorites will appreciate having them faithfully represented in unusually inviting illustrations. Delicate line and jewel tones successfully convey the hummingbird's graceful, hovering flight and its incessant activity. Especially interesting in the text are an explanation of the bird's iridescence and a comparison of its mode of flying to that of a helicopter. Attention is given also to physical characteristics, species and their locations, and life habits. Unforgivable and unscientific is the absence of any indication that Miss Simon's more elementary, less expensive—and therefore very useful—book is derived from Mr. Greenewalt's definitive work on the subject. It is hoped that children may be privileged to enjoy the exquisite photography and fine text in Crawford H. Greenewalt's *Hummingbirds.*

Evelyn Shaw

SOURCE: A review of *Wonders of Hummingbirds,* in *Natural History,* Vol. LXXIV, No. 9, November, 1965, p. 14A.

Wonders of Hummingbirds, by Hilda Simon, is an improvement on a book by the same author, which was reviewed here several years ago. Miss Simon, who also did the illustrations, has moved away from explaining behavior as occurring through mysterious instinct, toward more acceptable biological fact. I am not sufficiently familiar with hummingbird classification to evaluate the scientific accuracy of some of her statements on distribution and identification.

My general impression is that the book does not quite

come off. It does not give a true picture of the humming-birds' vitality or coloring. The latter, like their evanescent movement, is lost in the colored line drawings, for it is the iridescence of the birds that makes them especially exciting. Color photographs would have captured these qualities much more effectively.

📖 *INSECT MASQUERADES* (1968)

Science Books: A Quarterly Review

SOURCE: A review of *Insect Masquerades,* in *Science Books: A Quarterly Review,* Vol. 4, No. 1, May, 1968, p. 49.

The four-color paintings that illustrate examples of insect "traps and trickery," "camouflage," "warning signals," and "nightmare insects" are as beautiful and accurate as color photographs. The descriptive text is factually correct and typifies good expository writing that sustains reader interest. It also includes suggestions for collecting "masquer-aders" in the garden, has diagrams of the three major types of insect development, a list of references, and an index. Even a professional entomologist will enjoy this layman's exposition of some of the most interesting and unusual phenomena of nature.

Kirkus Service

SOURCE: A review of *Insect Masquerades,* in *Kirkus Service,* Vol. XXXVI, No. 9, May 1, 1968, p. 524.

Where does the insect begin and the flower (or leaf or branch) end? Which is the dangerously armed insect and which is the mimic? Exploring three classic forms of camouflage—to disappear and entrap, to attract and en-trap, to disappear and avoid attack—and the startling imitation of a stronger by a weaker species, Miss Simon illustrates her examples with such acuity that the reader is left blinking. This is neither a dossier of disguises nor a guide to the species mentioned; rather it's an introduction to an intriguing aspect of evolution which focuses on the why and how of adaptations within characteristic groups (especially the mantis among the cannibals, moths and butterflies among the defensive disappearers, other butterflies, moths and beetles among the mimics). A disjunct chapter displays various insects of bizarre appearance (resulting from hypertrophic growth); the concluding section offers tips on spying the more common species among the masqueraders. Not essential but it might be a ball for the entomologically-alert youngster.

Harry C. Stubbs

SOURCE: A review of *Insect Masquerades,* in *The Horn Book Magazine,* Vol. XLIV, No. 5, October, 1968, pp. 574-75.

[*Insect Masquerades* is] written and most beautifully il-

lustrated by Hilda Simon. The principal sense concerned here is, of course, sight; and two entirely different problems connected with this sense are involved.

The first is that of defeating sight—the problem of camouflage, of merging with the background. The second is that of emphasizing sight, a problem for animals which are poisonous or distasteful or which are imitating those that are. These creatures want to be recognized as quickly as possible; as Miss Simon points out, being spat out afterward is not much consolation.

This book . . . is descriptive rather than explanatory. We are shown very effectively how the insects solve their problems, but there is no discussion of the physical and neurological aspects of vision which make the solutions possible.

Miss Simon, however, gives her readers a wonderful chance to consider these aspects for themselves. Her art work supplements and supports the text admirably.

Zena Sutherland

SOURCE: A review of *Insect Masquerades,* in *Bulletin of the Center for Children's Books,* Vol. 23, No. 4, December, 1969, p. 65.

A very good book on imitative patterns or adaptations in the insect world, all operating to increase the survival potential whether the imitation serves to hide or to attract (and repel) or to entrap victims. The text is well-organized and well-written, save for an occasional remark that imputes purposiveness: "Instinct tells the monarch, the hornet, and the milkweed beetle that their best protection lies, not in trying to hide, but rather in showing their bright colors" or "The purpose of this masquerade is . . ." The illustrations are superb: clear and informative, beautifully detailed. A brief reading list, morphological diagrams, a guide to finding masquerading insects in the garden, and a relative index are appended.

📖 *FEATHERS, PLAIN AND FANCY* (1969)

Anne Greenwood

SOURCE: A review of *Feathers, Plain and Fancy,* in *School Library Journal,* Vol. 16, No. 1, September, 1969, p. 133.

A wealth of information on birds is packed into this attractive, well-written book about feathers. Beginning with a discussion of how birds evolved from amphibians, Simon carefully explains and diagrams the development and functioning of feathers, from buds on the embryo to the molting patterns of adult birds; also, the difference between coloration by pigment and by diffusion of light through a structure is clarified. Expanding the text are illustrations which are accurate and unusually well drawn and colored. One small criticism—a very well executed diagram showing barbs and barbules on a shaft does not identify the barbicels, which are mentioned in the text. Even Peterson's extensively detailed *Birds* (Time-Life, 1967) does not include the fine points on structure and coloration covered by Simon. For information on the subject, readers will flock to this book.

Ruth P. Bull

SOURCE: A review of *Feathers, Plain and Fancy,* in *The Booklist,* Vol. 66, No. 1, September 1, 1969, p. 59.

In a delightful, nontechnical account illustrated with beautiful four-color drawings and instructive diagrams, the author of *Insect masquerades* discusses theories concerning the possible origin of feathers and describes the growth, structure, function, color, and pattern of different types of bird feathers. A final chapter touches on the unusual plumage of such birds as the lyre bird, ostrich, and bird of paradise. Distinctive in format and content, the book should have appeal for the general reader as well as for bird lovers.

Harry C. Stubbs

SOURCE: A review of *Feathers, Plain and Fancy,* in *The Horn Book Magazine,* Vol. XLV, No. 5, October, 1969, p. 549.

Good as the descriptions and drawing are in Hilda Simon's *Feathers plain and fancy,* all is not simple reporting. There is explanation, or attempted explanation, too. The feather, as the author points out, is one of the major puzzles of evolution. While no biologist seriously doubts that birds developed from some featherless, flightless predecessor, no really satisfactory path has been proposed for the process. Fossil records fail to furnish the "missing links," which we would like to see connecting the birds with the reptiles or amphibians; no living creature has a covering suggesting at all convincingly a link between scales or hair and feathers.

Esther L. Steffens

SOURCE: A review of *Feathers, Plain and Fancy,* in *Appraisal: Children's Science Books,* Vol. 3, No. 2, Spring, 1970, p. 21.

Another beautiful, fascinating, and informative book from Hilda Simon. *Feathers* . . . begins with the evolution of feathers and their mysteries. The other chapters are entitled Growth and Structure, Form and Function, Colors and Patterns, and Unusual Feathers and Plumes. The colored illustrations are attractive and to my eye, accurate, and the diagrams are most helpful. Miss Simon's style is pleasing, at all times interesting, and to repeat, informative. The author has obviously done a lot of research. I like the way she does not take a stand on some of the still unproved theories of the earliest birds and feathers; she

presents both—or all—substantial views. An outstanding book.

Isabelle Behr

SOURCE: A review of *Feathers, Plain and Fancy,* in *Appraisal: Children's Science Books,* Vol. 3, No. 2, Spring, 1970, p. 21.

The author has illustrated with beautiful paintings and well-executed drawings a book on feathers in five chapters. The first describes a feather and discusses evolution and theories of the development of feathers. The second and third take up growth and structure, and form and function respectively. The information in these two chapters is clearly written but would be hard going for most students in the 10-14 age group for which the book is suggested. However, a well-motivated student or adult would find a wealth of valuable material. The last two chapters on colors and patterns and unusual feathers and plumes contain fascinating facts on the varieties and beauty of color patterns of birds of the world. The pictures and accompanying captions reveal many ways in which feathers contribute to variations and adaptations. One of the good features of this book is that it will increase a reader's interest in closer observation of the birds around him. A good index makes it possible for him to check out facts as needed.

MILKWEED BUTTERFLIES: MONARCHS, MODELS, AND MIMICS (1969)

Anne Greenwood

SOURCE: A review of *Milkweed Butterflies: Monarchs, Models, and Mimics,* in *School Library Journal,* Vol. 16, No. 8, April, 1970, p. 124.

After a brief introduction describing butterflies in general and their place in the insect world, Miss Simon writes in detail about the family of milkweed butterflies and its most famous member, the monarch. Coloration, mimicry, and migration are well explained and further clarified by helpful diagrams. Throughout the book lovely, accurately drawn and colored pictures of butterflies delight the eye and elucidate the text. There is no dearth of titles on butterflies for the young, but nothing quite like this is available for this age group.

Mary M. Burns

SOURCE: A review of *Milkweed Butterflies: Monarchs, Models, and Mimics,* in *The Horn Book Magazine,* Vol. XLVI, No. 4, August, 1970, pp. 403-04.

The meticulously executed book with magnificent full-color illustrations and clear diagrams is an in-depth study of the life cycle of the American monarch butterfly. However, the author does not treat the monarch in isolation. Rather, she begins with a fascinating introduction which analyzes the characteristics of butterflies in general before narrowing its focus to the Danaids or milkweed butterflies—the family to which the monarch belongs. A discussion of the monarch's topical relatives presents the principles of mimicry in readable prose, which makes this complex subject and its relationship to Darwinian theories comprehensible to young naturalists. Because of the clarity of the introductory material, the chapters dealing specifically with the breeding, growth, and seasonal migrations of the monarch can be more readily understood and appreciated. The concluding chapter, Raising Monarchs at Home, may encourage the ecology-conscious to participate in the propagation of a species threatened simultaneously by the indiscriminate use of insecticides and the urban sprawl, which eliminates milkweed plants—the necessary food supply for monarchs during the larval stage. The appendix includes an index, a glossary of zoological terms used in the text, diagrams of insect anatomy and development, and an insect "ancestral tree." An outstanding example of a book of information which combines impeccable scholarship with artistry of design.

PARTNERS, GUESTS, AND PARASITES: COEXISTENCE IN NATURE (1970)

Science Books: A Quarterly Review

SOURCE: A review of *Partners, Guests, and Parasites: Coexistence in Nature,* in *Science Books: A Quarterly Review,* Vol. 6, No. 2, September, 1970, p. 135.

Symbiosis, parasitism, and commensalism comprise the basic stuff of Hilda Simon's new book, which she has illustrated herself in talented drawings that are as accurate scientifically as photographs. Withal, she has prepared a readable, accurate exposition of these complex interdependent relationships among various species which constitute a vital aspect of the balance of nature and of biological cycles. This excellent study takes its place as worthwhile collateral reading for biology students with the author's two previous books, **Insect Masquerades** and **Feathers, Plain and Fancy**.

Ruth P. Bull

SOURCE: A review of *Partners, Guests, and Parasites: Coexistence in Nature,* in *The Booklist,* Vol. 67, No. 1, September 1, 1970, pp. 58-9.

In lucid, scientific text enhanced by handsome, accurately drawn colored illustrations, the author examines a variety of natural partnerships and associations formed for convenience, gain, or survival between different kinds of animals or organisms. The account emphasizes the vital role such cooperation plays in the balance of nature and also mentions some of the difficulties encountered by scientists in trying to discover the basis of these many interesting and often complex relationships. A noteworthy addition to books on symbiosis for older readers.

Douglas B. Sands

SOURCE: A review of *Partners, Guests, and Parasites: Coexistence in Nature,* in *Appraisal: Children's Science Books,* Vol. 4, No. 3, Fall, 1971, pp. 23-4.

Symbiosis, commensalism, and parasitism are all described in this book about animal relationships. The benefits of coexistence in nature are mentioned. Scientifically accurate, the anecdotes will introduce the reader to many strange cooperative ventures that spell life or death to its participants. In retrospect, however, much that is offered here has been offered before, and the sense of initial discovery is somehow lacking.

LIVING LANTERNS: LUMINESCENCE IN ANIMALS (1971)

Kirkus Reviews

SOURCE: A review of *Living Lanterns: Luminescence in Animals,* in *Kirkus Reviews,* Vol. XXXIX, No. 7, April 1, 1971, p. 384.

Living Lanterns shines with beautiful illustrations, but they do not succeed in putting a somewhat dull text in a better light. Beginning with fireflies ("Fireflies are members of the family lampyridae, which in turn is part of the suborder of Malacodermatidae, or soft skinned beetles"), the reader is taken from flying animals to earth-bound animals to swimming animals to those living on the ocean floor. Frequently there is commentary on the uncertainty or incompleteness of scientific knowledge. Several opportunities are taken to voice ecological concerns, although sometimes these are left hanging. The book, moreover, is uneven. The colorful, non-technical illustrations suggest that it is for the 4th to 6th grader. On the other hand, Simon uses terms such as symbiotic with neither definition nor contextual cues as to meaning. Animals are identified in terms of order, family, genus, and species with no effort made to let the reader know what taxonomic systems are all about. These are shortcomings not found in H. Arthur Klein's *Bioluminescence* (1965). Klein covers essentially the same subject matter, going into more detail—especially chemical detail—but also including explanatory background material for that detail. Klein discusses the same types of organisms, he gives more of the research on bioluminescence, and he gives equivalent explanations of the phenomenon. Although the level of **Living Lanterns** is inconsistent, it is generally aimed at a slightly younger reader than *Bioluminescence*. This, together with the excellent illustrations, would be the only basis for recommending it.

Zena Sutherland

SOURCE: A review of *Living Lanterns: Luminescence in Animals,* in *The Saturday Review,* New York, Vol. LIV, No. 34, August 21, 1971, p. 27.

Meticulous four-color drawings of animal forms balance the informative text of an unusually good book in the field of natural science. Intriguing enough to catch the interest of the general reader, the subject of bioluminescence is handled here with a simple informality that demands no background, yet *Living Lanterns* is accurate and comprehensive enough to be useful to those already acquainted with the topic. Although most of the book is devoted to descriptions of specific light-emitting creatures, it is buttressed by discussion of theories, knowledge, and research in the field.

Science Books: A Quarterly Review

SOURCE: A review of *Living Lanterns: Luminescence in Animals,* in *Science Books: A Quarterly Review,* Vol. 7, No. 3, December, 1971, p. 231.

It is highly unusual to find so complex and specialized a subject covered at such an elementary level. The author is to be commended for undertaking the task. The material is clearly presented. However, the writing style is somewhat authoritarian and may create problems for young readers for there are some oversimplifications and a slight tendency toward Lamarkianism. There are some minor errors in scientific accuracy, but, as a nontechnical book, it is rather good. One source of irritation to scientists will be the improper form of using scientific names. In spots, young readers will tend to lose interest. The repetition of material about so many animals becomes a little boring. The illustrations are ample although some would be more meaningful if they were more clearly labeled. One excellent factor throughout the book is the soft-sell for future natural history research. Pointing out how much is left to learn will be most challenging to young readers. The book's uniqueness in subject matter would recommend it for all advanced elementary and junior high school natural history libraries.

Judith E. Trenholm

SOURCE: A review of *Living Lanterns: Luminescence in Animals,* in *Appraisal: Children's Science Books,* Vol. 5, No. 3, Fall, 1972, p. 33.

This informative introduction to luminescence considers such insects as the firefly, click beetle, and fire beetle; and others such as the hatchet fish, squid, and shark. These and other species are discussed in depth. Although the text is quite comprehensive, whenever a new species is introduced, it should be indicated in dark type or in italics. The chapter, "Flying Flashlights," is rather confusing for this reason. Three-fourths of the chapter is devoted to fireflies, and the rest to click beetles, fire beetles, and other luminous beetles. Several controversial cases conclude the chapter. Despite this, the text is lucid. The four-color illustrations are clear and informative.

John J. Padalino

SOURCE: A review of *Living Lanterns: Luminescence in Animals,* in *Appraisal: Children's Science Books,* Vol. 5, No. 3, Fall, 1972, p. 33.

The illustrations are superb. The introductory treatment of "light in the night" is a succinct history of the study of bioluminescence which is brought up to date in the final chapter. The text is enhanced throughout by the inclusion of many of the scientific binomials as well as the common names for the organisms discussed. The species discussed range from insects, mostly beetles, to marine organisms and bacteria. The child who is fascinated by "glow worms" and "lightning bugs" in the out-of-doors will find the text a fountain of information and delight. I recommend this highly descriptive work for the emerging entomologist aged ten or older.

THE SPLENDOR OF IRIDESCENCE: STRUCTURAL COLORS IN THE ANIMAL WORLD (1971)

Science Books: A Quarterly Review

SOURCE: A review of *The Splendor of Iridescence: Structural Colors in the Animal World,* in *Science Books: A Quarterly Review,* Vol. 7, No. 1, May, 1971, p. 34.

The epilogue recalls the assertion of the German physicist and philosopher, Carl Friedrich von Weizsaecker, that color is "at home in a kind of no man's land bordered by physics, physiology, psychology, philosophy, and art." The book has been classified under "physics" by the editor but it also could have been classed under art, physiology, or other headings. One of its special features is revealed in the dust-jacket blurb. Most colored illustrations in books, be they photographs or paintings, are produced by engaging an engraver or lithographer to produce color separations in the four or five basic printing colors by means of elaborate photographic equipment employing various color filters. Miss Simon, who thoroughly understands color, has produced superior results through the preparation of her own color separations, one separation in black pencil for each of the four or five basic colors used, based on her own analysis of the percentage of the component colors in the tints and shades in her original paintings. The results portray the best reproduction of iridescence in color the reviewer has seen. The first part of the book, *The Anatomy of Structural Colors,* is an accurate analysis which will be intelligent to the lay reader but satisfying also to the physicist specializing in optics. The second part, *The Beauty of Iridescence,* includes a study, with microscope and electron microscope, of pigmented scales, integument, and feathers. The electron microscope was used for a detailed study of the structure of barbules of feathers of the Guatemalan quetzal, the Old World's sunbirds which are similar to humming birds in size and habits but of more brilliant coloration and iridescence, as well as of the New World's hummingbirds. Butterflies, beetles, fishes, and mollusks have their share in the study of the nature of iridescence. Following the epilogue, mentioned above, there are biographical sketches of Bernard Altum, Robert Boyle, Sir William Henry

Bragg, Le Comte de Buffon, Charles Darwin, Albert Einstein, Joseph von Fraunhofer, Karl von Frisch, Johann von Goethe, Augustus A. Gould, Herman L. F. von Hemholtz, Christian Huygens, Maurice Maeterlinck, Sir Isaac Newton, Max Planck, John Tyndall, Charles Waterton, and Thomas Young, each of whom made some contribution to the study of color. There is also a selected bibliography of books, periodical articles, and an adequate index. This book obviously is the result of long painstaking research, much consultation, and patient, skillful artistry. It is a book that all naturalists, many physicists, physiologists, and artists, and most people who like beautiful books will want to own. It is recommended for college libraries and public libraries.

The New Yorker

SOURCE: A review of *The Splendor of Iridescence*, in *The New Yorker*, Vol. XLVII, No. 13, May 15, 1971, p. 148.

Color is light, and iridescent color is light reflected and refracted by an interfering substance. The skin of film on a soap bubble or an oil slick is such a substance, but there are others. These include submicroscopic structures of infinite variety in the feathers or scales of certain birds, fish, and insects. It is these phenomena that particularly interest Miss Simon, and it is their examination and elucidation that form the subject of this engrossing book. Miss Simon's interest is understandable: she is an artist specializing in natural-history illustration, and the daughter of a physicist specializing in optics. Her mind is clear and her hand is firm, and her book is lucid in expression and beautifully (and lucidly) illustrated with brilliantly colored drawings of hummingbirds and scarab beetles and Urania moths and gold bugs and birds of paradise and cuckoo wasps and peacocks and pheasants and neon tetras and flower flies.

John D. Buffington

SOURCE: A review of *The Splendor of Iridescence: Structural Colors in the Animal World*, in *Library Journal*, Vol. 96, No. 13, July, 1971, p. 2334.

This book's desirability rests upon the quality of its plates, for anything the author might have chosen to say of her subject pales to insignificance alongside the beauty of her illustrations. Structural iridescence is an extremely difficult quality to capture in a picture, but Simon has done an admirable job. Her depictions of birds and insects, done by a special process, approach the richness of the living organism. The text itself is a primer on those aspects of optics which result in the structural colors of living organisms. Simon devotes extensive space to discussion of those groups best known for their iridescence, such as hummingbirds and Morpho butterflies. The orthodox biologist will find her paeans to the mysteries of life somewhat distasteful, but I suspect she couldn't care less. Her subject is life's beauty, not reductionist analysis. She has treated it well.

Philip Morrison

SOURCE: A review of *The Splendor of Iridescence: Structural Colors in the Animal World*, in *Scientific American*, Vol. 225, No. 5, November, 1971, pp. 129-30.

Hilda Simon is a professional illustrator of birds and insects, with both an artist's devotion to the eye and a scientist's curiosity. She thanks her late father, a physicist at Zeiss, for encouraging her widespread interests. How much she is involved with color is suggested by a fact she is too modest to mention but appears in the publisher's jacket biography: she prepares her color drawings, which are not merely the illustration of this handsome book but its essence, neither in colored inks nor in paint but in black pencil alone. She makes a separate pencil drawing for each of the four or five plates used for the superposed halftone impressions that make up the full-color printed picture. Her selection of the relative values of gray at any point in her several pencil drawings is what determines the final subtle color made up by the many tiny halftone dots in the colors of printer's inks. Color arises anew out of the structure of her drawings in black and white.

This is the theme of her book. The halftone structures she describes, however, are not the flat planes of printed dots each 100 microns across. Instead they are the breathtakingly intricate three-dimensional lattices of protein that make feathers and scales and give structural color to the animal world.

After a couple of chapters that provide a simplified account of physical optics and of the evolutionary history of color in the living world, Miss Simon reaches her central interest. Birds that are blue have color by structure, not by pigment. If a blue feather is crushed, it becomes dark; even if it is only soaked in a transparent liquid that fills its interstices, it loses its blueness. A red feather, on the other hand, is a set of hollow tubes filled with a carotenoid pigment; grind it and it stays red. A white feather is transparent under the microscope; its whiteness is the multiple-reflection whiteness of snow. A blue feather resembles a white one in that its texture scatters light; it preferentially scatters blue light because there are dark absorbing cores of the black pigment melanin within its horny keratin structures. Green birds add a yellow pigment to a structural blue; thus does a green shell parakeet produce mutant offspring that are blue or yellow. In birds that are blue the yellow pigment has been lost; in birds that are yellow the subtle "blue" structure is missing. (Green bird pigments are known; one pigmented green bird is the African plantain-eater the touraco.)

The peacock feather is the paradigm of intricate color-producing structure. Electron micrographs show that the entirely modified barbules of the feather hold a regular space lattice of parallel rods of melanin, arranged in a square array with a sixth of a micron between elements. At each molt the lattice must grow again; it takes seven months for this marvelous pattern to form. In the immature bird the melanin is randomly scattered through the feather. Different tiny structures differ in the number of melanin-rod layers; the brown of the eyespot is an intimate mixture of multi-layered violet and gold barbules that looks brown at a distance. The green-gold plumes of the sacred quetzal have a microstructure marked by layers of elliptical platelets of melanin separated by clear layers of keratin. Other birds of the same family, the trogons, have a simpler feather microanatomy: one bird, the Ecuadorian peacock, has barbules formed of close-packed hollow tubes of melanin, the smaller tubes in blue-violet zones and the larger ones in coppery places.

The blue butterflies, the Morphos, are perhaps the most striking. That the color is surface-generated is plain; transmitted light never shows those marvelous blues of the upper wing, only the concealing browns of the lower surface. The butterfly's beauty is skin-deep—a depth of less than half a micron. These wings gleamed for the naturalist Henry Bates, watching the butterflies in the sun "from a quarter mile." The colors are purer and brighter than those of the subtler birds; this is light scattered from a regularly carved surface, not from the more complex partly absorbing space lattices of the feather. The tiny butterfly-wing scales are lined with long ridges whose cross section resembles a Christmas tree or perhaps some magical microwave antenna. Every ridge has on each side some eight or ten regularly spaced branches; they produce their interference blues with an air spacing of about a quarter of a wavelength.

Gold bugs and ground beetles, swordtail fish and the rainbow boa, abalone shell and hummingbirds—all are quite beautifully depicted here. To be sure, flat absorbing ink spots, however cunningly arranged, cannot fully represent colors formed in space, colors whose play of motion and variation with angle add so much to iridescent reality. These approximations are nonetheless vivid and generally satisfying; a few of them, mostly showing the small beetles and the Morphos, closely evoke their source.

Structural color is unfading in the collector's cabinet, but pigments often do not last. Of course pigments too are structural. Their structure is on a scale even the electron beam cannot reach: the scale of the atom. A structure so delicate does not last because it is responsive to the impact of light and of the atoms of the air. On that scale the structural colors appear gross and static.

Miss Simon is no scientist, but she is an ally worth having. She sees what too many have overlooked, both the critics of the laboratory and the preoccupied workers within it. The world is indivisible, and knowledge and feeling interact. The wonder of the Morphos wing is not made commonplace by an understanding of its elegant fabric.

📖 OUR SIX-LEGGED FRIENDS AND ALLIES: ECOLOGY IN YOUR BACKYARD (1971)

The Booklist

SOURCE: A review of *Our Six-Legged Friends and Al-lies: Ecology in Your Backyard,* in *The Booklist,* Vol. 69, No. 3, October 1, 1972, pp. 151-52.

Writing with conversational verve and scientific accuracy the naturalist-author examines the physical appearance, habits, habitats, and usefulness to man of six insect predators—dragonflies, lace-wings, ladybird beetles, parasitic wasps, and flower and tachina flies—that live on some of the most destructive plant pests. As in her ***Milkweed butterflies; monarchs, models, and mimics,*** Simon's meticulous illustrations, including attractive full-color drawings of insects and diagrams of insect parts and forms of development, greatly enhance the lucid account. A glossary and a guide to observing and studying insects in the field and in captivity are appended.

Mary M. Merrel

SOURCE: A review of *Our Six-Legged Friends and Allies: Ecology in Your Backyard,* in *School Library Journal,* Vol. 19, No. 4, December, 1972, p. 62.

This discusses five insects which help maintain the balance of nature: dragonflies, lacewings, ladybird beetles, parasitic wasps, flower and Tachina flies. For each insect, the author notes the scientific classification and describes its characteristics, including slight differences among species. The text is followed by a guide to observing insects, a diagram of insect parts, a chart showing the development of various insects, a glossary and an index. Stressing the ecological importance of insects, this is clearly-written, has attractive illustrations and makes a good addition to library collections of insect books

📖 DRAGONFLIES (1972)

Kirkus Reviews

SOURCE: A review of *Dragonflies,* in *Kirkus Reviews,* Vol. XL, No. 9, May 1, 1972, p. 548.

An admirably thorough study of dragonfly physiology and habits, accompanied by Simon's characteristically careful, jewel-like drawings. Whether you find these representations more useful than Ross Hutchins' photographs of *The World of Dragonflies and Damselflies* (1969) is a matter of taste, but Simon is impeccably well organized (a "Guide to North American Dragonflies" and, for aesthetes, a "Picture Gallery of Dragonfly Beauties" follow chapters on general characteristics) and invariably clear (her discussion of mating rituals includes separate illustrations and a double-page recap showing the five stages in sequence). Mary Phillips (*Dragonflies and Damselflies,* 1960) and Hutchins have already done quite well by the Odonata; Simon offers a third attractive alternative.

Science Books: A Quarterly Review

SOURCE: A review of *Dragonflies,* in *Science Books: A*

Quarterly Review, Vol. 8, No. 2, September, 1972, pp. 151-52.

Dragonflies and damselflies populate Hilda Simon's book. The reader might well be sitting at the edge of a cattail pond watching the damselfly nymphs undulate through the water, the dragonfly nymphs creep up on likely prey, and the winged insects feed and mate in the air. All of these activities, and more, are vividly portrayed in both word and picture. Seventy realistic and colorful drawings perfectly complement the text. Although this is a rather technical subject and the writer has aimed at young readers, there is no trace of condescension. The facts are stated simply, accurately, and adequately. The bulk of the book is given over to descriptions of the essential activities of nymphal and adult dragonflies and damselflies: flight, sight, feeding, courtship, mating, oviposition, metamorphosis. The evolutionary history of the group is described and recognition characteristics are given. Several species from around the world are illustrated, but special attention is given to North American forms. The index is adequate, but there are no references to assist the curious reader in further inquiry into the subject.

Beryl B. Beatley

SOURCE: A review of *Dragonflies,* in *Appraisal: Children's Science Books,* Vol. 6, No. 3, Fall, 1973, p. 35.

From the very first pages where the adult dragonfly emerges from its nymphal shell, Hilda Simon has us enthralled and does not release us until the last page is turned. *Dragonflies,* like the author's other nature books, is a visual delight, for not only is it profusely illustrated in color but each illustration belongs so exactly with its text, each one is so clear it is impossible not to understand it, and the artistic positioning of the illustrations on each page lures the browser to read the text. In sequences such as the mating ritual, or the structure of the compound eye of the insect, the diagrams and drawings are exceedingly important in understanding the particular concept correctly. After a chapter on the historic development of dragonflies and damselflies, the author describes in some detail the life cycle of the insects. Of the two final chapters one describes some of the more common Odonata found throughout the world, and another is a useful guide to the North American species showing where they are to be found. As an appendix there are charts on insect evolution and development and a good index.

SNAKES: THE FACTS AND THE FOLKLORE (1973)

Kirkus Reviews

SOURCE: A review of *Snakes: The Facts and the Folklore,* in *Kirkus Reviews,* Vol. XLI, No. 20, October 15, 1973, p. 1175.

Simon's luminescent, almost hypnotically delicate drawings will of course be the main attraction here (surprisingly enough, the style works as well with the intricately patterned, exotically colored reptiles as it did with *Dragonflies* and *Living Lanterns*); yet her text, despite its formal reticence, holds its own as well. In addition to introducing the major groups of poisonous, semi-poisonous and non-poisonous snakes with an informal summary of their most salient characteristic—their swallowing of food, reproduction, danger to man, etc.—Simon investigates popular snake folklore—such as the idea that constrictors kill their prey by crushing their bones and the belief that a rattler's age corresponds to the number of segments in his tail—and even delves into the literary incarnations of snakes, searching in one case for a possible connection between the Biblical story of Aaron's rod and the performances of modern snake charmers in North Africa. Libraries still relying on Ditmars' scholarly *Snakes of the World* (1931) will find that this less academic (even if less personal) approach is better suited to the interests and attention spans of most upper grade readers.

Science Books: A Quarterly Review

SOURCE: A review of *Snakes: The Facts and the Folklore,* in *Science Books: A Quarterly Review,* Vol. X, No. 1, May, 1974, pp. 43-4.

The introductory chapter of this attractive little book sketches the myths, folklore and position of the serpent in human history and gives some of its attributes, mythical and otherwise. Next, the evolution and distinctive anatomical features of snakes are described. In subsequent chapters, certain giant snakes, nonvenomous snakes, rearfanged snakes and venomous snakes are briefly characterized. Examples are chosen for their interesting features—appearance, structure, habits, reproduction, etc.—or for their relationships with humans. Biologists will find only a few points of interpretation with which to disagree. A final chapter on how to keep a pet snake is based partly on the author's experience. Snakes are exceedingly difficult for an artist to delineate in truly lifelike form and position, and Ms. Simon's success is variable. Some portraits are well done; others lack some of the subtleties of the given kind. The approach is sympathetic, however; no snake is portrayed as a sinister or repulsive animal. Many drawings have the charm of some of the beautifully lithographed plates illustrating expensive monographs of the 19th century. A few drawings are reproduced with some colors overly brilliant—perhaps not the fault of the artist. Latin species names, with one exception, are omitted, but in view of the present lack of stability in English names of snakes, an appendix giving generic and specific names would have increased the usefulness of the book for the more advanced reader. Acknowledgements of the sources of geographic data are lacking. This book will provide readers with general knowledge, painlessly, of these often misunderstood animals, and it may help to overcome some of the fear and revulsion still in the minds of many people.

CHAMELEONS AND OTHER QUICK-CHANGE ARTISTS (1973)

Lola Dudley

SOURCE: A review of *Chameleons and Other Quick-Change Artists,* in *Library Journal,* Vol. 99, No. 3, February 1, 1974, p. 374.

This beautifully illustrated book about color adaptation in animals, birds, and fish is a delightful blend of scientific fact and humor. Written in a popular, highly readable style, it nevertheless contains a wealth of information on its fascinating topic. Simon points out that through the study of the chromatophores, the "how" of the color changes has been much easier to determine than the "why." The camouflage theory of protective coloration is now thought to be only part of the answer, with evidence pointing to color change as a kind of animal "language." To support this theory, Simon cites many utterly enchanting examples of animals exhibiting stress and other emotions through dramatic color changes. An intriguing study for both students and lay persons.

Science Books: A Quarterly Review

SOURCE: A review of *Chameleons and Other Quick-Change Artists,* in *Science Books: A Quarterly Review,* Vol. X, No. 2, September, 1974, pp. 132-33.

The text of this lively book contains anecdotes about the author's own experiences with various kinds of animals, including several varieties of fishes, lizards and frogs. Examples of animals from terrestrial, aquatic and marine environments illustrate color adaptation, and often there are series of drawings to demonstrate the dramatic color changes which can occur. The drawings are attractive, well executed and accurate. A theory of color changes for both camouflage and communication purposes is cogently argued. This excellent book is suitable for either reference or continuous reading. An additional, important feature is Ms. Simon's emphasis on the science which can be learned by careful observation in the reader's own home or yard.

Philip Morrison and Phylis Morrison

SOURCE: A review of *Chameleons and Other Quick-Change Artists,* in *Scientific American,* Vol. 231, No. 6, December, 1974, p. 159.

Aristotle did it; no reptile is better known than the wonderful chameleon, the "dwarf lion" of the Greek (it is not clear whence the name), a small tree-dweller found all along the southern coasts of the Mediterranean. He is fascinating in many respects, with his ratchet motions, independent eyes, dinosaur look and projectile tongue. He does not, however, change color to match his background. That skill is held by many forms, say the common flounder, shown here colorfully matching first a

From Chameleons and Other Quick-Change Artists, *written and illustrated by Hilda Simon.*

uniformly yellow sand, second a mottled substrate with red and blue pebbles, and third, heroically, black-and-white checkerboard! (Color, size, and mean spacing are matched, but the squares are rounded off.)

The chameleon can change color, all right. Here he is, painted from the life, in a tweedy red-brown, a smooth green and in between, with tasteful dark spots. Even the circus vendor's "chameleon," a small Mexican lizard properly called the anole, changes wonderfully. Here is a *Romeo and Juliet* scene, the ardent anole Romeo a fine golden green, his scarlet throat fan puffed out, while in the little plastic palm six inches above is Juliet, demurely brown. During mating she remains brown, save "for a small piece of skin on her neck which the male grasped . . . : that small area was bright green." The main inducers of color change in lizards are behavioral: mood, emotion, changes in environment, general health. These lizards have a coded color language, and protective coloration is for them quite secondary. So it is with frogs and cuttlefish, "cleaning" fish and crabs.

This remarkable book discusses, very often from direct observation, many more examples of color change. Each one is painted by the artist in her meticulous and sensitive style. The mechanisms are teased out as far as we know them, and redrawn microscopic views help us understand. When we see that a chromatophore cell can unfold from a pea shape to that of a spider chrysanthemum, we begin to understand. The anole provides an example of relatively simple color-change equipment: directly under the thin, clear outermost layer of its skin there is a static layer of droplets of yellow pigment, filling the space between the cells. Then follows a thick layer of cube-shaped cells filled with purine crystals, whose structural iridescence provides much angle-dependent blue and violet scattering, by no means simple. Below these lies a deep layer of dark melanin-bearing cells, whose intricately branched processes reach up through the layers above to the outermost skin itself. Add hormonal and direct nervous control, and you can begin to explain what the anole does, even a sick one that in distress will display a black spot behind each eye!

The author's own wide observation and experiment, careful study in the literature and plenty of paintings distinguish this work. To read it—or better, to try to extend it with anole or frog, if not squid or cuttlefish—will be a delight for any skillful reader who cares about living things.

📖 THE PRIVATE LIVES OF ORCHIDS (1975)

Elizabeth C. Hall

SOURCE: A review of *The Private Lives of Orchids*, in *Library Journal*, Vol. 100, No. 7, April 1, 1975, p. 680.

Simon's rather brief but well-written text is, in effect, an easy-to-read, informative essay on orchids. It has nothing to do with their cultivation, but does pull together a considerable amount of information on pollination and fertilization of orchids, mimicry, anatomy, geographical ranges, and much more. None of this will be new to orchid fans who have an interest in the botany of their favorites, but much of the information will be unfamiliar to most other gardeners. There are nearly 100 full-color illustrations, which seem quite creditable, though not up to the finest orchid portraits that have been published. Recommended.

The Booklist

SOURCE: A review of *The Private Lives of Orchids*, in *The Booklist*, Vol. 71, No. 16, April 15, 1975, p. 839.

The botanical diversity of the orchid family is examined in Simon's study of the fascinating variations in structure and behavior of some of the 25,000 orchid species which occur in nature. Biological history, anatomy, reproduction, and representative specimens are covered as the characteristics and oddities of the orchid are revealed in a brief text and in color drawings. Bibliography and maps of orchid ranges.

📖 FROGS AND TOADS OF THE WORLD (1975)

Kirkus Reviews

SOURCE: A review of *Frogs and Toads of the World*, in *Kirkus Reviews*, Vol. XLIII, No. 21, November 1, 1975, p. 1245.

Except for some introductory material on anatomy and a closing chapter on unusual breeding habits, this leisurely introduction to the world's anurans proceeds species by species, noting along the way unusual habits and adaptations—particularly coloration, which seems to be Simon's special interest. The prose—often redundant and overwrought in praise of "attractive colors, musical voices, acrobatic talents, elfin proportions" and other "exquisite" frog attributes—is offset somewhat by the appeal of Simon's luminous illustrations.

Margaret Bush

SOURCE: A review of *Frogs and Toads of the World*, in *School Library Journal*, Vol. 22, No. 6, February, 1976, p. 55.

Similar in format to Ommanney's *Frogs, Toads and Newts* (McGraw, 1974), this is much more skillfully illustrated and extensive in coverage. Simon includes physical characteristics, behavior, scientific and historical information, and geographical range. The scope and contents are similar to Blassingame's *Wonders of Frogs and Toads* (Dodd, 1975) but Blassingame includes a bit more detail on physical processes, which are particularly well demonstrated by photographs. Simon's book includes more species, and her handsome color drawings introduce a wider range of unfamiliar species than seen in any of the other available titles.

G. R. Zug

SOURCE: A review of *Frogs and Toads of the World*, in *Science Books & Films*, Vol. XII, No. 1, May, 1976, p. 41.

Of the more than 2500 frog species, none can be mistaken for anything other than a frog. Yet, while they may share similar shapes, they possess a multitude of life styles. This diversity is the thematic core of Simon's book. Her clear and interesting writing is aimed at a juvenile audience, but the book will also find enthusiastic readers in senior high school. In the first chapter, Simon surveys briefly the origin of amphibians, frog anatomy and development. The succeeding five chapters deal with five groups of frogs: primitive frogs and toads, toads, tree frogs, true frogs and maverick frog families. Each group receives a brief but adequate and accurate coverage. The final chapter contains a discussion of unusual breeding habits, a most fascinating feature of frogs. The great diversity of breeding is well represented and explained. The book is illustrated with over 60 color drawings, most of different frog species. The book will provide excellent supplemental reading for life science courses in junior and senior high schools, and it will be useful as a reference in the elementary grades.

Appraisal: Children's Science Books

SOURCE: A review of *Frogs and Toads of the World,* in *Appraisal: Children's Science Books,* Vol. 9, No. 3, Fall, 1976, pp. 39-40.

A strange mixture of the good and the bad. In one hundred twenty-eight pages no one could possibly cover all the frogs and toads of the world. What Ms. Simon does do is depict the marvelous diversity of form and habit of the anurans by choosing a representative few. Her drawings are very attractive and capture the essence of the creatures, while being scientifically accurate. The text, however, is a disappointment. It was supposedly written for children in grades four to six. Yet, according to Edward Fry's Readability Formula, the book is more suitable for children on a tenth grade reading level. The concepts are also not handled well for children in the upper elementary grades. The chapter on "Evolution, Anatomy, and Metamorphosis" is sketchy and misleading in its simplicity. Ms. Simon does not explain the difference between amphibians and reptiles or fish. Yet she tells us that amphibians "rank below" the reptiles. She writes that the earliest anuran ancestors appeared in the Jurassic period for which no dates are given. She also writes, "Despite the explanation of animal development offered in Darwin's theory of evolution we really have not the slightest idea how and why certain new animal forms appeared seemingly out of nowhere." This statement shows a lack of understanding of recent advances of knowledge in the fields of archeology, taxonomy, and physiology. Her classification scheme does not follow that used in modern zoological texts. It is confusing because it does not show the relationship between the different anurans. For all these reasons I can not recommend this text for fourth to sixth grade children, except as a picture book.

Selina Woods

SOURCE: A review of *Frogs and Toads of the World,* in *Appraisal: Children's Science Books,* Vol. 9, No. 3, Fall, 1976, p. 39.

The author is a combination science writer and artist, born in this country, educated in Germany, a teacher at the University of Jena, now living in New York. The sixty-eight four-color drawings by the author are a definite asset to this book, adding interest and usefulness to the text. An introduction mentions the roles of frog and toad in folklore, referring to the author's pet frog, Emil, and tracing the evolution, anatomy, and metamorphosis of the *Salientia* (leaping ones) order, here narrowed to the frog and toad families, the "anurans" (tailless ones). A fascinating chapter dwells on the primitive frogs of Africa, the Surinam toad of Venezuela, and those which prefer high

altitudes in the Pacific Northwest. The author then treats species of toads, tree toads, then true frogs, in the temperature climates of the world. Comments about experimentation on page thirteen hint at an emotional bias (i.e., frogs are "not even given the most rudimentary consideration by experimenters eager to discover new biological and medical facts"). Well-written, informative.

SNAILS OF LAND AND SEA (1976)

Barbara Elleman

SOURCE: A review of *Snails of Land and Sea,* in *Booklist,* Vol. 73, No. 11, February 1, 1977, pp. 837-38.

It is not only the discerning examination of her subject that marks Simon's text as exemplary, but also the meticulously drawn, finely colored illustrations that accompany the writing. As in *Frogs and Toads of the World,* the author generates interest and imparts information as she explores the various gastropods of land and sea: the air breathers—fresh water, ground, and tree snails—as well as those with and without shells that inhabit the ocean. Discussions include what snails eat, where they live, the growth and structure of their shells, an analysis of color pigmentation, and their courtship and egg-laying habits. Rounding out the narrative are fascinating remarks about unusual species such as the violet snails that construct rafts made of airfilled mucous bubbles and the pheasant snails that have a detachable portion on their foot, making a useful protection device. A top-quality science book for shell collectors, science researchers, and those interested in the unique designs of nature. Glossary and bibliography appended.

Zena Sutherland

SOURCE: A review of *Snails of Land and Sea,* in *Bulletin of the Center for Children's Books,* Vol. 30, No. 8, April, 1977, pp. 132-33.

As in other books by this naturalist and artist, the text is competently organized, comprehensive, clear, and authoritative, and the softly colored drawings are impeccably detailed and handsome. Simon begins with a discussion of the collecting of shells and the products used by people (snails as food, purple dye from the Murex group, shells used as money or ornaments) and provides two chapters of general information, "Evolution and Anatomy," and "Growth and Structure of the Shell," before discussing groups of snails in succeeding chapters: land, fresh-water, and marine snails as well as those gastropods that are less well known because they have no shells. Throughout the text, Simon describes structure, reproduction, habitat, diet, and—extensively—shells and shell color. Either the pictures or the text would stand alone; together they provide a valuable resource and an aesthetic tour de force. The writing style is direct and serious but not dry.

Cynthia K. Richey

SOURCE: A review of *Snails of Land and Sea,* in *School Library Journal,* Vol. 23, No. 8, April, 1977, p. 80.

Simon carefully describes all types of gastropods: land snails and slugs, fresh water snails, sea snails (both vegetarians and carnivores) and sea slugs, sea hares and bubbles (slug-like snails with thin, fragile, small shells). For each group the physical characteristics, reproduction, growth, feeding habits, etc. are meticulously explained, and the clear, logically developed text is profusely illustrated with finely drawn, accurate full-color, drawings and diagrams which will be of interest to shell collectors as well. This is broader in scope and for older readers than Zim's *Snails* (1975), Schisgall's *That Remarkable Creature, the Snail* (1970), and Hogner's *Snails* (1958), none of which discusses as many kinds of gastropods.

THE COURTSHIP OF BIRDS (1977)

Henry T. Armistead

SOURCE: A review of *The Courtship of Birds,* in *Library Journal,* Vol. 102, No. 18, October 15, 1977, p. 2174.

The author of several other interpretive nature books, Simon is also an accomplished artist. Her color illustrations make an already lucid text all the more stimulating. More than 40 species from all over the world are described here in depth. Most of these species exhibit spectacular plumage used in courtship or complex breeding behavior. Although Simon writes for a popular audience, her text makes no compromises with its subject matter. With the current interest in ethology of birds, this book should attract a following.

Richard Nicholls

SOURCE: A review of *The Courtship of Birds,* in *Best Sellers,* Vol. 37, No. 8, November, 1977, p. 256.

Hilda Simon has a remarkable talent for capturing, in prose and in color illustrations, the overlooked qualities or little-known patterns of life in the natural world. She has previously produced books on the incredible methods by which orchids propagate their kind, on the nature of color in the animal world, and on the almost totally ignored but quite fascinating snails of the world. *The Courtship of Birds,* her latest, is an excellent example of her ability to catch the uncommon in nature. It deals with one of the most fascinating and least known aspects of avian life: the manner in which a bird attracts, courts, and convinces another of its species to mate.

Courtship behavior in birds is often intricate, elaborate, colorful, and is even sometimes spectacular. Miss Simon recognizes four major courtship modes among birds, and she describes each by covering the courtship behavior of several species in depth. In some species males develop

impressively long or beautifully colored plumage, which is displayed to the greatest advantage during the mating season, for the benefit of the females. In other species the males stage elaborate acrobatic performances, during which they dance, leap, prance, sing, and demonstrate gymnastic feats. In yet other species males woo females by building elaborate bowers or nests.

The last of the four modes is composed of those species in which the male and female take an equal part in courtship rituals, engaging in graceful dances to celebrate the selection of a mate. I found it quite interesting that all of the species mentioned in this category are monogamous, selecting and keeping a mate for life. Most species of birds engage in brief unions, lasting only so long as it takes to carry out the essential functions of mating and rearing the young.

There are some 8500 species of birds now in existence, and while all of them follow either one or another of these methods of courtship, Miss Simon stresses that there is considerable variation in rituals from species to species. The many examples she cites bear this out. Her work is distinguished by a prose style of great clarity. The book is greatly enhanced by the detailed, beautifully rendered color illustrations Miss Simon has painted to complement the text. *The Courtship of Birds* is a splendid introduction to a complex but neglected aspect of avian life, for anyone interested in birds or in the behavior patterns of wildlife.

Roger F. Pasquier

SOURCE: A review of *The Courtship of Birds,* in *The New York Times Book Review,* December 18, 1977, p. 37.

This brisk survey of avian courtship behavior happily steers clear of most comparisons with human attitudes, but gives us much for speculation. Why should male bowerbirds elaborately decorate their nuptial structures when a female may chose a male with a simpler bower? Could the "eye spots" on the display feathers of the male great argus pheasant symbolize the kernels of grain that other pheasant cocks ritually present to prospective mates? Simon emphasizes the more elaborate courtship practices, such as extreme posturing, the display of fancy plumes, dancing and sparring among males, construction of special bowers and nests, and ceremonial posing of paired-off couples. Many of the descriptions are accompanied by illustrations, which further convey the behavior's drama.

The most spectacular courtship displays are often found in tropical birds, whose longer nesting season gives them the time for drawn out preliminaries, so only 20 of the approximately 70 species discussed are North American. "The Courtship of Birds" would provide a more complete picture if it suggested how to discern such behavior in the birds around us whose courtship may be less dramatic but no less interesting.

When describing ducks, for instance, Simon does not

mention that most temperate zone species begin their bobbing and head jerking displays in mid-winter, to save time during the short northern breeding season. They can be observed easily on any pond, lake or bay. And male pigeons bow and scrape before females on city streets every day of the year. An analysis of their behavior as good as the treatment of the birds of paradise would heighten our appreciation of courtship patterns in all birds.

John L. Zimmerman

SOURCE: A review of *The Courtship of Birds,* in *Science Books & Films,* Vol. XIV, No. 2, September, 1978, p. 96.

Some of the more spectacular courtship displays of birds are described and, in most cases, illustrated with drawings by the author. The book is divided into chapters on displays in which plumage is significantly used (e.g., birds of paradise, argus pheasant, peafowl); behavior patterns which emphasize the specific activities (e.g., grouse, greater bustard, ostrich); displays in which objects or construction play a role (e.g., bowerbirds, Adelie penguin, wrens); and exhibitions involving a mutual display between the sexes (e.g., cranes, waterfowl, albatrosses). This is not a book on the biology of behavior, an analysis of bird display or an interpretation of the evolution of behavior of birds. There are some statements that are not quite correct (e.g., regarding photoperiodism). The functional significance of the behavior is discussed, sometimes rather anthropomorphically, but this approach is in keeping with the book's apparent purpose of introducing the reader to the truly amazing behavioral repertoire of some species during courtship and mating. And toward this end the book is effective for the general reader.

📖 THE DATE PALM: BREAD OF THE DESERT (1978)

Kirkus Reviews

SOURCE: A review of *The Date Palm: Bread of the Desert,* in *Kirkus Reviews,* Vol. XLVI, No. 3, February 1, 1978, p. 114.

A sort of labor of love in honor of the author's father, who traveled in North Africa importing date palm offshoots for a California nursery—and who had intended to publish his *Notes on the Date Palm,* from which his daughter draws here. Illustrated with his own photos, Hilda Simon's summary of her father's 1913 "safari" is stiffer than might be expected (she refers to him repeatedly as "the young American") but it has its moments. Elsewhere the author details the date's importance in history ("even the vital and versatile coconut palm cannot compare") from its probable origin in Mesopotamia, its likely identity as the "honey" in the land of milk and honey, and its function through centuries as a staple food for millions. The Spanish first brought the date palm to the New World, but not until early in this century was successful commercial cultivation begun; Simon ends with a history and tour

of California's Coachella Valley where her father participated in establishing the industry. One quibble: the term "lifestyle" is already stretched when applied to animals; to refer (more than once) to a palm tree's lifestyle is ludicrous. Nevertheless, an informative survey, more serious and generally respectable than Meyer's *Coconuts* (1976).

Zena Sutherland

SOURCE: A review of *The Date Palm: Bread of the Desert,* in *Bulletin of the Center for Children's Books,* Vol. 31, No. 11, July-August, 1978, p. 185.

A substantial portion of the text here is based on the work of the author's father, who brought date palm shoots from Africa to California to contribute to the founding of a new industry. Simon describes the date palm's importance through the ages as a staple food in desert regions, and—accompanied by the meticulous drawings for which she has been noted—describes the plant botanically. She also discusses the spread of the plant, since other growers had sent agents like her father to obtain offshoots; their place in the ecology of which they became a part; and the date industry in the United States. The small print is a handicap; the photographs and drawings add greatly to the value of the book. An index is appended.

R. Gregory Belcher

SOURCE: A review of *The Date Palm: Bread of the Desert,* in *Appraisal: Children's Science Books,* Vol. 12, No. 1, Winter, 1979, p. 36.

"Here, then, was a story, not of war and strife, of conquest and slaughter, of cruelty, callousness, and inhumanity to man and beast, but rather of planting and tending, preserving and propagating the palm that, with good reason, was known as the Tree of Life." It is impossible to do greater justice to this very splendid book than to summarize it in the author's own words, as quoted above. I find no flaw in it. Its interest level is high and sustained. It tells a story, a history that should be a part of universal culture. Read it yourself, whether you are sixteen or sixty, and read it to your six year olds!

Gordon DeWolf

SOURCE: A review of *The Date Palm: Bread of the Desert,* in *Horticulture,* Vol. LVII, No. 2, February, 1979, pp. 9-10.

This well-written, pleasant book serves two purposes: First, it is a source of information about the date palm; second, it stands as a memorial to Hilda Simon's father, Henry Simon, one of the early American collectors and importers of Algerian date palms. The book is illustrated by the author with maps, drawings, and photographs that Mr.

Simon took during 1911-13 when he first brought the plants to the Coachella Valley of southern California.

The author takes us through a survey of the origin, history, cultivation, and distribution of date palms in Mesopotamia, Arabia, and Egypt, emphasizing the importance of the plant in the economy and nutrition of the area. The discussion of propagation is illuminating—seeds, more often than not, produce inferior dates, while vegetative offshoots from superior plants retain the parent plant's qualities. One such superior clone, Deglet Noor, was introduced by Ms. Simon's father and is now the principal variety cultivated in southern California.

A most interesting chapter describes Henry Simon's collecting trip in Algeria. He spent several months in the spring of 1913 traveling from one oasis to another, gathering the vegetative offshoots of several clones of desirable date palms. Travel and living conditions were often primitive, to say the least. And transporting the heavy and bulky offshoots, over 6000 in all, to the coast, loading a freighter, and shipping them to the United States and finally to southern California—alive and in good growing condition—was quite an arduous undertaking.

Other chapters describe efforts to establish the date palm in the Western Hemisphere by the Spanish, who planted date seeds in the Caribbean and Florida. Their efforts in these moist, humid areas failed; but under irrigation in Mexico and the arid Southwest they were successful. Hilda Simon emphasizes that these latter conditions come closest to the environment of the palms' origin in the Near East.

While the concluding chapters wind down with a brief treatment of the geological history of the Coachella Valley, the principal commercial source of dates grown in this country, one finds throughout *The Date Palm* an informative and entertaining presentation.

📖 *BIRD AND FLOWER EMBLEMS OF THE UNITED STATES* (1978)

Zena Sutherland

SOURCE: A review of *Bird and Flower Emblems of the United States,* in *Bulletin of the Center for Children's Books,* Vol. 32, No. 5, January, 1979, p. 88.

A double-page spread for each state includes color pictures of the bird and the flower that are emblems of their states; while painted with fine detail, the flower pictures . . . are—as are the bird pictures—sometimes less useful for identification, since some of the pictures have a repeat picture in other colors that overlap the accurate representation. For Nebraska, for example, the goldenrod is shadowed by a pink and blue goldenrod and the Western meadowlark's black and yellow is shadowed by a pink and blue bird. [The book] gives scientific information (scientific names are given separately, in appended lists) and the dates on which the emblems were officially des-

ignated by state legislatures, although the actual citation is not given. The one weakness of this useful and handsome book is variation of color; the cardinal, for example, is a rich scarlet when it is shown as the state bird of Kentucky and Virginia, but magenta in the North Carolina entry. An index is included.

Lois Foight Hodges

SOURCE: A review of *Bird and Flower Emblems of the United States,* in *School Library Journal,* Vol. 25, No. 6, February, 1979, p. 59.

For each of the 50 states (in alphabetical order) Simon has illustrated in color the representative flower and bird. Brief text (two pages per state) comments on how and when these emblems were chosen and presents a few facts and an appreciation of each. Where the same bird or flower represents more than one state, both illustration and text are repeated. An introduction discusses the use of emblems; there are scientific terms and an index at the end. Many official designations have been made since Earle's *State Birds and Flowers* (1951), and the black-and-white illustrations in the earlier title are not as compelling as Simon's.

📖 *THE RACERS: SPEED IN THE ANIMAL WORLD* (1980)

Margaret Bush

SOURCE: A review of *The Racers: Speed in the Animal World,* in *School Library Journal,* Vol. 27, No. 1, September, 1980, p. 78.

"Most large animal groups . . . include at least a few kinds that are built for speed and that are therefore much faster than others of their group." Simon's two-page essays on each of 14 selected species (dragonfly, marlin, ostrich and racehorse, et al.) consist of short bits of random information about appearance, behavior, and approximate speed. The introductory chapter, "The Mechanics of Animal Speed," draws a rather confusing analogy between animal physiology and machines. The idea of the relativity of speed is variously mentioned in the book but not clearly explicated, the text being a vague miscellany. Handsome colored drawings give an attractive appearance to the slim format, and there is a list of the scientific names of the animals and a brief index. It is disappointing to find this falling short of the previous standard of Simon's books, which have generally been considerably more informative and interesting.

Kirkus Reviews

SOURCE: A review of *The Racers: Speed in the Animal World,* in *Kirkus Reviews,* Vol. XLVIII, No. 18, September 15, 1980, p. 1235.

The title is more accurate than the subtitle of this one-by-one catalogue of 14 individual animals who are "outstanding within their groups for the speed with which they can move." Beginning with the dragonfly, Simon tells us that, although "its horizontal wings and internal flight mechanism are primitive . . . a dragonfly is able to capture in flight any of the more highly developed insects"—but she doesn't explain how its wings and flight mechanism work. Similarly, the dolphin (the fish), sand lizard, swift, greyhound, and other speedy animals are described in a general way, with miles-per-hour records noted (the peregrine falcon's dive takes the lead at 175), along with locomotive styles and any peculiarities of appearance, diet, or behavior Simon finds of interest. Unobjectionable but slack.

Mary M. Burns

SOURCE: A review of *The Racers: Speed in the Animal World,* in *The Horn Book Magazine,* Vol. LVI, No. 5, October, 1980, pp. 540-41.

Full-color, meticulously detailed drawings of fourteen animals remarkable for their swiftness are subtly executed to emphasize that form and function are interdependent elements of design in nature. A concise introduction presents the basic concepts underlying the selections which follow and states: "Fast-moving vehicles such as cars and planes are after all designed for only one thing: to move forward while carrying along those who want to be moved. . . . For the living 'speed machines' . . . moving fast is only one among many other life functions." Enthusiasm for the subject permeates the descriptions of such fascinating denizens of land, sea, and air as the dragonfly, whose ancestors predated the dinosaurs, the gazelle, whose name is derived from an Arabic word meaning "the beautiful one," and the marlin, which is capable of attaining swimming speeds of fifty miles an hour. Because of its simple presentation, selective focus, and thoughtful design, the book is a handsome addition to the growing number of artistically produced volumes on specific botanical or zoological concepts. An index and a list of scientific names are appended.

John R. Pancella

SOURCE: A review of *The Racers: Speed in the Animal World,* in *Science Books & Films,* Vol. 16, No. 5, May-June, 1981, p. 277.

In the opening chapter, Simon extols the complexity and efficiency of animals such as the hummingbird and is very negative on bionic and other devices such as computers, airplanes and telephone exchanges. She states that engineers have not found perfection in laminar flow vehicles while the porpoise obviously has. She does not acknowledge supersonic jets, rocket projectiles and the myriad of other things that are faster than animals. The rest of the book contains two-page, encyclopedia-like descriptions of the movement behavior of 14 mammals, birds, reptiles, fish and insects. Color line drawings enrich the text. The book is undistinguished; its single theme, however, makes it useful as a general library reference. The content and terminology are more suitable for younger children, but the sentence and paragraph structures are more demanding.

COLOR IN REPRODUCTION: THEORY AND TECHNIQUES FOR ARTISTS AND DESIGNERS (1980)

Julia M. Ehresmann

SOURCE: A review of *Color in Reproduction: Theory and Techniques for Artists and Designers,* in *Booklist,* Vol. 77, No. 6, November 15, 1980, p. 430.

Although directed to artists, illustrators, and designers as an introductory-level explanation of color theory and the standard process by which color is reproduced in book and magazine illustrations, this lucid book proves to be a highly satisfactory overview for the uninitiated. The sequence of material proceeds from a clearly expressed explanation of technically sophisticated color theory to methods of printing in color. Beginning with black, Simon describes historical processes leading to single-color photographic half-tones. In succeeding chapters, the addition of more colors is taken up: black plus one color, plus two colors, and finally the four-color range and separation process that is basic to full-color printing. An abundance of carefully conceived and prepared color charts and illustrations demonstrating points made in the text adds to the exceptional value—in both price and content—of this work.

Choice

SOURCE: A review of *Color in Reproduction: Theory and Techniques for Artists and Designers,* in *Choice,* Vol. 18, No. 6, February, 1981, p. 780.

Simon is clearly an authority on the subject, but her book is an unfortunate mixture. The first section, slightly more than 100 pages, deals admirably with one-, two-, three-, and four-color printing. It is accompanied by superb color illustrations that very rarely are out of register. The second section is a highly personalized description of another color reproduction method, the preseparation technique. The colored illustrations are excellent. The text in the latter section, however, is far too general and unclear to be sufficient for beginning students of color-printing techniques. Professional printers may find the text sufficient, but many details are omitted. The two sections are written in strikingly different styles: the former is clear, concise prose, the latter almost like a diary. No bibliography as such is included, although a few valuable texts are noted in the page of acknowledgements. The index is sparse.

📖 *THE MAGIC OF COLOR* (1981)

Kirkus Reviews

SOURCE: A review of *The Magic of Color,* in *Kirkus Reviews,* Vol. XLIX, No. 18, September 15, 1981, p. 1163.

A trim and simple introduction, ending with a practical application of the earlier basics. We say that a flower *is* red or a leaf green when it really just *looks* red or green, begins Simon, by way of explaining absorption and re-flection of different light waves. Next, aided by the prop-er diagrams, she shows how the primary and complemen-tary colors of light are the "exact opposite" of the prima-ry and complementary colors of paint, the primary colors of one being the complementary colors of the other. She shows us a few "color tricks" explained by after-images (the famous blue, black, and yellow American flag) and by the way a color seems to change according to the background. Finally we read and see how printers use screens and dots in combining three colors plus black to make full-color pictures. Neat, clear, and sufficiently illu-minating at its level.

Kate M. Flanagan

SOURCE: A review of *The Magic of Color,* in *The Horn Book Magazine,* Vol. LVII, No. 5, October, 1981, p. 554.

The author, drawing upon her extensive "background in color and optics," lucidly sets forth a basic explanation of color and the methods used by printers to reproduce it. She begins by discussing how white light can be separat-ed into bands of different colors according to their wave-lengths and continues with an examination of the rela-tionships among primary and complementary colors; dia-grams in brilliant full color aid immensely in making these concepts understandable. Further discussions show how different pigments reflect or absorb various portions of light. A large part of the book is devoted to the percep-tion of color; included are experiments with "afterimag-es" and "optical illusions." Finally, the author describes how color illusions are exploited in the printing of pic-tures in books and magazines. The combination of simply stated text with clear diagrams and illustrations results in a comprehensible presentation of a fascinating but poten-tially confusing subject. With subject and illustration in-dexes.

Zena Sutherland

SOURCE: A review of *The Magic of Color,* in *Bulletin of the Center for Children's Books,* Vol. 35, No. 3, Novem-ber, 1981, pp. 57-8.

Almost all books on color that have been designed for children focus on the colors in paint, so that blue and yellow always make green. Simon, skilled as an illustra-tor as well as a science writer, takes a broader approach

and shows not only some of the effects and relationships of paint colors, but also those of the colors of light. She gives, in a smoothly combined use of text and picture, a great deal of information about color and color vision, demonstrates some of the ways in which combinations of colors may be manipulated to achieve specific effects, and shows how printing techniques make it possible to produce many colors from a few basic ones. Lucid, infor-mative, and handsome.

Dana Whitney Pinizzotto

SOURCE: A review of *The Magic of Color,* in *School Library Journal,* Vol. 28, No. 3, November, 1981, pp. 110-11.

The peculiar relationship of prismatic color to pigmented color and how each relates to the technology of color printing is the sophisticated topic of this slim book. These concepts are not easily understood from print media, al-though Simon's text and illustrations are as clear as can be imagined. Most readers will need to read, reread and ponder before they truly comprehend the physics, physi-ology and psychology of color vision. Complementary colors, which are "opposite" for light and pigment, com-plicate matters further. Even for those who do not under-stand the scientific theory, there is much of interest to follow: why do some colors clash, why do some seem to change depending on the background color, why do oth-ers seem identical when they are not? A detailed explana-tion of multicolor printing concludes the text. A chal-lenge for interested, thoughtful readers.

Robert J. Stein

SOURCE: A review of *The Magic of Color,* in *Appraisal: Science Books for Young People,* Vol. 15, No. 1, Winter, 1982, pp. 60-1.

Few children's books offer as much excitement and ap-peal as does Hilda Simon's ***The Magic of Color***. Precise full-color photographs, and experiments the reader can quickly and easily perform, dramatically illustrate the nature of color, the behavior of light and pigments, the phenomenon of visual color perception, and the technol-ogy of full-color reproduction.

Though light refraction, color interactions, and visual perception are concepts not easily understood by young readers, Mrs. Simon's text is accurate and easy to under-stand. Under the guidance of a teacher equipped with a light source, color filters and variously colored pigments, the more abstract concepts described in the book can be demonstrated more clearly. ***The Magic of Color*** is de-signed to appeal to intermediate and junior high school aged readers, but the illustrations and experiment ideas contained in the book can easily be adapted for use in any grade level. The section dealing with color after-images provides exciting ideas and detailed instructions that young readers can follow in creating their own color "magic."

Joyce Swartney

SOURCE: A review of *The Magic of Color,* in *Science Books & Films,* Vol. 17, No. 4, March-April, 1982, p. 213.

The text adequately describes how four colors can be manipulated by a printer to produce a wide spectrum of color. Using several simple diagrams, the difference between colored light and pigment is explained. Unfortunately, the text and the diagrams are not always on the same page, and it is difficult to refer to the correct diagram. Young readers will probably find the section on afterimages to be the most interesting. In addition to the afterimages of the American flag, the author includes a blue cardinal and gives directions for other experiments with primary and complementary colors. Although this book appears simple, the explanations, especially about complementary colors, are quite complex. This book is very well illustrated by the four-color diagrams and pictures. *The Magic of Color* would be very useful as additional reading about light and color for the middle and junior high school student.

SIGHT AND SEEING: A WORLD OF LIGHT AND COLOR (1983)

Kirkus Reviews

SOURCE: A review of *Sight and Seeing: A World of Light and Color,* in *Kirkus Reviews,* Vol. LI, No. 10, May 15, 1983, p. 585.

Essentially, a survey of vision in different animals. Simon begins with the advantages and limitations of the "Mosaic Images" of insects' compound eyes, with emphasis on Karl von Frisch's studies of bees' vision and examples of other discoveries made, for example, by blinding dragonfly nymphs. A chapter called "Seeing Our Way" brings up the usual camera comparison, pointing out differences as well as similarities, and draws other parallels with TV pictures. There's a chapter on the superior eyesight of birds, who depend much on sight and have a poor sense of smell, and whose vision varies in diurnal and nocturnal, or seed-eating and prey-swooping species; and another on fish and amphibians who exhibit a range of specific peculiarities such as the bifocal eye of the periscope fish. The book ends with a survey of color perception in different species. The dry style is a deterrent: a typical sentence reads, "The 'double standard' which is the hallmark of amphibian life requires fundamental changes as the animals complete their metamorphosis from the fish-like larval to the terrestrial adult stage." For serious readers, though, there's a wealth of examples in a context of thoughtful generalizations and distinctions.

Margaret M. Hagel

SOURCE: A review of *Sight and Seeing: A World of Light and Color,* in *School Library Journal,* Vol. 30, No. 1, September, 1983, p. 139.

The world of sight, from that of the simplest life forms to the complex color vision of primates, is explored in this authoritative introduction for the non-scientist. Simon concentrates on vision and its importance in gathering information. The structure of visual organs—the simple eye of the mollusk, the compound eye of the insect, the detailed close vision of mammals and the farsighted eye of birds—is compared. The way an animal "sees" is related to his other habits, such as feeding and courtship. Bold color-coded diagrams, consistent throughout the book, aid the discussions of eye structure. Delicate pastel drawings of animals and plants add to the attractiveness and utility of the book.

Karen Stang Hanley

SOURCE: A review of *Sight and Seeing: A World of Light and Color,* in *Booklist,* Vol. 80, No. 1, September 1, 1983, pp. 91-2.

Precise, beautifully rendered colored pencil drawings are an elegant complement to Simon's fluid text about the miracle of eyesight. Emphasizing that acuteness and range of vision have enabled human beings to master the basic tasks required for survival, Simon observes that most of what we know as civilization—art, poetry, music, literature—has arisen more directly from our ability to see than from any of the other senses. The author's keen appreciation of the wonders of creation is reflected in seven thoughtfully written chapters focusing on light; the vision of insects, humans, birds, and underwater animals; and color perception. Experiments with animals' sight capabilities are reported in lively fashion, and diagrams of animal eyes and brains facilitate comparison. The book is indexed, but lack of a bibliography or suggestions for further reading is an unfortunate omission in so invigorating a presentation.

Ronald W. Everson

SOURCE: A review of *Sight and Seeing: A World of Light and Color,* in *Science Books & Films,* Vol. 19, No. 4, March/April, 1984, pp. 204-05.

This short, interesting, fact-filled essay describes the sense of sight and, occasionally, the senses of hearing and smell of selected members of the animal kingdom, ranging from insects to humans. Concerning sight, this volume offers numerous comparative diagrams of eye structure and descriptions of the light-dark discrimination ability, visual acuity, binocular vision, and color vision of various animals. Over 50 color drawings add to the expert illustrations. These drawings and their legends merit particularly careful study because they often contain details that add to the main narrative. The book is organized around structure and function. A chapter on the compound eye of insects and crustaceans focuses on honeybees and dragonflies. Three chapters are devoted to the camera-type eyes of mammals, birds, and fish. The final chapter is fascinating, describing the color perception of various animals. The approach throughout is comparison; thus, the visual characteristics of a given animal are usually revealed gradually rather than in one long paragraph, encyclopedia style. The more mature general science and biology students will appreciate this book.

Additional coverage of Simon's life and career is contained in the following sources published by Gale Research: *Contemporary Authors,* **Vols. 77-80; and** *Something about the Author,* **Vol. 28.**

CUMULATIVE INDEXES

How to Use This Index

The main reference

> Baum, L(yman) Frank
> 1856-1919 15

lists all author entries in this and previous volumes of *Children's Literature Review.*

The cross-references

> See also CA 103; 108; DLB 22; JRDA;
> MAICYA; MTCW; SATA 18; TCLC 7

list all author entries in the following Gale biographical and literary sources:

AAYA = Authors & Artists for Young Adults
AITN = Authors in the News
BLC = Black Literature Criticism
BW = Black Writers
CA = Contemporary Authors
CAAS = Contemporary Authors Autobiography Series
CABS = Contemporary Authors Bibliographical Series
CANR = Contemporary Authors New Revision Series
CAP = Contemporary Authors Permanent Series
CDALB = Concise Dictionary of American Literary Biography
CLC = Contemporary Literary Criticism
CLR = Children's Literature Review
CMLC = Classical and Medieval Literature Criticism
DA = DISCovering Authors
DC = Drama Criticism
DLB = Dictionary of Literary Biography
DLBD = Dictionary of Literary Biography Documentary Series
DLBY = Dictionary of Literary Biography Yearbook
HW = Hispanic Writers
JRDA = Junior DISCovering Authors
LC = Literature Criticism from 1400 to 1800
MAICYA = Major Authors and Illustrators for Children and Young Adults
MTCW = Major 20th-Century Writers
NCLC = Nineteenth-Century Literature Criticism
PC = Poetry Criticism
SAAS = Something about the Author Autobiography Series
SATA = Something about the Author
SSC = Short Story Criticism
TCLC = Twentieth-Century Literary Criticism
WLC = World Literature Criticism, 1500 to the Present
YABC = Yesterday's Authors of Books for Children

CUMULATIVE INDEX TO NATIONALITIES

CUMULATIVE INDEX TO TITLES

Title Index

Title Index

Title Index

Title Index

Title Index

ISBN 0-8103-9286-0